HISTORICAL DICTIONARIES OF RELIGIONS, PHILOSOPHIES, AND MOVEMENTS
Jon Woronoff, Series Editor

1. *Buddhism*, by Charles S. Prebish, 1993. *Out of print.*
2. *Mormonism*, by Davis Bitton, 1994. *Out of print. See no. 32.*
3. *Ecumenical Christianity*, by Ans Joachim van der Bent, 1994
4. *Terrorism*, by Sean Anderson and Stephen Sloan, 1995. *Out of print.*
5. *Sikhism*, by W. H. McLeod, 1995. *Out of print. See no. 59.*
6. *Feminism*, by Janet K. Boles and Diane Long Hoeveler, 1995. *Out of print. See no. 52.*
7. *Olympic Movement*, by Ian Buchanan and Bill Mallon, 1995. *Out of print. See no. 39.*
8. *Methodism*, by Charles Yrigoyen Jr. and Susan E. Warrick, 1996. *Out of print. See no. 57.*
9. *Orthodox Church*, by Michael Prokurat, Alexander Golitzin, and Michael D. Peterson, 1996
10. *Organized Labor*, by James C. Docherty, 1996. *Out of print. See no. 50.*
11. *Civil Rights Movement*, by Ralph E. Luker, 1997
12. *Catholicism*, by William J. Collinge, 1997
13. *Hinduism*, by Bruce M. Sullivan, 1997
14. *North American Environmentalism*, by Edward R. Wells and Alan M. Schwartz, 1997
15. *Welfare State*, by Bent Greve, 1998. *Out of print. See no. 63.*
16. *Socialism*, by James C. Docherty, 1997. *Out of print. See no. 73.*
17. *Bahá'í Faith*, by Hugh C. Adamson and Philip Hainsworth, 1998. *Out of print. See no. 71.*
18. *Taoism*, by Julian F. Pas in cooperation with Man Kam Leung, 1998
19. *Judaism*, by Norman Solomon, 1998. *Out of print. See no. 69.*
20. *Green Movement*, by Elim Papadakis, 1998. *Out of print. See no. 80.*
21. *Nietzscheanism*, by Carol Diethe, 1999. *Out of print. See no. 75.*
22. *Gay Liberation Movement*, by Ronald J. Hunt, 1999
23. *Islamic Fundamentalist Movements in the Arab World, Iran, and Turkey*, by Ahmad S. Moussalli, 1999
24. *Reformed Churches*, by Robert Benedetto, Darrell L. Guder, and Donald K. McKim, 1999. *Out of print. See no. 99.*

Historical Dictionary of Shinto

Second Edition

Stuart D. B. Picken

Historical Dictionaries of Religions,
Philosophies, and Movements, No. 104

The Scarecrow Press, Inc.
Lanham • Toronto • Plymouth, UK
2011

Published by Scarecrow Press, Inc.
A wholly owned subsidary of The Rowman & Littlefield Publishing Group, Inc.
4501 Forbes Boulevard, Suite 200, Lanham, Maryland 20706
http://www.scarecrowpress.com

Estover Road, Plymouth PL6 7PY, United Kingdom

British Library Cataloguing in Publication Information Available

Library of Congress Cataloging-in-Publication Data

Picken, Stuart D. B.
  Historical dictionary of Shinto / Stuart D.B. Picken. -- 2nd ed.
  p. cm. — (Historical dictionaries of religions, philosophies, and movements ; 104)
  Includes bibliographical references.
  ISBN 978-0-8108-7172-4 (cloth : alk. paper) — ISBN 978-0-8108-7372-8 (ebook)
  1. Shinto—Dictionaries—Japanese. 2. Japanese language—Dictionaries—
English. I. Title.
  BL2216.1.P53 2011
  299.5'6103—dc22   2010031382

∞™ The paper used in this publication meets the minimum requirements of
American National Standard for Information Sciences—Permanence of Paper for
Printed Library Materials, ANSI/NISO Z39.48-1992. Printed in the United States
of America

For Hongwen, William, and Lynn

Contents

Editor's Foreword

Shinto is different in many ways from other religions in this series of Historical Dictionaries of Religions, Philosophies, and Movements. Unlike most, it is not monotheistic. Quite to the contrary, it has a plenitude of divinities. There is no written or even oral text to which all can refer; instead, there are traditions. Theology is relatively unimportant and rites and rituals, festivals, and ceremonies all-important. There is no strict hierarchy; rather, there is an almost confusing decentralization. Despite efforts by the authorities over the centuries to capture and cultivate it, Shinto is still amazingly close to the grass roots. This may well explain its vitality, for it has withstood the encroachments of alien religions, not so much rejecting as blending with Buddhism, and to a lesser extent Confucianism and Taoism, and keeping Christianity to a tiny minority. It has undergone long periods of spontaneity and freedom, although the government frequently tried to claim and regulate it, and today it still thrives without much interference. Not only is it the largest religion in Japan, it has affected many of Japan's New Religions, and can be found abroad.

Given some of the features just mentioned, it must be obvious that Shinto is particularly difficult to define or even explain, and this is what makes the *Historical Dictionary of Shinto* so useful. The chronology traces its long history, with its many twists and turns, while the introduction places it in the overall setting. The dictionary section then tackles the real problems. One is to explain its development over the centuries, during which it assumed different forms—either spontaneously or imposed on it from the outside—with ample mention of countless religious and secular figures. Another is to show how it functions, through its various activities and countless rituals and festivals. A third is to show its limited structure and clerical personnel. Yet none seems more important for foreigners than simply to understand the terms and concepts applied, and this makes the section more of a true dictionary than usual. Of course, this book can only do so much, and it therefore refers readers to numerous other sources of literature and now websites in the bibliography.

This is now the second edition. Like the first, it was written by Stuart D. B. Picken, whose contacts with Japan are exceptionally close and long, having served on the faculty of the International Christian University in Tokyō for twenty-five years before moving to the Graduate School of the Nagoya University of Commerce and Business Administration, where he was dean. Even after returning home, he worked with Japan, serving as director of the Centre for Japanese Studies at the University of Stirling and helping found the Japan Society of Scotland, of which he is presently chair, and a council member of the Japan-British Society. His greatest accolade came in 2007, when he received the Order of the Sacred Treasure from the emperor of Japan for services to Japan-British Relations. All the while Dr. Picken has been explaining Japan to foreigners. This has been done in various ways, through teaching and lectures, interreligious dialogs, and writing with more than two hundred academic papers and articles as well as two books, *Shinto: Japan's Spiritual Roots* and *The Essentials of Shinto*. Several things make him a particularly good author for this volume: first, obviously his long acquaintance with Japan; second, his own studies and understanding; but also that he is not focused solely on religion or culture but also economics and business, which gives him a wider view.

Jon Woronoff
Series Editor

Preface

The opportunity to produce a historical dictionary of Shinto was a challenge I could not refuse. To update and expand it has been equally exciting. I deem it a privilege to add to the growing research and literature on Shinto in English that began appearing during the last decade of the 20th century. I felt also, and still do, that a historical dictionary approach would be not only valuable, but also one that very much suited Shinto, which lends itself more readily to empirical than purely theoretical investigation. I am also honored to try to assist in the process of helping researchers find meaning in the many aspects of Shinto.

Shinto remains extremely controversial, and there are as many opinions as there are observers. Unlike Buddhism and Christianity, it does not have a debatable rational core. It does not consist of agreed-upon doctrines from which implications can be drawn to deal with moral or social problems of life, or attitudes to the environment, for example. Consequently, arguments tend to turn on what Shinto is and what it is not.

Shinto's place in Japanese history and culture is also a major source of contention among scholars. Opinions range from the extreme position that it was a 19th-century invention to the equally radical view that it grew out of Taoism that came from China. Some 19th-century scholars labeled it a primitive religion, while some mid-20th-century scholars blamed it, in its guise as State Shinto, for Japan's entry into World War II. Some believe that it will make a return in its political form, or at least that there is a lobby in Japan trying to resurrect its nationalistic character.

This preface presents four simple observations that arose while this volume was being written, each of which is significant in some way for the future study of the subject. First, a new generation of serious scholarship is emerging that seems less influenced by the prejudices against Shinto that were common among many earlier scholars, as well as intellectually more balanced in its approach. I have referred to several of these scholars in the introduction to the bibliography.

Second, there now appears to be a growing international interest in Shinto as a religion that goes beyond academic study. Although viewed by most observers as purely a Japanese phenomenon, Shinto's attraction to non-Japanese points to overlooked features that have universal appeal. Shinto is awakening new curiosity, if not respect, in part because it represents a way of viewing religion that is different from the dogmatic stance of major, historical, revealed religions.

Shinto is perhaps the last representative of a way of thinking that the Western world lost when the so-called higher religions began to dominate its culture. Also, the kind of religious studies that have been generated from those positions have effectively narrowed the basis of interreligious dialog by excluding most of East Asian religious culture. I think it is safe to predict that theological and religious interest in Shinto will develop in parallel with the scholarly.

Third, in reflecting on Shinto's roots, I have become much more aware of the imperial institution's active role over the centuries, particularly as it tried to define its legitimacy through Shinto traditions and rites. This is a complex issue, but it suggests that alongside Shinto's folk tradition, or as a cultic form nurtured by governments at different periods, there is a dimension that belongs almost exclusively to the imperial tradition. How that complex issue can be researched will probably raise more questions than it will ever answer, but it is one worth examining more thoroughly.

Fourth, on a more personal level, in the process of assembling these materials, particularly in creating the bibliography, I have become acutely aware of a great watershed in the flow of time. Sadly, my preparatory notes came to look like an obituary column. The names of Nakamura Hajime and Joseph Kitagawa, to name but two of the individuals I have known personally and with whom I have had discussions over the thirty years lived and worked in Japan, remind me that Japan Studies in general and Shinto Studies in particular have lost many luminary figures. I have tried to represent the contemporary and rising generation as far as information was available. If anyone is omitted, I apologize.

It is my hope that Shinto Studies in the 21st century will continue to concentrate on Shinto itself, and not on the 19th- or 20th-century–imposed agendas referred to earlier. Shinto is alive and interest is growing. It has demonstrated its vitality through its introduction to North America not by Japanese, but by white Americans. This further defines the division between the 20th and the 21st centuries. This development,

I am sure, will have a considerable impact on the intellectual and spiritual map of world religions.

Many people have assisted, directly and indirectly, in the production of this work. A full list would include students, researchers, and Shinto priests with whom I have spent time over the past three decades. I would mention, in recent years, particularly the Japan Chapter of the International Association for Religious Freedom, which provided a model of how Shinto and the other religious traditions of Japan interact locally and how they combine their resources globally in the endeavors of interfaith dialog and cooperation. That has been a pilgrimage as well as an academic experience, and a model to me for developing inter-religious understanding. Jon Woronoff, as always, was exceptionally helpful as series editor, as has been the staff of Scarecrow Press. To my friend and former colleague at Nagoya University of Commerce and Business Administration, Vice-Dean William R. Acton, a descendant of Lafcadio Hearn, I am grateful for numerous comments on content and style in the first edition that helped to make the text more readable and intelligible. Finally, to Hongwen, William Daoyuan, and LynnWen, for their patience during the preparation of the first edition, I dedicate this second edition with my deepest gratitude.

Reader's Notes

ROMANIZATION

Romanization basically follows the Kenkyusha *New-Japanese English Dictionary* (1974), which uses a modification of the Hepburn system. The following exceptions to that system bring the text into line with the Kodansha *Encyclopedia of Japan*.

- m instead of n is used before p, b, or m as in Mommu or Kemmu.
- n is retained as in words such as Genpon (instead of Gempon) or Shinbutsu (instead of Shimbutsu). These are sometimes found hyphenated.
- The final syllable n is distinguished with an apostrophe when it comes before a vowel or y as in Man'yoshū.
- Macrons are used to indicate the long vowels a, u, and o, with the exception of the following cases:
  1. The seven well-known place names, Tokyō, Kyōto, Osaka, Kobe, Kyushū, Honshū and Hokkaido.
  2. In the case of Japanese words that have come into English usage, such as Aikido, Bushido, Judo, Shinto, or Shogun.
  3. Where established forms of romanization exist, such as Motoori Norinaga.

JAPANESE WORDS AND NAMES

Italicization has been dropped except for the untranslatable term *kami*. In the names of the *kami* and in technical expressions, hyphens are included to indicate Chinese characters where considered helpful (e.g., *Honji-suijaku-setsu*). For personal names, the following rules apply:

(a) For transliteration of Japanese names, Library of Congress catalog cards are the standard of reference. Where no reference exists, the most common form in use is listed.
(b) The order of names is as in Japanese: family name first and given name second (e.g., Hirata Atsutane).

NOTE ON HISTORICAL PERIODS

The dating of Japanese historical periods varies slightly from discipline to discipline. This volume follows the most common that reflects broad cultural divisions. Edo is the most debated. G. B. Sansom took 1615 as the starting date, while Edwin O. Reischauer preferred 1260. Emperor Komei died in 1866, but the Meiji Restoration is dated to 1868. For simplicity, 1868 is taken as the termination of Edo and the commencement of Meiji.

CROSS-REFERENCING

In order to facilitate the rapid and efficient location of information and to make this book as useful a reference tool as possible, extensive cross-references have been provided. Within individual dictionary entries, terms that have their own entries are in **bold type** the first time they appear. Further cross-referencing is shown through *See* and *See also*.

Major Shinto Sites in Japan

Chronology

10,000 B.C.E.   The ancient residents of Japan, along with their origins, largely remain mysterious. Pre-10,000 B.C.E. pottery exists, which is among the earliest in the world.

7000 B.C.E.   The Jōmon (Neolithic) period evolves, defined by pottery with rope-markings found in pit dwellings typical of Stone Age culture. Artifacts include male and female figurines and Nonaka-do, flat stone circles with an upright to the northwest of center, probably used for communal rituals.

661   Descent from the High Plain of Heaven of Ninigi-no-Mikoto, great grandfather of the first legendary emperor, Jimmu Tennō (r. 660–585 B.C.E.).

250   The Yayoi (Bronze-Iron) period was named after a Tokyō district where pots found in 1884 identified a culture that spanned the Neolithic and protohistoric periods. Artifacts include swords and mirrors, suggestive of the origins of the imperial regalia, along with dotaku (metal bell-shaped objects) and deer bones that appear to have been used in fortune telling.

The people of this period appeared to have first felt awe and wonder at the powers of nature, creating the concept of *kami*, divine reality or divine being, to express it. Basic terms such as spirit (tama) and object (mono) appeared, along with the idea of the festival (matsuri), and the unity of reverence and order were developed.

97   Emperor Sujin (r. 97–30 B.C.E.), according to the Nihon Shōki (Records of Japan, 720), institutes the distinction between the *kami* of heaven and earth and identifies lands and estates for their worship.

PROTOHISTORIC PERIOD (SECOND CENTURY–552 c.e.)

c. 100   The period was named after the large burial mounds (called kofun) built for Japan's early leaders, which emerged between the second and the sixth centuries. The rise of the Yamato clan and its cults, early Shinto, commences here. Some of the oldest Shinto sites, such as Isonokami and Mt. Miwa in Nara Prefecture (unrelated to the kofun), date to this period. The island of Okinoshima (Fukuoka Prefecture) was a guardian *kami* of traders plying between Japan and Korea. Mirrors, beads, and horse-related items are among Shinto's oldest known artifacts. As Japanese society formed itself, the basic roots of Shinto integrated, probably unselfconsciously, to create the various features of the cult, namely, animism, nature worship, ancestral reverence, shamanism, the cycle of the rice-growing calendar, and the ritual power of lustration as a cultural paradigm.

c. 250   Empress Jingū (r. 201–269) subdues Korea, according to the Nihon Shoki, leaving after offering worship at Sumiyoshi Taisha in Osaka.

c. 300   Emperor Ōjin (r. 270–310) introduces technology from the Asian mainland. He was interred in a kofun in Osaka.

c. 400   Emperor Nintoku (r. 313–399) is interred in the largest kofun yet discovered.

ASUKA PERIOD (552–710)

In response to the arrival in Japan of Buddhism—initially through the Korean Peninsula—the undefined indigenous cult came to articulate its basic concepts. Himorogi (sacred spaces) and iwasaka (circles of stones) became places to revere *kami*.

c. 580   Emperor Yōmei (r. 585–587) is noted in the Nihon Shoki to have respected the way of the Buddha and to have revered the way of the *kami*.

600   Legends circulate of En no Gyōja and his ascetic practices on Mt. Katsuragi (Nara Prefecture).

604   A 17-clause "Constitution" is promulgated by Imperial Regent Shōtoku Taishi (574–622) as a set of moral guidelines for the nation. The hegemony of the Yamato clan becomes established in Nara as a sacral monarchy that combined the duties of *kami* worship and government (matsuri-goto).

645–646 The Taika Reform, the first recorded code of laws in Japan, is drawn during the reign of Emperor Kōtoku (r. 645–654).

672–686 Emperor Temmu (r. 673–686) institutes the practice of rebuilding the Grand Shrines of Ise on adjacent sites every 20 years.

698 First recorded instance of the use of Shinbutsu Shugo to maintain harmony between Shinto and Buddhism.

c. 685–705 Kakinomoto no Hitomaru authors numerous poems found in the Man'yōshū collection.

699 The removal of the Taki Daijingu, recorded in the *Zoku Nihongi* as having taken place during the second year of the reign of Emperor Mommu (r. 697–707).

701 The Taiho Ritsuryō (Code) creates the first system of shrine rankings.

709 Kasuga Taisha is recorded as having been established.

NARA PERIOD (710–794)

Japan's new capital, Nara, was built on the grid model of a Chinese city. The immigrant cult of Buddhism began to emerge and grow, posing a threat to the older cult. The term Shinto was created to distinguish the way of the *kami* from the way of the Buddha.

711 Legends refer to the founding of Fushimi Inari Taisha.

712 Kojiki (Records of Ancient Matters) is completed and presented to Empress Genmei (r. 707–715).

720 Nihon Shōki is completed.

724 Nara Buddhism grows under the influence of Emperor Shōmu (r. 724–749), the first Japanese emperor to become a Buddhist priest.

733 Wake no Kiyomaru is born (d. 799), the courtier who brought the oracle from the Usa Hachiman-gū that condemned the Buddhist monk Dōkyō.

749 The Great Buddha of the Tōdai-ji is successfully cast in bronze, with the blessing of the *kami* Hachiman, and finally dedicated in 752. An oracle from the Usa Hachiman-gu Shrine rejects the claim of the Buddhist monk Dōkyō to become consort to Empress Kōken (r. 749–758).

759 The last items of the Man'yoshū poetic collection are completed.

767 Saichō, later known as Dengyō Daishi, the founder of Tendai Buddhism, is born (d. 822).

774 Kūkai, later known as Kōbō Daishi, the founder of Shingon Buddhism, is born (d. 835).

787 The *Shoku Nihongi* records that, four years earlier, Emperor Kammu performed worship of the heavenly *kami* at Kitano in the form of a Taoist ritual.

791 An ordinance decrees the termination of rituals in which animal sacrifices are offered to heavenly beings. Rejection of Taoism suggests a growing reaction to excessive Sinification of the culture.

HEIAN PERIOD (794–1185)

The court was removed to Kyōto by Emperor Kammu (r. 781–806) to prevent further Buddhist political interference in politics. The world's first novel, the *Tale of Genji*, was written by Lady Murasaki. Esoteric Buddhism (Shingon) was introduced from China by Kūkai (774–835) and semi-esoteric (Tendai) by Saichō (767–822).

797 *Shoku Nihongi* is completed.

804 The *Kotai-Jingū Gishiki-chō* and the *Toyouke-gū Gishiki-chō*, books of rituals and ceremonies along with other important information about the Grand Shines of Ise, are lodged with the Jingikan, the earliest collection of the records of Ise. They are evidence of an organized system of Shinto that is intelligible in modern terms.

806 Shrine Endowment is approved in a document which records that 4,870 agricultural households had been assigned to Shinto shrines, shinpo (or kanbe as noted earlier), showing that concern existed for the nationwide endowment and financial stability of shrines.

810   In addition to the imperial princess sent as *saio* to the Grand Shrines of Ise, another is sent to the Kamo Shrines in Kyōto as *saiin* (high priestess to the shrines of Kamo). This occurred during the reign of Emperor Saga (r. 809–823).

845   Sugawara Michizane is born (d. 903), the courtier who eventually was enshrined as Tenjin, the *kami* of learning.

863   The first recorded instance of pacification rites known as Chinkon takes place when a service is held at the Shinsen-en gardens in Kyōto to calm numerous distressed spirits of the imperial household.

901   *Nihon Sandai-jitsuroku* (Chronological Description of the Three Generations of Emperors) is completed during the first year of Engi (901) and dated August 28th of the first year of Jogan (859).

903   The calming of the soul of Sugawara Michizane takes place upon his death, after which he becomes Tenjin, the *kami* of learning.

905   *Kokinshū* collection of poems (Poems Ancient and Modern) is completed and presented at court to Emperor Daigo (r. 897–930). Emperor Daigo ordered the creation of the Engishiki.

921   Onakatomi no Yoshinobu is born (d. 991), courtier, Shinto liturgist, high priest of the Inner Shrine of Ise, and great influence upon Shinto ritual matters.

927   Engishiki, the system of *kami* and rituals, is compiled as the first attempt to standardize ritual practice and liturgy of priestly duties.

1081   The twenty-two shrines (Ni-jū-ni-sha) around the Kyōto area are singled out for special recognition. The number was initially 14, but was increased to 22. The district first shrines are also identified, as important locally revered old shrines came to be known as Ichi-no-miya (or first shrine). The first reference to this system appears in the *Konjaku Monogatari*. The creation of shrine/temples (jingū-ji) as an expression of the assimilation between Buddhism and Shinto began to express itself more concretely in the early Heian period. Harmonization of *kami* and Buddha expanded in the concept of honji-suijaku (literally "original essence, descended manifestations"), which can be viewed, in a general way, as the natural outcome of the process of Shinbutsu Shūgō, the close identification of interests between Buddhism and Shinto. Ryōbu Shinto (Shinto of the Two Parts) carried the principle of honji-suijaku further to the stage of actual unity between branches of Buddhism and Shinto. Tendai Shinto originated through the influence of Saicho. The *kami* known as Oyamakui-no-kami was worshipped at the Hie Jinja on Mt. Hiei and came to be known as Sanno Gongen (Mountain King avatar), a system that followed a similar model in T'ang China.

1133 Hōnen, founder of the Jōdo Sect of Buddhism, is born (d. 1212).

1173 Shinran, founder of the Jōdo-Shin Sect of Buddhism, is born (d. 1262). Kumano Shinto develops three religious centers in Kumano: the Hongū, Shingū, and Nachi, which collectively became known as the Kumano Sanja. Emperor Shirakawa (r. 1072–1086) undertook the pilgrimage 23 times after retiring. The Urabe family, one of the official hereditary houses within the Jingikan, served as priests of the Matsuo Shrine and later at Hirano, Ume no Miya, and the Yoshida Shrines, laying the foundation for the later development of Yoshida Shinto.

KAMAKURA PERIOD (1185–1333)

1185 Battle of Dannoura (April 11, 1185) takes place, resulting in the death of the boy emperor, Antoku, (r. 1180–83), who was lost in the sea along with the Imperial Sword. Popular religion and the imperial regalia subsequently become closely linked during the Kamakura period on the meaning of the mirror, the jewel, and the sword. Antoku had been effectively deposed by Emperor Gotoba, who was installed as rival in 1183, reigning until 1198.

1192 The establishment by Minamoto Yoritomo of his military government (bakufu) in Kamakura, moving the nation's capital to that city. The imperial court remains in Kyōto until the Meiji Restoration of 1868.

1205 The *Shin Kokinshū* (New Collection of Poems Ancient and Modern) are compiled. The Pure Land Buddhist sects, Jōdo and Shin, emerge under the local leadership of Honen (1133–1212) and Shinran (1173–1262), representing the reduction of Mahayana Buddhism to a very simple form of belief and rituals more in keeping with Japanese tastes and values.

1222 Birth of Nichiren (d. 1282), a radical figure in Japanese Buddhism emphasizing the *Lotus Sutra*. From the tradition he established, Hokke (Lotus) Shinto developed.

1232   The Joei law (or Goseibai Shikimoku) is drafted by the Council of State under the leadership of Hojo Yasutoki; the first lines mandate that shrines are to be maintained in good order and dedicated to worship.

1250   The *Yamabushi-chō*, a register of Shugendō practitioners, is compiled.

1255   Watarai Ieyuki is born (d. 1356?), founder of the tradition of the Outer Shrine of Ise. Zen Buddhism arrives from China.

1274, 1282   The Mongols under Kublai Khan twice fail to invade as Japan is saved by the weather and the divine winds (the kami-kaze, as Nichiren designated them). Urabe Kanekata composes the *Shaku Nihongi*, establishing the scholarly reputation of the Yoshida Shinto tradition. Shugendō, which emerged during the Heian period, begins to flourish during the Kamakura period.

1293   Kitabatake Chikafusa is born (d. 1354), author of the *Jinnō Shōtōki* (Descent of the Divine Emperors, 1340), which is famous for its opening declaration that Great Japan is the land of the *kami*.

ASHIKAGA OR MUROMACHI PERIOD (1333–1568)

1334   The capital returns to Kyōto. A new military government takes control of national affairs: the Ashikaga clan, which lived primarily in a district of Kyōto called Muromachi, from which the period takes its name. The Muromachi bakufu was more restricted in its area of authority, and consequently could pursue policies only as far as its power extended.

1336   The period of the two courts. Noh drama begins to evolve from shrine rituals, while the tea ceremony and black-and-white painting develops under Zen patronage.

1435   Urabe (Yoshida) Kanetomo is born (d. 1511), founder of Urabe Shinto. He advanced a theory of Shinto called Yuiitsu Genpon Sogen Shinto ("the one and only original essence Shinto"), also called Yuiitsu Shinto or Yoshida Shinto, which had a remarkable influence upon shrines and the entire culture of Shinto. He began the overt rejection of the honji-suijaku, Buddhist/Shinto syncretism.

1462–1500   Owing to severe economic decline, many Shinto-related practices are either postponed or abandoned. The Ōname-sai is postponed. Offerings to the 22 major shrines end, with only the Grand Shrines of Ise receiving offerings from the Jingikan. The rebuilding of the Inner Shrines at Ise (shikinen sengū) is discontinued from 1462 to 1585, and the Outer Shrines from 1434 to 1563.

1467   Beginning of the period of Sengoku Jidai, the period of civil wars that lasted until 1568.

1484   Yoshida Kanetomo completes the construction of the Daigengu.

1534   Oda Nobunaga is born (d. 1582), the first of the three generalissimos who united the country and the first destroyer of Buddhist power.

1536   Birth of Toyotomi Hideyoshi (d. 1598), who gradually achieved unification after extensive civil wars.

1541   Hasegawa Kakugyo is born (d. 1646), founder of the Kyōha Shinto sects, Fusō-kyō and Jikkō-kyō.

1542   Tokugawa Ieyasu is born (d. 1616), founder of the Tokugawa Shogunate and third of the unifiers of the nation.

1549   Francis Xavier, the Jesuit missionary, begins the introduction of Roman Catholic Christianity to Japan.

1561   Birth of Fujiwara Seika (d. 1619), scholar of his tradition who rejected not only the concept of honji-suijaku, but also the concept of Yuiitsu Shinto because Buddhist theories were included within it.

1568   End of the Sengoku Jidai.

AZUCHI-MOMOYAYA PERIOD (1568–1615)

1576   Oda Nobunaga builds his headquarters at Azuchi in Kyōto.

1579   Jesuit visitor to Japan, Alexandri Valignano, arrives.

1581   Rebellious priests on Mt. Koya killed by order of Nobunaga.

1582   Toyotomi Hideyoshi takes over upon the death of Nobunaga.

1585   Rebuilding of the Inner Shrines at Ise, discontinued in 1462.

1587   First persecution of Kirishitan (Christians) in Japan.

1594   Hideyoshi secures his headquarters at Fushimi.

1597   Death of the 26 Nagasaki martyrs.

1598   Tokugawa Ieyasu rises to power upon the death of Hideyoshi.

TOKUGAWA OR EDO PERIOD (1615–1868)

1600   Battle of Sekigahara, which confirms the ascendancy of the House of Tokugawa and the establishment of the Tokugawa Shogunate.

1608   Hayashi Razan (1583–1687) becomes Confucian advisor to the Tokugawa Shogunate, creating the basis for a Confucian/Shinto rapprochement.

1614   Anti-Kirishitan (Christian) edicts formally proclaimed.

1615   Watarai Nobuyoshi is born (d. 1690), also known as Deguchi Nobuyoshi, leading priest of the Outer Shrine of Ise. Founder of the tradition of Watarai Shinto, he formally rejected any synthesis with Buddhism or Confucianism, proposing instead a return to the simpler forms of the Shinto of Ise.

1616   Tokugawa Ieyasu dies. He had ordered a Shinto funeral, that his remains be interred in Mt. Kuno, that Buddhist rituals be conducted at the Zojo-ji in Edo (near the modern Tokyō Tower), and that a memorial be placed in the Taiju-ji in Mikawa (his birthplace). He also decreed that after the first annual memorial service following his death, a shrine was to be built at Nikko and his spirit revered as a *kami*. This became the famous Tosho-gu, where he is enshrined as the Tosho-Dai-Gongen (Great Avatar Light of the East). The shrine belongs to the Tendai-Shinto tradition. Yoshikawa Koretari (d. 1694), who founded Rigaku (Yoshikawa) Shinto using the Confucian cosmology of the Chinese scholar Chu Hsi (1132–1200), is born.

1618   Yamazaki Ansai is born (d. 1682), founder of the "Shinto of Divine Revelation and Blessing" (Suiga Shinto), which in time provides some solid academic support for the imperial loyalists and anti-bakufu movements of the late Edo period.

1619   Kumazwa Banzan (d. 1691), an important influence in the meeting of Confucianism and Shinto, is born.

1622   Yamaga Soko is born (d. 1685), founder of Seikyō Shinto (Teaching of the Sages, referring to Confucianism), which is described as being based on imperial reverence.

1630 Kaibara Ekken is born (d. 1714), the last major figure in Confucian Shinto.

1640 Keichu is born (d. 1701), scholar of the Japanese classics who prefigured the Kokugaku (National Learning) movement.

1650 First of the Okagemairi (Thanksgiving) Pilgrimages to the Grand Shrines of Ise, repeated in 1705, 1771, and 1830, eventually involving as many as two million people.

1655 Masuho Zankō is born (d. 1742), popular street orator and proponent of a Japanism that placed Japan above other cultures.

1666 *Daijingū Shinto Wakumon* is completed by Watarai Nobuyoshi.

1675 Watariai Tsuneakira is born (d. 1752), author of *Shinto Meiben*.

1685 Ishida Baigan is born (d. 1744), founder of the Heart Learning movement (Shingaku).

1691 Engelbert Kaempfer, the German scholar visits Japan.

1697 Kamo no Mabuchi is born (d. 1769), early influential scholar of the Kokugaku movement.

1699 Kada no Azumamaro is born (d. 1736), student of Kamo no Mabuchi and influence upon the work of Motoori Norinaga.

1705 The second great Ise pilgrimage.

1707 Last recorded eruption of Mt. Fuji.

1730 Motoori Norinaga is born (d. 1801), central figure of the Kokugaku movement.

1770 Kodera Kyōmitsu is born (d. 1843), writer on popular Shinto.

1776 Hirata Atsutane is born (d. 1843), principal ideologist of the Restoration Shinto movement.

1780 Kurozumi Munetada is born (d. 1850), founder of the Kyōha Shinto (Sect Shinto) sect Kurozumi-kyō.

1786 Gamo Kumpei is born (d. 1813), famous scholar of the imperial household tradition.

1787 Ninomiya Sontoku is born (d. 1856), founder of the Repayment of Virtue movement (Hotoku) which subsequently found favor with the Ministry of Home Affairs and the Ministry of Education.

1792 Okuni Takamasa is born (d. 1871), a Kokugaku scholar who was active in the early period after the Meiji Restoration until his death.

1798 Nakayaka Miki is born (d. 1887), founder of the Kyōha Shinto sect Tenri-kyō.

1801 Motoori Norinaga dies, central figure in the Kokugaku movement.

1814 Kawate Bunjiro is born (d. 1883), founder of the Kyōha Shinto sect Konkō-kyō.

1815 Hiragawa Shosai is born (d. 1890), founder of the Kyōha Shinto sect Taisei-kyō.

1836 Birth of Deguchi Nao (d. 1918), foundress of the Shinto-based sect Omoto-kyō, and Kannagibe Tsunehiko (d. 1910), founder of the Kyōha Shinto sect Shinri-kyō.

1839 Yoshimura Masamochi is born (d. 1916), founder of the Kyōha Shinto sect Shinshū-kyō.

1853 United States naval Commodore Matthew Perry arrived in Edo Bay on board a kurofune (black ship).

MEIJI PERIOD (1868–1912)

1867 The 15th shogun, Tokugawa Yoshinobu, recognizes that he can no longer maintain a viable government and yields to a group of young samurai who invade the Imperial Palace in Kyōto, proclaiming the young Emperor Mutsuhito "restored" as ruler as well as sovereign. The nation then begins a process of modernization that crushes the samurai and creates a modern state.

1868–1871 The reconstitution of Shinto as a state-controlled system commences. Taikyō Senpu (Proclamation of the Great Way) is declared to further the teachings of the Great Way and to revive the earlier notion of saisei-itchi, the unity of government and reverence. Shinbutsu-bunri, (the separation of Buddhism from Shinto) is implemented (March 28, 1868) by the government, to allow for a return to "pure Shinto."

1869   The Jingikan of the Nara period is re-established and put in charge of Shinto rituals. The head is made Dajōkansei (member of the Council of State), to ensure respect for Shinto and reverence for the emperor. A system of propagandists (senkyōshi) is set up to educate the people in the policies of the new government and to cultivate Shinto.

1870   In January, an imperial edict proclaims the enshrinement of the *kami* of heaven and earth, the eight central *kami* and the imperial ancestors by the Jingikan. In October, a system of imperial and national shrines is instituted, with each category divided into three classes based on size. A shrine ranking system is established, plus a listing of rituals to be performed, and a system of ranking for priests is formalized. Local governments are ordered to compile records of shrines in their area. Yasukuni Jinja is established on its present site at Kudanshita in Tokyō, near the old castle of Edo which had become the Imperial Palace. The land is secured and the shrine buildings erected in the following year. Emperor Meiji names it Yasukuni (Peaceful Country) Jinja. The Taikyō Senpu Undō, the campaign to advance the Great Teaching, is initiated.

1871   Shrines are declared national institutions and the system of hereditary priesthood is formally abolished, although many families and their shrines are not quite so easily separated. In August, the Jinkigan is abolished in response to criticism and replaced by a new Ministry of Shinto affairs (Jingishō) immediately below the Council of State (Dajōkan). The Council of State issues a proclamation on May 14, according to which all shrines are ranked in a new comprehensive system ranging from imperial shrines at the top to unranked shrines at the bottom. The favored position of Shinto is challenged; in reply, the idea is circulated by the government that Shinto is not a religion, but that there is a patriotic duty to show reverence at shrines.

1872   Jingū-kyō is established. The Kyōdōshoku is established as an agency of spiritual guidance for all shrine priests, to make them civil servants; training was the work of Shinto Taikyō-in. Imperial Rescript on Rituals for Enshrinement of *kami* is issued. Under the influence of Shimazu Mokurai and with pressure from the Jōdo-Shin sect, the government is forced to form the Kyōbushō (Ministry of Religious Instruction) to replace the Jingishō, whose functions were transferred there. The senkyōshi system is abolished because most were ultra-nationalists who often launched unreasonable attacks on Buddhism, ignoring both local feelings and the needs of Japan in a changing world. Heavy criticism from Buddhists and independent intellectuals forces a change of policy.

1873 The Shinto Taikyō, the leading Kyōha Shinto sect, is formed.

1877 The Kyōbusho is renamed Shajikyōku, which is under the Ministry of the Interior (Naimushō).

1878 The Saijin Ronsō debate on the enshrinement of the *kami* commences.

1880 Yasukuni Jinja is designated a Bekkaku-Kampeisha, the highest rank of shrine where the *kami* receive gifts from the emperor. The Ministry of the Interior becomes responsible for the administration, finances, and appointments of the shrine staff.

1882 The separation of religion and politics (seikyō-bunri) becomes a major issue since many religious instructors actually appear to be promoting their own teachings or those of cults unrelated to the objectives of the government. Kokugakuin University is founded.

1889 The Constitution recognizes Shinto, Buddhism, and Christianity as official religions, the first step toward a special status for Shinto.

1890 The Imperial Rescript on Education (Kyōiku Chokugo) is issued.

1891 Otsuka Kan'nichi is born (d. 1972), founder of the Kyōha Shinto sect Shinri-kyō.

1894 Many of the former government ranks are restored to the people's shrines (minsha). These had been removed as the government drew back from full state control of Shinto. The government begins giving official civil servant status to all priests, even those of unranked village shrines. By denying that Shinto is a religion, every citizen can be compelled to visit shrines and show respect.

1898 Kaisan Jinja is established in Taiwan.

1900 The Bureau of Shinto Affairs (Jinjakyōku) is set up within the Ministry of the Interior (Naimushō) to handle Shinto affairs separately from the Bureau of Religion, which dealt with Buddhism, Christianity, and the Shinto sects. The logic is that there should be a ministry teaching the enrichment of the whole body politic based on Shinto. This would encourage the following of the national way, the traditional way of the emperor, to counter the growing social and political unrest that came in the wake of the wars against China and Russia, which had been fought at enormous cost to the developing economy. The Bureau of Shinto Affairs raises the status of shrines dramatically, emphasizing that Shinto is simply a patriotic institution. This leads to the Shrine Merger (Jinja Gappei) movement. Jinja Kyōku, the department overseeing shrines, is set up in the Ministry of the Interior (Naimushō). Kitamura Sayo is born (d. 1967), founder of Tenshō Kōtai Jingū-kyō.

1901 Emperor Shōwa is born (Hirohito, d. 1989), longest-reigning emperor in Japanese history. Taiwan Jinja is established. Okada Kotama is born (d. 1974), founder of the Shinto-based sect Mahikari.

1903 Shrine Merger movement commences.

1906 The Hōtoku (Repayment of Virtue) movement becomes government supported.

1908 The Boshin Rescript on Thrift and Diligence is issued, one of a series of government measures designed to deal with the economic situation and to strengthen national vision and national goals.

1909 Chiho Kairyo Undō (Local District Improvement movement) is established.

1910 The revision of school textbooks is started. The formation of the Teikoku Zaigo Gunjin-Kai (Imperial Rural Military Association) is created to generate social stability, to recreate national values, and to add weight to the national ideology.

1911 Number of Shōkonsha (shrines for the war dead) reaches 105 nationwide (two are in Yamaguchi, the home of the Choshū clan, and fifteen in Kagoshima, the home of the Satsuma clan). While some predate the Meiji Restoration, all are integrated into the system and help to bolster local community commitment to the imperial system and the state.

1912 Death by seppuku (ritual suicide) of General Nogi Maresuke (1847–1912), veteran of the Meiji Restoration and national hero, along with his wife, on the day of the funeral of Emperor Meiji, 12 September.

TAISHO PERIOD (1912–1926)

1913 The Bureau of Religion is moved to the Ministry of Education, while all other religious groups were supervised by the Ministry of Education. Shinto affairs are left in the hands of the Shinto Honkyōku (Office of Shinto Affairs) department of the Ministry of the Interior, which exists until the end of the Pacific War.

1919 Enshrinement of General Nogi at Nogi Jinja in Akasaka, Tokyō.

1920 The Shrine Merger plan reduces the total number of shrines to fewer than 100,000.

1921 The construction of the Meiji Shrine (Meiji Jingū) is completed.

1923 Great Tokyō earthquake.

SHOWA PERIOD (1926–1989)

1931 The Manchurian Incident and Japan's departure from the League of Nations.

1932 Student protest about paying homage at Yasukuni Shrine as a violation of the constitutional right to religious freedom leads to the Ministry of Education declaring that Shinto is not a religion.

1935 Sekai-Kyūsei-Kyō (Church of World Messianity) is founded by Okada Mokichi.

1937 The *Kokutai no Hongi* (the Essence of the Body Politic) is published by the Ministry of Education as a basic text for moral and political education.

1940 Nationalism is actively promoted through the use of Shinto rituals. The Jingiin (College of *kami*) is established within the Ministry of the Interior. Kigensetsu (National Founding Day) is established to mark the accession of the first recorded emperor, Emperor Jimmū, 2600 years earlier.

1945 In August, United States Army General Douglas MacArthur, Japan's first foreign "shogun," becomes Supreme Commander of the Allied Powers. In December, the Shinto Directive is issued, ordering that shrines be disestablished from the state and that Shrine Shinto is not to receive any national support and is not to be under any kind of state control. Shinto was thereafter to remain a recognized religion for the individual Japanese citizens to practice or not at personal discretion.

1946 In February, the establishment of the Jinja Honchō (Association of Shinto Shrines) takes place. The Emperor makes his Tenno Ningen Sengen (declaration of humanity), stating that the emperor and people are linked by history and common concerns, not by myth or legend.

1947 Revised Constitution is promulgated.

1949 The Annai-kyō sect is formed by Nakano Yonosuke.

1950 Law for the Protection of Cultural Properties is enacted.

1952 The Treaty of San Francisco restores Japan's independence.

1953 The 64th rebuilding of the Grand Shrines of Ise (shikinen-sengū).

1955 The Religious Juridical Person Law is adopted.

1965 The Tsu legal battle commences over the use of the local government budget to finance a ground-breaking ceremony (Jichinsai).

1973 The 65th rebuilding of the Grand Shrines of Ise.

1979 Enshrinement in Yasukuni Shrine of 14 "Class-A" war criminals designated at the Tokyō War Crimes Trials, including General Tojo, the original war-time Prime Minister.

1985 The first branch shrine (bunsha) created outside of Japan since 1945 is set up in Stockton, California, as a point of intercultural meeting. Outside of the former Japanese Empire proper, only two other areas worldwide have shrines, both built voluntarily by Japanese immigrants of the Meiji period and therefore having nothing to do with State Shinto. The islands of Hawaii have several shrines plus a number of Buddhist temples, as does Brazil, where many Japanese settled. California, which had a large immigrant Japanese population, boasts numerous temples going back to the Meiji period, but no shrines.

1988 The Jinja Honchō moves from its location in Tokyō's Shibuya district near Kokugakuin University to a new site near Meiji Jingū.

HEISEI PERIOD (1989–)

1989   Crown Prince Akihito becomes emperor on January 24 upon the death of his father, Emperor Hirohito. The naming of imperial eras (Nengō) has a long tradition: 1989 begins the era of Heisei, meaning, loosely, "Peace and Development."

1990   In November, the accession ceremonies of Emperor Akihito are held. To deal with the same problem encountered in the funeral of Emperor Shōwa, namely, how to provide for the rites at public expense without violating Article 39 of the Constitution, the government declares the Sokui-nō-Rei part to be a state matter to be funded by the government. The Daijosai is declared to be a Shinto rite that is the prerogative of the imperial family and, as such, is considered to be an imperial household rite which the state funds because it is also of national interest and because the imperial household budget comes from the government. The Association of Shinto Shrines publishes a brochure to explain the Daijosai to the public, which simply describes the role of the emperor as revering the *kami* on behalf of the people, suggesting nothing about any special status of the emperor as was expounded in the doctrine of the Shōwa period. It closes with a sentiment considered appropriate to Japan's place in the modern world: "A new era has begun. The Emperor together with his people will work for the well-being of the nation and for the peace of the world."

1991   The Supreme Court in Tokyō, in dealing with an appeal by the right-wing Iwate Prefectural Assembly against a Sendai High Court decision that it acted unconstitutionally, rules on September 25 that official visits by either the emperor or prime minister to the Yasukuni Shrine violate the Constitution's separation of government and religion according to the terms of Article 20. The ruling, however conclusive, has resulted in the demand, from various quarters, for constitutional revision.

1993   The 66th rebuilding of the Grand Shrines of Ise.

1994   Shinto Kokusai Gakkai (Shinto International foundation) is formed by Umeda Yoshimi on May 31.

1996   The Grand Shrines of Ise celebrate their 2000th anniversary.

1997   Tsubaki Ōkami Yashiro celebrates its 2000th anniversary. Kannagara Jinja is established in Granite Falls, Washington State, U.S., under the direction of High Priest Koichi Barrish, the first non-Japanese ever to be licensed as a Shinto priest. The International Shinto Foundation (*Shinto Kokusai Gakkai*) endows the first professorship of Shinto Studies anywhere in the world, at the University of California, Santa Barbara. Professor Allan G. Grapard of the University of California, Santa Barbara, becomes the first endowed professor of Shinto Studies in the United States.

1998   First Cyber Jinja, Sakura Jinja, Setagaya Ward in Tokyō, goes online.

1999   Tsubaki Grand Shrine's second non-Japanese bunsha (branch shrine) is established in Victoria, Canada.

2000   In May, Prime Minister Mori Yoshiro makes a controversial remark to a group of Shinto-affiliated Diet members, that Japan was a land of the *kami* with the emperor at the center. Mistranslation of the expression "land of the *kami*" as "divine country" or "Kingdom of God" sparks off both domestic and international controversy. In August, senior religious leaders from Japan, including the high priest of the Grand Shrines of Ise and the high priest of Tsubaki Grand Shrine, in the company of some Buddhist leaders, attend the United Nations Center in New York for a summit of world religious leaders.

Introduction

PROBLEMS IN APPROACHING SHINTO

How can Shinto be described so it can be understood by anyone coming to it with criteria or expectations about religion? Shinto has nothing comparable to the official doctrinal positions and formal scriptures **Buddhism** or Christianity. It has no doctrines, and there are no sacred texts from which religious authority can be derived. It has no identifiable historical founder and has survived the vicissitudes of history through **rituals** and symbols rather than through continuity of doctrine. If it were set alongside Western religions, the only possible comparison would be with a class of religious culture that no longer exists overtly in the West: Celtic Christianity, which was eliminated in 667 by the Synod of Whitby in England. This was a hybrid religion, in some respects analogous to the combination of Shinto and Buddhism that developed in Japan during the **Heian period** (794–1185). The demise of Celtic Christianity preceded the creation of the Holy Roman Empire in Europe, which affirmed the political ascendancy of a form of Christianity that was theologically hostile to all nature-based religion. Consequently, Western models of religion cannot readily be applied to the study of Shinto.

Shinto survived not only Buddhism but also the deviant **Kokka Shinto** (State Shinto) era, which lasted from the early **Meiji period** (1868–1912) to 1945. It was forced to appear like a state religion, on a par with the state churches of Europe, which resulted in shrines (**jinja**) suffering from intense disruption. But even during that process, the basics of Shinto survived within the life structures and daily consciousness of the people. It adjusted to the context of the new industrial society, re-inventing aspects of itself to meet the needs of its new surroundings but still preserving the simple inspiration of its spiritual roots. Consequently, Japan is perhaps the only modern industrial nation with a native religious culture that has been preserved in spite of the powerful invasion and presence

1

of what 19th-century scholars term "higher religion" and the impact of technology on an agrarian society. In the tradition of Shinto, the past has survived and is both visible and intelligible.

Accordingly, the best way to commence an account of Shinto is not to speak of belief but rather to depict origins, and from them to describe the manner of the religion's existence throughout the history of Japanese society and culture.

THE ORIGINS OF SHINTO

Shinto is primarily a religion of nature centered on the cultivation of rice, one with which the Western world is not familiar in terms of either its annual cycle or the lifestyle it generates. The roots of Shinto reflect an awareness of the natural order. The oldest shrines are located in places that created a sense of awe and wonder in their observers, such as majestic mountains or the great Fall of Nachi in Kumano. But people were also inspired by rocks, trees, animals, unique human beings, and, in modern times, even inanimate objects such as industrial robots. This is the origin of *kami*, the divine as it is identified in the world of Shinto.

The 18th-century **Kokugaku** (National Learning) scholar **Motoori Norinaga** (1730–1801) penned a famous passage in which he tried to explain the meaning of the term *kami*. He began by rejecting the entire range of spurious etymological explanations, ranging from *kami* as a prefix for above or superior, to *kami* as an abbreviation of kagami meaning mirror, or kashikomi meaning reverence.

> I really do not fully comprehend the meaning of the word *kami*. Generally speaking, *kami* denotes, in the first place, the deities of heaven and earth that appear in the ancient texts and also the spirits enshrined in the shrines; furthermore, among all kinds of beings—including not only human beings but also such objects as birds, beasts, trees, grass, seas, mountains and so forth—any being whatsoever which possesses some eminent quality out of the ordinary, and is awe inspiring, is called *kami*. Eminence here does not refer simply to superiority in nobility, goodness or meritoriousness. Evil or queer things, if they are extraordinarily awe-inspiring, are also called *kami*.[1]

Whatever else may be said, it is clear that, among the principal historical or cultural origins to which the development of Shinto may be attributed, a sense of awe and mystery is important. Much of what has become Shinto has been inspired by this kind of awareness.

ANCESTRAL REVERENCE

Like most of Asia, Japan is profoundly steeped in the idea of **ancestral reverence**, another notion that was eliminated from the Western mind in its long transformation by the Judeo-Christian tradition. The 19th-century observer **Lafcadio Hearn** (1850–1904)—criticized by some as a romantic but in reality probably the most sensitive Western writer on Japan during the transition from feudal to industrial state—saw ancestral reverence as another great wellspring from which Japanese religious culture evolved. But in keeping with the natural sense of awe at the roots of Shinto, ancestors are considered in some sense to be present, like *kami*.

While teaching English in the town of Matsue, where he lived after marrying the daughter of a samurai family, Hearn corrected some sentences in which a boy wrote about performing rites "for his ancestors." Hearn, with Western values in mind, edited this to "in memory of our ancestors." But when speaking with the boy, he came to perceive the boy's understanding of his ancestors as alive and with him. This awoke him from his dogmatic slumber and enabled him to move toward a more profound appreciation of Japanese spirituality. In this regard, the Japanese have added a unique spiritual touch to the idea of ancestral reverence in Asia.

FROM RICE TO RITUAL

The introduction of rice cultivation from the Asian mainland brought with it the primitive historical beginnings of Japanese civilization that included settled life and a calendar of events. In Japan , it was believed that ancestors lived in mountains, coming down in spring to assist with planting rites and returning to the mountains in the fall once the rice had been harvested. Ethnological studies conducted by the **Nihon Minzoku Bunka Eizo Kenkyujo**, on communities in islands off Hiroshima, have shown that this basic pattern survives to the present. Documentation of the cycle took seven years to complete.

At this point, rituals began to be devised to mark these watershed times of the year. As immigrants entered Japan from the Asian mainland and elsewhere, they doubtless brought with them ideas, artifacts, and even rituals from their homeland, which they integrated with whatever they found already in existence in Japan. Japan has been described as having created a bricolage culture, meaning one which has absorbed and assimilated, on a selective basis, many features of other civilizations as they were seen necessary or useful. This is one reason why a search for rational consistency of concepts, rituals, and forms will always be fruitless. The culture did not originate, as did much of Western civilization, out of a handful of values or rational principles from a unitary religious source of authority. Japanese culture grew and expanded as new elements were introduced, often for their appearance. For example, the stylization and painting of shrine gateways (**torii**), in vermilion, was in imitation of Chinese forms.

One distinctive approach detectable even in the ancient Japanese character seems to have been a penchant for ritual, something that engagement with China elevated to the level almost of a science and from which, in due course, many Japanese performing arts developed. Indeed, it is arguable that it is the preservation of elaborate rituals that has perpetuated the life of the Shinto tradition. The regulation of Shinto rituals was always a part of the earliest attempts to create codes of government and law. From the **Taika Reform** of 645 to the composition of the **Engishiki** (procedures of the Engi era) completed in 927, and from thereafter, through all the periods of Japanese history to the **Meiji Restoration** in 1868, governments of Japan have tried to order rituals, classify shrines, and identify their place within national life, although the emphasis is always on ritual and not on doctrine. It has been argued, quite convincingly by some Japanese scholars such as Iwamoto Tokuichi, that the only "belief" common to all shrine traditions is that the most important duty of shrines is to perform and perpetuate ancient ceremonies. In so doing, the power and the dignity of the *kami* are manifest and honored. **Festivals**, in the sense of Mircea Eliade's concept of "ancient ontology," reenact the events surrounding an original enshrinement and consequently recapture the age when the *kami* was visible in all his or her power. This renews the bond between the *kami* and worshippers, and makes the benefits of the *kami* available to the community, whether within the framework of the agricultural year or related to other aspects of community life. Western scholars who have taken an interest in Shinto rituals have found them a fruitful source of understanding.

FROM RITUAL TO MYTH

Perhaps it is presumptuous to make a general affirmation in such a simple and unequivocal manner. In the case of Shinto, however, the evolution appears relatively clear. The oldest texts recording Japan's mythological beginnings are composite and complex. They do not appear until the eighth century and are steeped in Chinese imagery, being written in classical Chinese form. The **Kojiki** (712) and the **Nihon Shoki** (or Nihongi, 720) are relatively late in their compilation. Indeed, one of the tasks set for themselves by the Kokugaku (National Learning) scholars of the Edo period (1615–1868)—for example, Motoori Norinaga, quoted above—was to analyze the classical texts and try to distinguish within them what was Japanese from what was Chinese.

For Motoori Norinaga, the doctrine of **Amaterasu-ōmikami**, the *kami* of the sun, was the basis of Japanese culture. Hence, the fundamental mythological framework of Shinto came to be that of a solar deity, female, in possession of certain powers, and associated with white horses, among other things. It is at this point that the universal elements of Shinto can be seen and, in comparative studies with other ancient cultures, better understood. In Japan's case, of course, the doctrine of Amaterasu was not merely a solar myth, but evolved into the origin of the **imperial household** and supported its claim to power: being in direct descent from the *kami* of the sun. The greatest symbol in the heavens became the ancestor of the greatest family on earth. The political claims built into the **mythology** were designed to buttress the status of the **Yamato** clan in its drive for hegemony over the other competing clans, a project in which it was successful. Of particular importance are the claims to authority by virtue of conquests of different parts of the country by "relatives" of the ancestral *kami*. For example, **Ōkuninushi-no-mikoto** conquered the land around Izumo, which is a stage in the unification of the kingdom, while the travels of **Yamato-takeru-no-mikoto** took him to the Kanto plain.

While one role of the mythology was to justify the Yamato clan's standing, another was to provide the populace with some form of identity and self-understanding, again related to rituals. The predilection for purification (**harai**), which clearly belonged to the character of the ancient Japanese, is found in mythology and became a paradigmatic form of the developed culture. While Freudian ideas of taboo may be somewhat relevant here, what developed in Japanese culture is far and away one of the most elaborate practices of purification rituals found anywhere.

The narrative of **Izanagi-no-mikoto** and **Izanami-no-mikoto**, procreators of the Japanese archipelago, is at quite a different level from the myths of Amaterasu-ōmikami. They reflect ideas of fertility, the procreative act itself, and phallicism in the form of the Jeweled Spear of Heaven which was dipped into the ocean; according to the mythological narrative, the brine drops that fell from it coagulated, thus creating the islands. Izanami died giving birth to the *kami* of fire and went to **Yomi-no-kuni** (the Land of the Dead), a filthy and polluted place, as Izanagi discovered when he visited there. He was chased out, pursued by some ugly creatures, and upon leaving the land of pollution and death and reentering the world, he felt impure because of the experience, and washed himself in the River Tachibana. This was the first act of **misogi**, the generic form of all kinds of purification rituals ranging from the symbolic use of the harai gushi (a wand with an abundance of white paper streamers) to misogi performed in a river, in the ocean, or under a waterfall, which became popular in mountain areas. The incident is still recited in **norito** (ritual invocations). From those beginnings the tradition grew, developed new forms, and still manifests itself in many practices such as placing small piles of salt outside restaurants each evening before business commences, or washing doorways and entrances to buildings every morning.

FROM RITUAL AND MYTH TO DRAMA

The mythology of Japan provided sources for two kinds of ritual activities that derived from Shinto. One was the festivals that grew to celebrate the bounties of nature, the plentiful rice harvest, and the power of fertility. While the ritual part was conducted with dignified restraint, the celebratory aspects were often robust and boisterous. Many of them had a focus on fertility, such as the famous Henoko Matsuri (or Phallus Festival) of the **Tagata Jinja** in Komaki, near Nagoya Airport in Aiichi Prefecture, which is one of the best known. Nearby Inuyama city's **Oagata Jinja** hosts the Ososo Matsuri (Vagina Festival). These festivals are intended to protect crops, to guarantee business success, and to enrich fertility. On the other hand, there is the sedate tradition of **Noh**, which came to be one of Japan's highly aesthetic **dramatic arts**.

The roots of Noh within Shinto culture have preserved and perpetuated another dimension of the tradition.

The purification rituals that linked the ancient Japanese rice culture to its self-understanding were themselves symbolic re-enactments of the primal act of Izanagi-no-mikoto in the River Tachibana. It is from this source that religious drama evolved from Shinto rituals, which, in turn, expressed themes from Japanese mythology. These appear to have arisen from lengthy rituals performed initially by priests, whose roles were subsequently taken over by actors. Eventually, these actors performed only the early parts of the total sequences, which came to be performed as separate artistic modules.

Although it is performed in a secular context in modern times, many Noh performances still take place at shrines. Even when they do not, the actors, chorus, orchestra, and stage assistants all receive **oharai** (ritual purification) before performances, as do costumes and masks. The oldest plays deal directly with themes from the age of the *kami (kami-yo)*, as recorded in the aforementioned classical texts the Nihongi (720) and the Kojiki (712). As the art form developed, new themes were introduced from time to time, but in spite of its evolution, many of the ancient features still remain highly visible.

The earliest Noh plays were performed outdoors, with nature as the setting and the earth as the stage, not unlike classical Greek drama. When **Kagura**, sacred dances, were first performed, particularly after Chinese costumes were introduced, stages were erected outdoors. Hence, the Kagura stage became very important for the subsequent development of Noh. Dance rituals, such as the **Shishi-mai**, a harvest divination dance of Chinese origin using a lion costume, is still performed outdoors, on large reed mats, with the audience surrounding the dance area. While modern Noh theaters (Noh-gaku-do) have a shared roof for the audience and the actors, several reminders of tradition remain: first, there is a separate roof over the stage, as in the past; second, white gravel, known as shirasu, is spread on the ground between the stage and the audience that goes back to the time when the plays were performed outdoors and when the gravel reflected the natural light of the sun on to the stage; finally, the floor of the stage is made of Japanese cypress, from which all shrine buildings are constructed.

There are several types of Noh, among which the *waki* are the most relevant for the understanding of Shinto. Plays in this category are preceded by the performance of Okina in its entirety, a Shinto purification ceremony consisting of three dances. The visual symbolism of Shinto is very much in evidence in Waki-Noh plays: for example, orchestra members dress in the **eboshi** (a Heian period courtier's headdress).

The shite (the principal performer) is always a *kami* or the messenger of a *kami* who tells the story of the origin of a shrine in a poetic narrative. In the second scene, he appears as the *kami* of that shrine and performs a dance. Once the dance is finished, he removes the mask, shows proper respect and reverence toward it, replaces it in its box, and leaves the stage. The performance concludes with a lively stick drum performance and a dance, in which the actor himself vocalizes loudly as he stamps his feet. He wears a black mask, the koku-shiji-jo, and carries a suzu, a purification implement with bells attached, which he shakes during the dance. The dances are performed at important occasions, such as at New Year, festival, and other times, and are a request to the *kami* for a good harvest and good fortune, the core purpose of all Shinto rituals and festivals.

The written forms of Waki-Noh date to the eighth century, although the themes of earlier centuries are to be found in the famous poetic collection the **Man'yōshū**, the Thousand Leaves Collection. The shite actors of the Kongoryu School who perform Waki-Noh are all priests. This format of their performances is typical of the oldest genre of Noh, and demonstrates again the origins of Noh in the rituals of Shinto.

HISTORICAL BEGINNINGS OF INSTITUTIONAL SHINTO

The mythological roots having been planted, Shinto's first experience at articulating self-identity was in response to the introduction of Buddhism to the imperial court. It was during the **Kofun** (Proto-Historic) period (circa second century to 552 C.E.) that the first physical evidence of the impact of continental influences on Shinto practices may be observed. The Chinese Wei Dynasty Chronicles refer to almost one hundred small fiefdoms in Japan that were gradually subsumed under the authority of the Yamato clan. Clan leaders were buried in stone chambers covered by earth mounds known as kofun. Some of those excavated suggest leadership that used swords, curved stones (magatama), and mirrors as symbols of authority, akin to the elements of the **imperial regalia** of a later age. The **Grand Shrines of Ise** and **Izumo Taisha**, for example, probably date their major development to this period.

The term Shinto is a combination of two Chinese characters *kami* (*shen* in Chinese) and *dō* (*dao* in Chinese). In Japanese, it means the way of the *kami*. It was first used in the reign of **Emperor Yōmei** (reigned 586–587), who was recorded as having believed in the law of the Buddha and having revered the way of the *kami*. Buddhism was referred to initially in Japanese as Butsudo, the way of the Buddha, and Shinto consequently identified as the way of the *kami*. Buddhism is now referred to as Bukkyō, the teaching of Buddha. Shinto remains a *dō,* a folkway. Buddhism's first formal recognition in court about 538 challenged Shinto to develop a structure to support the indigenous rites, into which, doubtless, some continental elements were incorporated.

As the hegemony of the Yamato clan grew, legitimacy in the form of ritual, myth, and religious unity led to the claims of divine descent, as expressed in the Kojiki and the Nihon Shōki. Following the Taika Reform of 645, the **Ritsuryō System** established the **Jingikan** (the Office of Shinto *Kami* Worship) on the basis of the concept of **matsuri-goto**, the unity of worship and government (**saisei-itchi**). The term **matsuri** is the ordinary word for a Shinto festival, but in those early days, it referred also to government. Specific clans were appointed to deal with these matters, and these were the ancestral figures of later Shinto families such as **Nakatomi**, Imbe, and **Urabe**. It is fairly clear from the evidence that during this period Shinto moved from a loosely structured set of practices, beliefs, and attitudes embedded in community rituals toward an organized religious system at the level of the state. As **Allan G. Grapard** has stated the point, "These two basic aspects are, however, not entirely separate and are responsible for, or reflect much of, the Japanese national character as it is expressed in sociopolitical structure, psychological attitudes, and aesthetic criteria."[2]

THE RAPPROCHEMENT WITH BUDDHISM

Buddhism, as the great intellectual historian **Nakamura Hajime** has stated, was introduced to help manage the state, not in the interests of the salvation of people's souls. A system of state-supported temples was instituted, known as Kokubunji, and the populace at large was told to place a Butsudan, a Buddhist altar, inside their homes. Buddhism, as well as Shinto, was receiving state patronage and therefore there was little either could do except accommodate the other through peaceful coexistence and ritual interaction. There is clear evidence that this was happening at the local level long before any philosophical theories were generated to explain one in terms of the other. By the eighth century, **jingū-ji** (shrine-temple) complexes were being created, such as the **Kashima Jingū-ji** created by the monk Mangan in 749 and the Tado Jingū-ji in 763. The great bronze Buddha of Nara, housed in the Tōdai-ji (the Great Temple of the East, which is the largest wooden building in the world), was completed during the reign of **Emperor Shomu** (reigned 724–729) under both the *kami* **Hachiman** and the patronage of the **Usa Hachiman Shrine**, which donated funds in 745. This in turn earned Hachiman the title of Bosatsu (bodhisattva) in 783. When the capital removed to Kyōto, the **Iwashimizu Hachiman-gū** was established as a center of syncretistic practice. It took a leadership role in this respect during the period when the Hachiman cult flourished. These developments were spontaneous and not in any way governed by an apparent central policy.

However, it was the Heian period that saw the flowering of a syncretistic philosophy that embraced both Buddhism and Shinto. Two important Japanese Buddhist monks visited China to study continental Buddhism. **Saichō** (767–822) introduced the semi-esoteric cult known in Japan as **Tendai Buddhism** (named after Mount T'ien-T'ai in China), and **Kūkai** (774–835) introduced Tibetan-style Buddhism known in Japan as **Shingon Buddhism** (true word). Both of these sects favored mountain locations for temples, and their rites were introduced into the culture of the mountain shrines that were already in place. Cults of an ascetic nature known as **Shugendō** grew out of these movements. Centers sprung up in Kumano, Yamagata, and other parts of the country. **Yamabushi**, mountain ascetics and practitioners of various rituals, lived on these mountains, and engaged in the pursuit of supernatural powers through diet, purification under waterfalls or in rivers (misogi), meditation, climbing, fire rites, and numerous other activities. They were a product of the many theories that combined Buddhism and Shinto, central among which was the **Honji-Suijaku** theory, according to which Shinto *kami* became manifestations of Buddhist figures.

So syncretic were these movements that it is in reality impossible to discuss either Shinto or Buddhism adequately in isolation. However, it should be noted that each of these communities had its own theory, sets of beliefs, rituals, and figures of reverence. In this way, the particularity of Shinto remained and manifested itself. These movements can be broken into various groups. Broadly speaking, the Tendai tradition gave rise to **Sannō Ichijitsu Shinto** centered on Mount Hiei near Kyōto, while the Shingon tradition gave rise to **Ryōbu Shinto**, found typically in Kumano or Kasuga.

Sanno Ichijitsu Shinto relates to three groups of *kami* worshipped on the east side of Mount Hiei and were associated with three groups of Buddhist avatars worshipped in three temples on top of the mountain. One famous feature of this cult was the practice of **sen-nichi-kai-hō-gyō**, a discipline consisting of running at night around a fixed circuit of sacred places for 1000 days, broken into stages and spread over a period of seven years. The total distance covered is equivalent to almost the circumference of the earth. During the Tokugawa government's control, this cult became important and useful to a government suspicious of any religious group. Many Yamabushi were recruited as spies. The syncretism had its appeal, and Ieyasu himself was enshrined, after his death, in the **Nikkō Tōshūgō** as the "Great Incarnate Illuminator of the East."

Ryobu Shinto was an attempt to bring together Shingon Buddhism and the Shinto of Ise. The principal Buddha of Shingon was Dainichi Nyorai, the Great Sun Buddha, making links with Amaterasu-ōmikami quite overt. The term Ryobu (both parts) refers not, as is often mistakenly assumed, to Buddhism and Shinto, but to the two great mandalas of Shingon Buddhism, cosmograms that were created to teach the truths of enlightenment. These were linked with the **Gekū** (Outer) and **Naikū** (Inner) Shrines at Ise in the framework of a complex system consisting of ritual, diagrams, philosophical ideas, and a code of numbers, which had the effect of proving that, in essence, Buddhism and Shinto were identical. Ryobu Shinto had a brief existence, then went into decline as a result of two factors. One was the Shinto counter-thesis that, rather than *kami* being manifestations of Buddhas, the reverse was true. The second was that Shinto felt challenged with the emergence of more radical forms of Buddhism in the Kamakura period (1185–1333), particularly those advocating belief in Buddha alone as adequate. By the end of the Kamakura period, Shinto studies had slowly recommenced, preparing the way for the movements of the Edo period.

Two other schools of Shinto of the Heian period call for brief mention. One was that of the **Watarai** family, hereditary priests of the Outer Shine of Ise. By the end of the 13th century, they had compiled a set of texts known as the Five Canonical Writings of Shinto (**Shinto Gobusho**). **Watarai Ieyuki** (1255–1351) compiled a massive text in

1320 known as the **Ruiji jingi hongen** which had an enormous influence on the imperial loyalist **Kitabatake Chikafusa** (1293–1354), who was also a scholar of imperial history. There are traces of Chinese **Confucian** cosmology in the Watarai tradition, which fed into the Confucian varieties of Shinto that emerged in the Edo period. **Watarai (Deguchi) Nobuyoshi** (1615–1690) was a teacher of **Yamazaki Ansai** (1618–1682), the founder of **Suiga Shinto**.

Yuiitsu Genpon Shinto was another major tradition, associated with the distinguished, priestly, Yoshida family. The leading figure was **Yoshida Kanetomo** (1435–1511), descended from the Urabe family, diviners in the imperial court whose lineage went back to the seventh century. The disruption of the Onin War in 1467 and the destruction of some old shrines led to him advocating their reconstruction, the re-establishment of imperial authority, and the supremacy of Shinto in Japanese culture. While the school had syncretic elements, including Confucian, Taoist, and Buddhist elements, Shinto was the true origin of all of these. As in Buddhism, he distinguished between exoteric teachings, as found in the Kojiki and the Nihon Shoki, and his own esoteric teachings, derived from sacred texts transmitted by the *kami* to the Yoshida family. By the beginning of the 16th century, Yoshida Kanetomo had risen to become the most important single personality in Shinto. The funeral rites of **Toyotomi Hideyoshi** (1536–1598) in 1598 were arranged by the Yoshida family, along with his enshrinement at the Toyokuni Jinja. The family's influence lasted all through the Edo period, controlling the ordination and appointment of priests in many shrines throughout the country. The Meiji government's seizure of control in 1868 ended the dominant role of Yoshida Shinto.

The turbulence of the era of civil war ended with the ascendancy of the House of Tokugawa, which enforced a peace that permitted more scholarly pursuits to proceed. As part of the philosophical background to his rule, Tokugawa Ieyasu actively imported Neo-Confucian values from China. This meeting of **Confucianism and Shinto** in turn provided yet another context for Shinto's development.

THE SHINTO REVIVAL

It was during the Edo period that the serious study of Shinto in its own right commenced with the work of a number of scholars who formed various schools. **Hayashi Razan** (1583–1657), the Confucian adviser to Ieyasu and to his three successors, was the first to try to unite Shinto and Neo-Confucian thought. His rejection of Buddhism led also to his attack on Yoshida Shinto, which he considered impure. In his work *Shinto Denju* (The Transmission of Shinto), he stressed the unity of Shinto and the imperial way, the presence of the *kami* within the human heart, and the proper administration of government as evidence of divine virtue.

His work was continued by **Yoshikawa Koretari** (1616–1694), who was originally a student of Yoshida Shinto and rose to the most prominent position within it by 1657. With the support of a number of daimyo (provincial lords), he became the government's Shinto adviser, and in keeping with the tendencies of the Tokugawa system, he reconsidered his Shinto doctrines and brought them more into line with Neo-Confucianism. He saw **Kunitokotachi-no-mikoto** at the center of the pantheon, preceding the separation of heaven and earth. The human and divine could meet within Yoshikawa's system, through people showing the attitude of **tsutsushimi** (reverence and humility). In this way, they could rejoin the supra-rational absolute that existed before thought had emerged. Although his work did not generate a school, it was highly influential, finding its way into the thought of those who sought to unite Neo-Confucianism with Shinto.

Yamazaki Ansai, originally ordained as a Zen monk, was "converted" to Shinto and received as his reishago, or initiation name, Shidemasu, also read as Suika, from which the name of his school was derived, Suika Shinto. He saw Neo-Confucianism and Shinto as, in effect, the ways of earth and heaven, which he felt were completely in harmony. In praising the merits of revering the emperor, he offered the most famous account of the imperial regalia since that of Kitabatake Chikafusa. He declared that the divine is a force residing in the heart, symbolized by the jewel. The radiance of the divine is represented by the mirror, and its awesome virtue by the sword. The only limitation of Yamazaki's thought was its sheer abstraction. It was not linked to any particular rituals or shrines; therefore, his successors had the task of both developing his ideas and in some way giving them institutional embodiment. The Yoshida tradition wielded enormous influence, and in spite of serious efforts by Yoshimi Yukikazu (1673–1761), who belonged to the priestly family that cared for the Tokugawa family mausoleum in Nagoya, Yoshida power could not be usurped. Consequently, it was left to the scholars of the National Learning movement (Kokugaku) to examine and build on the work of Yamazaki.

Restoration or **Fukko Shinto**, which began with **Keichu** (1640–1701) and **Kamo no Mabuchi** (1697–1769), was developed by Motoori Norinaga (1730–1801) and linked to the Meiji Restoration by **Hirata Atsutane** (1776–1843). It focused on a revived study of the classics beginning with the **Man'yōshū**, respected on account of the spontaneity of its style and its antiquity. Kamo no Mabuchi encouraged Motoori Norinaga to work on the Kojiki. Norinaga devoted 30 years to the task; as a result, he came to reject Neo-Confucianism and Chinese culture in general, and found Buddhism equally unacceptable. He longed for a return to the classical age of virtuous emperors and people. The core of Japanese culture he located in the doctrine of Amaterasu and the notion of divine descent. Hirata Atsutane promoted Shinto as the only way to restore Japan's identity and fortunes amidst the domestic crisis of the last days of the shogunate, and the imminent threat posed by the Western powers. His son, Kanatane (1799–1880), was active in the early days of the Meiji government, advocating the implementation of his father's ideas.

The Kokugaku movement did not by itself create the Meiji Restoration, which was very much a response to an external threat. However, it did help enrich the Japanese sense of national identity, always a useful strategy when a nation is threatened, and it offered some features of an ideological basis for the new government. It is not difficult to see the link between Hirata Shinto and some of the excesses of the Meiji government, but it must always be remembered that the Meiji government's agenda was not the proper understanding of either Shinto or the National Learning movement, but the creation of a national ideology strong enough to unite the people and enable them to deal effectively with the foreign challenge they were facing.

THE MEIJI RESTORATION

In 1868, the last shogun surrendered his power to a group of young samurai who were committed to restoring imperial rule and to bringing the country up to modern standards. By this means they hoped to avoid the fate of China, which had been ruthlessly carved up by the aggressive and technologically advanced Western powers. The capital was swiftly moved to Edo and renamed Tōkyō (Eastern Capital), and the emperor set up in residence within what had been the Tokugawa castle, thereafter the Imperial Palace. The idea of a system of national shrines was reintroduced and the steps to State Shinto initiated.

Before discussing State Shinto, it is perhaps useful to try to imagine the mood and concerns of the Meiji period leadership. These are best captured in the slogans of the period. **Wakon-Yōsai** (Western techniques–Eastern spirit) is probably the best known, reflecting the desire to import Western technology, but as far as possible, on Japanese terms. **Fukoku-Kyōhei** (rich country–strong army) articulated the need for a competent defense in the event of invasion or attack. This was to be built on the basis of a strong economy. A third and rather explicitly xenophobic one was **Sonnō-Joi** (revere the emperor—expel the barbarians). Each of these three represents one facet of the period; all, however, are basic features of the modernization process that arises when technological change begins to challenge the old order. Modernization, for the purposes of this brief essay, may be defined very simply as a process brought about by the impact of technology on what has hitherto been a predominantly agricultural economy. In Japan's case, education was quickly perceived as a pre-condition to achieving some of these goals, and consequently, compulsory education was instituted. In these respects, Japan was no different from any other states that were undergoing, or have subsequently undergone, the same process of transformation.

Along with adaptation to technology and the implementation of educational programs, one further basic ingredient of any modernizing program is an ideology that serves to unify the nation concerned and enrich its sense of common purpose. It is in this general context that the role of State Shinto should be understood.

STATE SHINTO

Nationalism by itself is usually effective as a stimulant to modernization, but it is more effective if combined with a system of symbols and rituals. Ironically, the state churches of Europe provided one model for the Meiji leadership. A section of the leadership came to think that Shinto could be adapted to the role of guardian of the nation's soul and the basis of national morality. Thus, Kokka Shinto (State Shinto) was the work of a government and, subsequently, a Ministry of Home Affairs extremely unenlightened in matters of religion and its relationship to culture.

The separation of Buddhism from Shinto was the first step, accomplished through the **Shinbutsu-Bunri** instruction of 28 March, 1868. The proponents of the view that State Shinto, and indeed Shinto itself, was an artificial creation of the 19th century are guilty of not paying attention to the facts of Japanese history. Firstly, there is a clear distinction between shrines and *kami* that received government support and recognition from the Heian period onward and those that were more clearly rooted in local community and agricultural origins. Hachiman, for example, played a decisive role in the eventual removal of the court to Kyōto. Other *kami* were clearly favored, especially those to whom imperial messengers were sent at festival times.

Second, moving to the popular level, there is the question of the organizing and running of festivals that continued all through the period of syncretism, encouraged by the Edo government. It was the people's religion and the people's culture. The excesses of Shinto fertility festivals that had continued through the Edo period were curbed in response to the criticism of Western missionaries and diplomats who argued that their continuance would hinder Japan's recognition as a modern state.

Third, Buddhism's association with funerals is not a post-Edo development, but dates back to the Kamakura period. Taboos involving death are as old as the roots of Japanese culture; that was one clear area where overlap would simply not be possible. In short, in spite of syncretism, the two elements had separately defined areas of responsibility, and these were easily detached in 1868.

Therefore, the basis of State Shinto was conceived by its proponents to lie in already existing structures which they judged could be separated from Buddhism, and revised (or updated) to meet contemporary needs. In other words, there was a perceived basis upon which the concept could be built and a group of shrines readily available for the idea to be developed. Further, the creation of the **Yasukuni Jinja** and the shrines to honor the war dead, the **Shōkonsha**, was the manipulation of ancestral reverence, an area ceded partly to Buddhism. Therefore, in a way, these shrines were more like Butsudan (Buddhist family altars) than Shinto shrines. This does not enhance the case for Buddhism being the reality and Shinto some kind of ethereal phenomenon, but merely illustrates how the power of an underlying "ethnophilosophy," as it has been called, can quite unselfconsciously manipulate any elements of a culture in the interest of a desired result. To call this either Buddhism or Shinto is a little naive.

So what was State Shinto? It was a politically engineered attempt to use the shrines as symbols of nationalism on the basis that it would stimulate the Japanese spirit to greater levels of self-sacrificial endeavor. And it failed miserably. Why did it fail? Firstly, the shrine authorities themselves had virtually nothing to do with it. It was decreed by the government and handed to the Ministry of the Interior to manage. Even a superficial survey of the number of organs of government successively assigned to deal with the issue illustrates how ill-conceived was the idea and how impossible its implementation. For example, the **Jinja Gappei** movement to merge lesser shrines into more impressive ones failed to recognize the deep roots of highly localized village culture, and virtually collapsed after 1920. The plan to prevent aristocratic families from becoming hereditary priests succeeded in some instances but was not totally effective, because many old shrines—for example, those referred to in the Nihon Shoki or other classics—intimidated the military police sent to harass their priests. Finally, the great argument that Shinto was not a religion but a "folk way," while true in terms of Western definitions of religion as something with doctrines and founders and rules, failed to recognize that within the world of Japanese spirituality, it is a distinction without a difference.

How did State Shinto work? The emotional role of the Yasukuni Jinja became central. The emperor himself actually bowed to the spirits of Yasukuni, and therein is both the argument for the theory of renewed nationalism and its answer. But set in a wider context, the modern issue of Yasukuni Jinja is much more complex than many Western critics are prepared to admit. Over three million souls are enshrined in Yasukuni Jinja. Whatever the reason they died, they believed they were giving their lives for a worthy cause. An incident from a different context might help to demonstrate how sensitive an issue war dead can be. Former British Prime Minister Harold Macmillan, in a careless statement on television in 1958, remarked that World War I had not only been a mistake, but had been actually unnecessary and probably avoidable. Bereaved relatives of war veterans were outraged—and they were on the victorious side. Japanese bereaved have faced loss, defeat, and war crime trials. Small wonder that Yasukuni Shrine has been a sensitive issue for domestic politicians of the post-World War II period. Perhaps it is difficult to persuade people that the deaths of their friends and relatives and the deaths of people of another culture are of equal value, especially if they perceive the other as an aggressor. But if such an attitude continues to prevail, emotional prejudices will always displace objective historical judgments. That is one reason the Yasukuni Jinja remains controversial.

THE POSTWAR DEBATE ON STATE SHINTO

After the end of the Pacific War (World War II), many critical and polemical writings about State Shinto appeared that were inspired by the idea that even after the war, there was, and still remains, a "plot" or "conspiracy" to restore State Shinto. Dr. Ernest Lokowandt gave a controversial presentation to the Asiatic Society of Japan in Tōkyō in September 1982 entitled "The Revival of State Shinto," in which he gave reasons that he thought a conspiracy existed. One of the main arguments, for all observers like him, is based on the controversial status of the Yasukuni Jinja. Any public activity surrounding the Yasukuni Shrine is closely monitored, particularly by the governments of Korea and China, to both of which it remains a sensitive issue. This is understandable, as they had the state shrines imposed on them along with the requirements of emperor worship. However, they forget that the war dead of any nation remains an emotional issue. Some subjects should be handled with great sensitivity, and the war dead is one.

Claims that militarism is being stimulated and revived by people performing **sampai** (reverence) at the Yasukuni Jinja are difficult to substantiate. A mood of pacifism has pervaded Japanese society since 1945, and Yasukuni Jinja is a part of the past that many people are still trying to come to terms with. One central issue for the Japanese is how the shrine can be supported. After 1945, the Yasukuni Shrine became a private religious juridical corporation (**shūkyō hōjin**). Some argue that the state should take responsibility. Opponents to this view counter that any state support would be against the constitution. Therefore, the question of constitutional revision is closely linked with the Yasukuni problem. That there has been a move toward seeking government support for the shrine is clear; however, local public and international reaction has so far made this impossible. Fuel was added to the flames of criticism by two controversial events that were immediately seized upon, both of which stirred up feelings on all sides.

First was the enshrinement in the fall of 1979 of 14 men, all of whom were designated as Class-A defendants at the Tōkyō War Crimes Trials, including Prime Minister General Hideki Tojo, the perceived war leader. Western journalists were caught up in the reaction, and there were stories of the bones having been smuggled in at night. This was utter nonsense: No human remains are to be found at any shrine, because death is pollution. The souls of the men were moved at night from a local shrine for the war dead to Yasukuni, because enshrinement that entails moving spirits from one place to another normally takes place at night. While desiring to see the men enshrined along with the others who died is natural from a Japanese point of view, it distressed critics in Japan and led to extreme verbal outbursts from the governments of China and Korea.

Prime Minister Nakasone Yasuhiro (born 1918; prime minister 1982–1987) was responsible for the second incident. He visited the Yasukuni Shrine in the company of several cabinet members, an event that takes place annually. Until Nakasone's visit, previous prime ministers signed the book with their name only, and donated from their own pockets. Nakasone signed "Prime Minister (Sori Daijin) Nakasone Yasuhiro," making the visit official and consequently stirring up considerable controversy. His successor, Prime Minister Takeshita Noboru, felt forced to cancel the visit in the following year. The complexity of the issue is seen in the fact that former Foreign Minister Matsuoka Yosuke, one of the architects of the Berlin-Rome-Tōkyō Axis, was Christian (Presbyterian), along with numerous others. Nakasone is well known for his right-wing views, and that alone to some was grounds for argument.

Studies of militarism in general suggest that it is seldom traceable to a unitary source. Economic and other factors come into play. But Shinto, because it had been raised to the status of a national ideology, was an easy target. However, a week-long symposium held in March 1994 outside Santa Fe in New Mexico focused on the relationship between Japanese nationalism and intellectuals in the Kyōto school and the world of Zen Buddhism. Revelations about the association of Martin Heidegger (1889–1976), the German-born existentialist philosopher, and the Nazi Party challenged conventional views of the apolitical image of intellectuals and of Heidegger. This "rude awakening" transferred itself to Japan, and questions were asked about the philosophy of the Kyōto school of Zen and the culture of Zen Buddhism itself. The proceedings of the symposium were published under the title *Rude Awakenings: The Kyōto School and the Questions of Nationalism.*[3] A book by Brian Victoria, *Zen at War*,[4] followed shortly after, dealing with the link between Zen Buddhism and Japanese militarism. The problem of the relationship between Zen and nationalism may not have been completely resolved; it is indeed ironic that the famous Suzuki Daisetsu went around the world after 1945 popularizing Zen as a philosophy of enlightenment, peace, and love, while Shinto was blamed for the rise of militarism in keeping with U.S. wartime political propaganda that centered on State Shinto.

Conspiracy theories that have existed for over half a century and that have not demonstrated much evidence of substance are better considered as anxieties in the minds of their creators than genuine predictions of the future. At any rate, the Yasukuni Jinja issue, while intriguing in its own right and a part of the history of Shinto, is not capable of being the basis for an illuminating discussion of the Shinto tradition in all its diversity. It is perhaps appropriate to return to the original plan: to describe Shinto as it is, and, from how it exists and functions, infer back to the meaning it sets forth in its rituals and its artifacts. The physical presence is perhaps the simplest starting point.

SHRINE ART AND ARCHITECTURE

The character of Shinto is seen very clearly in its architecture, which is perhaps justifiably describable as its ultimate artistic expression. Architects from around the world have observed and studied the Grand Shrine of Ise skyline. While many features of shrine architecture were borrowed from China, such as the use of vermilion on shrine gateways (torii) after the Nara period, certain characteristics remain Japanese. The gateways are unique to Japan, and no indisputable origin has been discovered to explain their form. The oldest may have been simply a rope strung across two trees, intended to mark the entrance to a sacred space. However, under Chinese influence the gateways began to take many forms, made of different materials. Buildings also took new forms through time, and eventually, different *kami* came to be worshipped in buildings whose design became particular to that *kami*. For example, Hachiman shrines are easily noted by the sweeping roof line in which the three separate buildings are joined by verandas. The **chigi** (protruding gables) and the **katsuogi**, the rounded blocks laid along the roof apex, may be the remains of a lean-to roof style of an ancient pit dwelling, but it has been refined by time and effort into a work of art.

Jinja in Japanese refers to a location, and not to a building. Shrines began as places of divine manifestations, like the burning bush Moses saw, or the place where Jacob dreamed of a ladder stretching up to heaven; the Japanese of old felt that those places were the residences of *kami*. Consequently, Japan's oldest and most impressive shrines are located in places of dramatic natural beauty. Early worship centered upon these sacred spaces, the precursor of the **himorogi**, marked off initially by a rope but later fenced by trees, rocks, or carefully laid-out stones. These were the locations where eventually buildings were raised to house acts of worship. This system continues today as new buildings are erected. When **jichinsai** is performed to pacify a *kami* of the earth, a himorogi is marked with branches of **sakaki** and plaited straw rope known as a **shimenawa**. The area inside is considered sacred for that time and the ceremony is conducted by a properly purified priest.

The earliest shrines were probably little more than rock piles that marked a sacred spot; in time, structures were built in front of them or at the foot of the mountain where these spaces were identified. Some jinja of very ancient origin have no **honden** (main worship hall), and some even had no buildings whatsoever. The island of **Okinoshima** was the center of the worship of **Munakata-ōkami**, protector of the ocean waterways. Between the fourth and seventh centuries, the government energetically promoted this cult, which prospered because of Japan's domination of the southern part of the Korean peninsula. The entire island is dotted with numerous altars. The huge amount of artifacts and treasures found at them suggest the vitality of the cult, yet there is no evidence of any building ever having been erected there.

It is from such simple beginnings that the modern shrine developed. It was a indeed the "place of the *kami*," a **yorishiro**, because the space was perceived as sacred and thus himorogi and **iwasaka** developed. Some shrines have no main buildings even today. The Omiya (great shrine) near Nara has Mount Miwa as its honden and its *kami*. It is topped by a large rock that serves as a yorishiro. The **Isonokami Jinja** in Kyōto and the upper **Suwa Jinja** in Nagano had no honden until the Meiji period.

Once buildings began to appear, probably around the fifth century, **jinja shaden** (shrine buildings) came to provide another example of the particularity of Shinto in its tendency to identify *kami* with particular places. Not only are *kami* worshipped in specific localities, but they are also worshipped in specific types of buildings whose form is associated with them. It would be incongruous to see the worship of Hachiman taking place inside buildings that looked like an **Inari** shrine, for example.

It is quite possible to have **massha** (subordinate shrines) to another *kami* inside shrine precincts. Inari massha are found in many shrines of other *kami*. While there are historical reasons for the differences of design, these designs also help to identify the *kami* being worshipped. It is believed that the *kami*, rather than the worshipers, determine the locations of jinja and buildings. For example, a community or family might believe that their need to worship a particular *kami* is itself a sign from that *kami* that it is to be worshipped by them. An auspicious site is chosen, and the location then becomes sacred. Shrines or their buildings are seldom relocated except under the most exceptional circumstances.

The details of individual shrines extend beyond buildings to the types of torii (gateway) and to the kinds of **shinsen** (food offerings) that the various *kami* prefer. There are about 16 main styles of architecture of varied historical origins and over 20 types of torii associated with different *kami* and locations. These are described with the names of principal exemplary shrines and *kami*, some of which have been identified earlier.

Some scholars claim, on the basis of mythological arguments, that the first shrine building was erected by Okuninishi-no-mikoto to revere his own kushi-mitama (**soul** of mysterious virtue). Shortly thereafter, **Nininigi-no-mikoto**, grandson of Amaterasu-ōmikami, is said to have erected a shrine modeled on his palace to honor Okuninishi-no-mikoto at Obama in Izumo. This became the famous Izumo Taisha. Also according to legend, in February 657 B.C.E., Emperor Jimmu enshrined the **tama** of Amaterasu on Mount Tomiyama in Yamato, although no buildings were erected. In 92 B.C.E., the sacred mirror (formerly kept in the Imperial Palace) was enshrined by Emperor Sujin (reigned 97–30 B.C.E.) at Kasanui in Yamato. In another legend, Emperor Suinin (reigned 29 B.C.E.–70 C.E.) constructed Ise Jingu in 5 B.C.E. for the sacred mirror, and from that date shrine buildings came to be erected. This is, of course, mere legend, because the dating is beyond verification; however, much of this mythology was incorporated into the teachings of State Shinto.

Alongside the politically inspired legends of shrine origins, many old shrines have independent folk origins. There are shrines for the *kami* of earth and other shrines which predate politicization. No imperial sanction was involved in setting up these shrines, which reflected the spiritual aspirations of an agricultural people to have their own places of veneration.

Many old buildings around the countryside, local to a community, belong in this category. Most have no names and would have been part of the 100,000 that were eliminated by government ordinance during the era of State Shinto, when the wholesale destruction of local folk shrines was undertaken in order to strengthen government shrines.

The earliest buildings were examples of stark beauty and simplicity, constructed, as in the case of Ise Jingū, of plain Japanese cypress with no decoration and using few if any nails. Polynesian rice stores are thought to be the nearest similar buildings. The various styles of architecture that emerged reflect the different ages of Shinto and the periods through which the development of its traditions passed. The use of curved lines did not appear until after the eighth century, about the time that Chinese and Korean influences began to seep into Japan.

The architecture and traditions of shrines reflect two deep traits of the Japanese character: the love of purity and the love of newness. The periodic rebuilding of shrines (usually replicating the existing form) expresses the spirit of endless renewal that seems to lie at the root of the culture, along with the desire for purity and brightness. The buildings in which the *kami* are revered should not be decrepit, dirty, and neglected, but fresh, clean, and well kept.

The capital has been moved from time to time for the same reason. Emperor Kammu (reigned 781–806) moved it from Nara to Kyōto in 794, ushering in not only a new age of Japanese history, but also new styles in building, manners, and dress. From that time onward, the styles of shrines, matching the mood of the ages, began to change. Nevertheless, in spite of historical change, the ideals and values expressed in, for example, the simple, graceful form of the Grand Shrines of Ise remain a classical product of Japanese aesthetic values.

SHINTO RITUALS

The continuity of Shinto is seen in its rituals. A shrine, of course, is a sacred place and not a building, although buildings are erected to house activities of various kinds. Principal among these activities is the performance of purification ceremonies. Purification (harai) is the core paradigm of Shinto.

The philosophy of ritual is a relatively new field, but can be effectively applied to Shinto. The ultimate value embodied in its rituals is purity, derived from the act of purification of Izanagi-no-mikoto when he escaped from the Land of Pollution, Yomi-no-kuni, where he found his dead wife, Izanami-no-mikoto, decomposing. After escaping, he purified himself in the River Tachibana, performing the first act of misogi, water purification, which became the basis of meaning in all Shinto rituals. This incident is a central reference point in most Shinto ceremonies, and in the norito, the liturgical incantations. The centrality of purification is also reflected in the normal sequence of ritual acts in almost every Shinto ceremony, whether ground-breaking (**jichinsai**) or purification of a car for road safety.

Stage one is **shūbatsu**, in which the officiating priest purifies himself or herself. This is followed by the invocation of the *kami* to alight on the evergreen sakaki branch. The offerings are then uncovered and the ceremony may commence. The principal act is the Norito-Sojo, the reading of the norito which includes an account of what is taking place, the date, the event, the people concerned, and whatever is relevant to identifying it. After the norito has been intoned, the ceremony is performed: the ground is broken, a car or airplane is purified, or a building opened. When this is over, the principal participants offer a **tamagushi**, a sakaki branch with **gohei**, paper strips attached, as an act of reverence. Once this is completed, the order of events at the beginning is reversed. The offerings are covered, and the invocation of appreciation permits the *kami* to leave the site. This pattern of ritual is widely practiced in Shrine Shinto rituals. Sects have their variations, but the pattern is almost standard, irrespective of the *kami* invoked. This description does little justice to the reality, which is reverent, colorful, dignified, and intense. The uniqueness of the development of Shinto is reflected in the fact that the ritual described is performed by priests wearing Chinese T'ang Dynasty dress, reading Heian period formulas, and relating all this to contemporary reality.

Of course, purification is not the only basis of ritual. Regard for sacred space is also most important. The website of Professors James W. Boyd and Ron G. Williams, who have spent time in Japan studying Shinto rituals, offers some interesting and original accounts of the meaning of what they observed. They are among the first attempts to articulate in philosophical terms the meaning implicit in the rituals of Shinto.

Why is ritual important, and why is attention to rituals especially important in the case of Shinto? It is precisely because Shinto as a tradition takes ritual so seriously. The link between ritual and the development of drama in Japan makes it possible for a researcher to see back into the earliest form of consciousness in which the first concepts of self-understanding were created. Art forms such as Noh and **Bugaku**, discussed earlier, are simply ritual segments that became detached modules through time, and eventually dramatic forms in their own right. Many shrines stage Noh performances of the mythological stories surrounding their own foundation.

These points should offer some approaches to Shinto by examining its rituals and ceremonies in order to infer back to the meaning or concepts they seek to express.

THE PHENOMENOLOGICAL APPROACH

At the risk of becoming excessively technical in a philosophical sense, the approach to Shinto thus far taken does have an academic identity. The Gottingen school of neo-Kantianism developed a methodology on such studies which was best exemplified in Rudolf Otto's phenomenological approach to religion in his work *Das Heilige*,[5] which speaks of the *mysterium tremendum* at the core of religious experience. The sense of awe that Motoori Norinaga identified seems well matched to Otto's ideas, and may therefore be a useful approach to the discussion of Shinto in Western terms. Also of use might be Martin Heidegger's famous definition of philosophy in *Sein und Zeit* (*Being and Time*) as "universal phenomenological ontology proceeding from the hermeneutics of human existence." From phenomenological observation, interpretation leads to the existential meaning.

By making reference to these thinkers, there is no appeal to the authority of Otto or Heidegger. However, with reference to the study of Shinto within the field of religious studies, they successfully juxtapose a number of terms that clarify some methodological issues in the study of the subject. These terms move the discussion away from theoretical questions of belief into the area of experience, and how experience may contain belief without it having been articulated in intellectual terms, a basic characteristic of not just Shinto, but of Japanese culture as a whole.

Scholars of religion who do not understand the difference between articulated and unarticulated belief—belief that is, in David Hume's words, more felt than judged—raise meaningless questions when they ask, "What do Shintoists believe about God, or worship, or the environment, or gay rights?" They assume that there are agreed-upon doctrines from which positions may be logically deduced—a false assumption in the case of Shinto.

Returning to Motoori Norinaga, it is interesting to note that in a phenomenological sense, he speaks of different kinds of *kami*. First of these are human *kami*, an idea that belongs to ancient times. Aside from emperors as "distant kami," he speaks of ordinary people in villages who were accorded the status of *kami* in their community on account of status or good works. In the same context he writes:

> Needless to say, among the human beings who are called *kami* all the emperors in successive generations are the first to be counted. For, as is indicated by the fact that the emperors are called totsu kami (distant *kami*), they are aloof, remote, august, and worthy of reverence. The human beings who are referred to as *kami* in a lesser degree can be found in antiquity as well as today. There are also men who are respected as *kami*, not throughout the whole world, but within a province, a village, or a family, according to their respective status. The *kami* in the age of *kami* were for the most part human beings of that time, and the people of that time were all *kami*. Therefore it is called the age of *kami*.

This resembles Teilhard de Chardin's idea of hominization, and the return to *kami* status through disciplines that heighten spirituality—an idea of his shared by later Shinto thinkers—might suggest a correspondence with his idea of deification after hominization. With regard to non-human *kami*, Motoori Norinaga comments:

> Among things which are called *kami*, thunder is evidently included, since it is usually referred to as narukami or kaminari (pealing *kami*). Also such things as dragons, kotama, foxes, and so forth, which are eminently wonderful and awe-inspiring, are *kami*. Kotama is what people today call Tengu, and in Chinese writings it is referred to as a mountain goblin. . . . In the Nihongi and the Man'yoshū, we see the tiger and the wolf, too, called *kami*. There are also the cases in which peaches were given the divine name Okamuzumi-no-mikoto, and a necklace was called Mikuratana-no-kami. Furthermore, we often find cases in which rocks, stumps of trees, and leaves of plants spoke audibly. All these were *kami*. Also, frequently, seas and mountains are called *kami*. It is not that the spirit of the sea or the mountains is referred to as *kami*, but that the sea or the mountain itself is regarded as a *kami*. This is because they are exceedingly awe-inspiring.

The fact that the phenomenological approach seems to fit the raw materials of Shinto leads now to one final point—namely its formal recognition as an outstanding, surviving example of ethnophilosophy.

SHINTO AS ETHNOPHILOSOPHY

Ethnophilosophy is a relatively new concept, but, like the philosophy of ritual, considerably helpful in discussing Shinto. Both involve a probing of the symbols or rituals and activities of a cultural system to identify the meaning behind them, without requiring them necessarily to fit the meaning thus disclosed into any rational framework. The term ethnophilosophy is currently a subject heading used by the Library of Congress, replacing terms such as folk philosophy or primitive philosophy.

Dr. Fidelis U. Okafor summarizes the concept of ethnophilosophy as follows:

> Ethnophilosophy is so called because its focus is on the thought that underlies the life patterns and belief system of a people. It is folk philosophy insofar as it is an exposition of the philosophical thought undergirding the way of life of a people as a collectivity. African and Japanese philosophy belong to this tradition. Western philosophy, however, is based on reason and logic; in contrast with ethnophilosophy, it developed ab initio as a critique of folk thought and worldviews. Both traditions are not contradictory but complementary. Each bears the marks of its peculiar culture and history.[6]

Therefore, scholars requiring, in the Western sense, a rational core in either Japanese culture or Shinto will probably be disappointed. Japanese culture evolved empirically and through adapting imported culture to Japanese needs. Unlike Western civilization, with common roots in Greek and Roman concepts, Japan was an island off Asia that created its own values and ideals and then incorporated whatever seemed to have some quality of fascination, as was felt appropriate. That is not to say that either Japanese culture or Shinto is in any sense "irrational." The appropriate word is "a-rational" or "trans-rational." It has evolved a form of logic that gives its activities meaning not derived from a set of concepts from which principles are established and implications are drawn.

In this regard, Shinto embodies in ritual form the self-understanding of the ancient Japanese and the paradigmatic values of the culture,

namely, the concept of people and objects being pure. In this sense, it
a form of ethnophilosophy. It was a working rather than intellectual response to experience. It also provides an answer to the question "What
is Shinto?" raised by those who argue that, during the Edo period, or
even before, syncretism was the normal state of affairs and that Shinto
lived within a Buddhist worldview. That approach must answer several
serious questions.

First, why must a rationally structured worldview be presupposed at
all? This is itself a Western assumption, based on a rational understanding of religion and philosophy, as Dr. Okafor points out. To the Western
mind, Buddhism possesses such a framework, and therefore must have
been the receptacle in which the amorphous cult was contained. This
is solid Western logic but specious in its assumptions, which actually
beg the question.

In addition to this, there is the issue of Buddhism itself: "What was
the nature of the Buddhism whose worldview encompassed Shinto?"
It became a Buddhism that did not believe in reincarnation, that practiced ancestral reverence, and that permitted married priests to inherit
temples. Can this be described as Buddhism at all, if the southern tradition is taken as the norm? Further, if Mahayana, with all its Chinese
modifications is considered "Buddhism," then it must be conceded that
there are as many varieties of Buddhism as there are varieties of any
major religious tradition. In other words, there is not, nor ever could
have been, a standard worldview that Buddhism provided for Shinto.

Ergo, the assumption that a Buddhist worldview absorbed Shinto is
merely positing on behalf of Buddhism what is forbidden to apologists
of Shinto. The late Professor **Joseph Kitagawa** has relevant observations that naturally fit here.

> Some people hold that Japan became a Buddhist country during the He-
> ian period when Buddhism in effect absorbed Shinto. Yet is it not equally
> true that Buddhism surrendered to the ethos of that nebulous religion of
> Japan, which lay deeper than the visible religious structure, commonly
> referred to as Shinto?[7]

Professor Kitagawa is making the point that in order to accommodate to the Japanese ethnophilosophy, Buddhism had to surrender its
essential content in order to preserve its form. While the process began
in China, where Buddhism and Chinese philosophy met, in the case
of Japan, it was not a rational philosophical system that challenged

and changed Buddhism, but an ethnophilosophy that had enormous spiritual energy to integrate alien ideas on its own terms, giving the impression that it had succumbed in the process, while, in actuality, it had conquered.

This relates to the argument, advanced by some philosophers, that everyone has a philosophy. Even someone saying "I have no philosophy" is admitting to have a philosophy. In the context of Shinto, the answer would be "I have no worldview philosophy. I have an ethnophilosophy, the collective and empirically acquired self-understanding of my life and my society derived from its collective experience."

Ethnophilosophy has the merit of giving more formal status to the kind of local thought and behavior too readily dismissed by modernized Western civilization on account of its own technological advances and its confidence of total superiority over all other forms of civilization on the planet. Shinto is evidence that an ethnophilosophical culture can survive in the modern world and that, therefore, the term "primitive" should be used with extreme caution.

Shinto survives as a reminder of how human beings articulate their experience when Nature alone is the guide. It may be transcended by more sophisticated systems, even those originating from its own matrix, but its continuing vitality and place in Japanese culture, however difficult to characterize, cannot be ignored. Shinto may be one of the last great truly natural, human, a-rational philosophical systems. It is a reference point for all cultures and, as such, should command more and more attention and interest as an ethnophilosophy, as its next millennium flows into the future.

SHINTO IN CONTEMPORARY JAPAN

One of the most difficult aspects of Japanese religion for the Western mind to comprehend is how religious affiliation is defined. Statistics issued by the Ministry of Cultural affairs issues lists that usually read: Shinto, 90 million; Buddhism, 80 million; Christian, 1 million; **New Religions**, 35 million. The total comes to 195 million. The population of Japan, however, is approximately 130 million. Why is there such a discrepancy? The answer is in observing how these figures are compiled. According to the Voluntary Association of Shinto Shrines (**Jinja Honchō**), there are over 80,000 shrines registered with it.

There are 20,000 others that are either too small to be registered or for various reasons have chosen not to affiliate. At New Year, for example, around 90 million people visit shrines for **hatsu-mode**, the first event of New Year. Many visit Buddhist temples; the majority, however, visits shrines, evident in the numbers attending shrines for **hatsu miya-mairi**, the first shrine visit for newly born babies (32nd day for girls and 33rd day for boys), or for **weddings** (shinzen-kekkon), or for festivals (**matsuri**). Large shrines have an **ujikokai**, a local, or sometimes nationwide, support group; Buddhism, after the removal of state support when the capital moved from Nara to Kyōto in 794 by Emperor Kwammu, was forced to find new sources of revenue, which it did by institutionalizing the funeral. Temples also created support groups, and these became an indicator of the level of local support. While shrines and temples have always had some separate identity, there have been various types of overlap of interest and activity over the centuries. The esoteric forms of Buddhism imported from China during the Heian period (794–1185), Tendai Buddhism by Saichō and Shingon by Kūkai, formed a relationship with mountain shrines and created hybrids such as Shugendō, the mountain cults that combined rituals from both religions. The Edo period government (1615–1868) encouraged the syncretistic practices of these cults in order to blur the distinction and discourage any religious challenge to political authority. Hence there grew up the mentality of not "either-or," as Western religions perceive loyalty, but of "both-and," an outlook that is not highly regarded in the West but is the norm in Japan. Even some New Religions suggest that their role can include the support of other religions.

With regard to the New Religions, generally, their statistics are based on actual numbers of committed believers who subscribe to them by providing financial support. While sometimes these numbers may be exaggerated, they indicate the relative strength or weakness of each group. More difficult to assess are the "New-New Religions" (shin-shin shūkyō, in Japanese). Kōfuku no Kagaku (the Science of Happiness) founded by Okawa Ryuho (born 1956) is one example. Its existence is based on the leader, whose income comes largely from the vast number of books he has written. He claims to have the insights and enlightenment of Buddha, Christ, Mohammed, and Confucius, an extreme form of syncretism. The New Religions and the Christian churches are the only groups that report statistics based on documented numbers of subscribing believers.

These facts are frequently used to argue that the Japanese are not religious. However, this statement is dependent upon the Western model of religiosity—that is, attending places of worship regularly at fixed hours for prayer and worship—being invoked as universally valid. Monks who engage in disciplines such as sen-nichi-kai-hō-gyō (running 25,000 miles around Mount Hiei at night over a period of seven years) and who practice austerities and rituals that combine Buddhist and Shinto elements can hardly be discounted because of syncretism. Religiosity and spirituality must be distinguished if the contrasts between Japanese and Western religions are to be appreciated.

Since state support for any religious group is unconstitutional, and because of fiscal pressure on shrines and temples during the recession of the 1990s, temples and shrines were forced to examine new approaches to finance. A magazine of long standing exists that offers advice to Buddhist temples on how to raise extra income. One widely used method has been through the creation of hoiku-en, kindergartens for preschool children. Temples with land in valuable locations have either sold it for housing development or created new businesses of their own ranging from paying parking lots to convenience stores (konbini in Japanese). Pet graveyards have become popular, and pet funerals range from the simple to the elaborate. When people die, the temple will give them a kaimyo, a posthumous name. Kaimyo is the title of the name given to a newly ordained Buddhist priest, the first step to Buddhahood. The deceased therefore becomes a priest and then a Buddha (or in Shinto a *kami*) at death. The kaimyo can cost as much as US $1,000 for each Chinese character used. Cremation in Japan is mandatory, but graveyards for ashes can also be provided by temples at a price, creating another source of income. Both shrines and temples sell artifacts for use at home. Shrines sell *kami*-dana (*kami* shelves) that are often in the form of replica shrine buildings. The offerings of water, salt, and rice are changed daily. Buddhist temples sell butsudan, small altars containing a statue of a Buddha in front of which incense is burned to show reverence for ancestors.

The staffing of shrines varies from place to place. The Voluntary Association of Shinto Shrines, which licenses priests, has a roll of 20,000. These are clearly unevenly distributed nationwide, since some shrines with a long history can have a dozen or more priests while others have none. Where there are no permanent staff, volunteers and lay leaders form a **miya-za** to oversee its affairs and bring in priests for special events. Some priests make a living by serving ten or more small shrines in rotation, in much the same way that many Christian clergy in rural areas carry responsibility for more than one parish.

In the entry **Shinto outside of Japan**, detailed information is provided about how Shinto in particular has spread internationally since the Meiji period (1868–1912), when Japan's first wave of immigrants went to Hawaii and Brazil. Numerous overseas shrines were built by the imperial army during the occupation of East Asia that ended in 1945. Following the liberation of all religious groups from any state control, many New Religions have spread into North and South America, Europe, and other parts of the world. Non-Japanese believers affiliated to the New Religions are reported to be growing, although no reliable data is available. Only one shrine in Japan has established itself abroad: In North America, the **Tsubaki Grand Shrine** has a **bunsha** (branch shrine) in Granite Falls, Washington State, headed by a white American priest. While at present this is unusual, with the spread of **Aikido** and other Japanese **martial arts**, who knows what the future may bring?

NOTES

1. Motoori Norinaga. *Collected Works* (in Japanese), I, 135–136.

2. Alan Grapard. *The Protocol of the Gods: A Study of the Kasuga Cult in Japanese History* (Berkeley: University of California Press, 1992).

3. *Rude Awakenings: the Kyōto School and the Questions of Nationalism* (Honolulu: University of Hawai'i Press, 1995).

4. Brian Victoria. *Zen at War* (Tokyō: Weatherhill, 1998).

5. Rudolf Otto. *Das Heilige—Über das Irrationale in der Idee des Göttlichen und sein Verhältnis zum Rationalen (The Idea of the Holy)* (1918).

6. Fidelis J. Okafor. "In Defense of Afro-Japanese Ethnophilosophy," in *Philosophy East and West* 47 (4 October 1997), 363–382.

7. Joseph Kitagawa. *History of Japanese Religion* (New York: Columbia University Press, 1966), 85.

The Dictionary

– A –

AIDONO-NO-KAMI. The practice in which several *kami* are enshrined together in an aidono (joint hall), the invited *kami* subordinate to and usually enshrined to the right and left of the principal *kami*. Aidono-no-kami dates back to 649 C.E., when joint enshrinement took place at **Kashima Jingū** in what is now Ibaraki Prefecture. **Katori Jingū** is also in this category, as is **Kasuga Taisha**. Joint enshrinement became especially popular during the **Heian period** (794–1185), when various forms of **syncretism** were developing.

AIKIDO. A Japanese self-defense art developed originally by Takeda Sokaku (1860–1943) and developed in its modern form by **Ueshiba Morihei** (1883–1969). It is based on use of **ki**, or energy, and is linked to the idea of Shinto spirituality. Because of its non-aggressive nature, as a form of self-defense it has become popular internationally since the early 1960s.

Aikido uses the **Taoist** idea of the virtue of non-action in the concept of the underlying passivity and non-aggression in what is essentially a self-defense form of martial art. Unlike other martial arts, such as kickboxing or karate, that have become global sports because they can be competitive, there are no aikido tournaments, contests, or world championships. Dōjō aikido practitioners work at their skills in order to heighten them but not in a competitive context. Ueshiba Morihei began as a student of jujitsu, a popular style of martial arts, at the end of the 19th century. He claimed to have had a vision in which he saw the truth that the purpose of the martial arts is universal love rather than combat. His principles of harmony and gentleness were embodied in his new art called aikido and employed in the first **dōjō** he opened in Tokyō in 1927. Unlike jujitsu and judo, where

33

the opponent waits for a strike, in aikido, the opponent is absent, in the sense of being passive. There are no offensive strikes, only locks and holds that protect. Ueshiba is commemorated at Aiki Jinja and greatly revered by aikido practitioners. Aiki Jinja was for many years under the tutelage of **Tsubaki Ōkami Yashiro**. The head dōjō, or training hall, is located in Shinjuku Ward in central Tokyō.

Aikido has spread far beyond Japan, and various federations now exist. There is an International Aikido Federation, but also individual national federations in the United States, Canada, the United Kingdom, and various European and Asia countries, including France, Germany, Bulgaria, Lithuania, Singapore, Australia, New Zealand, Hong Kong, and in Africa and South America. The U.S. actor Steven Seagal is perhaps the best-known foreign practitioner who began one of his early movies leading a training session in a dōjō that had a picture of Ueshiba Morihei on the wall. *See also* MARTIAL ARTS; ŌMOTO-KYŌ.

AINU. Considered by some scholars to be the original inhabitants of the Japanese archipelago, the Ainu are now confined to the northern island of Hokkaido, where they try to retain the remnants of their culture. Their situation is often juxtaposed with that of Native Americans or the Aborigines of Australia, but that is perhaps an incorrect analogy. However old the Ainu may be, other parts of Japan have been inhabited for almost 10,000 years, from the early **Jōmon** period. This is stated not to dismiss the plight of the Ainu, but merely to point out the problems that arise when a stone-age culture is forced to co-exist with modern civilization. Some features of Ainu religion resemble Shinto, suggesting that there may have been some meeting. However, the two cultures remain distinct and separate, as do those of mainland Japan and Okinawa.

AKAKI KIYOKI KOKORO. The four virtues in Shinto relate to the heart, and their existence is considered essential in order for people to have unity with the *kami*. They are also known as **sei-mei-shin**. They prize the brightness and the purity of the **kokoro** (or the heart as the seat of the moral virtues). *See also* ETHICS IN SHINTO; SHINGAKU.

AKAMA JINGŪ. Located in Shimonoseki City in Yamaguchi Prefecture, this shrine (**jinja**) enshrines **Emperor Antoku** (r. 1180–1183), who died at the age of seven at the battle of **Dannoura** in 1185. It is recorded that he drowned in the arms of his grandmother. An annual festival for him is celebrated on 23–25 April.

AKAZAWA BUNJI (1814–1883). Founder of the **Kyōha Shinto** (Sect Shinto) movement **Konkō-kyō**, the teaching of the Golden Light, which continues to have a large, committed following in modern Japan of around half a million believers.

AKIBA JINJA. Located on Mt. Akiba in Shizuoka Prefecture, it enshrines Kagutsuchi-no-kami, the *kami* of fire, who, according to legend, was slain by **Izanagi-no-mikoto**, his father, because his birth killed **Izanami-no-mikoto**, his mother. The shrine dates to the early **Heian period** (794–1185), during which, under the prevailing tendency of the **assimilation of Shinto and Buddhism**, the *kami* of the shrine (**jinja**) became associated with the bodhisattva **Kannon**. The shrine is known for its famous fire festival held in December. Under the popular name Sanjakubo, the cult of the shrine spread into east Japan during the Edo period (1615–1868).

AKI-MATSURI. Also known as the Kannamesai and the **Niinamesai** as well Aki-Taisai, it is the Autumn **Festival** of harvest thanksgiving in which the first fruits of the harvest are offered to the *kami.* This is the most solemn festival of the Shinto year. At the **Grand Shrines of Ise** (Ise Jingū), where it is known as the Kannamesai, offerings are made to **Amaterasu-ōmikami** on 15 and 16 October at the **Gekū** (Outer Shrine), and at the **Naikū** (Inner Shrine) on 16 and 17 October.

The first harvested grains of rice are presented by the emperor himself on 23–24 November at the Niinamesai. When this becomes the first ritual act of a new imperial reign, it is simultaneously an accession rite, and is referred to as the **Daijōsai**. Records of proper procedures are found in the **Engishiki** of the **Heian period** (794–1185), and the background is recorded in the **Taihō Ritsuryō**, or Taiho Code of 701. At that time, the new emperor sends officials to determine the location of the yuki and suki fields from which offerings are brought to the Yuki-den and Suki-den erected within the Imperial Palace for the purpose of performing the various rituals that make up the complete ceremony.

AKITSUMI *KAMI*. A *kami* in human form. In the past the title was used especially for the emperor, but it is also used for common people who were judged to be worthy. There were numerous instances of the enshrinement of living persons who performed great deeds, both in political and in folk contexts. **Emperor Meiji**, for example, was enshrined in at least three places during his life before the **Meiji Jingū** was established after his death. *See also* ARAHITO-GAMI; IKIGAMI.

AKU. Evil, not simply in the Western moral sense, but in a broader frame encompassing unhappiness, disaster, or misfortune, all things from which people may be protected by purification, **harai**. Since Japanese thought does not rest on a metaphysical dualism of good versus evil, the translation of aku as evil should be used with discretion. *See also* ETHICS IN SHINTO; KEGARE; TATARI; TSUMI.

AMAGOI. Traditional invocations for rain to ensure a healthy rice harvest. When Buddhism entered Japan, Buddhist sutras were first read for this purpose in the sixth century. In Shinto, **Inari** is frequently petitioned because of the connection with rice. *See also* RYŪJIN; WATER IN SHINTO.

AMATERASU-ŌMIKAMI. *Kami* of the sun, principal *kami* of Shinto (literally, Great Kami Lighting the Heavens). According to the **mythology** in the **Kojiki** (712), she was born from the left eye of **Izanagi-no-mikoto** while he was purifying himself in the Tachibana River. The later **Nihon Shōki** (720) account of the incident has her as the child of Izanagi and Izanami. She was appointed as ruler of the High Plain of Heaven (**Takama-no-hara**, or sometimes Takama-ga-hara). From there, she dispatched her grandson, **Ninigi-no-mikoto**, to descend and rule the land of reed plains, bearing the **imperial regalia**, or **sanshū-no-shinki**, the three imperial treasures that are symbols of office: the jewel, mirror, and sword. His grandson became the first emperor, **Jimmu Tennō** (r. 660–585 B.C.E.) The imperial family is considered to be descended from Amaterasu, demonstrating its primal position in the firmament of heaven and earth. Amaterasu is worshipped principally at the **Naikū** (Inner) of the **Grand Shrines of Ise** (Ise Jingū), although she is enshrined in numerous other locations. The *yata*, the mirror of the sanshū-no-shinki, is enshrined in Ise.

Interpreted in broader academic terms, Amaterasu is a solar female deity, accompanied by the almost universal symbols of similar deities. Extant continuation of these symbols may still be seen, such as the white horse kept at the Grand Shrines and in other shrines. The government of Australia formally presented a white horse to the **Nikko Toshūgu** during the 1980s as an act of respect and friendship. The solar aspect made early **syncretism** with **Buddhism** possible, although the cult of Ise resisted, and by the end of the 16th century had established its identity in unmistakably and unambiguously Shinto terms.

While the Amaterasu cult is clearly ancient, according to the mythology, it did not become widely popular until the development of the famous **Okagemairi Pilgrimages** of Thanksgiving during the Edo period (1615–1868), when as many as three million people walked to the Grand Shrines of Ise. As the ancestral *kami* of the imperial family, Amaterasu receives reports of all events in the **imperial household**. Amaterasu-ōmikami is also referred to as Ohirume-muchi. *See also* AME-NO-IWATO; EMPEROR SYSTEM.

AMATSU-KAMI. The *kami* of **Takama-no-hara** (the Plain of High Heaven), supreme among whom is **Amaterasu-ōmikami**. *See also* *KAMI* OF HEAVEN AND EARTH.

AME-NO-IWATO. The cave in which **Amaterasu-ōmikami** hid herself, according to the mythology as recorded in the **Kojiki** (712) and the **Nihon Shoki** (720). Distressed by the bad behavior of **Susano-o-no-mikoto**, she plunged the world into darkness by disappearing into a cave. A ribald dance performed by **Ame-uzume-no-mikoto** created such hilarity among the other *kami* that she came out to see what was happening. As soon as she had emerged, the other *kami* strung a rope across the entrance to prevent her returning. The world was again filled with light, and cosmic order was restored. *See also* NOH; SARUTAHIKO-ŌKAMI.

AME-NO-MINAKA-NUSHI-NO-KAMI. Central *kami* of the Plain of High Heaven (**Takama-no-hara**) and primal member of the **Zoka-sanshin**, the three original creative *kami* who brought the universe into being. *See also* COSMOLOGY IN SHINTO.

AME-NO-MURAKUMO-NO-TSURUGI. The imperial sword presented to each new emperor. It was lost, according to legend, by the deposed boy emperor, **Antoku** (r. 1180–1183), when he died at the battle of **Dannoura** in 1185. The first reference to it was in the **mythology** when it was presented to **Ninigi-no-mikoto**, the grandson of **Amaterasu-ōmikami** and subsequently to his grandson, **Jimmu Tennō**, the legendary first emperor (reigned 660–585 B.C.E.). The famous imperial loyalist scholar **Kitabatake Chikafusa** (1293–1354) in his text, **Jinnō Shōtōki**, (1339) claimed that it was a replica that vanished into the sea, and that the original survived. The official sword (or its replacement) is currently kept at **Atsuta Jingū** in Nagoya City, and is brought together with the other two **imperial regalia (sanshū-no-shinki)**, the mirror and the jewel, to each new emperor following the death of his predecessor. *See also* KUSANAGI-NO-TSURUGI.

AME-NO-UKIHASHI. The Floating Bridge of Heaven referred to in the **mythology** of the **Kojiki** (712) and the **Nihon Shōki** (720) as the place from which **Izanagi-no-mikoto** and **Izanami-no-mikoto** dipped the jeweled spear into the ocean. Drops of brine from the spear hardened into landmasses that became the Japanese archipelago.

AME-TSUCHI. An expression derived from the Chinese Classics, certainly found in the classic of **Taoism**, the *Daodejing*, in which it has the meaning "heaven-earth." It refers to a cosmic principle, according to which, at creation, the light and pure elements remained in heaven—ame—while the heavier remained on earth—tsuchi. Traces of the concept are found in the imagery and conceptualization of the early accounts of the mythological origins of the Japanese islands in the **Kojiki** (712) and in the **Nihon Shōki** (720). Ame became the home of the **Amatsu-kami** (the *kami* of heaven), while tsuchi became the home of the **Kunitsu-kami** (the *kami* of earth). The role of the Amatsu-kami is to help pacify the world.

AME-UZUME-NO-MIKOTO. Wife of **Sarutahiko-ōkami**, head of the **earthly** *kami*. She performed in front of the **Ame-no-iwato** the dance that brought **Amaterasu-ōmikami** out of hiding. She is the guardian *kami* of entertainers, and remains popular in the world of geisha. She is also known as the guardian *kami* of defense, especially in the martial arts, and in modern times, of lawyers. *See also* KAGURA; TSUBAKI OKAMI YASHIRO.

ANANAI-KYŌ. A neo-Shinto **New Religion** started in 1949 by Nakano Yonosuke, based on reverence for **Kuni-tokotachi-no-mikoto**, but which he widened into a syncretistic vision that embraced **Buddhism**, Christianity, **Confucianism**, Islam, and **Taoism**. It also uses the Shinto practice of **chinkon**, calming the soul in order to effect union with the *kami*.

ANCESTRAL REVERENCE. Although Shinto funerals are rare, ancestral reverence remains an important principle of the tradition. The souls of the dead were traditionally thought to reside in mountains, according to the beliefs of **sangaku shinkō**, from where they could descend to assist in the yearly cycle of agricultural events, **Nenchū-gyōji**. Attention to the spirits of the dead has been a long and important part of Japanese religious ceremonies. Later evidence from the **Heian period** (894–1185) is in the form of the elaborate pacification rites (**chinkon**) developed to calm the souls of unhappy or unjustly treated people. The most famous case was that of **Sugawara Michizane** (845–903), whose angry spirit wreaked vengeance on the city of Kyōto until he was subsequently elevated to the status of the *kami* of learning, **Tenjin**.

Some shrines (**jinja**) contain the souls of famous people, such as Sugawara, while the numerous shrines for the war dead tend the souls of those who died for Japan since the **Meiji Restoration**. The Meiji period (1868–1912) government tried to make explicit links between ancestral reverence, filial piety, and devotion to nation and emperor. The various shrines for the war dead were part of this, along with the creation of the **Yasukuni Jinja** at the apex of the hierarchy. After **Buddhism** developed, the **Bon Matsuri** (Bon Festival), found all over Asia was introduced, again as an ancestral reverence event. While Buddhism came to exercise a great influence on the treatment of the dead, the older and deeper origins of ancestral reverence should never be forgotten.

Robert J. Smith, a U.S. researcher on ancestral reverence in postwar Japan, demonstrated over two research periods that despite modern sociological changes, ancestral altars were still common even in a nuclear family environment such as Tokyō. His second period of study found that Buddhist statuary had all but vanished, suggesting that the tradition is not necessarily dependent upon Buddhism. These roots appear to remain a profound, albeit subconscious, dimension of Japanese spirituality. *See also* HEARN, LAFCADIO.

ANCIENT LEARNING SCHOOL. The name for classical Japanese studies used in the Edo period by **Motoori Norinaga** (1730–1801), leading figure of the **Kokugaku** (National Learning) movement. It became steadily influential in the 18th and early 19th centuries, especially with regard to revived reverence for ancient emperors and the **emperor system.** In this respect it helped to lay the intellectual and moral foundations of the **Meiji Restoration** of 1867 and the **modernization** process ushered in by it.

ANDO. Literally meaning "undisturbed possession" of real estate granted by a feudal lord to vassals to guarantee their subservience and loyalty. Extended to certain shrines, it meant ownership rights to land given to them, especially the **Grand Shrines of Ise** (Ise Jingū) for the purpose of earning income. It evolved into a political tool designed to maintain social stability.

ANESAKI MASAHARU (1873–1949). Internationally known scholar of Japanese religion in the early to mid-20th century. Those is work was principally focused on **Buddhism**, he made numerous contributions to the better understanding of Shinto through his discussion of the relationship between religion and human feelings for the natural order. Much knowledge about the unique nature of Japanese religion can be attributed to his work. His major book was the *History of Japanese Religion*, published in London in 1930.

ANIMISM IN SHINTO. As in all religious traditions that remain close to nature, Shinto retains a degree of animism. Sacred energy can be stored and retained in rocks, rivers, trees, and mountains, as well as borne by certain animals. **Mitsumine Jinja** in Saitama Prefecture reveres wolves as sacred guardians of the mountain, while the cult of **Inari** has a deep relationship with foxes (**kitsune**).

The giant black crow (**yatagarasu**) is revered in the **Kumano** cult, and a varied but limited number of animals are acknowledged at other shrines. Inanimate objects (as categorized in Western thought) may also possess energy, particularly mountains and waterfalls. The concept of life force and energy (**ki**) is much more comprehensively understood in Japanese than in Western thinking, partly because of its importance in Chinese thought, but more so because of the way in which spirituality in Japan is deeply rooted in the awareness of nature. *See also* NATURE IN SHINTO.

ANSHIN RITSUMEI. This doctrine, common in much of Japanese religion, teaches people not to worry about daily life concerns, but to pursue their religious goals. While not attributable directly or exclusively either to Shinto or to **Buddhism**, it is found in both, and seems to be part of the **ethnophilosophical** outlook of the Japanese people toward life.

ANTHROPOLOTARY. A term invented by **D. C. Holtom** (1884–1962), the American missionary scholar of the early 20th century who wrote extensively about Shinto. He used the expression to refer to the practice of the enshrinement of living persons as *kami* throughout Japanese history. They were known as **ikigami**, living human *kami*.

As evidence of how some of the basic concepts of Shinto found expression in the incoming tradition of Buddhism, there is the matching concept of **ikibotoke**, or living human Buddha. The title could be conferred honorifically, in the same way as in Shinto, or after a period of lengthy and severe discipline. There were two varieties in Buddhism. One developed in the tradition of **Shingon Buddhism** known as Soku-shin-jo-butsu but has not been practiced since the end of the Edo period (1615–1868). It entailed the self-mortification of the body through discipline and diet, followed by special interment that resulted in Buddhahood through a perfect death, confirmed by the fact that the mummified body was absolutely intact. Equally demanding is the other discipline of **Sen-nichi-kai-ho-gyo**, the marathon running around the peaks of Mount Hiei over a period of seven years. Unlike its Shingon counterpart, which was never revived after the period of **modernization**, this discipline is still undertaken from time to time. *See also* ARAHITO-GAMI; KATO GENCHI.

ANTOKU, EMPEROR. Famous boy emperor (born 1178; reigned 1180–1183) drowned at the battle of **Dannoura** in 1185. At the closing confrontation of the war between the Taira and Minamoto clans, when the Taira clan was routed, the young emperor's grandmother, the widow of Taira no Kiyomori, jumped into the ocean with him in her arms, drowning them both. The imperial sword was lost because she was said to have taken it with them when she leapt overboard.

In 1183, when Antoku was with the Taira clan in west Japan, retired emperor Go-Shirakawa (reigned 1155–1158) presided over the accession rites of Emperor Go-Toba (reigned 1183–1198) without any of the **imperial regalia**. The result of these events was dramatic and the significance of the imperial regalia came to be taken very seriously. From the point of view of **Buddhism** of the time, the chaos was evidence that the world was to end the era of **mappō**. Antoku is enshrined in **Akama Jingū** in Shimonoseki and is listed as 81st emperor of Japan. Some of his toys are preserved at **Itsukushima Jinja** in Hiroshima. *See also* AME-NO-MURAKUMO-NO-TSURUGI.

AOI MATSURI. Festival of Hollyhocks (*Asarum caulescens*), celebrated in Kyōto on 15 May. The seventh-century origin is obscure, but the **Heian period** (794–1185) costumes, the commencement from the Kyōto Imperial Palace, and moving to the Shimo-Gamo and Kami-Gamo Shrines suggests some links with the community that preceded the Heian court. Along with the **Gion Matsuri** and the Jidai Matsuri, it is the third of Kyōto's three famous festivals. *See also* KAMO JINJA.

ARABURU KAMI. Like **magatsuhi-no-kami**, they are troublesome *kami* who are able to inflict various types of harm on human beings. Holding regular festivals (**matsuri**) is thought to keep them calm and make them more benevolent. *See also* AKU; MAREBITO; NAMAHAGE.

ARAHITO-GAMI. A living human *kami*. The term formerly was used of emperors but now also includes other distinguished persons being honored for their achievements. *See also* AKITSUMI KAMI; ANTHROPOLOTARY; IKIBOTOKE; IKIGAMI; KATO GENCHI.

ARAMITAMA. The wilder or more spirited aspect of the character of a *kami*, in contrast to the **nigimitama**, the more peaceful or calm side. **Empress Jingū** (reigned 201–269) is said to have taken the aramitama of **Amaterasu-ōmikami** with her on her Korean campaign, leaving the nigimitama in the **Sumiyoshi Taisha** in Osaka. *See also* SOUL IN SHINTO.

ARCHERY IN SHINTO. Distinct from the **martial art** called Kyudo, the way of the bow, Shinto makes use of two kinds of archery for the purposes of **divination**. One is **yabusame**, which consists of Heian period-costumed riders firing arrows at three standing targets. The second is **omato-shinji**, in which the high priest (**gūji**) of a shrine, attired in formal priestly robes, fires an arrow at a standing target. Both are practiced in order to divine the fortune of the year. *See also* BOKUSEN.

ARCHITECTURE IN SHINTO. Architectural styles are important in Shinto, beginning with the distinctive **torii** or gateway, whose origins are unknown. One feature of Shinto architecture is its variety, and the fact that different styles are associated with different *kami*. There are over 20 styles of torii and the appropriately matching buildings that identify the *kami* enshrined. There are normally at least two buildings: one exclusively for the *kami*, the **honden** (inner sanctuary); and another for the worshippers, the **heiden** (hall of offerings). There also may be a **haiden** (public hall of worship).

The original purpose of erecting buildings was to provide a place in which the *kami* could descend and where both the *kami* and worshippers could be, in some sense, united. Once erected, shrine buildings house the *kami* that has descended and the ground is sacred. **Tatari**, misfortune, threatens any who violate that sanctity by removing the shrine (**jinja**) or damaging the grounds, of which there are many records. There is a large red torii that stands in the middle of the public parking area at Haneda International Airport in Tōkyō that dates to the mid-20th century. It stands on the site of a shrine that had to be moved to make room for the car park. Several accidents occurred in the wake of the removal. A decision was made to restore the torii to its original site in order to pacify the troubled *kami* in the same way that troubled spirits are pacified by the rituals of **chinkon**. The string of incidents ended, and the airport functioned as normal.

The honden of a shrine need not always be a building, but may instead be a mountain. In some cases, the mountain itself may also be the *kami*, underlining the point that there is no consistent doctrinal position or even standard use of basic terms.

ART IN SHINTO. Shinto has almost nothing comparable to the art of **Buddhism**, with its elaborate statuary and pictographic arts, such as the **mandala**, which depict various doctrines.

Some shrines of the **Tendai** or **Shingon** Shinto have elaborate paintings on the ceilings of the worship halls. These are reminiscent of mandalas, and usually depict some historical event or spiritual them. The only mandalas in Shinto would be those created by combined shrine-temple culture such as in Kumano.

Shinto's artistic spirit is manifest supremely in its **architecture** and in the way in which shrines are located in settings that have an aura of the sacred around them. The sacred objects in the innermost part of the honden, **go-shintai**, the symbols of the *kami*, are rarely seen, even by priests. When the go-shintai has to be moved—for example, because of a rebuilding—it is done in secret at night and completely covered. Ordinary worshippers are never permitted to be close enough to even catch a glimpse of one.

Prayer tablets known as **ema**, however, have become folk art in their own right and are on sale at all shrines for worshippers to write petitions to the *kami*. These prayers range from requests for **healing** to success in entrance examinations for prestigious high schools or universities. Collections of these in various sizes may be found in shrine (**jinja**) halls especially of the 15th and 16th centuries.

Emakimono are Chinese-style long scrolls that recount auspicious events such as the founding of a famous shrine, and these can be seen on display. The famous Tosa School of the Edo period (1615–1868) continued to produce them, but the emakimono was superceded by other art forms.

Saifuku, priestly vestments, modeled on court dress of T'ang Dynasty China (618–907), are elaborately designed and stylized to indicate rank and status. They may also be considered part of the artistic dimension of Shinto. *See also* MUSIC IN SHINTO.

ASAGUTSU. Wooden clog-style shoes worn by priests (**kannushi**) performing important ceremonies that were originally shoes worn by nobles in the Heian period (794–1185) and earlier. Originally made of leather, they are now made of hollowed paulownia wood and finished with a black lacquer surface.

ASAMI KEISEI (1652–1711). Scholar of **Confucian Shinto** and disciple of **Yamazaki Ansai** (1618–1682). At one point he was expelled from the school for allegedly criticizing Yamazaki's views on Shinto, but was subsequently considered orthodox. *See also* CONFUCIANISM AND SHINTO.

ASCETICISM IN SHINTO. Spiritual discipline, **gyō**, involving rituals of severe endurance or effort. Shugyo (activities designed to achieve a particular spiritual objective) or kugyo (severe discipline and austerity to achieve a defined objective) are the normal Japanese terms used. Shinto thought understands human nature as pure, but affected by **tsumi** (impurity), which can be removed by purification (**harai**). Various forms exist, probably the oldest being purification under a free-standing waterfall. **Misogi** is the generic name given to these forms. **Buddhism** also employed the principle that enlightenment could be attained by various kinds of discipline, such as in **Shingon** and **Tendai Buddhism** because of their esoteric elements.

Ascetic practices were prohibited by the **Meiji Restoration** government because they seemed to make Japanese inferior and primitive in comparison to more intellectualized Western religion. Many practices were resumed after the liberation of religion from state control in 1945. *See also* MISOGI SHŪHŌ; SEN-NICHI-KAI-HŌ-GYŌ; SHUGENDŌ; YAMABUSHI.

ASO JINJA. Located at the base of Mount Aso, Kumamato (Kyushū), it enshrines the son and grandsons of Japan's first legendary emperor, **Jimmu Tennō** (reigned 660–585 B.C.E.). It served to strengthen claims about the link between the first emperor and the southern island of Kyushū. Members of the Aso family continue to be part of the Japanese political establishment.

ASSIMILATION OF BUDDHISM AND SHINTO. This process took over six centuries to reach a completed form. It began with **Shinbutsu-Shugō**, the consolidation of temples and shrines (**jinja**), and continued with **Honji-suijaku-setsu**, the principle of assimilation.

Initially, Shinto was considered subordinate to **Buddhism**, but as time passed, Buddhism began to take on many characteristics of the Shinto tradition it had seemingly displaced. For example, the introduction of Buddhist fire rituals into Shinto was balanced by the introduction of water purification rituals (**harai** and **misogi**) into Buddhism. Esoteric Buddhism and Shinto created a range of interesting symbiotic practices that flourished especially in mountain **asceticism** such as **Shugendō** and in the ascetic practices of the **yamabushi**.

Buddhism and Shinto were separated officially at the **Meiji Restoration** (1868) on the principle of **Shinbutsu-bunri**, and have remained so ever since, although there is a cordial relationship between most shrines and temples.

ASSOCIATION OF SECT SHINTO. *See* KYŌHA SHINTO RENGŌKAI.

ASSOCIATION OF SHINTO SHRINES. *See* JINJA HONCHO.

ASTON, W. G. (1841–1911). British scholar and diplomat of the 19th century who first translated the Japanese classics into English, along with portions of the **Engishiki**. His famous work on Shinto concluded with a prediction of its impending demise, presumably because the Shinto he was observing had been robbed of its vitality as a result of the strictures imposed by the Meiji government. However, it proved durable and continued to flourish through festivals and other events of the Shinto calendar, the **nenchū-gyōji**.

ASUKA PERIOD. The early phase of Japanese cultural growth from circa 552 to 710 C.E., during which many Korean and Chinese cultural forms entered Japan. The entry of **Buddhism** and the Chinese model of bureaucracy were effected during this period.

ATAGO JINJA. Shrine (**jinja**) located on Mt. Atago in Ukyō Ward, Kyōto. **Izanami-no-mikoto**, according to the mythology recorded in the **Kojiki** (712) and the **Nihon Shōki** (720), co-procreator of the Japanese islands, is enshrined in the central shrine (**hongū**) along with Wakamusubi-no-mikoto. The fire *kami* is enshrined in the **wakamiya**, or subsidiary shrine. According to the principle of the **assimilation of Buddhism and Shinto**, the figure of **Jizō** was linked to the shrine, particularly Shogun Jizō, who protected the souls of dead samurai. Protection from fire remains one of the shrine's major attractions.

ATHEISM, SECULARISM, AND PLURALISM IN JAPANESE RELIGIOUS CULTURE. One major misunderstanding on the part of many observers of Japan arises from the assumption that religious phenomena is subject to universal categories of analysis, and therefore that what applies in the West must apply to Japan. On this basis, it is argued that Japanese religion can be "deciphered" through the use of Western models. This is as untrue of religion as it is untrue of business. Forces such as atheism and secularism that have emerged to challenge the dominant place of Christianity in Western civilization have not appeared in Japan in quite the same manner. In the first place, Japan never evolved any single religion that could parallel the role of Christianity in the West or Islam in the Middle East. Japan never developed the notion of one single, transcendent divine being. Without theism, there is no natural role for atheism. Secularism falls into a similar category. With no dominant religious culture to exercise a strong political influence and give form and order to society, a secular reaction to religious authority becomes impossible.

In the past, though the governments of Japan, like China, showed generosity to shrines (**jinja**) and temples, they were at the same time very suspicious of popular religious movements or indeed any movement that might even appear able to mount a challenge to central authority. Japan's three great feudal leaders, **Oda Nobunaga** (1534–1582), **Toyotomi Hideyoshi** (1536–1598), and **Tokugawa Ieyasu** (1543–1616) dealt mercilessly with any religious movements showing signs of aspiring to power. The **Buddhist** monasteries on Hiei-zan (Mount Hiei), with their armies of soldier monks, were destroyed. The foreign religion of Christianity, which had made inroads during the time when central government was weak, became the target particularly of Ieyasu's concern.

A farmers' revolt that had the appearance of a religious uprising was the last major act of suppression. Some 50,000 hapless farmers and their families took refuge in Hara castle at Shimabara in what is now Nagasaki Prefecture. Ieyasu responded by sending an army that numbered almost a quarter of a million to exterminate them. The rivers, according to eyewitnesses, ran red for days, and, not surprisingly, Ieyasu's authority was never challenged again.

Great shrines and temples existed by grace and favor. Tokugawa Ieyasu in particular encouraged the rise of **syncretism**, which involved the mixing of Shinto and Buddhism in an amalgam that kept both under strict control and limited in influence. The later use of **ninja** as spies enabled his successors to monitor every movement in the country. Japan's government has always been fundamentally secular, using religion merely as a decoration. **State Shinto,**, the invention of the **Meiji Restoration** government, was formally abolished in 1945 in the **Shinto Directive** issued by the **Supreme Commander Allied Forces**, but was more symbolic than substantial. The only positive outcome was that, since the government was not permitted to provide support for any religious body, it could not influence them, either. The one exception to the Shinto Directive remains the place of **imperial household** rites and the close relation of the rituals to the **Grand Shrines of Ise**. The funeral rites for the late Emperor Showa and the accession rites of Emperor Heisei were conducted according to tradition, justified partly on the basis of freedom of religion, to which the imperial family was equally entitled alongside the rest of the people.

Pluralism, the mutual co-existence of different worldviews, is a good description of a culture that produces a large number of **new religions**. Emperor Akihito (reigned 1989–), when he was crown prince, made a speech at Conference of World Religions in 1955 in which he described Japan as a "living laboratory of religious culture." In religious terms, Japan is very much pluralistic, although something Japanese seems to run through even the new religions. The Japanese can justifiably be described as people possessed of a distinctive type of spirituality, often associated with sacred places. Young people in modern Japan are still struck by places that exhibit what Rudolf Otto, in his book *Das Heilige* (translated as *The Idea of the Holy*), described as the "mysterium tremendum et fascinans." The spiritual atmosphere that **Ueshiba Morihei** sensed at **Kumano**, where he found inspiration and motivation, seems typical of what many have felt.

Throughout history, this has infused itself into formal rituals in Shinto, the funeral ceremonies in Buddhism, and in countless other forms. Indeed, it could be argued that this is the pre-condition of any new movement's survival in Japan. None of the monotheistic religions have a great appeal to the Japanese. Protestant Christianity briefly flourished in the **Meiji period** (1868–1912) because it was associated with the technological superiority of the West. It remains, however, like an alien form of rice that seems unable to take root in Japanese soil. The Christian population has never exceeded one percent. It seems unable to grow beyond that level, and is unlikely that it ever will.

ATSUTA JINGŪ. Historical shrine (**jinja**) located in Nagoya City which houses and enshrines the sword of the **imperial regalia**. A local legend has it that the enshrined *kami* is the famous Yang Guifei, the beautiful concubine of Emperor Xuan Gong, an eighth-century emperor of T'ang Dynasty China. He was thought to have planned an invasion of Japan, but because of his obsession with Yang Guifei, he failed to govern properly, and so Japan was saved.

There is also a narrative in the **mythology** recorded in the **Kojiki** (712) that **Yamato-takeru-no-mikoto** transformed himself into a beautiful woman in order to distract the Kumaso clan of Kyushū, which he succeeded in subduing. Perhaps by an association of ideas, the Atsuta Daimyōjin was thought to have become Yang Guifei in order to save Japan, being at the same time a re-incarnation of Yamato-takeru-no-mikoto. Although historians believe she died during a revolution, legends survive that she escaped to Japan, and lived near Atsuta.

Whether or not it is true, the legend illustrates many of the complex themes that lie in the background of almost all of Japan's major shrines. There is continental influence of one kind or another, syncretism, eclecticism, and selective admixing of myth, legend, and history.

AWA JINJA. Located in Tateyama city, Chiba Prefecture, the enshrined *kami* is Ame-no-futodama-no-mikoto, ancestor of the Imbe family, early court ritualist, and assistant to **Ame-uzume-no-mikoto** when she enticed **Amaterasu-ōmikami** from the **Ame-no-iwato**, the cave in which she was hiding to escape from the other *kami*. The *kami* was also associated with the descent of **Ninigi-no-mikoto**. It was given the status of a district first shrine (**Ichi-no-miya**) during the **Heian period** (794–1185) and ranked as a Myōjin Taisha, an eminent shrine (**jinja**), in the **Engishiki**.

AZUMA-ASOBI. Music, songs, and entertainment from the eastern provinces of Japan that were offered to the imperial court as evidence of fealty. The musical notation used was fixed by order of **Emperor Daigo** (reigned 897–930). The songs that belonged mostly to Sagami and Suruga provinces are still in use at shrines (**jinja**) and at the imperial court.

– B –

BACHI. Term referring to retributive punishment experienced by people who have not shown a proper attitude of reverence to the *kami* or who have offended them by inappropriate behavior. *See also*

ETHICS IN SHINTO; HARAI; KEGARE; SHINBATSU; TATARI; TSUMI.

BAN NOBUTOMO (1773–1846). Disciple of **Motoori Norinaga** (1730–1801), the leading **Kokugaku** (National Learning) scholar and specialist in the study of the text of the **Nihon Shōki** (720). He was adopted by Ban Nobumasa, a samurai of Wakasa Province (now in Fukui Prefecture). In 1801, he became attached to the school of Motoori Norinaga, and became a student of Motoori Ohira, Norinaga's adopted son. Described as a prolific writer, a careful scholar, and a thorough researcher, he was one of the finest members of the Kokugaku tradition.

BEKKA. Abstinence by a priest (**kannushi**) from various activities prior to performing an important ritual. *See also* SAIKAI.

BEKKAKU KAMPEISHA. A special category of **Kokka Shinto** (State Shinto) shrines (**jinja**), created in 1872 to give recognition to their role within the government-defined hierarchy of shrines during the Meiji period (1868–1912). Some were very old, but others date to the Meiji period, such as **Yasukuni Jinja**. The **Nikkō Tōshōgū**, which enshrines **Tokugawa Ieyasu** (1543–1616), was listed in 1873. It was, in effect, a compromise list that integrated shrines of great historical status with those revering heroes that the government considered good examples of the heroic ideals it sought to promote.

BEPPYŌ JINJA. A **Jinja Honchō** (Association of Shinto Shrines) list of the principal 244 shrines (**jinja**) nationwide, most of which were considered central shrines during the Meiji period (1868–1912).

BOKUSEN. Historically ancient form of **divination**, probably originating in China, that uses tortoise shells and other artifacts. Futomani, for example, was the practice of heating the shoulder bone of a deer and reading meaning into the configuration of cracks that appeared. Bokusen is still in use for the divination that precedes the building of the two special pavilions, the Yuki Den and the Suki Den, used in the imperial accession ritual known as the **Daijōsai**. The details are recorded in the **Engishiki** text of the **Heian period** (794–1185). It is also referred to by the term uranai.

BON-MATSURI. Festival celebrated from mid-July to early August to welcome back the **souls** of ancestors. Found also in other parts of Asia, it most likely derived from these Asian origins. Anthropological studies have demonstrated that **ancestral reverence** is one common binding feature of all eastern Asian civilizations, north and south, and that it takes different forms in different environments. It also seems to have become closely linked with **Buddhism,** from the time when the conflict between the Buddhist doctrine of reincarnation and the Asian predilection for ancestral reverence reached confrontation, initially in China. The Chinese Buddhists had to answer questions from Confucian scholars about behavioral requirements of Buddhists that were considered anathema to Chinese.

In a sixth-century text entitled *The Settling of Doubts* (known in Chinese as *Li huo lun* and in Japanese as *Riwaku ron*), questions about Buddhism were raised and answered. It asked, for example, why Buddhism was not mentioned in the definitive Confucian classics, how someone could be "reborn," and why ancestors should not be revered. By a method of analogy, both Confucian and **Taoist** meanings found their way into the translation of all Sanskrit terms into Chinese. Thus, the Chinese vocabulary of Buddhist thought and culture was formed, and this process made the transmission of Buddhism to Japan much easier than it otherwise would have been. Chinese culture effected a powerful transformation of Buddhism into a religion of ancestors, changing its fundamental character, and it is in this form that Buddhism entered Japan.

Arguments that Japanese ancestral reverence preceded Buddhism would merely indicate that Japan's earliest Asian immigrants brought the ancestral cult of the Bon festival with them, making its link with Buddhism in Japan. In the Japanese version, a mukae-bi (welcoming fire) is lit, followed later by an okuri-bi (sending fire). Between these occurs the Bon Odori, the dance with the ancestors that in modern Japan has become a form of communal entertainment with members of the community wearing the summer yukata and dancing in a circle to traditional music.

The overall association of Buddhism with death and funerals, also part of the Chinese heritage, was carried further in Japan because of the meticulous way in which ancestral reverence came to be practiced. It is significant that in modern Japanese society, the (normally) early August Bon festival ranks second only to the celebration of the New Year, when about 80 percent of the population visit shrines (**jinja**) and temples, most of them visiting shrines. While the celebration of Bon probably does predate Buddhism in Japan, because of the association of Buddhism with death, it was appropriated by Buddhist temples in the same way that funerals became the province of Buddhism after state support had been withdrawn in the Kamakura period (1185–1333). It opens another window of perception on the issue of **death in Shinto** and Buddhist thought.

BOSHIN SHŌSHŌ. One of numerous imperial rescripts issued at different times in the name of **Emperor Meiji** (reigned 1868–1912). This one was promulgated on 13 October 1908, on the themes of thrift and diligence, urging the Japanese people to unite and to show both economic and academic self-restraint. The main objective was to raise capital to cover the cost of Japan's very costly wars against China and Russia by stimulating national savings, a familiar device of Japanese governments when dealing with cash-flow problems.

It was, however, also a key theme built into pre-war moral education. It became further linked with the values of the **Hotoku** movement, which was based on the ideals of repayment of and indebtedness to ancestors and founded by **Ninomiya Sontoku** (1787–1856), a farmer and philosopher of the Edo period (1615–1868). The government promoted the creation of Hotoku societies nationwide in order to stimulate patriotism and self-restraint. The Ministry of Home Affairs (Naimushō) was so vigorous in this exercise that it earned the tag "Hōtoku Naimushō."

BUCHANAN, DANIEL CRUMP (1892–1982). Early 20th-century teacher, Christian missionary, and scholar of Japanese life who conducted research on the cult of **Inari**, publishing his work in the *Transactions of the Asiatic Society of Japan* in 1935. He was born in Japan of American parents, and was a 1914 graduate of Washington and Lee University. He subsequently became a Presbyterian minister and missionary.

The Daniel Crump Buchanan Papers are housed at Washington and Lee. Included in the collection are materials from his work with the Office of Strategic Services during the **Pacific War** (World War II), including position papers, studies, and internal memoranda; manuscripts of his books; and printed materials he collected on

Japan. The collection is valuable for the study of the U.S. wartime relationship with Japan.

BUDDHISM. Immigrant religious cult founded in India about the sixth century B.C.E, which entered Japan through China and Korea. Based on information in the **Nihon Shōki** (720), 552 C.E. is normally acknowledged as the date of imperial court recognition. The interaction with Japanese culture took six centuries to complete, after which Buddhism became fully indigenized and distinctively Japanese forms of Buddhism began to develop. While Buddhism at its inception in India was deeply concerned with the problem of individual enlightenment, its travels north into China changed it radically through its encounter with the eastern Asian tradition of **ancestral reverence** and the values of **Confucianism**. Its cross-fertilizing with **Taoism**, for example, in China, led to what became Zen in Japan.

Similar encounters with Tibetan Buddhism produced a hybrid with Tantric Indian thought which created more new forms of Buddhism, known subsequently in Japan as **Tendai** (partly esoteric, or *ken-kyō*) **Buddhism** and **Shingon** (fully esoteric, or *mikkyō*) **Buddhism**. This became known as the northern Buddhism (Daijō Bukkyō in Japanese), the Buddhism of the Great Vehicle. Buddhism in southern Asia, as in Sri Lanka, and Southeast Asia, as in Myanmar and Thailand, Cambodia and Vietnam, remain more orthodox, and are referred to as Hinayana Buddhism (Shōjō Bukkyō in Japanese), meaning the Buddhism of the Smaller Vehicle. The southern tradition follows the Pali Canon, while the northern tradition accepts both sutras and sastras, written in Sanskrit, as basic texts. The Mahayana tradition and its eclecticism enabled new concepts to be incorporated and developed at various stages of history as Buddhism traveled from one culture to another.

The traditional historical listing of Japanese Buddhism identifies 12 schools. First came the six Asuka/Nara period (552–794) schools. The oldest, Jō-Jitsu-shū (shū means sect), dates to 623 C.E. in Japan, being transmitted (at the request of Empress Suiko, reigned 592–628) by two Korean philosopher priests. It was developed in China as a bridgehead school between the Mahayana and the Hinayana traditions. The Kusha-shū tradition goes back to the *Abhidharma-kosha Sastra* (*Book of the Treasury of Metaphysics*). It was never a major school in China, and when transmitted to Japan it was closely related to the Hossō-shū, which continues to exist as a sect with 42 temples. The Horyu-ji in Nara (originally a Sanron-shū temple) was taken over and remains Hossō-shū. The Indian origin of the school was Yogachara, from the school of the scholar Asanga. In China, it was known as the school of Fa-hsiang. The last of the early four schools is the Sanron-shū, the dates of which are uncertain. Whether this school was historically earlier than the others is not as important as the fact that it is logically prior (in its foundation ideas) to many aspects of Japanese Buddhism and its influence on Japanese thought and culture.

The shift of early civilization from the **Yamato** region to the formal capital in Nara from 710, plus the patronage of **Emperor Shomu** (reigned 724–749) led to the integration of Buddhism into the emerging culture of Nara civilization. The introduction of the Kegon-shū belongs to this period, as does the building of the Tōdai-ji in Nara to house the great Buddha (Nara-no-Daibutsu). In the same way that Kegon marks the beginning of popular Buddhism, the rules and regulations of the Ritsu School provided the basis for the emergence of state Buddhism in Japan. Buddhism was introduced primarily in the interests of modernizing Japan, bringing its culture into line with the great civilization of China, and the protection of the state. Consequently, Buddhism remained very much the property of the court to the end of the Nara period.

Indeed, Japan wished to be part of the Pax Buddhica that the Chinese saw as a key concept to unify Asia. In 691 C.E. the Chinese emperor ordered the building in Luoyang of a Hall of World Government (*mingtang*) and the construction of the Great Regulator (probably the world's first mechanical clock). They were designed to be symbols that China was the true center of the new Buddhist world order, a goal supported by intense international diplomatic activity. Japan's removal of the capital to Nara was accompanied by the acceptance of many aspects of Chinese civilization, including Chinese standards. However, to emphasize Japan's distinctive identity, the Tōdai-ji in Nara was built to be the world's largest building housing the world's largest bronze Buddha. It was also completed with the protection of the *kami* **Hachiman**.

The Tendai-shū is one of the small group of schools that belong to the **Heian period** (794–1185) after the capital had been removed to Kyōto. It originated in China based on the *Saddharmapudarika*

(Hokke-kyō, or **Lotus Sutra**). The Lotus tradition is very important for Japan, especially for Tendai Buddhism. In Japan, it was introduced from China by **Saichō** (767–822), posthumously known as **Dengyō Daishi**. He entered a temple in 779 but became disillusioned by lax practice of the monks. **Emperor Kammu** (reigned 781–806) gave him permission to go to China in 804, where he learned the Tendai teaching on Mount T'ien-T'ai. He made the Enryakuji, a temple that he had founded around 788, the headquarters of his new school. It has remained so ever since. It remains also one of the most important temples in Japanese Buddhism.

The other great school of the Heian period was the Shingon-shū, that originated in the Tantric tradition of India. It made its way to Tibet where it combined with the Tibetan way of thinking to produce Lamaism, the uniquely politicized form of Buddhism containing elements and aspects not found in other Buddhist traditions. It is known in China still as Tibetan Buddhism. Its transmission to Japan was the work of **Kukai** (773–835), posthumously remembered as **Kōbō Daishi** (Propagator of the Law). From early days, he showed an interest in Chinese thought and culture, and in 789, went to Nara to study the Chinese Classics. While respecting the ethics of Confucius, the mystic-philosophical ideas of Taoism attracted him more, and after his firm conversion to Buddhism, he tried to integrate the various traditions of thought into one broad cosmo-theistic understanding of the universe. He received permission to go to China, arriving there in 804. By 807 he had been made eighth patriarch to transmit the tradition to Japan. From 805 to 815 he gradually increased his position of privilege with the emperor and became superintendent of the Tōdai-ji in Nara. Disdaining politics, he returned to Mount Kōya, and with a grant from the emperor, established the Shingon Buddhism central temple, the Kongobuji, on Mount Kōya in what is now Wakayama Prefecture. Among his many achievements are included improvements to the infrastructure of the nation, and the Japanese writing script, hiragana.

The late Heian period saw the rise of Jōdo Shu and Jōdo Shin Shu, which belong to the group of sects that focus on the worship of Amida. The worship of Amida was known in Tendai, but it was not until Genshin (942–1017) and later Hōnen (1133–1212) that the idea emerged of a simple Buddhist faith for ordinary people. He emphasized the Pure Land, the original vow of Amida, and the idea of rely-

ing on the other power, tariki of Amida, and the Nembutsu (the invocation of Amida) in the formula "Namu Amida Butsu." This became
the basis of the Jōdo Shū in Japan. The work of Shinran (1173–1262)
was to combine this with a simplified form of Shinshū or true school,
to form the modern popular movement known as Jōdo-shin-shū, the
most popular Buddhist tradition in Japan.

The establishment of a military government that marked the beginning of the Kamakura period (1185–1333) led to a kind of eschatological mood in Japanese society. The waning influence of Tendai
and Shingon plus the rather worldly mood of Amida pietism left room
for a strong, puritanical type of Buddhism to emerge with a sense of
historical destiny that related to Japanese hopes for the age. Nichiren
(1222–1282) developed such a type of Buddhism. The Lotus Sutra of
the Tendai School was the basic text on which the new Buddhism of
Nichiren was based. Thereafter it became one of the most important
texts in Japanese Buddhism which it remains to the present.

Over 40 older sects claim the ancestry of Nichiren. Three important **New Religions** in particular that emerged from the Nichiren
tradition of thought are Reiyūkai (Society of Spirit Friends), Sōka
Gakkai (Value Creating Society), and Risshō-Kōseikai, which is
liberal in contrast to the conservatism of the first two.

Finally, **Zen Buddhism** made its appearance also during the
Kamakura period 1185–1333), and found favor with the warrior
classes. Its origins are mythological, coming from the era of Bo-
dhidharma, who is said to have meditated for nine years until his
arms and legs withered and fell off. The origin is probably within the
Yogāchāra tradition, in combination with Taoism in China and the
idea of the abrupt way to enlightenment produced in the Southern
tradition of Zen in China.

During the Kamakura period, several Chinese scholars were invited to visit Japan, and these included teachers of Zen. Zen ideas,
however, had already been propagated by Eisai (1131–1215), the
Rinzai School and **Dogen** (1200–1253), the Sōtō School. The
Chinese teachers were able to develop the school from already
established foundations. The goal of discovering the Buddha as
mind (bushin) was to be achieved by a method of thinking that
transcends ordinary thinking and methods of logic and reasoning.
The objective was to awake an intuitional level of knowledge and
understanding that could be the source of satori (enlightenment).

The transmission of the tradition is therefore from mind to mind by indirect communication rather than by written or oral teaching. Training to hear a voice in silence, the state of mu-shin (empty mind) peace and fearlessness before death commended it as a means of discipline to the samurai to whom it became the basis of **bushidō** (the way of the warrior).

In the 1960s, Zen attracted much attention, mainly through the popularizing work of Suzuki Daisetsu in Japan and Alan Watts outside of Asia. It became identified with Japan, in popular Western writings, in a way that totally belied its reality and obscured the study of the other major traditions of Japanese religion and philosophy. Subsequent scholarship and research has demonstrated evidence of clear links between the so-called Kyōto School of Zen, an academic rather than a priestly tradition, and pre-war ultranationalism, more identifiable links than ever existed with Shrine Shinto (**Jinja Shinto**) in its totality. *See also* ASSIMILATION OF BUDDHISM AND SHINTO; SHUGENDŌ; TAOISM.

BUGAKU. A form of classical Japanese **music** used in **Noh** drama, in Shinto rituals, and at ceremonies in the **imperial household**. Classical instruments and rhythm are accompanied by stylized vocalization that is highly distinctive to the genre. This provides the background to dancers who perform the steps and stages of a narrative. There are many forms of bugaku that were developed in Japan over the centuries. More than 80 percent of the various forms derive from China, which in turn drew on its links with Tibet, India, and other parts of the Asian mainland. The remainder is of Korean origin. *See also* AME-UZUME-NO-MIKOTO; DANCE IN SHINTO; DRAMATIC ARTS; GAGAKU; KAGURA.

BUNREI. A branch of the soul of a *kami* separately enshrined to create a new place of worship. A bunrei is normally enshrined in a **bunsha**, or branch or subordinate shrine (**jinja**). The creation of branch shrines throughout Japanese history is principally associated with clan migration, although the popularity of various cults at different times led to the same result.

One of the best known is the expansion of the **Hachiman** cult. From the origins at the Usa Hachiman Shrine in Kyushū, the Hachiman cult spread first to Kyōto, when the capital was moved at the beginning of the **Heian period** (794–1185). The Iwashimizu Hachiman-gu was established. Subsequently, it expanded to Kamakura at the beginning of the Kamakura period (1185–1333), when **Minamoto Yoritomo** (1147–1199) set up his military government in Kamakura, resulting in the Tsurugaoka Hachiman-gū. The splitting of the mitama, the soul of the *kami*, in no way diminishes it; rather; it enhances its greatness. *See also* SOUL IN SHINTO.

BUNSHA. A branch shrine of a major shrine (**jinja**) in which a branch spirit, or **bunrei**, is enshrined in a new locality. Bessha (separate shrine) and betsugu are virtually synonymous terms. *See also* MASSHA.

BUSHIDŌ. General name given to the warrior cult that emerged at the time of the civil wars and that was institutionalized in the Military House Codes (bukeho) of the period and the subsequent Edo period (1615–1868). While not related directly to Shinto, Bushidō's **Zen Buddhism** background retained some of the aesthetic sensitivity of Shinto, particularly in the concept of **death** as a form of "purification" (**harai**), not a Shinto concept in that form, but one in which a Shinto motif is certainly present. The glorious death of the warrior is frequently identified with the cherry blossom (sakura): The flower falls when it reaches the fullness of its flowering beauty; so it was with the warrior.

BYAKKŌ-SHINKŌKAI. A **New Religion** with Shinto roots that dates to the mid-20th century. It was founded in1955 by Go Masahisa (1916–1980), a follower of Taniguchi Masaharu (1895–1985), founder of **Seicho-no-ie**, the House of Growth movement. The heart of the miraculous in all religion is centered in Japan and from there, peace will emanate. A ritual prayer is chanted to produce special energy in the form of "white light" (byakko). The presence of the sect is known by the placement of its famous peace poles that are found worldwide, bearing the inscription "May Peace Prevail on Earth."

The present chairperson is Masami Saionji (1941–), a descendent of the royal Ryukyu family of Okinawa. She met Goi when she was 16 and became deeply inspired by his vision for world peace. She became his adopted daughter, and now leads the movement.

– C –

CHAMBERLAIN, BASIL HALL (1850–1935). Scholar of Japanese culture who taught at the Imperial Naval Academy in Tokyō from 1874 to 1882. In1886, he became professor of Japanese at Tokyō Imperial University. It was there that his reputation was established as an authority on Japanese language and literature.

He was the first translator of the **Kojiki** (712), a translation famous for his attempts to eliminate what he considered improper sexual references in the text by rendering them into Latin. His health was always poor, and after leaving Japan, he retired to Geneva in Switzerland in 1911. He was a close acquaintance of **Lafcadio Hearn**, for whom he procured a position teaching at Tokyō Imperial University.

CHICHIBU JINJA. One of three important shrines (**jinja**) in the north of Saitama Prefecture, famous for its principal festival, the **Chichibu Yo-Matsuri.** The other two are equally famous. **Hodo-san Jinja** contains a **kiyome-no-ike,** which was used by the mythological figure **Yamato-takeru-no-mikoto.** The third, **Mitsumine Jinja,** was a visited by **Kukai** (774–835), the founder of **Shingon Buddhism**, as he traveled around mountain shrines introducing various Buddhist rituals and ideas to create a synthesis of Shinto and Buddhist culture. He worked hard to further the **assimilation of Buddhism and Shinto** that had begun in the early Nara period (710–794). It came to be known as **Shinbutsu-Shūgō** and evolved, eventually, into the tradition of **Shugendō.**

CHICHIBU YO-MATSURI. This **festival,** related to silk merchants of the Edo period (1615–1868), is held in Chichibu, Saitama Prefecture, on 2–3 December. It commences from Chichibu Jinja and traverses the town, and is famous for the giant carts, known as **dashi,** that are dragged through the streets and finally hauled up a very steep slope as the evening's climax. They are followed by the portable palanquin (**mikoshi**) before the event is brought to a conclusion by a massive display of fireworks. It is listed as one of Japan's great festivals, having all the essential ingredients including some drama, classical dances, and sake-drinking.

CHIEN-SHIN. The *kami* of the land of a small, local agricultural commune. During the Meiji period (1868–1912), a large percentage of these were integrated into an **ujigami**, a larger family grouping of *kami*. Chien-shin usually refers to communities in even smaller geographical areas more appropriate to a **dozoku-shin**. *See also* UBUSUNA-NO-KAMI.

CHIGI/KATSUOGI. The distinctive gable posts and roof beams on shimmei-zukuri shrine (**jinja**) roofs, such as those found at the **Grand Shrines of Ise** (Ise Jingū). *See also* ARCHITECTURE IN SHINTO.

CHIGO. The term, which literally means "young child," perhaps originated in **Buddhism**. It came to identify child mediums whose role in divination was possible because of their purity. The term Shin-do (literally *kami*-youth, or divine child) most likely originated in the use of children in Shinto harvest divining rites, as still practiced in the Tohoku region. Children prior to the age of puberty are widely used in rituals, dances, and other festival events where a medium is required. After puberty, in some areas, they climb a local mountain as the first act of adult purification (**harai**). *See also* BOKUSEN; SHAMANISM IN SHINTO.

CHINJU-NO-KAMI. Protective *kami* of a clan. Military houses, such as that of **Minamoto Yorimoto**, always had a protective *kami*. The Hata family of Kyōto is thought to have introduced the cult of **Inari** to the Kanto plain in the context of setting up business operations in Edo. Most major families were associated with one specific *kami* for whom a shrine (**jinja**) would be established on land belonging to them. The movement of military and business houses and the setting up of branch houses was one way in which Shinto cults spread to other regions throughout Japanese history. *See also* DOZOKU-SHIN.

CHINKI-SHIKI. A **fire calming ritual** in which believers walk barefooted on hot coals. The ritual is one of several practiced by the **Ontake-kyō** and **Shinshū-kyō** of the **Kyōha Shinto** (Sect Shinto) groups. The hot coals lie on a straw bed about five meters long and one meter wide and covered with sand. The entire area is marked off as a sacred space by surrounding it with a **shimenawa** (straw rope) hung with **shide** (paper streamers in a zigzag formation). The goals of the discipline are two-fold. First, it is to invite the *kami* of the moon or of water to "calm" (**chinkon**) the *kami* of fire, demonstrating the power of the believers. Second, it is viewed as an act of ritual purification (**harai**) through fire. Once the officiating priests have undergone the ritual, the believers may follow. In the rituals of **Shugendō**, the Shinto-Buddhist amalgam that existed until the separation of **Buddhism** and Shinto after 1868, fire rituals such as **goma** were interpreted both in Buddhist and Shinto terms as purification and as the enhancement of human powers to greater levels.

CHINKON. A ritual or ceremony to calm the **soul**, popular especially during the **Heian period** (794–1185). Its practice began in the Heian court, a place of superstitions, intrigue, and scandal, and where malicious rumor could lead to the sudden rise and fall of courtiers and politicians. When they died, as they often did, in exile or from the assassin's knife, any subsequent natural disasters were frequently attributed to their vengeful spirits.

The idea of pacifying vengeful spirits by reverencing them led to worship known as **goryō-e**. The most famous historical example of the Heian period is that of **Sugawara Michizane** (845–903). At the level of general shrine (**jinja**) rituals, chinkon, whose form varies according to shrine traditions, is still practiced at the conclusion of **misogi** and other forms of purification (**harai**), where the calming of the soul is considered the appropriate conclusion to a sequence of rituals. It is also referred to as tama-shizume or mitama-shizume. **Iresai** is a ceremony to console the souls of the dead, particularly dead soldiers. *See also* SHŌKONSHA; YASUKUNI JINJA.

CHI-NO-WA. A large ring, at least three meters in diameter, made of twisted miscanthus reeds through which people pass on 30 June, at the time of the **Ōbarae**, the great purification (**harai**), to avoid misfortune by removing impurities (**tsumi**).

CHINZA. Rituals involving the enshrinement or removal of a *kami* are particularly solemn, and are performed usually at night and in near total darkness. If reference is being made to the initial enshrinement of a *kami*, it is formally styled as go-chinza, and the date of the first enshrinement is referred to as go-chinza followed by the number of years. The **Grand Shrines of Ise** (Ise Jingū) date the go-chinza of **Amaterasu-ōmikami** to 4 B.C.E.

CHOKUSAI. A shrine (**jinja**) **festival** celebrated in the presence of an imperial messenger, dating to the **Heian period** (794–1185), when imperial patronage of certain important shrines began to develop. A **chokushi**, an imperial messenger, attended such highly ranked festivals and presented missives from the emperor along with supporting gifts. The shrines thus honored varied from time to time. In the postwar period, the head of the **Jinja Honchō** (the Association of Shinto Shrines) replaced the imperial messenger.

CHOKUSHI. A messenger dispatched from the Imperial Palace to take greetings, along with monetary gifts, to important shrines (**jinja**) on the occasion of their principal **festival**. Some shrines conducted their festival rituals in the presence of such a messenger. During times of economic restraint, when gifts were not possible, imperial greetings were still delivered. Only a limited number of major shrines were accorded this privilege. *See also* CHOKUSAI.

CHU HSI (1132–1200). (Also known as Zhu Xi). Founder of a neo-**Confucian** intellectual movement in China that was imported by the government of **Tokugawa Ieyasu** (1543–1616) as the basis of its sociopolitical system of thought. It was known as **Rigaku** (the Study of Rational Principles). Chu Hsi's social thought became the basis of the entire Edo period (1615–1868) social order, and with some changes, it also became the foundation of **Yoshikawa Shinto**. Until the Edo period, Confucian values had been closely linked to **Buddhism** from the time of the Seventeen Clause Constitution of **Shōtoku Taishi** (574–622). After the early Edo period, **Confucianism and Shinto** became linked as the values and cosmology of Chu Hsi became associated with Shinto.

CHŪKOGAKU. The technical name given to Heian Studies during the Edo period (1600–1868) by the **Kokugaku** (National Learning) scholar **Motoori Norinaga** (1730–1801).

CHŪNAGON. Middle-court rank of the **Heian period** (794–1185), frequently a pivotal position of political significance because occupants of the office were able to communicate freely with ranks above and below.

CONFUCIANISM. The conservative Chinese philosophical and ethical system created by Confucius (551-479 B.C.E.) that came to define the character of Chinese society. It organized society into ranks and established relations that were to be observed. Filial piety was observed by following the relations, namely, the precedence of ruler over ruled, father over son, husband over wife, elder brother over younger brother, and finally friend to friend. Various versions of the Confucian system existed. The teaching of **Chu Hsi** (1130–1200), which stressed that form of the five relationships, was particularly congenial to **Tokugawa Ieyasu** (1543–1616), who successfully created a warrior code that stressed loyalty to a feudal master as the basis of a civilized society. The warrior code of **Bushidō** grew from this and provided Edo period (1615–1868) society with an enormous degree of stability. *See also* CONFUCIANISM AND SHINTO.

CONFUCIANISM AND SHINTO. Confucian values entered Japan with **Buddhism**, and are evident in the Seventeen Clause Constitution of **Shōtoku Taishi** (574–622), which was, in reality, a set of moral guidelines for national wellbeing. The emphasis upon harmony is one of the lasting traces of Confucian influence in Japanese culture.

Confucianism may never have existed independently after its initial entrance to Japan along with Buddhism, and it may also have been more closely linked to Buddhism during its first few hundred years in Japan. However, by the Edo period (1615–1868), a Shinto-Confucian synthesis had begun to emerge that came to be highly influential in creating the values of pre-modern Japan and that helped to provide the foundations of modern Japanese social values. This integration of Shinto and neo-Confucian values began during the early Edo period and was based on the thought of **Chu Hsi** (1132–1200). The Tokugawa government found his system of thought extremely congenial to government goals. It was encouraged and developed by the government philosopher **Hayashi Razan** (1583–1687), who created a syncretistic system of thought that linked Confucian values with Shinto *kami*.

As the era progressed, various expressions of the basic concepts began to appear at the popular level, and in this way seeped into popular consciousness. Thinkers such as **Ishida Baigan** (1685–1744), **Kaibara Ekken** (1630–1714), and **Ninomiya Sontoku** (1787–1856) created movements and fostered ideals that reflected Confucian values, distilled for consumption at the popular level. It is through the values created by these thinkers that Japan found ideas that contributed substantially to the ideological and psychological basis for the development of the **modernization** program of the Meiji period (1868–1912). Scholars have even tried to draw comparisons between these and the Protestant work ethic that early sociologist Max Weber identified as an essential ingredient of the modernization of the Western world.

COSMOLOGY IN SHINTO. Cosmology in Japanese thought is in reality cosmogony, and is found primarily in the ancient writings the **Nihon Shōki** (720) and the **Kojiki** (712), both of which contain narratives of the coming into being of the Japanese archipelago through the procreative act of **Izanagi-no-mikoto** and **Izanami-no-mikoto.**

The introduction and adaptation of various Chinese concepts that came to Japan with **Buddhism,** and their integration into the mainstream of Japanese thought, produced a syncretistic system of thought that has survived to the present. It has flourished particularly in the area where esoteric Buddhism and Shinto overlapped, creating movements such as **Shugendō,** a form of mountain asceticism.

– D –

DAIDŌ. Meaning the great way, an old name for Shinto, Daidō is synonymous with **Kodō,** the ancient way, and **Teidō,** the imperial way. Shinto has been known under different names, depending often upon the point of view of the person referring to it. The first use of the term Shinto is found in the **Nihon Shōki** (720), where **Emperor Yōmei** (reigned 585–587) is reported as having believed in the law of the Buddha and revered the way of the *kami.*

There was much discussion of the great way during the 17th and 18th centuries. Amano Nobukage (1660–1733) described it as the way to revere the *kami* of heaven and earth, a view followed subsequently by Ise Teijo (1714–1784). **Hayashi Razan** (1583–1657) referred to it as the way of true government, a position supported by Confucian Shinto thinkers such as **Yoshikawa Koretari** (1616–1694). The **Kokugaku** (National Learning) scholars, principally **Motoori Norinaga** (1730–1801) and **Hirata Atsutane** (1776–1843), spoke of it as the way of **Amaterasu-ōmikami**, *kami* of the sun and divine ancestress of the imperial family. Kannagara no michi is also still used. The term **Tai-kyō**, the great teaching, was used widely in the Meiji period (1868–1912). *See also* TAIKYO SENPU UNDO.

DAIGENGŪ. The Palace of Great Origins, the name of a great shrine (**jinja**) constructed in 1484 by **Yoshida Kanetomo** (1435–1511), which employed **architectural** features as symbols of his syncretistic view of Shinto, **Taoism**, and **Buddhism**. A central pillar made of 3,132 stones represented the number of *kami* named in the **Engishiki** and symbolized the unity and ultimacy of Shinto.

DAIGO, EMPEROR. Listed as the 60th emperor (born 885; reigned 897–930), he tried to maintain his independence from the Fujiwara regency. Palace infighting resulted in the exile in 901 of one of his ministers, **Sugawara Michizane** (845–903), who was later enshrined to calm his spirit. He was responsible for the Engi Reform of 902. The **Engishiki**, the historical text, the *Nihon Sandai Jitsuroku*, and the poetic anthology, the **Kokinshū**, were compiled during his reign. *See also* CHINKON.

DAI-GŪJI. The special rank of Supreme High Priest that exists only at the **Grand Shrines of Ise** (Ise Jingū). Along with the Dai-guji, there is also a **Sho-Guji**, a position also unique to the Grand Shrines, who is the associate or deputy high priest. *See also* GUJI; KANNUSHI.

DAIJINGŪ SHINTO WAKUMON. Questions concerning Grand Shrine Shinto (1666) was a text authored by **Watarai Nobuyoshi**, (1615–1691). It was the Shinto of the later rather than the earlier Ise cult, and part of his work was trying to restore the old texts of the **Grand Shrines of Ise** (Ise Jingū) that had been destroyed or simply lost during the long period of civil war.

The work itself revived the study of the **Ise Shinto**; in particular, with the aid of some of the high priests of the Grand Shrines, he set up the **Toyomiyazaki Library** for the training of senior priests at the **Gekū** (the Outer shrine). He also worked tirelessly for the rebuilding of the sessha and **massha**, the branch shrines that had been destroyed during the civil war. In his efforts to improve the weakened reputation of the Outer Shrine, he came into conflict with the high priest of the **Naikū** (the Inner Shrine) on the subject of what kind of inscription should be written on good fortune amulets distributed by the shrines (**jinja**). He lost the debate, and shortly thereafter, much of his own personal library was destroyed by fire.

The concept of "propriety," about which he was concerned, was very much a value of **Confucianism**. There is much in his thought that is Confucian, and in that regard, he is more typical of the early Edo period (1615–1868) and has some traits in common with the Confucian-style Shinto that grew up at the time. Nevertheless, his vigorous assertion of the claims of Ise Shinto marks him off from the other thinkers of the period. The order in which he discussed the Confucian relationships is that preferred by the Edo government, particularly the shogun, **Tokugawa Ieyasu** (1543–1616). Obedience to the ruler was the prime relationship to which the rest deferred. He introduced the discussion in order to strengthen the moral grip of the government upon the social order. He also composed a two-volume work that interprets Shinto in terms of **divination**, and another that argues that the Shinto practiced at Ise was the true origin of Shinto in Japan.

DAIJŌSAI. Also known as Ōnie-no-Matsuri, this ceremony relating to the accession of a new emperor dates to the reign (673–686) of **Emperor Temmu**. It is the **festival** at which a newly installed emperor offers, for the first time, the first fruits of the harvest to **Amaterasu-ōmikami**, *kami* of the sun and the Imperial Ancestor. He continues to do this every autumn in the **Niinamesai** for the entire length of his reign.

Daijosai is the third ritual to mark the Senso, the accession. The first act is the formal declaration by the emperor of his status and his receipt of the mirror, jewel, and sword. This ceremony is called the Kenji Togyo no Gi and was televised for the first time in 1989. Second comes the Sokuirei, the imperial declaration of status, traditionally performed in the Shishinden of the Imperial Palace in Kyōto. Although it is not specified in the Imperial Household Law of 1947, in the case of Emperor Akihito in 1989, the same style as that of the accession of Emperor Shōwa was followed, using the procedures for the ceremony recorded in the **Engishiki**. Using an ancient Chinese system of **divination**, two **rice** fields, east and west of Kyōto, the Yukiden and the Sukiden, are selected. Rice from these is brought to the two wooden buildings erected inside the Imperial Palace, known as the Yuki Pavilion and the Suki Pavilion. In the center of each is a kind of bed called a **shinza**. The ritual is performed after elaborate purification (**harai**) rites have taken place.

The new emperor enters the Yuki Pavilion and makes offerings. A ceremony of **naorai** takes place, and after midnight, the ritual is repeated in the Suki Pavilion. The event is reported on the day to the **Grand Shrines of Ise** (Ise Jingū), to the shrines inside the Palace, and to the old government and prefectural shrines. The two halls are dismantled the following day by men from the region of the two fields. During the accession rites of a new emperor, the regular annual Niinamesai is not held. Theories of the daijosai vary from the idea of a ritual in which the new emperor communes with the **soul** of Amaterasu-ōmikami to the radical idea of **Origuchi Shinobu** (1887–1953), who argued that there was only one imperial soul which was transmitted from emperor to emperor through the ritual, an idea closer to Tibetan Buddhism than to Shinto. *See also* AKI MATSURI.

DAIKOKUTEN. The *kami* of wealth and prosperity, thought to have originated in India, introduced to Japan by **Saichō** (767–822) as a guardian of the Buddhist Treasures. Because readings are homophonous with **O-kuni-nushi-no-kami**, the identification led to the association of the two figures. During the medieval period, he become a *kami* of prosperity, being associated with **Ebisu** as one of the seven *kami* of prosperity (**Shichi-fuku-jin**). In southwestern Japan, he is known as **Ta-no-kami**, *kami* of **rice** fields. He is portrayed holding a mallet, a sack, and wearing a black cloth cap.

DAINAGON. First ministerial rank in the **Heian period** (794–1185) imperial court.

DAINICHI NYORAI. The Buddha Mahavairochana, the Buddha of great light. The Nara period (710–794) Great Buddha (Daibutsu) statue is of this figure. In the early synthesis with Shinto, Vairochana was quickly associated with the *kami* of the sun, **Amaterasu-ōmikami**, with the Buddha being the reality and the sun being the manifestation. Vairochana is the central Buddha of the **Shingon** Buddhist tradition, and was also linked with *kami* of both the **Naikū** (Inner) and the **Gekū** (Outer) of the **Grand Shrines of Ise** (Ise Jingū). Eventually, the roles were reversed, as Shinto began to reclaim the territory it had lost to **Buddhism**. *See also* ASSIMILATION OF BUDDHISM AND SHINTO; HONJI-SUIJAKU-SETSU; RYŌBU SHINTO.

DAI-NIPPON-JINGIKAI. Pre-War Organization of Shrines, abolished in 1945 and replaced by the **Jinja Honcho** (the Voluntary Association of Shinto Shrines, as it was known initially).

DAISAI. Annual ritual marking the death of the previous emperor, and one of the **imperial household** rituals within the annual calendar of Shinto ceremonies of the imperial household performed by the reigning emperor as an institutional figure.

DAISHIZEN. Meaning "Great Nature," the term goes beyond merely nature (shizen in Japanese) to more of a comprehensive cosmological nuance that includes the stars and planets as well as the earth and its natural order. It is found also in the *Daodejing*, the classic text of Chinese **Taoism**. *See also* COSMOLOGY IN SHINTO; NATURE IN SHINTO.

DAJŌKAN. The Great Council of State in the early Japanese Court system was known also as Omatsurigoto no Tsukasa, illustrating the early links between religious rituals (**matsuri** meaning **festival**) and the government of the country. Along with the **Jingikan**, it was the main organ of government, the Jingikan dealing with worship of the *kami*. The early **Meiji Restoration** government of 1868 employed the ancient system until a modern form of cabinet government was developed around 1885. *See also* MATSURI-GOTO; SAISEI-ITCHI.

DANCE IN SHINTO. Shinto **rituals** make extensive use of **music** and dance. Dance is nearly universal in religion as a means of worship and celebration, from the culture of Native Americans to the tribal culture of Africa, or the rituals of China to the ceremonies of Thailand. Japan has been prolific in the creation and use of dance in the religious culture of Shinto. The earliest reference to dance in the mythology is of **Ame-uzume-no-mikoto** attracting **Amaterasu-ōmikami** (*kami* of the sun) out of the **Ame-no-iwato**, the cave in which she was hiding, by performing a ribald dance. The evolution of ritual into drama, when **Noh** emerged as an art form out of **saru-gaku**, involves dance of a different type, namely, measured steps and careful movement similar to the kind of steps taken by priests (**kan-

nushi) when they are performing ceremonies of purification (**harai**) at shrines (**jinja**). Ceremonial dancing accompanied by special music is known as **bugaku**, and is another classical form of dance.

Other forms of Shinto culture have produced several different genre of dance according to the needs of the situation or event. Communal dance at **festivals (matsuri)** has a long history, and these are usually associated with local popular folk songs that have become symbolic reminders of community life and history. The **Bon-Matsuri**, a festival to welcome back the **souls** of ancestors, involves various versions of bon-odori, the dance of villagers with their ancestors. Since the festival is celebrated in mid-summer, the image that comes to mind is of people in yukata, cotton kimono-style robes, waving fans and moving through the steps in a huge circle to the intoxicating sound of the **taiko** drums and the Japanese flute.

Shamanistic dances are also very much part of the folk culture of Shinto. The **Shishi-mai**, which is derived from masked dances known as Gigaku, was introduced from China toward the end of the seventh century. These evolved in Japan into **kagura**, a sacred dance ritual, often performed by boys who have not yet reached puberty, dancing inside a lion costume in order to animate it. There is also the **Otome-mai**, a dance by young girls, of which the Gosechi-no-mai is the oldest. It is a five-movement dance that depicts an incident in the life of **Emperor Temmu** (reigned 673–686). Many of these classic dances have a famous historical incident in their background that they were created to commemorate.

Within the **New Religions**, shamanistic dance is also found. **Nakayama Miki** (1798–1887), founder of the sect **Tenri-kyō**, is reported to have died performing her **Kagura Zutone** (salvation dance) at the headquarters of the sect in 1887. Kitamura Sayo (1900–1967), founder of **Tenshō Kōtai Jingū-Kyō**, developed a dance called the muga-no-mai, or "no-self" dance, based on the **Buddhist** concept of no-self. From ancient times, Japanese religion has found expression in many forms of art and culture, among which the use of dance in many forms has a long and important history. *See also* DRAMATIC ARTS IN SHINTO; MASKS.

DANNA. Disciple of a **Shugendō** master of the **Heian period** (794–1185) who learned the esoteric and physically demanding ways to purification (**harai**) and enlightenment.

DANNOURA NO TATAKAI. A sea battle fought at Shimonoseki on 25 April 1185, at which the Minamoto (Genji) clan defeated the Taira (Heike) and the seven-year-old **Antoku**, the boy emperor (reigned 1180–1183), was drowned and the sword of the **imperial regalia** lost. The battle's outcome enabled **Minamoto Yorimoto** (1147–1199) to establish a new regime based at Kamakura in 1192.

DASHI. A large wagon pulled at **festivals**, differently named in various areas of the country as yatai, hiki-yama, odori-guruma, or yama-boko. They are normally kept by the residents of the wards they represent and are used to carry the *kami* around the town or city during festivals. *See also* CHICHIBU YO-MATSURI; OMIKOSHI.

DAZAIFU TENMAN-GŪ. Shrine (**jinja**) located near Fukuoka in Kyushū, established in 905 to pacify the angry spirit of **Sugawara Michizane** (845–903), where he was renamed **Tenjin**, the *kami* of learning. *See also* CHINKON; GORYŌ-E.

DAZAI SHOCHI. Title of a provincial governor in the **Heian period** (794–1185) political system.

DAZAI SHONI. Title of provincial vice-governor in the **Heian period** (794–1185) political system.

DEATH IN SHINTO THOUGHT. The earliest reference to death is found in the **mythology**, which narrates how **Izanami-no-mikoto** died while giving birth to the *kami* of fire and how she is pursued by her grieving husband, **Izanagi-no-mikoto**. She goes to **Yomi-no-kuni**, an underworld of decay similar to Hades in Greek mythology. It is described as a land of pollution and filth horrific to Izanagi. who is forced to purify himself in the River Tachibana after his escape. This was the first recorded instance of **misogi**, performed as an act of ritual purification (**harai**).

Death, therefore, was perceived to be a source of impurity. Wei Dynasty records in China note that Japanese went to purify themselves in a river after attending a funeral, a practice symbolically continued into modern times in the form of a little packet of salt mourners receive to throw into the entranceway of their homes upon returning, in order to prevent infection by impurity. Taboos of avoidance (**imi**) also remain. Those who have suffered a bereavement normally refrain from attending celebratory events for several months, again because of their contact with death. They also send out a simple message to all friends and relatives stating that they will not be sending New Year greetings cards (nengajo) in that year because of the bereavement. This is to ask politely that no greetings cards, which are congratulatory about the coming year, be sent to them.

Since the evolution of Shinto was concerned mostly with ritual and ceremony, little eschatological speculation developed within the tradition. It was left to **Buddhism** to capitalize on this when state patronage was withdrawn. During the highly superstitious **Heian period** (794–1185), from the ninth century, vengeful spirits known as goryō or onryō were the object of pacification rituals (**chinkon**). From the late Heian period onward, Buddhism became the culture of the funeral, with even 14th-century writers on **Zen Buddhism** spending more time writing about funeral rites than about enlightenment.

One topic on which the mythology is almost silent is the status of the **soul** (**tama**) after death. In the mythology, *kami* die, and later people and emperors die, yet they continue to be *kami*. The only observation that can be made on this fact is that, since Shinto is concerned with development and stages of growth, it really views death as simply a stage in a longer process. Certainly there is no kind of Shinto eschatology, and little about life after death in the Western sense in which this is conceived. Later concepts, such as the idea of the Pure Land, belong entirely to Buddhism.

Shinto funerals (sōsai) are not unknown, but the bulk of funerals were traditionally, and still remain in the hands of, Buddhist priests. As to what happens to people when they die, the vague identification of them as *kami* or hotoke (a Buddha) really does not address the issue in any existential sense of the term. It may simply be the case that the power of the ancestral cult and the reassurance it offers of respect being paid to the deceased has rendered speculation on life after death unnecessary.

Since by law cremation is now mandatory in Japan, traditional burial is possible only for families who already possess land reserved for that purpose. The ashes of a cremated Shinto priest (**kannushi**), for example, may be interred close to the shrine (**jinja**) precincts, but never inside them. A **bessha** may be erected inside the grounds in order to show reverence to the *kami* now present. Very rarely, the "grave" of a *kami* from the mythology may be found within shrine grounds. *See also* ANCESTRAL REVERENCE; TOKOYO-NO-KUNI.

DEGUCHI NAO (1836–1918). Foundress of the **New Religion** known as **Omoto-kyō**, now part of **Kyōha Shinto** (Sect Shinto), although not one of the original 13 sects. From 1892, she began having visions of Ushitora Konjin, a great deity whose messages she began writing and which became known as the *Ofudesaki*. Her eschatological message about the corrupt age of the present being replaced by a coming golden age implied public criticisms of the **emperor system** and **Kokka Shinto** (State Shinto), which had a later impact on the sect.

In 1898, she made the acquaintance of Ueda Onesaburo (later to become **Deguchi Onesaburō** [1871–1948] after he married Nao's daughter Sumi), who successfully translated her ideas into a Shinto conceptual framework. His leadership enabled the movement to effect its transition to a legitimate branch of Sect Shinto.

DEGUCHI NOBUYOSHI (1615–1690). Also known as **Watarai Nobuyoshi,** a distinguished priest of the **Naikū** (Outer Shrine) of the **Grand Shrines of Ise** (Ise Jingū) and a leading figure in the development of **Watarai Shinto**.

DEGUCHI ONESABURŌ (1871–1948). Early leading figure of the **New Religion, Ōmoto-kyō.** Born in Kameoka (Kyōto Prefecture) of a poor family, he showed considerable potential but was unable to receive formal education. After a traumatic experience in 1898, he devoted himself to religious contemplation and discipline, through which he developed charismatic and shamanistic skills.

A chance meeting with **Deguchi Nao** (1837–1918), foundress of Ōmoto-kyō, led to an alliance in which he used his Shinto theological framework to interpret Nao's ideas. This led to the development and formation of Ōmoto-kyō as a sect. He formed a close friendship with Ueshiba Morihei (1883–1969), the founder of **aikido**, with whom he went to China to spread his ideas. The trip proved disastrous; both were repatriated to Japan in chains, accused of having caused civil unrest in China.

Similarly, Onesaburō's announcement in Japan of an eschatological age led to a backlash from the authorities, because they perceived the movement as revolutionary. In 1921, and again in 1935,

Ōmoto-kyō was brutally suppressed and its headquarters destroyed. Onesaburō was imprisoned until 1945; upon his release he was able to rebuild the movement and is now active in interfaith religious activity, especially with Episcopalian Christians in North America.

DENGAKU. Music that originated in **rice**-planting **rituals.** Satome (rice planting maidens) sang songs as they planted rice shots. Instruments used were flutes, drums, and sasara (wooden blocks) that were struck against each other. The popularity of this music resulted in the emergence of dengaku-hoshi, professional musicians who incorporated it into shrine festivals **(matsuri). Sarugaku** performances evolved out of these. Dengaku performances, however, may still be seen at some shrines **(jinja)** in older areas such as downtown Asakusa in Tokyō.

DENGYŌ DAISHI (767–822). Posthumous name conferred on the founder of **Tendai Buddhism, Saichō.**

DEWA-SANZAN JINJA. A group of three shrines **(jinja)** located on three adjacent mountains, Gassan (Jinja), Hagurosan (Ideha Jinja), and Yudonosan (Jinja), in Yamagata Prefecture. The mountains are home to **yamabushi,** mountain ascetics who combine **rituals** from **Buddhism** and Shinto in their esoteric practices. Provincial governors visited them regularly in the eighth and ninth centuries while trying to establish the hegemony of the central government in eastern Japan. The Dewa-Sanzan remain centers of **Shugendō,** and still attract both pilgrim ascetics and general tourists.

DIVINATION. Communication with the supernatural in order to determine propitious times and places for events to assure their success. Numerous methods exist, including futomani, interpreting the cracks on the heated shoulder bone of a deer; kiboku, using turtle shells, as is done at the time of the **Daijōsai;** the use of Yi jing, confined isolation to receive oracles; and the use of shamanistic mediums. The first three can be traced to Chinese origins; the latter appear to be local to Japan, although similar forms exist in other cultures, notably Korea.

In popular Shinto, there are numerous versions still in use, such as **yabusame, matoi,** and **omato-shinji,** all forms of fortune-telling that use archery. Many shrines **(jinja)** provide fortune-telling guides based on the traditional Oriental (originally Chinese) Zodiac, which runs in cycles of 12 years, each one named after an animal. There are also o-mikuji (fortunes printed on sheets of paper). If these contain words of good fortune, they are taken home. If they do not, they are usually tied to trees in the shrine grounds in the hope that the no ill will come to their recipients.

There are numerous forms of fortune-telling, some practiced separately by professionals quite unconnected to shrines. Even at modern university culture day events, the fortune-teller regularly appears, and many are found on the streets of big cities such as Tokyō, catching clients on their way home from work. *See also* BOKUSEN; SHAMANISM IN SHINTO.

DŌGEN (1200–1253). Buddhist priest and poet, philosopher and scholar of the Zen tradition, and author of the *Shobo-genzo*. While not directly linked to Shinto thought, his unique appreciation of **nature** and his understanding of it helped to bridge the gap between the natural as understood in Shinto and the more austere perception found in **Zen Buddhism**. His name in Chinese characters means the root of the Dao (**Tao**) which is also the character for way (do) in Shinto.

DOHYO. Sumo wrestling ring that is a sacred space used only in the performance of sumo rituals and tournaments. The earth is specially selected and the entire edifice stands a few feet above floor level. Various items are buried in the center of the ring, and before any tournament commences, priests perform the Dohyō **Matsuri** in order to purify it. Dohyō may be found in the grounds of many country shrines, especially in the north of Japan and in the precincts of the **Yasukuni Jinja** in Tokyō. Tournaments are staged in it for the calming (**chinkon**) of the **souls (tama)** of the war dead.

The throwing of salt by the rikishi (wrestlers) before each bout is also an act of purification. The two great tournaments in Tokyō are held in the Kokugikkan. *See also* MARTIAL ARTS.

DOJIN. Mythical child attendants of the *kami* in the culture of Japanese **folk religion**.

DŌJŌ. Technical term for a gym used for practicing the **martial arts**, such as **aikido**, judo, and kendo. **Sumo** wrestlers train in the **dohyō**

located in the heya, or stable, to which they belong. All of these may have a **kami-dana**, a small Shinto altar (usually in the form of a shelf), on which are placed offerings of water, salt, and sake to show respect to the protective *kami* of the organization.

DŌKYŌ (DIED 722). Buddhist priest and confidant of Empress Koken (reigned 749–758). He aspired to imperial status, but his claim was refuted by an oracle from the **Usa Hachiman-gū**, delivered by courtier **Wake no Kiyomaru** (733–799). The incident is significant because it accentuated the attempted intrusion of Buddhist priests into court politics, leading eventually to the removal of the capital to Kyōto. It also demonstrated the importance of the Hachiman cult and its relationship with the **imperial household**, and raises the issue of the importance of Kyushū in the rise of the **Yamato** hegemony.

DŌSOJIN. Also known as sae-no-kami (or sai-no-kami) and dorokujin, Dosojin are worshipped on village borders, mountain passes, crossroads, and bridges to protect travelers, and is one example of the outstanding folk roots of Shinto. They are sometimes identified with **Sarutahiko-ōkami**, *kami* of pioneering and guidance. In modern times, their protection became extended to children, marriage, and childbirth. Consequently, children came to play a key role in **festivals** to Dosojin. Sometimes they are linked to phallic worship, and thereby become associated with procreation. *See also* FOLK RELIGION; HENOKO MATSURI; OAGATA JINJA; SEX IN SHINTO.

DŌTAKU. Bronze bell-like objects found in parts of Japan, mostly in the Kyōto-Osaka-Nara region, and dating to the Yayoi period (circa 300 B.C.E.–300 C.E.). Some have been found along with bronze mirrors. Probably functional at first, they likely evolved into ritual items over time. They have assisted archaeologists concerned with analyzing the roots of various aspects of Japanese culture.

DŌZOKU-SHIN. Kinship-*kami*, meaning the *kami* of a family or group with strong kinship ties in a common ancestor, providing in some cases the historical foundations of a shrine (**jinja**). As branch houses (bunke) were set up, a **bunrei**, or branch spirit, of the Dozoku-shin might be enshrined. In this way, the cult of the family would spread. This was not uncommon among the merchant houses of Osaka whose guardian *kami* was taken with them to wherever they established a new business. *See also* BUNSHA; INARI; UBUSUNA-NO-KAMI.

DRAMATIC ARTS IN SHINTO. Shinto rituals and **mythology** gave rise to various art forms that came to be performed at festival times. **Dengaku** and **Sarugaku** both emerged from **rice**-planting celebrations. **Noh** and **Kyōgen** evolved later into specialized dramatic arts depicting famous incidents or events. Various types of dance (such as Gigaku, masked **dance**) also developed in a similar stylized manner derived from presentation of mythology at **festivals**. Many shrines (**jinja**) had stages that were designed for such performances and many still perform plays annually that depict the origins of the shrine itself. *See also* ART IN SHINTO; MUSIC IN SHINTO; RITUAL AND DRAMA; SARUGAKU; SHISHIMAI.

– E –

EARTHLY *KAMI*. The *kami* of earth are distinct from the *kami* of heaven, paralleling the distinction between heaven and earth as described in the **mythology**. The *kami* of heaven are the **Amatsu-kami**; the **Kunitsu-kami** are the *kami* of earth, headed by **Sarutahiko-ōkami**. The two groups are jointly invoked, along with the **Yao yorozu no kami**, the myriad of *kami*, in all Shinto rituals. *See also* AMATERASU-ŌMIKAMI; *KAMI* OF HEAVEN AND EARTH.

EBISU. One of the seven *kami* of good fortune (**Shichi-fuku-jin**). In cities it is the *kami* of merchants, in rural areas, of rice-fields. The name means "barbarian/alien" and may be linked to the idea of deities that come from beyond Japan or are considered **marebito** (strange visitors). Ebisu is also identified as Kotoshironushi-no-mikoto, the son of **Okuninushi-no-mikoto**, or as Ebisu Saburo, son of **Izanagi-no-mikoto** and **Izanami-no-mikoto**. He is usually depicted holding in his right hand a fishing rod and in the other a large sea bream (tai), a symbol of happiness. He normally wears a kimono and a hakama (divided trouser/skirt) along with a kazaori **eboshi** (folded cap). He is thought to be a little deaf, and so his attention must be drawn by loud noises when paying respect to him. The ebisu-mawashii puppeteers appeared to have originated from Nishinomiya, in modern Hyogo Prefecture, traditionally regarded as being the center of the Ebisu cult. *See also* DAIKOKUTEN.

EBOSHI. Part of Shinto priestly dress that originated in Chinese court dress of the T'ang Dynasty (618–907), part of the infusion of culture that took place during the Nara (710–794) and **Heian** (794–1185) periods. The eboshi was prominently displayed in the national media when the son of Emperor **Heisei** (reigned 1989–) reached adulthood at the age of 20, in celebration of which he wore complete traditional court dress, including the black eboshi and the matching asa-gutsu, clog-style shoes made of hollowed paulownia wood and finished with a lacquer surface. *See also* SAIFUKU; SAIKIGU.

EIREI. The **souls** of the war dead enshrined at **Yasukuni Jinja** and at other **Gokoku Jinja**, shrines for the protection of the nation. The ceremony to console the souls of the war dead is called an **iresai**, and regional shrines for the war dead are referred to as **shōkonsha**.

EMA. Wooden tablets offered at shrines (**jinja**) with special prayers written on them. White horses were the vehicle of solar deities in cultures where deities of the sun were revered. Evidence of this may be seen in those shrines where white horses are kept, such as the **Grand Shrines of Ise** (Ise Jingū).

The term E-ma means picture of a horse, and most likely, the ema became a substitute gift to a *kami* on which worshippers were permitted to write requests. They may be seen at most shrines in the Ema-den, usually a large frame from which they are hung. It is also customary for them to be painted with the animal of the Oriental Zodiac whose year it is. The widespread existence and continued use of Ema underlines the importance of horses in early Shinto, and of the significance of communication between the two worlds of *kami* and people which horses were thought to be able to bridge.

The Ema has also become a distinctive form of folk art. Alongside the Ko-ema, or small Ema, are the Ō-ema, or large Ema, displayed in Emado, or Ema Halls, which date to the 15th and 16th centuries. These are more in the form of monumental depictions of the life and the times and the role of horses in shrine ceremonies. Various schools grew up, the study of which is a research field in its own right. *See also* ART IN SHINTO.

EMAKIMONO. Literally, a rolled object containing pictures. They are long, horizontally laid-out scrolls depicting a famous incident such as the founding of a shrine (**jinja**) or Buddhist temple, the life of a great religious teacher, or some miraculous happening. The pictures are often accompanied by a text containing the narrative displayed. They were created mostly during the **Heian** (794–1185) and Kamakura (1185–1333) periods although they were modeled on similar Chinese scrolls of the first to sixth centuries. The origins of the Kitano Tenmangu are preserved in the Kitano Tenmangu Engi.

The genre was steadily displaced by the rise of black-and-white **Zen Buddhist** art, although the Tosa School of artists of the Edo period (1615–1868) continued to thrive. The Tōshōgū Engi Emaki (Legends of the **Nikkō Tōshōgū**, which enshrines **Tokugawa Ieyasu**, [1543–1616]), painted by Kano Tan'yu, is one of the most celebrated of the Edo period. *See also* ART IN SHINTO; EMA.

EMMA. Ruler of the spirit world who confronts the dead with the record of their lives for punishment or reward. Emma entered Japan via the tradition of **Taoism** in China, where Emma was one of the presiding ten kings of the nether region. *See also* DEATH IN SHINTO; JIGOKU.

EMPEROR SYSTEM. The imperial system of Japan (**Tennōsei**) is the oldest hereditary monarchy in the world, and the world's oldest continuously occupied office. It can be historically dated to at least the fourth century C.E., originating much earlier in what was most likely a shamanistic role. In due course, the emperor came to be viewed as the high priest of the nation in the Shinto hierarchy, a role that modern emperors continue to fulfill.

The modern Constitution calls for the role of the emperor to be symbolic, but even emperors in the past seldom exercised political power, which was traditionally delegated elsewhere. According to the mythological register, Emperor Heisei (Akihito), is the 125th. His father, **Emperor Shōwa** (reigned 1926–1989), had the longest reign in Japanese history, 63 years. Women emperors were not unknown in the early centuries, particularly the legendary **Empress**

Jingū (reigned 201–269). After the incident in the early eighth century involving the Buddhist monk **Dōkyō** and his designs on the imperial office, Empress Kōken (reigned 749–758), Dokyō's sponsor, became the last female to occupy the office, which was thereafter closed to **women**.

In 1945, a statement of the "renunciation of divinity" was made, as some uninformed Western critics like to describe it. It was, in Japanese, **Tennō no Ningen Sengen**, meaning "declaration of humanity." It was read by the emperor and couched in the style of a traditional **imperial rescript**, although the language was rather less formal. It was stated that it was intended to dissolve any mythological status of divinity in the Western sense and to provide reassurance that Japan desired to return to the family of nations, purified of extremism. The status of the emperor nevertheless remains controversial in many circles because of the seeming association of Emperor Shōwa with the pre-war military establishment. The most radical book published that is critical of Emperor Showa appeared in early 2000: *Hirohito and the Making of Modern Japan* by Herbert P. Bix, a Harvard historian.

An incumbent mayor of Hiroshima was shot by a rightist for suggesting that Emperor Showa bore some responsibility for the Pacific War, thereby sharing in war-guilt. Most Christian groups are critical, if not openly hostile, to the emperor system, and some go so far as to claim that it is a device used to manipulate national consciousness. Pre-war, most of these groups cooperated with the system. However, as history moves on, it is to be expected that these issues will slowly recede into the past. *See also* FUKKO SHINTO; HIRATA ATSU-TANE; KITABATAKE CHIKAFUSA; KOKUGAKU SHINTO; MEIJI RESTORATION; MODERNIZATION AND SHINTO.

ENGISHIKI. Based on a collection of government regulations that evolved between the seventh and ninth centuries, it was formally compiled by order of **Emperor Daigo** (reigned 897–930) between 905 and 927. It consists of 50 volumes, the first 10 of which deal with Shinto rituals. Worship was detailed for specific occasions and times. There were regulations regarding the **Grand Shrines of Ise** (Ise Jingū), the Saigū-ryo, the **Jingikan** department that handled the business of the office of Saiin and the proper performance of the **Daijōsai**, the imperial accession rites. The liturgies (**norito**) were also written down or composed, and lists were compiled of the 2,861 shrines (**jinja**), along with the 3,132 enshrined *kami* that which were acknowledged by the Jingikan and designated as qualified to receive offerings.

A system of ranks was introduced for the shrines listed for these special shrines, collectively referred to as kansha. Powerful shrines came under the management of the government, and a period of intense state control began. During the Kamakura period (1185–1333), the old imperial administration of the **Heian period** (794–1185), the **Ritsuryō Seido** (Ritsuryo System), fell into disuse and was replaced by the law of military households, the Bukehō. Nevertheless, the ritual portions of the Engishiki relating to shrines and worship remained the model of standard practice, particularly in the wording of norito, as it does to the present.

Unfortunately, neither of its predecessors, the Konin or the Jogan, are extant. They were earlier compilations of the same type of records and would have been invaluable resources had they survived.

ENNICHI. Day of affinity or relation (en) for a particular *kami* whose blessing may be received by performing **sampai** (formal worship) on such a propitious day.

EN NO GYŌJA. Also known as En no Ozunu, a partially legendary seventh-century holy man possessed of remarkable powers. His wild ascetic adventures on Mount Katsuragi in Yamato (now Nara Prefecture) led to him becoming identified as the founder of **Shugendō**, the mountain ascetic cult combining Shinto and **Buddhism**. He also became revered as Shimpen Dai Bosatsu. He was exiled to Oshima in 699 on account of accusations by a former disciple, Karakuni no Muraji Hirotari, who envied his prestige.

ETHICS IN SHINTO. It is a standard criticism made of Shinto by Western religions that it has no system of ethics similar to **Buddhism**, Judaism, or Christianity, and consequently it offers no guidance for life. This is also asserted to be evidence of the primitive nature of the tradition. However, to claim that there is no ethical content to Shinto whatsoever is to argue from an inadequate understanding of both Shinto and of how values evolve within a cultural tradition.

When Shinto representatives are asked in interreligious contexts to express views on various pressing issues, they do so; from these expressed opinions and ideas, the elements of a system of ethics are being made explicit. It is not being created, nor is it being copied; it is being drawn from the resources of the tradition and formulated to meet the needs of the age, as was the custom of the past.

However, one basic contrast with the West should be noted. The Western approach has traditionally viewed humanity as created by a God who issues a moral code. Hence ethics and values have been understood as derived from religion. Shinto holds to the idea that humanity is in some way descended from the *kami* and therefore possesses something of a divine awareness that precedes any religion. While this is less common, it is not unknown in the West.

If the Shinto approach to ethics were to be classified within the Western framework, it would belong to the minority group of moral sense theories associated with the names of Francis Hutcheson (1694–1747), David Hume (1711–1776), and Adam Smith (1723–1790). From the premise that reason cannot lead human beings to action, they concluded that some kind of intervening moral sense was required to motivate people to act. In recognition of a similar insight, **Motoori Norinaga** (1723–1801), the **Kokugaku** (National Learning) scholar of the Edo period (1615–1868), made the following observation on ethics:

> Human beings having been produced by the spirit of the two creative *kami* are naturally endowed with the knowledge of what they ought to do and what they ought to refrain from. It is unnecessary for them to trouble their heads with systems of morality. If a system of morals were necessary, men would be inferior to animals, all of whom are endowed with the knowledge of what they ought to do, only in an inferior degree to man.

Hirata Atsutane (1776–1843), in a similar vein, made the observation that the Japanese who have been brought into existence through the creative spirits of the sacred ancestral *kami* are, each and every one, in spontaneous possession of the *kannagara-no-michi*. This means that we are equipped naturally with the virtues of reverence for the *kami* and for rulers and parents, and with kindness toward wife and children—the moral principles which in **Confucianism** are called the five great ethical principles.

To follow these in a natural way, he declares, is conforming to the teaching of the *kami*. There is also implied here the assumption that human nature is basically good. This is the concept of **sei-zen-setsu**, as it is known in neo-Confucian thought. There is a Japanese proverb that says, *Honshin ni oite wa akunin wa inai* (In their heart of hearts, no one is really evil).

Its counterpart and opposite—namely, that human nature is fundamentally evil—is the doctrine of **sei-aku-setsu**. This doctrine has little support in the Japanese tradition. Doctrines that assume evil in human nature obviously take a different view of the necessity and role of a system of ethics from those that begin from the opposite assumption.

The fundamental moral value in Shinto is purity, maintained by purification (**harai**). The paradigmatic act was performed by **Izanagi-no-mikoto** when he has escaped from **Yomi-no-kuni** where, according to the **mythology** recorded in the **Nihon Shōki** (720), he was visiting his deceased wife. The purpose of purification is to remove **tsumi** (impurity) and **kegare** (impurity caused by various human conditions) and restore human nature to its primal and pure state. Thus the idea that human nature can in some sense return to its divine origins lies behind all other related concepts.

Among the principal terms associated with moral values in Shinto, the most important is **makoto**, which is translated usually as sincerity. **Kamo no Mabuchi** (1697–1769) stressed the status of **makoto no kokoro**, a sincere heart, as the ideal virtue in Shinto. The term remained extremely important and a generic concept of the tradition. Junsui, meaning pure, is used (in addition to its non-moral usages) to refer to people who are "pure in heart" or pure in the sense of simple, honest, and uncorrupted by the world.

Other terms are **sei-mei-shin**, the pure heart; **akaki kiyoki kokoro**, which is used to describe brightness with regard to the human heart; and naoki kokoro, which refers to uprightness of character. All of these were defined individually by the Kokugaku (National Learning) scholars based upon the usages of the **Man'yōshū** and other ancient Japanese texts.

Human nature can also be defined in terms of **shinjin-gōitsu** and **shinjin-kiitsu**. The former term refers to the organic unity of human and divine (literally: *kami*-person-meeting-one), and the latter refers to the restoration of the divine (literally: *kami*-person-return-one). Behind this are the ideas of the original innocence of human character and its periodic restoration throughout life. Human beings are born able to live in harmony with the divine and with nature, but because of the various forms of impurity that overtake life, purification becomes necessary. Hence the importance of purification to effect restoration.

The goal to be achieved by the performance of **misogi shūho**, purification using water, is the cultivation of **reisei**, the Shinto ideal of spirituality. As the spirit is purified again and again, it can rise to the level of the divine as its spiritual sensitivity is heightened. The repairing and remaking of the **kokoro** is called **tsukuri katame naosu**.

Kansha, or thanksgiving, is a term used widely in the Japanese language, but especially in Shinto to express human gratitude for its dependence upon the divine. It frequently appears in statements of corporate philosophy in Japan, with a semi-religious nuance. People are "thankful" to customers, suppliers, workers and the invisible powers that bless them, and this is fostered as a basic attitude toward society. Individuals are encouraged to express kansha even when things may not be going too well in order to maintain a positive outlook.

Related to human effort is tsui-shin (hard work), which is praised in Shinto as a virtue. If there is anything in Japan that resembles a work ethic such as that identified in the West by the sociologist Max Weber (1864–1920), it is this ideal. Life means life in the widest sense of people being within the processes of **Daishizen**, or great nature, where they find a mission or a clear set of purposes in the form of duties and responsibilities toward society and other people. In fulfilling these, destiny is achieved in the sense of the realization of the best and highest of which humanity is capable. In order to keep their ideals and their sense of mission alive, purification is necessary. That is the task of Shinto ethics: not indeed a system of ethics that arises from a moral theology, but from a kind of universal moral sense believed to be the property of all human beings.

ETHNOPHILOSOPHY. A term used in the Library of Congress as a subject classification to cover traditional cultures that have ways of thinking peculiar unto themselves. Ethnophilosophical ideas are deduced by making explicit the thought forms that underlie the behavioral patterns in a culture. Many forms of culture worldwide do not readily fit Western intellectual models, which are based on logic and reason, and these are the object of ethnophilosophical study. Shinto, while perhaps capable of being analyzed in other ways in many of its features, falls into this category. *See also* The Introduction.

– F –

FAITH HEALING. Healing is frequently found in the **New Religions** and in charismatic groups. Occasionally, female shamans can be seen performing healing acts near mountain shrines (**jinja**). Among **Kyōha Shinto** (Sect Shinto) groups, healing is part of the belief of **Tenri-kyō, Kurozumi-kyō**, and **Konkō-kyō**, for example, and more recent groups such as **Mahikari** and **Shinrei-kyō**. *See also* SHAMANISM IN SHINTO.

FEMINISM AND SHINTO. It has been charged that Shinto discriminates against **women**, on the grounds that it appears male-dominated like the rest of Japanese society. While there may be some justification for this argument, it should not be forgotten that Japan was ruled by some powerful women such as **Empress Jingū Kogo** (reigned 201–269). Empress Koken (reigned 749–758) was the last female to occupy the throne because of her liaison with the Buddhist monk **Dōkyō** (died 722). During times of war, when men were away from home, women fulfilled the role of priests, and, in some places, continue to be available. Women have featured prominently in some of the Shinto-based **New Religions**. Even the Japanese Presbyterian church ordained women in the early years of the 20th century, partly because there was the Shinto precedent to follow, while it took until the 1960s to achieve this in most Western churches. Accusations of male chauvinism should perhaps be addressed to the social ethics of the **Tokugawa** style of neo-**Confucian** thought and to the influence of the male-dominated culture of **Buddhism**.

FERTILITY RITES IN SHINTO. In addition to rites for the cultivation of **rice**, human fertility is also central to the **rituals** of some shrines (**jinja**). Because the roots of Shinto are those of a religion of nature, Shinto has a very down-to-earth and realistic approach to matters pertaining to fertility and sex. The Japanese archipelago comes about as the result of the procreative act of **Izanagi-no-mikoto** and **Izanami-no-mikoto**, an act described in graphic detail. It so distressed the 19th-century translator of the **Kojiki** (720), **Basil Hall Chamberlain** (1850–1935), that he rendered the entire narrative into Latin. He did the same when translating the passage in which Susano-o-no-mikoto so frightened some workers in the palace when he threw a flayed horse through the roof that one young **woman** struck her genitals against a loom and died.

Shinto, in its worldview, is quite open in its treatment of fertility and sexuality, and shows no sign of either the prudery or the puritanical morality associated with some Western values. Again in the mythology, **Izanagi-no-Mikoto** performs a crude erotic dance in order to draw the *kami* of the sun, **Amaterasu-ōmikami**, out of the **Ame-no-Iwato**, the cave of heaven in which she was hiding from the boisterous *kami* outside who were causing her distress. The Jeweled Spear of Heaven referred to in the mythological text in the **Kojiki** (712) and **Nihon Shōki** (720) is regarded by some scholars as a phallic symbol.

Infertility has always been a source of anxiety in rural communities that depend on sons and daughters for labor. Therefore, it is hardly surprising that some shrines have made provision to meet these needs. The Japanese *kami* are understood as having two aspects to their makeup: There is the **nigimitama**, the gentler side; and the **aramitama**, the rougher or more boisterous side, visible particularly at **festivals**. In popular entertainment at village festivals, overt sexual themes were frequently depicted. Normally after a major project had been completed, banquets at which people ate and drank freely and entertained each other with song and dance of a ribald nature were a normal practice.

Festivals in Shinto were traditionally occasions when promiscuous sex was openly tolerated, rather like the Bayern Oktoberfest in southern Germany or the medieval Holy Fairs. While the agricultural background of Japanese culture may have weakened, the tradition continues into the kind of drinking gatherings of various groups, social or corporate, where language and behavior is tolerated that would be regarded as politically incorrect by modern standards, but which is forgotten by the next morning. While fertility is fundamental to all festivals, in some shrine rites, at certain festivals, phallic symbols take pride of place during the celebrations.

The famous **Henoko Matsuri**, or Phallus Festival, of the **Tagata Jinja** in Komaki near Nagoya Airport in Aiichi Prefecture is one of the best known. Nearby Inuyama city's **Oagata Jinja** hosts the **Ososo Matsuri**, or Vagina Festival. These festivals are intended to protect crops, cure sterility and impotence, and guarantee business success and fertility. The touching and kissing of the sacred objects, the phallus at the Tagata Jinja Matsuri, by women assures pregnancy, while at the Oagata Jinja, the clam, a symbol of the vagina, guarantees a good harvest, as well as marital harmony, conception, and the cure of sexual diseases. In the case of the Henoko Matsuri, a huge wooden phallus at least five meters long is enthusiastically carried around the shrine grounds and into the streets outside as part of the celebrations. The vagina symbol is often a v-shaped part of a tree, and where this is in a prominent place, it can be worn smooth by generations of young would-be mothers hoping to acquire some of its properties.

The very survival of these festivals indicates how deeply rooted in agricultural motifs Japanese culture remains. In spite of pressure exerted by the Meiji period (1868–1912) government to abandon these festivals because they were not considered sophisticated enough for the vision of **Kokka Shinto** (State Shinto) being entertained by the government, much of the traditional fertility culture survived at the level of folk culture. It may not have as much relevance to the present as it did in the past, but it opens another window to the understanding of the evolution of Japanese culture. It could perhaps be argued that the wilder side of the *kami* is still released at the festival, but that the gentler side expresses itself in more refined **ritual and drama** such as **Noh**.

FESTIVALS IN SHINTO. Japanese festivals (**matsuri**) originated in the rituals of a **rice** culture, and were related to the growth and protection of the rice crop. The festival is an act of communication with the *kami*, the protective divine beings at the core of Shinto belief. While some modern festivals have been created to encourage tourism and have no religious significance, the traditional festivals of Japan are all rooted in the Shinto tradition.

The structure and meaning of the festival follows a basic tripartite sequence, namely the invocation of the *kami*, the offerings to the *kami*, and the final communion with the *kami* at the shrine (**jinja**). At the invocation of the *kami*, the priests in full ceremonial dress purify themselves (**shūbatsu**) in order to take part in the **rituals**. The inner building (**honden**) of the shrine complex is opened up and the **go-shintai** (symbol of the *kami*) is viewed by the priests. Priests are also expected to practice abstinence (**saikai**) before major festivals. With the participating leading laymen in robes of state, the priests form a procession that moves down the **sando** (the approach road to the shrine) to meet the *kami* at the appointed place. It is here that the duly purified laypeople become responsible for transporting the *kami* around the shrine precincts and throughout the community, in an **omikoshi**, for example.

Offerings to the *kami* (**shinsen**) come next, normally comprising rice; salt; water; rice wine (sake); rice cakes (omochi); fish, usually tai (seabream); seaweed (konbu); vegetables; grain; and fruit. Speeches are made, after which the ritual part of the festival is closed. Classic forms of entertainment have long been associated with shrine festivals, particularly **kagura**, a dance performed by shrine maidens (**miko**). **Bugaku** is another genre of classical Japanese dance with special **music**. The entire cycle of **Noh** drama has its roots in Shinto myths, rituals, and festivals. *Kami* are portrayed in the introductions to the various epics.

Finally, there is communion with the *kami* (**naorai**). Casks of sake are broken open and drunk from a wooden masu (a square cup made of Japanese cypress). The combination of the aroma of the wood and the taste of the sake is probably one fragrance uniquely associated with Shinto and Japan. This aspect of the festival is especially important in Japan: social drinking as a religious act to commune with the *kami* in addition to the ritual use of sake. This happens after any major festival and often becomes a major party with the organizers, the high priest, and other priests present for as long as worshippers remain. In past eras, a liberal view was taken of sexual activities during such periods of celebration. *See also* FERTILITY RITES IN SHINTO; MUSIC IN SHINTO.

FINANCE OF SHRINES. Since the Constitution prohibits the government from supporting any religious bodies, shrines (**jinja**), like **Buddhist** temples, have had to find sources of income to cover their needs. Among the most prominent of these are weddings, shinzen kekkon, as they are called. They are offered by many shrines as a total package, including a wedding ceremony performed by a priest; a reception party, usually in an adjacent building; and presents for the guests, who normally bring cash gifts for the newlyweds. A honeymoon plan can also be added. Prices vary, depending upon the level of service required. The average price of a wedding during the first decade of the 21st century was around $30,000. First shrine visits (**hatsu miya mairi**) of newborn babies might cost $100 or more, again depending on whether or not the family is given private or group treatment.

New cars are purified (**harai**) in a ceremony called kotsu anzen harai: literally, purification for road safety. Groundbreaking ceremonies (**jichinsai**) are usually performed before a construction project commences to calm the *kami* of the land. The building is also purified when completed, and these services are paid for by those involved. Corporations make donations for various purposes. Airplanes, cars, production lines, and other facilities and products are normally purified. One grey area concerns the Japanese Self-Defense Forces. Any member who dies while on duty is enshrined locally in a shrine for the war dead (**shōkonsha**). This has taken place even against the express wishes of the family; therefore one assumes that the military pays the cost, which could be a violation of the Constitution. One family went to court, but the enshrinement could not be "undone."

Festival (**matsuri**) days are profitable, as is New Year (**hatsu mōde**), and occasional visitors will usually buy souvenirs such as lucky charms, postcards, talismans, and other mementos. Corporate religious persons according to the law (**Shūkyō Hōjin Hō**) can be tax-free, which is a benefit to those shrines that own restaurants and guest facilities. The higher ranked the shine, the higher the charge. Shrine finances might be stretched with buildings to maintain and priests to pay, but so long as the cycle of life and yearly events continue, the shrines will have sources of income. *See also* SAIMOTSU; SAISEN.

FIRE CALMING RITUALS. As evidence of enhanced spiritual power, firewalking and rituals involving boiling water (**yudate**) are performed in some shrines (**jinja**) and in the rituals of the **New Religions**. These are usually linked to **festivals**, frequently attracting large numbers of spectators. *See also* AKIBA JINJA; CHINKI-SHIKI; KUGATACHI-SHIKI.

FIRST DISTRICT SHRINES. *See* ICHI-NO-MIYA.

FLOATING BRIDGE OF HEAVEN. The **Ame-no-Ukihashi** from which **Izanagi-no-mikoto** and **Izanami-no-mikoto**, according to the **mythology** recorded in the **Kojiki** (712) and the **Nihon**

Shōki (720), dipped a jeweled spear into the ocean as part of the procreation of the Japanese archipelago. *See also* FERTILITY IN SHINTO.

FOLK RELIGION. Minkan Shinto, as it is referred to in Japanese, was first researched academically by **Yanagita Kunio** (1875–1962) and became the object of study of folklorists throughout the 20th century. Folk religion usually arises out of the understanding of communal experience: in the case of Japan, it is hard to separate from Shinto, because Shinto itself is the expression of the self-understanding of a rice culture. As the culture developed, so did the **rituals** that accompanied its annual cycle of events (**nenchū-gyōji**).

Japan shows at least one clear pattern of the evolution of organized religion, in the form of its seasonal **festivals.** Most important of these is the **daijosai**, the first harvest thanksgiving ceremony of a new imperial reign and a traditional event of the agricultural year. Many traditional trades and occupations practiced local religious rites appropriate to their activities. Other events celebrated in folk religion, such as **New Year** or rites of passage, are recognized and often staged at shrines (**jinja**), which have served as a support for the local cultic practices. Hence the variations of styles and dates nationwide. In the 60 years of intense urbanization following the end of the **Pacific War** (World War II), the **New Religions** have become for many people, according to some sociologists of religion, a substitute for the culture of the countryside they left behind. Since many festivals are highly spectacular, attracting very large numbers of spectators, it is unlikely that they will disappear.

However, various ethnological groups are actively documenting and filming rituals and festivals in more isolated areas so that records will remain. But because continuity and change overlap so much in Japanese history, it is quite likely that these traditions will in due course re-invent themselves to suit the needs of the times. *See also* FOLK SHINTO; TSŪZOKU SHINTO.

FOLK SHINTO. Minkan Shinto is the name given to features of Shinto at the local community level, as distinct from rites that were government supported in the past, and rituals dictated by the Meiji government during the period of **Kokka Shinto** (State

Shinto). Tradition and modernity in Japan are not as clearly distinguished as they are in the West, and neither are the folk level and the institutionalized level very clearly distinguished. Folk Shinto also is closely integrated with folk religious culture in general. It is community based and grew out of the experiences of history and agriculture. Ironically, religious charismatics emerged from some of these folk contexts, some of whom became founders of Shinto sects, dating as far back as the last century of the Edo period (1868–1912). Indeed, it might be argued that one appeal of the **New Religions** lies in their ability at the local "church" level to replicate the sense of community that people lost in the process of uprooting and moving to dense urban areas like the Kanto Plain or the suburbs of Osaka. *See also* FOLK RELIGION.

FORTUNE-TELLING. *See* DIVINATION.

FOXES. The fox is thought to have many strange powers, including the power to bewitch people. A whole culture has grown up around the fox in **Folk Religion**. *See also* KITSUNE.

FUDOKI. Reports from local governors that contain information on geography, local names, soil quality, regional products, and local traditions, created by an imperial order of 713. Many of these were lost, but the complete record of **Izumo** still exists. Fudoki were also compiled during the Edo period (1615–1868). *See also* FUSHIMI INARI TAISHA.

FUJI-SAN. The daily language way of referring to **Mount Fuji**.

FUJIWARA SEIKA (1561–1619). Neo-**Confucian** scholar of the early Edo period (1615–1868). He began his career as a **Zen** Buddhist monk, but subsequently became profoundly influenced by the thought of the Chinese neo-Confucian scholar **Chu Hsi** (Zhu Xi, 1132–1200). His work prepared the foundation for the integration of Confucian thought with Shinto that took place at a later date. His most influential disciple was **Hayashi Razan** (1583–1657), who became adviser to **Tokugawa Ieyasu** (1543–1616) and who implemented the complex system of neo-Confucianism that gave form and order to Tokugawa society.

FUKENSHA. Prefectural shrine (**jinja**) ranking within the **Kokka Shinto** (State Shinto) system during the Meiji period (1868–1912).

FUKKO SHINTO. The religious nature of Shinto based on the principle of the unity of worship in government, also known as Restoration Shinto. It was largely the work of **Hirata Atsutane** (1776–1843), whose thought greatly influenced the declining samurai class and drew many of them toward the imperial cause. It left an indelible impression upon the political thought of the early Meiji government and upon the concepts of the nature of Shinto and the of **kokutai**, the body politic, which eventually was defined as the emperor in union with the people. It was these, among other influences, that gave Japanese nationalism its own unique flavor once the ideology of the Meiji period (1868–1912) had been generated. *See also* MODERNIZATION AND SHINTO.

FUKOKU KYŌHEI. A Meiji period (1868–1912) slogan that means "strong country [economy] and a powerful army." It was used to inspire national aspirations to international greatness and was intended to encourage people to work toward these ends. The implicit message was that Japan could only survive pressures from the stronger Western nations by being able to match them in strength. The **Yasukuni Jinja** in Tokyō and the regional **Shōkonsha** (shrines for the war dead) were created to show respect for the military. It became particularly significant after the emperor began visiting the Yasukuni Jinja in person to show respect for the dead of the Meiji Restoration and those who had died thereafter. While the emperor no longer visits the Yasukuni Jinja, controversial visits have been made by postwar prime ministers, especially Nakasone Yasuhiro, who signed the record book as Prime Minister Nakasone Yasuhiro. *See also* GOGOKU JINJA; MODERNIZATION AND SHINTO.

FUKUBA YOSHISHIZU (1831–1907). Follower of **Ōkuni Takamasa** (1792–1871) and important Meiji period (1868–1912) scholar of the **Kokugaku** (National Learning) movement. He was the mastermind of the **Taikyō Senpu Undō**, the Great Teaching, the basis of Shinto as a national ideology. His competence became suspect after he disastrously mismanaged an 1897 memorial ceremony for Emperor Kōmei (reigned 1847–1866), the last pre-Meiji period emperor and father of **Emperor Meiji** (reigned 1868–1912). His vision of Shinto had a human face, unlike the Hirata faction, which claimed to be followers of **Hirata Atsutane** (1776–1843) but who in fact wished to confine Shinto to imperial rites only. *See also* KOKKA SHINTO; MODERNIZATION AND SHINTO.

FUNA-DAMA. A *kami* revered by fishermen to protect ships and to guarantee a good catch. Various items are inserted into the mast of the ship going to sea, including a woman's hair, dolls, two dice, twelve coins, and the five grains that sustain life.

Not relating to fishing but to travel by water, a funa-dama festival is held annually at **Hodosan Jinja** in Saitama Prefecture. It started in the Edo period (1615–1868) for the protection of people, likely silk merchants, making the trip from Chichibu to Edo on the river Ara (Arakawa).

FUNAKURABE. These are boat races between villages on the shores of Western Japan. They are a form of **divination** concerning the prospects of the coming year's harvest. The most famous are held in Iki, Tsushima, Sakurajima, and Nagasaki.

FUSHIMI INARI TAISHA. Located in Fushimi Ward, Kyōto, it enshrines Uka-no-mitama-no-kami, a deity of agriculture, along with several other *kami*. Collectively, they are known as **Inari**. It is said to have been established first in 711 on Mt. Inari, but after intervention by **Kūkai** (773–835), the founder of **Shingon Buddhism**, it was moved to provide protection for the Toji, a Shingon temple. It is the central shrine (**jinja**) of the Inari group, which consists of around 40,000 shrines nationwide. Their distinguishing feature is a large number of red gates (**torii**). They were patronized especially by the merchant class during the Edo period (1615–1868). *See also* KITSUNE.

FUSŌ-KYŌ. One of the officially and originally designated 13 Shinto Sects known as **Kyōha Shinto** (Sect Shinto) and one of those officially recognized during the Edo period (1615–1868) by the Tokugawa government. Said to have been founded by **Hasegawa Kakugyo** (circa 1541–1646), an ascetic who revered **Mount Fuji**. The sect **Jikkō-kyō** also claims Hasegawa as its founder.

It did not become an independent sect until 1882, by which time it was under the leadership of Nakaba Shishino (died 1884), who was born in Satsuma-gun in what is now Kagoshima Prefecture. The original name was Fuji-Ichizan Kyōkai (The One Mount Fuji Association) and it enshrined Sengen Ōkami, but was changed to Fusō Kyōkai as the result of a play on words. The change of title of the sect, Fuso, came from an old and poetic name for Japan, "fu" meaning "to save" and "so" referring to a Chinese legend of a mulberry tree that stood in the sea to the east of China. The meaning gradually changed to refer to the land of the sunrise, and the teaching of the sect that protects the country.

In 1878 it became known as Fuso Kyōha, and in 1883, it finally became Fusō-kyō. It aimed at revering the divine virtue of creation, especially the **Zōka-sanshin**, the three *kami* of creation, reverentially holding **festivals** for the *kami* **of heaven and earth**. The sect taught the mystical spirit and unique power of Mount Fuji. Its teachings were explained and practiced by **divination** and incantation, demonstrated by performing rituals that include removing the heat from fire in **fire calming rituals**, along with other ascetic rites. These rituals are still performed at various shrines (**jinja**) and festivals throughout the country. It has a following of about 80,000.

FUTAMIGURA. Coastal area in the town of Futami, Mie Prefecture. It faces the Bay of Ise, and is famous for the Meotoiwa ("wedded rocks"), usually taken to represent **Izanagi-no-mikoto** and **Izanami-no-mikoto**. The gate (**torii**) on top of the larger and the **shimenawa** (sacred rope) that joins them are indicative of their divine nature. The shrine (**jinja**) in which the rocks are located is Futami Okitama Jinja.

FUTARAYAMA JINJA. Two famous shrines (**jinja**) have this name. One is located in the vicinity of Nikko City in Tochigi Prefecture, and enshrines **Ōkuninushi-no-mikoto**. The main part of the shrine (**jinja**) is located within Nikko, but the **honden** (inner shrine building) sits on top of Mount Futara. It was a center of **Shugendō** as far back as the eighth century. The other is located in Utsunomiya, also Tochigi Prefecture, and enshrines Toyokiirihiko-no-mikoto, a son of the legendary Emperor Sujin (reigned 97–30 B.C.E.) who is said to have brought the eastern provinces under imperial control. *See also* MOUNTAIN WORSHIP; SANGAKU SHINKO.

– G –

GAGAKU. Ceremonial **music** and dance for use in imperial court rituals and ceremonies and at certain shrines (**jinja**) and temples. The **gakubu** (music department) of the division of ceremonies of the **imperial household** retains records of the form and style of these. The dance accompanying the music is called **bugaku**. The sources of these include elements from India and China, as well as Japanese forms. *See also* DENGAKU; DRAMATIC ARTS IN SHINTO; NOH; SARUGAKU; TAIKO.

GAKUBU. The ceremonial court **music** supervisory department of the **imperial household** responsible for organizing performance of traditional music and **dance** at the appropriate times of year. *See also* BUGAKU; GAGAKU.

GAKUHA SHINTO. Academic Shinto, particularly as referred to during the Edo period (1600–1868). *See also* FUKKO SHINTO; KOKUGAKU SHINTO.

GAMO KUMPEI (1768–1813). Classical scholar of the Edo period (1615–1868) who had a great interest in the **emperor system** and its perceived decline in significance during his lifetime. He reported imperial tombs in disrepair, and published his findings in an 1808 report which encouraged later imperial loyalists to claim him as an early restorationist.

GASHO. Warnings from God, such as suffering and misfortunes, as taught in **P. L. Kyōdan**, a **New Religion** founded in 1912 by Kanada Tokumitsu (1863–1919). Believers who recognize these may go to a Master (Miki) or a consultant to ask for a kokoroe (prescription) that can bring relief.

GEKŪ. Outer Shrine of the **Grand Shrines of Ise** (Ise Jingū). *See also* WATARAI SHINTO.

GION MATSURI. **Susa-no-o-no-mikoto**, referred to as Gion, is enshrined in the **Yasaka Jinja** in Kyōto. The **festival (matsuri)** is said to have been a form of **goryo-e**, a ritual like **chinkon** performed in order to purify the city, in this case from an outbreak of disease. It has become a popular tourist attraction, and is now celebrated as one of Japan's major festivals. *See also* AOI MATSURI.

GISHIKI-DEN. A building within shrine (**jinja**) precincts reserved for special ceremonies. While the principal **rituals** are performed in the **haiden** or the **heiden**, other events, including weddings, may be held in a separate location. **Nogi Jinja** in Tokyō has Nogi Kaikan adjacent to it for such events. This has arisen from popular interest in holding special events at shrines.

GOBUSHO. Shortened name for the **Shinto Gobusho**, a 13th-century set of texts produced by the **Watarai Shinto** tradition, which became a canon of Shinto scholarship.

GOHEI. Strips of paper—sometimes cotton, and sometimes also gilt metal—on a Shinto altar, in a zigzag formation, hanging down. They are attached to a wooden stick or to a **sakaki** branch and offered to a *kami*. Referred to also as **heihaku** or **hobei**.

GOKOKU JINJA. Shrine (**jinja**) for the protection of the state, originally branch shrines of the **Yasukuni Jinja**. The name follows the model of the Kokubunji, or state temples of the Nara period (710–794), built for the protection of the nation and the advancement of the state cult, which at that time was Buddhism.

GOMA. Fire Ceremony of purification (**harai**) used in **Shingon Buddhism** and in Shinto/Buddhist rites such as practiced by **yamabushi**, mountain ascetics.

GONGEN. Term in **Buddhism** that refers to avatars, or incarnations of a Buddha. The concept was widely employed in expounding the relationship between Buddhism and Shinto. From the latter part of the **Heian period** (794–1185), Shinto *kami* came to be designated as Gongen. For example, **Emperor Ōjin** (reigned 270–310) was depicted as an avatar and was represented as the *kami* **Hachiman**. The enshrinement of **Tokugawa Ieyasu** (1543–1616) in the **Nikkō Tōshōgū** designates him the great incarnation of the light of the East. A style of Shinto **architecture** grew out of this, easily recognized by the front roof of the main worship building **(haiden)** being in the normal rounded roof style of a Buddhist temple. The building is normally filled with elaborate art, carvings, and ceiling paintings. *See also* ASSIMILATION OF BUDDHISM AND SHINTO; HONJI-SUIJAKU-SETSU; RYŌBU SHINTO.

GORYŌ-E. Ritual of **chinkon** to calm angry souls (goryo, or onryo), practiced during the **Heian period** (794–1185). *See also* SUGAWARA MICHIZANE.

GOSHA. Village shrine **(jinja)**, according to the **Kokka Shinto** (State Shinto) rankings of the Meiji period (1868–1912).

GOSHIKI-BAN. Five-colored set of ribbons hung in shrines **(jinja)** in the altar area: kuro (black) or murasaki (purple) are accompanied by ao (green), aka (red), shiro (white), and kiro (yellow). The form originated in esoteric **Buddhism** and identifies directions and powers that may be invoked in rituals. *See also* SHINGON SHINTO; TENDAI SHINTO.

GOSHINETSU. Report by a new emperor to **Amaterasu-ōmikami** at the **Grand Shrines of Ise** (Ise Jingū) at the time of his accession. *See also* DAIJŌSAI; EMPEROR SYSTEM.

GOSHINSUI. Offering water charged with divine power, as practiced in the Shinto-based **New Religion Shinrei-kyō**.

GO-SHINTAI. Symbol of the enshrined *kami* kept in the innermost part of the **honden** (inner worship hall) of a shrine **(jinja)**. Also called mitama-shiro in older Japanese form. The go-shintai is never normally seen or removed unless the *kami* is being removed to permit new buildings to be erected. The actual object may be a stone, a mirror, or even nothing at all. In the Tenmangū near Hakone, the go-shintai is a statue of a Buddha, while in a company shrine in Yokohama, the go-shintai is an industrial robot. *See also* ART IN SHINTO.

GRAND SHRINES OF ISE. The widely known English designation for Ise Jingū. Also known as the Kotai Jingū, the Grand Shrines of Ise, located in Mie Prefecture, consist of a group of over 20 shrines (**jinja**). Principal among these are the Inner (**Naikū**) and Outer (**Gekū**) shrines, intimately linked with the **imperial household** and the worship of **Amaterasu-ōmikami** and **Toyoukehime-no-kami**. The shrines were originally closed to the public. All significant events of the imperial family are still reported to the Grand Shrines, and all new government cabinets are inaugurated by a visit to Ise. Such traditions continue as evidence of the status of the shrines.

However, Ise had more difficult times in the past. After hostilities in the Onin civil war had commenced in 1467, the imperial family lost both status and revenue, and the maintenance of the shrines had to be financed independently, through opening them to the public. The nationwide popularity of Ise therefore dates to the 15th century, partly due to the efforts of the **oshi**, missionary priests of the shrines. The oshi taught the merits of donating to the shrines and of making pilgrimages, known as **Okagemairi**, which peaked in popularity during the Edo period (1615–1868). They were not unlike the Canterbury Pilgrimages in Chaucer's England, designed to raise funds for needy buildings. As many as one million people took part in each one of these, growing an economy along the route consisting of guests houses, food stalls, and drinking parlors, along with less salubrious establishments.

In the period of civil instability prior to the establishment of the Tokugawa government, Ise found support. In spite of his hostility to religious institutions, **Oda Nobunaga** (1534–1582) actually donated large amounts of money to Ise to reestablish the reconstruction. **Hideyoshi Toyotomi** (1536–1598) and **Tokugawa Ieyasu** (1543–1616) continued high levels of support, presumably to assure that the continuance of imperial prominence as their guarantors would ensure their own power. During the Edo period, when the population of Japan was probably about 20 to 30 million, 2,500 pilgrims visited Ise every day between March and May of 1650. By 1705, the figure had risen to 40,000 each day for the same months. From March to August 1830, the total number was more than 4.5 million.

The **architecture** of Ise is world famous, and has brought architects from every corner of the globe to study its unique features. Its design and method of construction are the subject of continuous study. In the view of many, it is the eighth wonder of the world, not listed as such, but qualifying for that title. This, however, takes second place behind the spiritual centrality of Ise-no-kuni and the splendor of Ise in its imperial majesty.

The Grand Shrines celebrated their 2000th anniversary in 1996, although their present forms may date to a later era. By order of **Emperor Temmu** (reigned 672–686), to keep them perpetually new, they are rebuilt on adjacent sites every 20 years. The 66th **shikinen-sengu** took place in 1993, at which, for the first time in history, non-Japanese were invited to lay white stones within the grounds of the buildings and were permitted to walk through and view the new edifices from only a few meters' distance. *See also* EMPEROR SYSTEM; ISE PROVINCE; ISE SHINTO; OKAGEMAIRI; WATARAI SHINTO.

GRAPARD, ALLAN G. (1944–). French-born scholar of Shinto and professor at the University of California, Santa Barbara, campus. He is the occupant of the first endowed chair of Shinto Studies in the United States. The professorship was the gift of the **International Shinto Foundation** to the university in 1998. Grapard's scholarly work includes a translation of Yoshida Kanetomo's *Myōbōshū* along with a major work on the **Kasuga** cult.

GREAT NATURE. The cosmic environment and universal process in which all life and the universe are embodied. *See also* DAISHIZEN; NATURE IN SHINTO; TAOISM.

GŪJI. The high (or chief) priest of a shrine (**jinja**). This rank is conferred by the shrine itself, and should not be confused with the rankings issued by the **Jinja Honchō** (Association of Shinto Shrines) known as the **Kai-i.** In many old shrines, in spite of Meiji period (1868–1912) government efforts to break the system, the rank of Guji remains hereditary in many old shrines. Izumo Taisha claims 95, while Tsubaki Grand Shrine claims 97 generations of the same family. The **Grand Shrines of Ise** (Ise Jingū) have the unusual ranks of **Dai-Gūji** and **Sho-Gūji**, great high priest and lesser, or associate, high priest. *See also* SHINSHOKU.

GYO. The term used in both Shinto and **Buddhism** to refer to an ascetic discipline intended to heighten spiritual powers (**reisei**). *See also* MISOGI; SEN-NICHI-KAI-HŌ-GYŌ; SHUGENDŌ; YAMABUSHI.

GYOKI. The age of attenuation, a concept of an eschatological nature that had considerable influence on the mood of the latter years of the

Edo period (1615–1868), leading to the breakdown of society and the creation of popular radical movements such as the Eejanaika, which was basically a social rebellion against the government. *See also* MAPPŌ; OKAGEMAIRI.

– H –

HACHIMAN. Of obscure origins, including possibly being the protective *kami* of copper miners in Kyushū, Hachiman became and is still revered principally as a *kami* of battle. The **Shoku Nihongi** of 797 records many problems that occurred at the casting of the great statue of the Buddha and that the *kami* Hachiman was invoked for protection. An oracle reportedly delivered the promise in 749, "I will lead the *kami* **of heaven and earth** and without fail see to the completion of the Great Buddha." The germ of the later idea of the **assimilation of Buddhism and Shinto** can be seen by the way in which Hachiman was involved in protecting the construction of the Todai-ji in Nara and its famous statue. Following this precedent, Japanese *kami* were customarily invoked in the building of temples and monasteries and Buddhist sutras were read before them in shrines (**jinja**) as an act of appreciation. Shrines were usually created at the northeast extremity of the temple grounds, an area considered highly vulnerable.

The original Hachiman shrine is the **Usa Hachiman-gū** in Kyushū. It is dated by the Fuso Ryakki (Shortened Annals of Japan, 12th century), as having been established in 571. The Shoku Nihongi first mentions it in a reference that dates to 737. From there, a branch was established as the **Iwashimizu Hachiman-gū** in Kyōto, suggesting that the Heian court found it necessary to have a branch in Kyōto. Imperial links clearly suggest themselves to be authentic, but again obscure. This was followed by the **Tsurugaoka Hachiman-gū** in Kamakura, after Hachiman had become the tutelary *kami* of the Minamoto clan. Presumably **Minamoto Yoritomo** (1147–1199) took this branch to Kamakura to strengthen his claim as shogun to the emperor.

The meaning of the name "Hachiman" is equally obscure. The **Kokugaku** (National Learning) scholar **Motoori Norinaga** (1730–1801) pronounced it as yawata, employing a Chinese-style reading meaning eight (many) flags. This evokes the image of soldiers on the ground or on horseback carrying banners into battle. In art, he was depicted as **Emperor Ōjin** (reigned 270–310) and associated with his mother, the **Empress Jingū** (reigned 201–269), and Hime-okami, Ojin's empress. Whatever the origin, after the Kamakura period (1185–1333), Hachiman became firmly associated with war and governmental authority. He was subsequently enshrined in over 30,000 separate locations, and became the protective *kami* particularly of the Kanto plain. Hachiman shrines are easily distinguished by their **architecture**, which is composed of three buildings, a front hall, a middle worship hall, and an inner sanctuary (**honden**) in which the sacred symbol (**go-shintai**) resides. The appearance of continuity, because of the three sweeping roofs, is very distinctive.

In the postwar period, Hachiman, because of his associations, has probably been one of the more difficult *kami* to realign with modern Japanese attitudes and values. It is clear from Japanese history that various regional cults have waxed and waned. Hachiman may not vanish, but according to the views of some scholars, unless a meaningful and relevant role is rediscovered, the cult may find support declining among the generations of younger Japanese, who prefer to patronize the *kami* of economic prosperity and wellbeing, or who may defect to some of the ersatz cults that make such promises. One of Hachiman's virtues is national protection; this will probably ensure his survival.

HAFURI. Shrine (**jinja**) estates granted from early times to enable shrines to raise revenue for their support and maintenance. *See also* ANDO.

HAGA, YAICHI (1867–1927). Academic Shinto scholar and influential president of **Kokugakuin University** from 1919 to 1927. A graduate of the University of Tokyō, his principal work was the analysis of the Japanese national character through the literary tradition, based on his application of German philological methods to the study of the Japanese classics. His opus magnum was his *Kokubungaku-shi Jikkō* (History of Classical Japanese Literature) published in 1899, which was followed by his *Kokuminsei Juron* (Investigation into the Japanese National Character through Literature) published in 1907.

HAGIWARA KANEYORI (1588–1660). A **Yoshida Shinto** teacher who taught **Yoshikawa Koretari** (1616–1694) which in turn transformed him into a successor to the tradition.

HAGOROMO. Literally "Feather Robe," the term refers to mythological heavenly female persons wearing a robe of swan feathers who have miraculous powers, and that feature in tales and legends of the **Noh** drama *Hagoromo*. It narrates the story of a man who sees a Hagoromo bathing and steals her robe so that she must become his wife and bear his children. It ends when she recovers the feather robe and returns to her celestial home. *See also* FOLK SHINTO.

HAGURO-SAN SHUGENDŌ. Located in Yamagata Prefecture, Haguro-san **Shugendō** still retains a distinct identity within the general tradition of mountain asceticism. Haguro **yamabushi** are recorded as having visited Kyōto as early as the late 10th century, although the first historical references and the oldest records date to the 13th century.

While it claimed many grounds for an independent existence, it seems most likely that Haguro Shugendō originated from the Honzan-ha, or **Honzan Sect**, that developed in **Kumano**. The figure of **yatagarasu**, a great black legendary crow said to have guided **Ninigi-no-mikoto**, is the messenger of Haguro-**gongen** that further strengthens the possibility of links with Kumano. The additional fact that three mountains are revered may further parallel Kumano. The area functioned as headquarters for all Shugendō practitioners in the Tohoku area. By the late Edo period (1615–1868), over 4,000 yamabushi practiced on Haguro including priests of both **Shingon** and **Tendai Buddhism** who performed ascetic rituals with Tendai affiliated ascetics and **hijiri** practicing the nembutsu. Shugendō was proscribed by the Meiji government, with Haguro-san suffering like all other centers. Dewa-Jinja became the most important center of the revived **Dewa-Sanzan** after the **Pacific War** (World War II) (1941–1945), when Shugendō reestablished itself.

HAIBATSU-KISHAKŪ. A Meiji period (1868–1912) anti-Buddhist slogan inciting people to destroy the Buddha in order to advance the claims of **Kokka Shinto** (State Shinto). The slogan, never advocated by Shinto priests, created some violence, but had no serious impact on the massive support **Buddhism** retained because of its deep links with funerals and **ancestral reverence**. It came about after the enforced separation of Buddhism and Shinto on the principle of **Shinbutsu-bunri**.

HAIDEN. The worship hall of a shrine (**jinja**) in which members of the public or shrine believers may participate in ceremonies of purification. *See also* ARCHITECTURE IN SHINTO; JINJA SHADEN.

HAKAMA. The lower part of a priest's attire, consisting of a divided skirt-like article of clothing that covers from the waist to the feet. The three colors used are purple with insignia, plain purple, and light blue, which indicate rank. **Miko**, or shrine maidens, wear a distinctive bright red hakama.

HAKOZAKI-GŪ. Shrine located in the Hakozaki area of Fukuoka City in Kyushū. It enshrines **Emperor Ōjin** (reigned 270–310) and **Jingū Kōgō**, Empress Jingū, (reigned 201–269) along with Tamayorihime-no-mikoto. It was ranked in the **Engishiki** as a great shrine, and claims to date to the 10th century. The umbilical cord of Emperor Ojin is said to have been buried there by his mother in a box (hako), which gave the shrine its name.

HAKUSAN. The mother shrine (**jinja**) is Shirayamahime Jinja in Ishikawa Prefecture. Shirayama is a Chinese reading of the Japanese hakusan, meaning white mountain. Enshrined are **Izanagi-no-mikoto**, **Izanami-no-mikoto**, and Kukurihime-no-kami, who mediated a quarrel between the husband and wife that occurred at Yomotsuhirasaka. Branch shrines are referred to as Hakusan-miya.

HANAWA HOKI'ICHI (1746–1821). A mid-Edo period (1615–1868) **Kokugaku** (National Learning) scholar who became attached to **Kamo no Mabuchi** (1697–1769). In 1785, with government approval, he founded a Japanese Culture Studies Institute (Wagaku Kōdansho) from which he bequeathed to the nation a wealth of scholarship and learning, including texts relating to ancient Japan. His achievement is all the more remarkable because he lost his sight when he was only six years old.

HANIWA. Clay figurines used as funerary offerings in the protohistoric period of Japanese culture, from the second to sixth centuries, the **Kofun** period (second century—552 C.E.). The unglazed cylinders and hollow statues were used to decorate the surface of the kofun (burial mound). In contrast to other cultures, where such artifacts were buried with the deceased, these were placed outside, possibly to mark the area as sacred and further afford protection for the deceased.

Since there is no evidence of attendants of the deceased ever being buried alive, as was the case in other cultures, the notion of protection seems a likely explanation. Furthermore, on account of the vast differences between Haniwa and Chinese tomb figures, transmission from China has been ruled out by the majority of scholars, leaving Haniwa as an enigmatic part of Japan's pre-Buddhist culture.

HAPPYŌ-KAI. The normal term for a meeting to make a report, but in the case of the **New Religion** with Shinto roots, **Shinrei-kyō**, the purpose is to report the occurrence of miracles.

HARAE-DO. A building or other place provided for purification (**harai**) of body and mind prior to participation in Shinto ceremonies.

HARAI. Sometimes harae, it is the generic name for the act of ritual purification to remove impurities, of which there are several forms. The harai-gushi, a wand covered with paper streamers, is a familiar sight at shrines (**jinja**), as individuals, families, or businesses receive purification. Priests wave them in a left to right to left movement over the person, object, or site being purified. Salt is also considered a powerful purifying agent, and is given to mourners attending a funeral to sprinkle in the genkan, or entranceway, to their homes. It is believed that the salt is able to prevent contamination from the impurities arising from close contact with death. There are other forms of harai practiced in ascetic groups, involving immersion in rivers, waterfalls, or the sea.

The primal act was performed by the creative *kami* **Izanagi-no-mikoto** when he left the land of **Yomi-no-kuni**, the land of the dead, where he saw his wife, **Izanami-no-mikoto**, in a state of partial decomposition. The impurity he felt made him go to the **Tachibana** River and perform what became the first act of **misogi** harai. The words of the **Obarae-no-kotoba**, as do most **norito**, rituals addressed to the *kami*, contains a description of this event from the **mythology**.

Even **Buddhism** was induced to devise purification rites. The New Year Joya-no-kane, the ringing of the temple bell 108 times, is to remove the 108 forms of impurity that inflict people. And, of course, the use of fire in **Shingon** and **Tendai Buddhism** are forms of purification. *See also* ASCETICISM; DEATH IN SHINTO THOUGHT; ETHICS IN SHINTO; GYŌ; IMI; KEGARE; MISOGI; TSUMI; YAKUBARAI.

HARAIGUSHI. Paper or linen strips attached to a stick that is waved right to left to right in the performance of **harai**.

HARU MATSURI. Spring **festival** to pray for protection of crops. The cycle of **festivals** based on agricultural rites derived from **rice** cultivation are Spring, Summer, and Autumn, referred to collectively along with other rites as the **nenchū-gyōji**. Autumn becomes a harvest thanksgiving event. These are to be distinguished from other festivals, such as **New Year** or other occasions of significance that are derived from the concept of special purification (**harai**) rites to accompany an auspicious occasion. *See also* AKI MATSURI; DAI-JOSAI; NIINAMESAI.

HASEGAWA KAKUGYO (CIRCA 1541–1664). This ascetic practitioner is said to be the founder of the **Kyōha Shinto** (Sect Shinto) groups **Fusō-Kyō** and **Jikkō-Kyō**. He performed his discipline in the crater of **Mount Fuji**, through which he received supernatural powers.

HASHIRAMOTO-GOMA. Goma is a fire purification (**harai**) ceremony performed with piles of wood in esoteric **Buddhism**, in some Shinto ceremonies, and by practitioners of **Shugendō**. Prayers for the removal of sickness, misfortune, or other kinds of **tsumi**, impurity, are written on the wooden sticks, which are burned to destroy the causes of people's troubles.

HATSU-HI-NODE. Celebration of the first sunrise of the **New Year**, the continuity of which indicates how deeply the solar myth concept remains embedded in Shinto and in Japanese culture.

HATSU-MIYA-MAIRI. First shrine (**jinja**) visit of newly born children to be accepted as parishioners; for boys, it is the 32nd day, and for girls, it is the 33rd day. In view of the fact that the mother was considered impure after childbirth, it was traditional for the grandmother to present the child. While this is still common, the nuclear family has influenced the custom to the extent that it has become acceptable that mothers may also present their children in person.

HATSU-MŌDE. First shrine (**jinja**) visit of the **New Year**, made on average by over 80 million Japanese during the first two or three days of the New Year. Traditionally, people visited their own tutelary shrine, or a shrine located in a propitious direction for that particular year. In the postwar period, it has become a family event.

At popular shrines, such as the **Meiji Jingū** in Tōkyō, people are urged, often by policemen carrying loudspeakers, to offer their prayers as briefly as possible. Many kinds of talismans are on sale at shrines (and temples), and people dressed for the occasion in kimono may be seen carrying **sakaki** branches and arrows that are intended to break misfortune to their homes.

HATTORI NAKATSUNE (1757–1824). An Edo period (1615–1868) **Kokugaku** (National Learning) scholar and a disciple of **Motoori Norinaga** (1730–1801) who exercised a powerful influence on the development of features of the cosmological conceptualization of Shinto ideas within a comprehensive framework developed by **Hirata Atsutane** (1776–1843).

HATTORI NANKAKU (1683–1759). Confucian scholar of the Edo period (1615–1868) who became an eminent philologist and precursor of the **Kokugaku** (National Learning) methodology. He studied under Ōgyu Sorai (1666–1728), founder of the **Kobunjigaku** of Confucianism, and was therefore one of the figures who helped create a rapport between **Confucianism and Shinto**.

HAYASHI RAZAN (1583–1657). Confucian adviser to the government of **Tokugawa Ieyasu** (1543–1616) who linked the idea of reverence for the *kami* with the idea of the wellbeing of the nation and society. He actually identified the idea of the Confucian ultimate reality with the Japanese *kami* **Kuni-tokotachi-no-mikoto.**

It became an Edo period (1615–1868) version of **saisei-itchi**, the unity of worship and government, the classic concept of **matsuri-goto**. He rejected the alien cultures of Christianity and **Buddhism** and tried to align **Confucianism and Shinto** into one integrated belief and value system.

HEALING IN SHINTO. While several **New Religions** practice various forms of **faith healing** and promise the performance of miracles, **shamanistic** healing has a long history of its own. Healers, usually women, can be seen often in mountain shrines, and many claim to speak the words of a *kami* while they are in a trance. The blind women shamans, the itako of Osorezan in Aomori Prefecture, are the best-known surviving example of this type of culture. **Fortune-telling** and healing frequently accompany each other.

Some festivals related to **fertility** and **sex** have links to healing. The **Henoko Matsuri**, a phallic festival celebrated at **Tagata Jinja** a shine in Nagoya City, and the **Ososo Matsuri**, celebrated at **Oagata Jinja** in Inuyama City, are both concerned with conception and pregnancy. However, healing of sexual disease is also one property of observing the rituals at these events. **Mountain asceticism**, such as **Shugendō**, is intended to cultivate unique and even supernatural powers. People who have gained these powers are revered and often consulted for help and healing.

Water in special or sacred locations is thought to have powers to heal various medical ailments. Among the New Religions, **Shinrei-kyō** refers to itself as the fountainhead of miracles. Mitamura Sayo (1900–1967), who founded **Tenshō Kōtai Jingū-Kyō**, claimed to have performed numerous miracles of healing in her lifetime. Okada Kotama (1901–1974) recovered from an incurable disease that led to him founding the sect known as **Mahikari**. **Kurozumi Munetada** (1780–1850) was also dying when he was taken out to the veranda of his house to revere the sun for the last time. His recovery led to the founding of **Kurozumi-kyō** and its healing technique called **Majinai**. Healing in many forms lies at the heart of the shamanistic roots of Shinto.

HEARN, LAFCADIO (1850–1904). Authority on Japanese cultural behavior and customs. Although his work is tinged with a little romanticism, it remains an invaluable guide to understanding the deeper roots of the Japanese tradition, passed over all too frequently by superficial sociological observers of the late 20th century.

His major work, *Japan: An Attempt at Interpretation*, was intended to be a series of invited lectures at Cornell University. His observations about Shinto, buried at that time under the **Kokka Shinto** (State Shinto) system, remain a valuable guide as to how, in local contexts, the national system was little more than a government imitation of Western state religion, imposed on a vibrant folk tradition that not only survived, but continues in the present, demonstrating many of the characteristics that Hearn (later Koizumi Yakumo, after his naturalization) identified.

He is truly the forefather of the tradition that sees Japanese spirituality as the key to understanding the culture. Comments about his books and papers regaining popularity in fact imply that his work still has both meaning and validity. His empirical observations combined with his own intuitive grasp of the deeper structures underlying Japanese culture mark him out as a sentinel observer who was able to identify both change and continuity at a pivotal time in Japanese history.

His alleged dislike of **modernization** may say less about Japan and more about his critics, who wish to dismiss his earlier insights in favor of theories of modernization that were based on limited sociological premises. **Basil Hall Chamberlain** (1850–1935) enabled him to be appointed to teach English Literature at the University of Tokyō, where he worked until 1903. Apart from his house in Matsue, there is a memorial to him in Okubo, a district of Shinjuku Ward in Tokyō. *See also* MEIJI RESTORATION; MODERNIZATION AND SHINTO.

HEART. *See* KOKORO.

HEIAN JINGU. Established in 1895 to mark the 1100th anniversary of Kyōto becoming capital. Emperor Kammu (reigned 781–806), the first Heian emperor, and Komei (reigned 1846–1867), the last, are both enshrined. The famous Jidai Matsuri (Festival of the Historical Periods) takes place annually on 22 October, drawing large crowds of tourists. It was one of the imperial shrines (**jinja**) created during the time of **Kokka Shinto** (State Shinto), but one which had a genuine historical basis and which retains great popularity as a cultural feature of Kyōto life. Within its grounds there is the complete engine from an early steam train, reminding people that the technology that aided **modernization** was also a gift of the *kami. See also* FESTI-VALS IN SHINTO.

HEIAN PERIOD SHINTO. The removal of the court from Nara to Kyōto (Heian-kyō, capital of peace and safety) resulted in further changes in the relationship between Shinto and **Buddhism**. The introduction of the two new schools of Buddhism from China, **Tendai** by **Saichō** (767–833) and **Shingon** by **Kūkai** (773–835), made the connection between Buddhism and Shinto even more possible. Both were philosophically sophisticated and used rituals and ceremonies that must have been very impressive to the people of the Heian period (794–1185), particularly, the **goma** fire rite, which was quickly identified as a form of purification (**harai**). This further assisted the process of the **assimilation of Buddhism and Shinto**.

Both Buddhist sects had a preference for mountain locations for temples, and this made a rapport with Shinto very simple. Even the construction of the great esoteric temples such as the Kongobu-ji on Mount Koya, head temple of the Shingon sect, and the Enryaku-ji on Mount Hiei, head temple of the Tendai sect, required the co-operation and good will of the *kami* of their respective mountains. The ranking system of Buddhas, *kami*, and human beings seemed to be accepted, although the relationship was more complicated in practice.

For the ordinary people of the Heian period, Shinto and its agricultural rituals probably remained closest to their community life, since Buddhism always possessed the image of an aristocratic and courtly religion. The rapprochement between Buddhism and Shinto in the Heian period continued at the popular level, built around practices such as **chinkon** and various superstitious behaviors. Chinese influence continued to flow into Japan, and much of the stylization of buildings, priestly dress, **ritual**, and language in modern Shinto can be traced directly to this period.

HEIDEN. The hall of offerings in a shrine (**jinja**) where worshippers may present a **tamagushi**, a branch of **sakaki** with paper strips known as **heihaku**. *See also* ARCHITECTURE IN SHINTO; HAIDEN.

HEIHAKU. Paper strips in a zigzag formation attached to a stick that are offered to a *kami* during an act of purification (**harai**) at a shrine (**jinja**) or placed on an altar.

HEISEI. Meaning roughly "fulfillment of peace," this is the period of Emperor Akihito, which commenced in 1989. The year 2010 became Heisei 21. *See also* EMPEROR SYSTEM; GRAND SHRINES OF ISE; NENGŌ; TENNŌSEI.

HENOKO MATSURI. The famous **Henoko Matsuri** or Phallus **Festival** of the **Tagata Jinja** in Komaki, near Nagoya Airport in Aiichi Prefecture is one of the best-known festivals of its type. Nearby, Inuyama city's **Oagata Jinja** hosts the **Ososo Matsuri**, or Vagina Festival. *See also* FERTILITY RITES IN SHINTO.

HIE JINJA. Two shrines (**jinja**) bear the name. One is in Otsu, Shiga (also known as Hiyoshi Taisha), which enshrines Oyamakui-no-kami of Mount Hiei in the east side and Onamuchi-no-mikoto in the west. The establishment dates to Emperor Tenji (reigned 662–671). When **Saichō** (767–822) established the Enryakuji as his headquarters on Mount Hiei, the shrine was adopted as guardian of the temple in 788. **Sannō Ichijitsu Shinto** arose from this and the tradition grew.

The other shrine is in Tokyō, in Akasaka, and enshrines Oyamakui-no-kami of Mount Hiei as the protective *kami* of Edo (the former name of Tokyō), as respected by the Edo government. It dates to the order of Ota Dokan (1432–1486), issued in 1457, to build a shrine dedicated to **Sannō Gongen**. It subsequently became one of the two popular downtown shrines in the city of Edo, the other being in **Kanda**. Their annual **festivals** continue in alternate years and remain powerful reminders of the vigorous culture of the old Edo period (1615–1868).

HIGH PLAIN OF HEAVEN. *See KAMI* OF HEAVEN AND EARTH; TAKAMA-NO-HARA.

HIHON-HANSHI. A popular religious idea of the Edo period (1615–1868) concerning indebtedness to ancestors and return to beginnings. *See* HOTOKU; NINOMIYA SONTOKU.

HIJIRI. Holy man, mountain ascetic, dating before the Heian period (794–1185) and forerunner of the **yamabushi**. During the medieval period, the yamabushi were considered Buddhist priests, although they also used many Shinto rituals in their disciplines, particularly **misogi**, purification (**harai**) in water. *See also* SHUGENDŌ.

HIKAWA JINJA. The oldest shrine (**jinja**) in the city of Omiya, Saitama Prefecture, enshrining two *kami*, **Susano-o-no-mikoto** and **Amaterasu-ōmikami**. There are 162 branch shrines (**bunsha**) in Saitama Prefecture and a further 59 in the Tokyō metropolitan area. It is therefore very much an Edo period (1615–1868), Kanto-based cult, found almost nowhere else in Japan. It dates at least to the **Heian period** (794–1185), evidenced by its listing in the **Engishiki** of 972, but beyond that, the historical origins of the cult are virtually unknown.

HI-MACHI. Waiting for the sun on the 15th night of the first, fifth, and ninth months of the old calendar. Meeting in each other's homes, believers would pass the night talking until the act of devotion could be performed as the sun rose, as in **hatsu-hi-node**.

HI-MATSURI. A fire festival performed as an act of purification (**harai**) or **divination**. Some shrines (**jinja**), such as at **Nachi**, have famous **festivals** involving fire. It is not certain if fire festivals predate **Buddhism**, although it is very likely. However, the ritual employment of fire for purification developed especially during the **Heian period** (794–1185), with its introduction through esoteric Buddhism. *See also* AKIBA JINJA; CHINKI-SHIKI; HASHIRAMOTO-GOMA.

HIMIKO. Legendary empress of the of the second century C.E., referred to also as Pimiko, and discussed in the chronicles of the *Wei Zhi* (*Wei Chih*) a third-century document composed in China. Possessed of shamanistic powers, she is an early externally verified example of the sacral roots of Japanese society, and the place within it of the **emperor system** that remains to the present.

A civil conflict between 170 and 180 C.E. within the **Yamatai** confederation was brought to an end when she was made empress at the age of 13. The fact that Himiko's brother is recorded as having taken over the management of government affairs suggests that the transition had begun toward a more realistic understanding of government functions as distinct from the pure sacral society style, according to which the "divine personage" was made monarch.

HIMOROGI. A sacred space marked off by a rope in which **rituals** may take place. Since shrines (**jinja**) were initially sacred spaces on which buildings were erected to house rituals, it is not improper to infer that the setting up of a himorogi is the symbolic act from which the culture of the shrine itself grew. A *kami* could be asked to alight only on a sacred and purified place, surrounded by evergreens, symbolized by the **sakaki** tree branch. *See also* IWASAKA.

HI-NO-KAMI. The *kami* of fire, known as Homusubi-no-kami, revered as responsible for fire. Fire itself is not worshipped, but there are *kami* of the hibachi, the principal location of fire in a traditional household.

HINOKI. The Japanese cypress (*Chamaecyparis obtusa*), or "fire tree." It is a sacred tree used in the construction of shrine (**jinja**) buildings. It is marked by its distinctive aroma and is used also in making masu, cypress wooden cups, for drinking sake at festivals. Along with the **sakaki** and the matsu-no-ki, Japanese fir, it features in Shinto rituals, ceremonies, and symbolism.

HIOGI. Originating as a Heian period (794–1185) fan carried by the nobility, it is now carried by priests in formal dress. Thin strips of Japanese cypress, **hinoki**, are threaded together, the number being determined by rank. When it is carried by a priestess, it is called an akomeogi.

HIRANO JINJA. Transferred from Nagaoka in 794, it enshrines the *kami* of the city of Kyōto. *See also* YOSHIDA SHINTO.

HIRANO SHINTO. The Shinto tradition of a distinguished priestly family of Kyōto that held enormous influence until the end of the Edo period (1615–1868). *See also* YOSHIDA SHINTO.

HIRATA ATSUTANE (1776–1843). Principal ideologist of the **Fukko Shinto**, or Restoration Shinto, movement who remains a controversial figure because of the uncertain origin of many of his ideas. He has been accused by some of displaying Christian leanings and by others of being an ultranationalist, an odd combination of positions. He exercised a major influence on the early **Meiji Restoration** (1868) government policy.

Hirata Atsutane's perceived extremism by the Edo government resulted in his exile and death, which probably raised his value in the early Meiji period (1868–1912), only for his ideas to face the same fate when the Meiji government realized that his extreme views were not relevant to the thinking of the average person of the age.

He was born into a poor samurai family in Akita and trained in the **Confucianism** of **Yamazaki Ansai** (1618–1682), but at the age of 20 he ran away to Edo, where he became interested in **Taoist** thought. He was adopted by Hirata Atsuyasu, a Matsuyama retainer, in what became the modern Okayama Prefecture. In 1801, he first read the work of **Motoori Norinaga** (1730–1801), the key figure of the **Kokugaku** (National Learning) movement, inspired by whom he elected to devote his life to the study of Shinto.

Hirata followed Motoori's thought, but used an almost mystical approach to Shinto. He advocated a return to the ancient way, imperial reverence, and the rejection of **Buddhism**, Confucianism, and Christianity, although he used the logic of the latter to establish his case. This extremism proved too much for the Edo government. He was put under house arrest in 1841, and then forced to return to Akita, where he died in 1843. His ideology, referred to as **Hirata Shinto**, was used initially and effectively in the Meiji Restoration, but soon proved to be too extreme. Nevertheless, he helped to provide an intellectual and historical basis for nationalism, one vital ingredient of the modernization process. Studies of his ideas remain filled with controversy, but nevertheless, he was a significant figure in the process of Japan's 19th-century movement toward the modern world.

HIRATA SHINTO. The term is used in reference to the pro-**Kokka Shinto** (State Shinto) lobby within the early Meiji period (1868–1912) government that was concerned with the **rituals** and ceremonies performed at the **Grand Shrines of Ise** (Ise Jingū). Whether or not all the ideas were all legitimately derived from the thought of **Hirata Atsutane** (1776–1843) is a separate question. However, it was sufficiently identifiable to be known as Hirata Shinto. *See also* SAIJIN RONSO.

HIROHITO, EMPEROR (1901–1989). *See also* EMPEROR SYSTEM; NENGŌ; SHŌWA.

HIROSE JINJA. This shrine, located in Kita Katsuragi District in Nara Prefecture, was first recorded in 676. It enshrines Wakaukanome-no-mikoto, the *kami* of cereals, and was ranked in the **Engi-**

shiki of the **Heian period** (794–1185) as a Myōjin Taisha (the great shrine (**jinja**) of a gracious *kami*). Historically, it has links with the famous **Tatsuta Jinja**.

HIROTA JINJA. Located in Nishinomiya City in Hyogo Prefecture, it enshrines the *aramitama* (wild aspect of the soul of a *kami*) of **Amaterasu-ōmikami**. It was established to celebrate the success of **Empress Jingū** (reigned 210–269) during her famous Korean campaign and in appreciation of the help of this wild soul that she had taken with her when she left from **Sumiyosi Taisha**. Upon returning, she was instructed by an oracle to establish a shrine (**jinja**) to revere the wild soul. It also enshrines four other *kami* related to the Korean campaign.

HITO. In classical texts, human beings are described as aohitogusa, meaning "green-human-grass," something rich and capable of growing. Ame-no-masuhito is also used, implying that human beings can progress to the realm of the divine; thus reality is brought into the ideal world of the divine.

HITOGARA. A term meaning moral elegance of personality. Kunigara refers to the moral elegance of a nation, specifically meaning the Japanese. These were terms created by Edo period (1615–1868) scholars who wished to find appropriate defining terms for the national character of the Japanese people.

HIWADA. Bark of Japanese cypress used in roofing traditional shrines (**jinja**), such as the **Grand Shrines of Ise** (Ise Jingū). *See also* HINOKI.

HŌ. The outer gown-like robe worn over the other items of priestly dress when conducting an important ritual of purification (**harai**). The colors are black, red, and light blue, depending upon rank.

HŌBEI. The presentation of **heihaku**, special offerings made to a *kami*.

HODOSAN JINJA. Along with Chichibu **Jinja** and **Mitsumine Jinja**, it is one of the three principal shrines in the North of Saitama Prefecture. It contains a **kiyome-no-ike** (pond) in which **Yamato-**

takeru-no-mikoto performed **misogi** to purify himself on his travels throughout the country.

HŌGYO. Honorific verb meaning to die, used only to describe the passing away of an emperor or *kami* and in no other contexts. The normal term referring to a person passing away is shinu (die) or naku-naru (polite form). "Hōgyo" was used in the mass media to report the passing of **Emperor Showa**. *See also* DEATH IN SHINTO THOUGHT; EMPEROR SYSTEM.

HOKKE SHINTO. A syncretistic system that combines ideas from of **Tendai Buddhism** and Tendai Shinto with those of **Yoshida Shinto**, making use of the **Lotus Sutra** as a key text.

HOKORA. Originally meaning beautiful storehouse, hokora were storehouses within shrine (**jinja**) precincts. The term now refers to small wayside shrines.

HOLTOM, D. C. (1884–1962). U.S.-born missionary scholar who researched various aspects of Shinto, including imperial accession rites such as the **Daijōsai**, during the first half of the 20th century, and published extensively on various aspects of Shinto.

HONDEN. The inner sanctuary or worship hall within the building complex of a shrine (**jinja**). It houses the **go-shintai**, the symbol of the enshrined *kami*. Only purified **priests** may enter, although in some cases, where the honden fulfills more than one function, worshippers may enter also at certain times. In some special cases, the honden may be a mountain—for example, Kanasana Jinja in Saitama Prefecture—or some other natural phenomenon. The entire island of Okinoshima could be considered both *kami* and honden. *See also* ARCHITECTURE IN SHINTO; HAIDEN; HEIDEN; MUNAKATA SHINKŌ.

HONGU. The central or head shrine (**jinja**) for the worship of a particular *kami*, also sometimes referred to as honsha.

HONJI-SUIJAKU-SETSU. The principle of the noumenal (honji) and the phenomenal (suijaku) aspects of **Buddhism** and Shinto that enabled the one to be a manifestation of the other, making possible an explanation of the relationship between Buddha and *kami*. The doctrine is one stage in the long process of the **assimilation of Buddhism and Shinto**. Coming as it did from the high civilization of China, Buddhism was understood initially as the essence and the *kami* merely the manifestation. The theory led to the close identification of Buddhas and *kami* in the concept of honji-suijaku, which implied that the *kami* and Buddhas were one and the same beings.

Actual listings in many locations were drawn up to show how the identification was to be understood. The *kami* of **Kasuga Taisha**, for example, were listed in 1175 along with their Buddhist equivalents. Based on the idea that the understanding of Shinto *kami* and Buddhist deities could be in some way combined, it was first used, according to the great Shinto scholar **Muraoka Tsunetsugu** (1884–1946), in the *Nihon Sandai Jitsuroku* (Chronological Description of the Three Generations of Emperors), the compilation of which was completed during the first year of Engi (901) and started on 28 August of the first year of Jogan (859). Eryo, abbot of the of the Enryakuji, was granted two priests whom he requested to expound sutras for the *kami* at the **Kamo** and **Kasuga** shrines, respectively. At that time he stated:

> When the Buddha seeks existence he sometimes uses jitsu (truth) or gom (manifestation). The Nyorai reveals jaku (suijaku) and sometimes becomes a king or *kami*. Therefore when the noble king governs the nation, surely he will rely upon the help of the *kami*.

The further development of the theory during the **Heian period** (794–1185) accords historically with the shift of the court from Nara (where Hinayana and semi-Mahayana types of Buddhism had been introduced to Japan) to Kyōto, where Japanese religious thinkers such as **Saichō** (767–822), the founder of **Tendai Buddhism**, and **Kūkai** (773–835), founder of **Shingon Buddhism**, took the initiative to combine the traditions. Esoteric Buddhism was more readily able to express the integration, and this enabled Buddhism to come into contact with ordinary people, thus making it possible for popular forms to develop. Honji-Suijaku is probably best understood as a process that came about spontaneously for a number of reasons, resulting in the creation of a new type of Buddhism and a new relationship between Buddhism and Shinto. It was with the two esoteric forms of Buddhism that the first manifestations of the synthesis are seen, in **Ryōbu**

Shinto, in the Shingon tradition, and in **Sanno Ichijitsu Shinto** in the Tendai tradition. Its existence almost certainly saved Shinto from extinction: the fate, for example, of Celtic Christian culture in the Western world, a hybrid between a religion founded on a revelation and a religion derived from reverence for nature (see "Introduction").

By the 13th century, as Shinto struggled to maintain its ground, the balance within the relationship began to change. The complex doctrines of the Tendai and Shingon thinkers made possible the creation of **Yuiitsu Genpon Shinto** by **Yoshida Kanetomo** (1435–1511). This led, subsequently, to the reversal of doctrine by Shinto thinkers advocating the theory of han-honji-suijaku-setsu, or shimpon-butsuju-setsu.

Some apologists for Buddhism have claimed that the Japanese people as a whole accepted the idea of Buddhism as the true essence and Shinto as the manifestation until 1868, and that Shinto itself, and not merely **Kokka Shinto** (State Shinto), was an artificial creation of the Meiji period (1868–1912). This is a revisionist fiction. The meaning of the terminology, in Japanese, could be understood either way. Crucial for understanding is recognition of the fact that Buddhism discarded most of its central concepts, such as reincarnation, in order to find acceptance in Japan. The doctrine is also known as Honjaku-Engi Shinto.

HONZAN SECT OF SHUGENDŌ. The rise to prominence of the **Kumano** cult was very much the work of a **Tendai Buddhist** priest of the Mii-dera called Zōyo (1032–1116), who guided Emperor Shirakawa (reigned 1072–1086) on his 1090 Kumano pilgrimage. When he was subsequently appointed governor of Kumano, the **Kumano Sanja** became directly related to the Mii-dera and consequently to the Tendai sect. Jokei, the son of Emperor Go-Shirakawa (reigned 1155–1158), became a Tendai priest and abbot of the Shōgo-in, which in turn connected the abbacy to the governorship of Kumano. This important development enabled the Kumano **shūgenja** to become preeminent among **yamabushi**. Shugenja in Kumano came to be known as **sendatsu**, and their followers as **danna**.

Highly ranked teachers called **oshi** received stipends to guide people to mountain power places. Many sendatsu and oshi became very wealthy as a result of the large numbers of followers coming to their areas for purification (**harai**) and guidance. This added further prestige and power to the Shōgo-in, which in turn appointed a major shrine in Kyōto, one supported by the Ashikaga Shogunate, as the supervising shrine of the Kumano Sanja in the 14th century.

The system was expanded and remained under the administration of the Shōgo-in, which consequently became the headquarters of what came to be known as the Honzan sect. It declared itself the orthodox tradition, hence the name Honzan (original root, mountain), claiming **En no Gyōja** as founder and Zōyo as patron of the sect. The Tendai monk Enchin (founder of the Mii-dera) was said to have been engaged in ascetic practices at Omine and Kumano. A system was also created permitting each influential shūgenja an independent area of authority called a **kasumi**. Lower-ranked shūgenja were appointed with designated districts inside each kasumi.

By the 15th century, Shogo-in abbots began making nation-wide tours to all outlying centers to inspect shūgenja. Abbot Doko (1430–1510) was particularly active. The Honzan sect claimed in its biography of En no Gyōja that he had visited all these places, a propaganda claim to legitimize the efforts of the abbots of the Shogo-in and to enhance the status of the sect. The headquarters remains the Shogo-in in Kyōto.

HONZEN-NO-SEI. A philosophical term of neo-Confucianism, created by **Chu Shi** (Zhu Xi, 1130–1200). It referred to the primary nature of the universe, a concept of which the scholar **Itō Jinsai** (1617–1705) was highly critical.

HORIKAWA SCHOOL. An influential Edo period (1615–1868) Kyōto school of **Confucian** studies that combined the work of **Ito Jinsai** (1627–1705) and his son Togai (1670–1736).

HOTOKU. Repayment and indebtedness, a moral ideal put forward by **Ninomiya Sontoku** (1787–1856) a peasant philosopher, who taught four virtues: sincerity of mind (shisei), industrious labor (kinrō), a planned economy (bundo), and yielding to others (suijō). These values were encouraged by the Ministry of Home Affairs in the early years of the 20th century as part of the national cultivation of moral virtue. They were linked into the virtues of thrift and diligence as well as the virtue of perseverance against adversity, taught as the foundation of moral education in schools.

The idea was symbolized by the presence of a statue of Ninomiya Kinjirō, a little boy reading a book and carrying firewood on his back, placed in every school playground nationwide. He was taught as a model of virtuous endeavor who overcame difficulty and suffering to achieve success.

Mistaken by critics as another form a nationalism, the statues were ordered removed after 1945 as part of the **Supreme Commander Allied Powers** purge of education. In reality, the ideals and values in moral education were little different from what was taught, for example, in British schools at the time. The ideas of Ninomiya Sontoku still command the respect of many Japanese intellectuals.

A debate started within the Ministry of Education in the 1980s about restoring the statues because of the moral values they represented. *See also* BOSHIN SHŌSHŌ.

– I –

IBUKI. Breathing exercises practiced as a part of various ascetic activities, for example, before taking part in **misogi**. The concept and the practice probably originated in China, but was refined in Japan and incorporated into **Shugendō** and other Shinto/Buddhist rituals. Deep breathing as performed in **Ontake-kyō** is known as ibuki-ho.

ICHIJO KANEYOSHI (1402–1481). Classical scholar and member of the noblest branch of the Fujiwara family. He was the most important scholar of the Muromachi period (1333–1568), envisioning a philosophical system that combined Shinto, **Buddhist**, and **Confucian** ideals. He helped protect and promote the finest poetic genre of the era to preserve the best of Japanese spirituality and vision. He also assisted in saving and transmitting the finest Japanese culture during an era of serious cultural decline.

ICHI-NO-MIYA. The formally acknowledged oldest shrine (**jinja**) of a district, decided in the **Heian period** (794–1185). District first shrines (Ichi-no-Miya), also identified as important locally revered old shrines, came to be known as Ichi-no-miya (or first shrine). The first reference to this system appears in the *Konjaku Monogatari*, where the term was applied to the *kami* known as Suo-no-kuni-tama-no-ya-daimyōjin. The first shrine title was applied in each province (kuni) to the shrine that drew the most widespread worship of the ordinary people.

The Ichi-no-miya shrines still carry these titles, usually stated in the form of, for example, X-kuni-no-ichi-no-miya followed by the name of the shrine. Ni-no-miya and san-no-miya, second and third shrines, are also found. It meant that, in addition to the national and government-backed shrines, recognition was given to local shrines derived probably from tutelary and clan *kami* (both **chinju-no-***kami* and **ujigami)**, which were closely related to the daily lives of large numbers of the ordinary people. These were given special attention and respect by both government and lay people alike. A modern **Ichi-no-miya-kai**, an association of the existing traditional district first shrines, was inaugurated in 1985.

IKIBOTOKE. This title, meaning a living human Buddha, is given to priests who have undertaken severe disciplines such as **Sen-nichi-kai-ho-gyo** and survived. The term parallels **ikigami**, living human *kami* in Shinto, and indicates how much of the mentality of Shinto that Buddhism was required to absorb in order to be integrated into Japanese cultural life.

IKIGAMI. Living human *kami* is a title given to people, who, in their lifetimes, had achieved some remarkable feat. Numerous examples abound in Japanese, history, including **Emperor Meiji**, who was enshrined twice during his lifetime. **Katō Genchi** (1873–1965), the famous Shinto scholar, conducted extensive research and confounded skeptical scholars at a Conference in Oxford in the early years of the 20th century by citing numerous authentic historical case studies. *See also* AKITSUMI KAMI; ARAHITO-GAMI; IKIBOTOKE.

IKUKUNITAMA JINJA. Located in Tennoji Ward, Osaka, it enshrines Ikushima-no-kami and Tarushima-no-kami, protective *kami* of the Japanese archipelago. The shrine **(jinja)** was listed in the **Engishiki** and achieved imperial recognition after 850.

IMI. Avoidance as a form of purification (**harai**), particularly prior to the performance of important ritual functions. Imi-no-kotoba are words that should be avoided because their sound is not pleasing to the *kami*. At a wedding party, for example, the words deru (go out) and kiru (to cut) should not be used. *See also* HARAI; KEGARE; TSUMI; YAKUBARAI.

IMI-NO-KOTOBA. A list of words that should be avoided because they can bring misfortune if spoken. The practice of avoiding certain words is referred to in the **Engishiki**. *See* IMI; SEICHO NO IE.

IMPERIAL HOUSEHOLD. The term used to translate Koshitsu, which refers to the institution, residence, and **ritual** activities (**Kōshitsu Saishi**) of the members of the imperial family, principally the emperor. The affairs of the imperial household are regulated by a law enacted by the Japanese parliament, and financed by a budget similar to the Civil List in the United Kingdom. Over 40 rituals are performed by the emperor every year at various sacred sites within the grounds of the Imperial Palace, as well as a number performed at the **Grand Shrines of Ise** (Ise Jingū). The performance of these rituals on behalf of the imperial family and the people has been considered traditionally as a form of protection for the nation. *See also* DAIJŌSAI; EMPEROR SYSTEM.

IMPERIAL REGALIA. Known as the sanshū-no-jingi, sanshū-no-shinki, and sometimes sanshū-no-shimpo, they are the three sacred objects that guarantee the authority and legitimacy of the emperor: the mirror (**yata-no-kagami**), the jewel (**yasakani-no-magatama**), and the sword (kusanagi-no-tsurugi). Each was presented to **Amaterasu-ōmikami**, who in turn presented them to her grandson, **Ninigi-no-mikoto**, before his descent to the Japanese archipelago. They were to serve as the symbols of the ideals of wisdom, courage, and benevolence.

Many legends surround these, including the version that the originals are secretly enshrined in **The Grand Shrines of Ise** (Ise Jingū), and that the present ones are mere replicas. Another is that **Yamato-takeru-no-mikoto** used the sword to conquer eastern Japan. Having saved his life, it was renamed kusanagi-no-tsurugi and enshrined in **Atsuta Jingū**, Nagoya. The original sword was later reported lost at the battle of **Dannoura** in 1185, when the boy emperor, **Antoku**, died. Popular enthusiasm for the imperial regalia grew up during the Kamakura period (1185–1333), fired initially by **Kitabatake Chika-**

fusa (1293–1354), who composed a defense of the imperial line in his **Jinnō-Shōtōki**. Subsequently, **Ichijo Kaneyoshi** (1402–1481), a scholar and court official, published a dissertation on the imperial regalia in which he treated them as symbols of Shinto, **Buddhism**, and **Confucianism**, which could be integrated into one social, political, and religious system.

At the initial stage of the accession of a new emperor (senso), he receives the imperial regalia in the Kemji Togyo no Gi within the Imperial Palace. This event was televised for the first time in 1989 when Emperor Akihito (subsequently known as Emperor Heisei) succeeded his late father, **Emperor Showa**. The more ritualistic stages of the accession rites follow within the succeeding 12-month period, namely, the **Sokui-no-rei** and the **Daijōsai**. *See also* EMPEROR SYSTEM; TENNŌSEI.

IMPERIAL RESCRIPTS. During the Meiji period (1868–1912), numerous rescripts were issued on subjects such as education, thrift, and diligence, guides to the military and other organs of society. They were mostly, in essence, Confucian-style documents. The most famous is perhaps that on education (**Kyōiku Chokugo**), issued in the name of **Emperor Meiji**.

INARI. The protective *kami* of the cultivation of **rice** as well as the five basic grain cereals, popular among the merchant classes of the city of Edo (the old name for what is now Tokyō) and continues to be popular in the modern business community. The cult developed between the 13th and 16th centuries, and various accretions enabled it to grow and embrace different trades, professions, and social classes. Association with the **fox** as a messenger of Inari provided a visual image, and statues of foxes being offered fried bean curd are found at all Inari sites.

Tracing the roots of Inari to the Japanese **mythology**, the term refers to the collective identity of Uka-no-mitama, also known as **Toyoukehime-no-kami**, of the **Gekū** (Outer Shrine) of the **Grand Shrines of Ise** (Ise Jingū). The connection is clearly with food, suggesting that the etymology of inari means "becoming rice."

One historical lineage that has been suggested ties Inari to the powerful Hata clan of Kyōto, whose growing influence resulted in the district of Fushimi and the **Fushimi Inari Taisha** becoming equally important. Legends abound concerning the Hata family's wealth: for example, Hata no Kimi Irogu is said to have used rice cakes for archery target practice, one of which, after he hit it, became a swan which flew to Inariyama. Penitent ancestors brought a tree from Inariyama and planted it in a sacred spot, which became Inari Jinja. Inari could thus be linked with **Ta-no-kami**, deity of the rice fields and the family deity of the Hata clan.

According to ancient records, the enshrinement took place on the first day of the horse in the second month of 711. Traditionally, Inari festivals nationwide are celebrated on that day, giving credence to the mixture of myth and history. Edo-period merchants took to Inari as the *kami* of business success (shūsse Inari).

The two central shrines (**jinja**) of the main branches are the Fushimi Inari Jinja in Kyōto and the **Toyokawa Inari Jinja** in Toyokawa City, Aiichi Prefecture. The Fushimi tradition is extremely complex, with Inari as a *kami*, seen most probably as a composite figure. The Inari-gosha is a group of five shrines in Fushimi that enshrine nine *kami*. Myth, local legend, and history completely overlap to produce single identity. Mount Inari was the dwelling place of packs of foxes, creating yet another image of the fox as the messenger of the *kami*.

The Toyokawa tradition dates back only to the building of the shrine in 1930, but has links with **Buddhism** that go back to the 15th century. In addition, worship of the byakko (white fox), is associated with the Toyokawa tradition. Toyokawa shrines are usually a complex of shrine and temple: Inari is revered in both.

Perhaps the greatest moment of recognition of Inari was when **Emperor Meiji** invoked Inari to protect the nations against the menacing southern barbarians during the early Meiji period (1868–1912).

IN-EN-GA. The idea of a cause and effect cycle that affects human destiny, as taught by the Shinto-based **New Religion Shinrei-kyō**.

INOUE KOWASHI (1843–1895). A Meiji period (1868–1912) statesman who was influential in drafting the Constitution of 1889 and the Imperial Rescript on Education (**Kyōiku Chokugo**) of 1890. He became Minister of Education in 1893. *See also* BOSHIN SHŌSHŌ.

INOUE MASAKANE (1790–1849). Born Ando Kisaburo, founder of **Misogi-kyō**, one of the **Kyōha Shinto** (Sect Shinto) groups that practice **misogi**. Descended from a distinguished samurai family, Inoue was preoccupied by the issues of disease, suffering, death, how the poor could be helped, and how human health could best be preserved. He traveled, studied, became a disciple of Shirakawa Hakoke, a Shinto sect that taught misogi and breathing (**ibuki**), and received a teaching license. He made breathing a discipline, based on the idea that the world began with the breath of the *kami*. Consequently, he believed it is possible, through controlled breathing, to be in communion with the divine.

He went to Edo as head of the Shinmeigu and was licensed to teach and conduct rituals. However, he fell afoul of the government by expressing dissatisfaction with the religious policy of the Edo administration. He was arrested several times and imprisoned. Finally, in 1843, he was exiled to the volcanic island of Miyakejima, far south of Tokyō in the Pacific Ocean, where he died six years later.

INSEI. Retired emperors of the Heian period (794–1185) who usually became cloistered Buddhist priests but still remained active in the background of court politics while appearing to be distant from public affairs.

IRESAI. A ceremony to console the distressed spirits of the dead. *See also* SOUL IN SHINTO; YASUKUNI JINJA.

ISE JINGŪ. *See* GRAND SHRINES OF ISE.

ISE PROVINCE. Ise-no-kuni, also known as Seishū, was one of the 15 provinces of the Tokkaido in central Honshū. It was formally established under the Kokugun system of 646 and included most of what is now Mie Prefecture. From ancient times, it had deep associations with various Shinto cults, including the Uji-Yamada (now Ise City) cult of **Amaterasu-ōmikami** and the cult of **Sarutahiko-ōkami** in what is now Suzuka City.

In the "first shrine" rankings, **Tsubaki Ōkami Yashiro** (Tsubaki Dai Jinja, Tsubaki Grand Shrine) is listed as first shrine (**jinja**) of Ise province, rather than the **Grand Shrines of Ise** (Ise Jingū), which were closed to the general population, confirming the antiquity of the Sarutahiko cult. According to the **mythology**, Sarutahiko-ōkami stood at the crossroads of heaven and earth, and eventually guided

Ninigi-no-mikoto to the site of Ise. When the prefectural system was institutionalized in 1871, Ise was combined with Iga and Shima provinces to form Mie Prefecture. *See also* AME-UZUME-NO-MIKOTO; ISE SHINTO.

ISE SHINTO. The teaching of the **Grand Shrines of Ise** (Ise Jingū), but especially the ideas of the **Gekū** (Outer Shrine), as developed by the **Watarai** family, whose philosophical imagination and cosmological creativity enabled the Outer Shrine to achieve enormous prominence through its assimilation of concepts derived from **Buddhism** into a very clearly defined Shinto framework.

ISHIDA BAIGAN (1685–1744). Edo period (1615–1868) scholar and founder of the **Shingaku** (Heart Learning) movement that provided a popular morality based on Shinto ideals. He grew up in an agricultural household, and although briefly apprenticed to a Kyōto merchant, preferred to return to the land. He began preaching Shinto ideals in Kyōto in about 1708, and began studying under a scholar called Oguri Ryoun (1669–1729), from whom he learned meditation techniques.

At the age of 43, he became a professional teacher, and although being relatively unsuccessful initially, gathered a following that established his reputation. His key point was that the virtues of **Confucianism** were not arbitrarily imposed ideals, but conformed to the "true human heart" that could be discovered through knowing nature. He popularized the idea that enlightenment did not require the arduous study of Confucian values, nor even the chanting or reading of sutras, but could be achieved by knowing one's own heart and nature, and by committing unreservedly to whatever task was being undertaken.

As a practical philosophy emphasizing a lifestyle of virtue based upon following the flow of **Daishizen**, great nature, Ishida made a major contribution to Shinto ethics by demonstrating the existence of a moral sense that was a kind of ethical commonsense in all mankind. *See also* ETHICS IN SHINTO.

ISONOKAMI JINGŪ. A shrine (**jinja**) located in Tenri City, Nara Prefecture, enshrining the tutelary *kami* of the Mononobe clan, which administered to the nation on behalf of the imperial family during the fifth and sixth centuries. It enshrines Futsunomitama-no-okami, a sacred sword presented to the first legendary emperor, **Jimmu Tennō** (reigned 660–585 B.C.E.), after his conquest of the Japanese archipelago.

ITŌ JINSAI (1627–1705). Founder of the **Ancient Learning School**, whose work gave legitimacy to the study of the classical origins of Japanese thought. He was born into a merchant family in Kyōto, but developed as a scholar of **Confucianism**, particularly **Chu Hsi** (Zhu Xi, 1130–1200). He became very critical of Chu Hsi, particularly of his distinction between primary matter (**honzen no sei**) and physical matter (**kishitsu no sei**), which both have their origins in a supra-rational absolute (taikyōku), principle (li), and spirit, or energy (**ki**).

Self-cultivation in the Confucian moral tradition for Chu Hsi, according to Itō, was really a kind of progressive self-realization, something Ito considered to be derived more from **Buddhism** or even **Taoism** than from Confucianism. Ito argued that the traditional Confucian way was the Way of Heaven (Tendō), which was followed by cultivating humanity (jin) and not by metaphysical speculation.

His son Togai (1670–1736) continued in his father's footsteps, and together their work became known as the **Horikawa School** of Kyōto. Their work prepared the way for both the rapport of **Confucianism and Shinto**, as well as for the **Kokugaku** (National Learning) approach to the Japanese classics.

ITSUKUSHIMA JINJA. Shrine (**jinja**) located in Hiroshima Prefecture on the island of Itsukushima that enshrines Ichikichima-hime-no-mikoto, along with two *kami* from the **Munakata Jinja**; these protect seamen and fishing, particularly in the straits between Japan and Korea.

Tradition dates it to 593, following the manifestation of the three *kami*. Taira no Kiyomori, after becoming guardian of Aki province, ordered it to be built. Not unlike the Italian city of Venice, much of it is built over water, creating a floating impression at high tide. It has 6,000 branch shrines linked to it, all derived from the Shinto/Buddhist amalgam that the shrines came to represent in the medieval period. It is highly photogenic, and is easily recognized by the **Ryōbu Shinto** design of its famous red gateway (**torii**) set 160 meters into Hiroshima Bay.

Its museum contains some toys that belonged to the boy emperor, **Antoku** (reigned 1180–1183), who was drowned at the battle of **Dannoura** in 1185.

IWAKURA TOMONOMI (1825–1883). One of the leaders of the **Meiji Restoration** movement who supported the creation of the **Jingikan**, but who, after leading a mission to Europe and North America from 1871 to 1873, was aware of foreign pressure on the matter of religious toleration and therefore was critical of the anti-foreign movements in Japan. However, he was not an advocate of a people's democracy, preferring an order based on nobility and oligarchy. Although funds were raised to build a shrine (**jinja**), he was never enshrined; instead, a school was built with the money.

IWASAKA. A rock formation considered to be the residence of a *kami* or used as a sacred place for the performance of **rituals**.

IWASHIMIZU HACHIMAN-GŪ. Branch shrine (**jinja**) of the **Usa Hachiman-gū** of Kyushū, dating to 859, when the protective presence of **Hachiman** was considered to be necessary in Kyōto. The Usa shrine's links to the **imperial household** are obscure, but appear to be very deep. It was an oracle from Kyushū that destroyed the usurping monk **Dōkyō** (died 722), and it was the choice of **Minamoto Yoritomo** (1147–1199) to have another branch established in Kamakura to protect and authenticate his regime. The Hachiman cult thereafter spread throughout Kanto and beyond, and eventually produced a network of over 30,000 shrines in which Hachiman was revered.

IWAU. A word that meant practicing abstinence (**saikai**) before a festival, it now refers to words of congratulations or blessing. The modern form o-iwai refers to a congratulatory message, with or without a Shinto ceremony, although the invocation of protection by a *kami* is implied.

IZANAGI NO MIKOTO AND IZANAMI NO MIKOTO. According to the Japanese **mythology** as recorded in the **Nihon Shōki** (720), they were procreators of the Japanese archipelago. They stood on the **Ame-no-ukihashi** (the Floating Bridge of Heaven) and dipped a jeweled spear into the ocean. The coagulated drops or brine falling from the spear became the islands of Japan to which they descended and continued the activities that produced the entire archipelago.

Izanami died giving birth to the *kami* of fire and went to **Yomi-no-kuni**, the polluted land of the dead. Izanagi pursued her there, where he found Izanami decomposing and surrounded by the sight of decay and corruption. Izanami rebuked him for pursuing her, and threatened to kill a thousand people every day if he came back. He responded that he could cause more to be born, a point which **Motoori Norinaga** (1731–1800), the **Kokugaku** (National Learning) scholar, considered evidence of Shinto belief in the power of life over death.

Izanagi was threatened by some ugly decaying hags of Yomi-no-kuni and forced to flee. After he had escaped from the land of pollution, he purified himself in the River Tachibana, creating the paradigmatic act of **misogi**, ritual purification (**harai**) in water. He continued giving birth to various *kami*, including **Amaterasu-ōmikami**, the *kami* of the sun and ancestor figure of the imperial family. *See also* FERTILITY RITES AND SHINTO.

IZUMO ŌYASHIRO-KYŌ. Ōyashirō, or Great Shrine, is the other reading of the name of **Izumo Taisha**. The sect dates to 1874, when the 80th governor of Kuninomiyatsuko (Izumo Province) Senge Takatomi was also the **Gūji** of Izumo Taisha. He left the ujiko of Izumo-oyashiro, the shrine (**jinja**) supporters' organization, to form the Izumo Taisha Kei Shinko, which recognized Izumo no Kuni nomi yatsuko, Ame-ho-hi-no-mikoto as its head. Meiji Government policy to use Shinto for national goals centered on the worship of **Amaterasu-ōmikami** and the **Zōka-sanshin** but did not encourage the worship of **Okuninushi-no-mikoto**. It also placed restrictions upon the activities of all religious groups.

In 1882, Taisha-kyō was authorized as an independent sect under the leadership of Senge Takatomi. While the main purpose was to popularize the worship Okuninushi-no-mikoto, it also sought to promote the Great Way of the *Kami* for the purpose of cultivating national character. This brought it very much into line with the ideal of the state taught by the Meiji government.

After the end of the **Pacific War** (World War II), the organization was freed from state control; by 1951, Izumo Taisha had repossessed the organization, which became an independent sect. It has a separate existence, although it is under full control of the shrine authorities. It functions nationwide as a base for the support of the shrine. The Senge family, hereditary priests of the shrine, now also head the sect. It claims to have about 1 million supporters.

IZUMO TAISHA. The principal shrine (**jinja**) of one of the eight provinces of the south Honshū Sea of Japan area, now the eastern half of Shimane Prefecture. It was the center of religious and political activities that almost rivaled the Yamato clan of Nara. It is located in Taishamachi, which bears its name.

It enshrines **Ōkuninushi-no-mikoto**, along with **Ame-no-mi-nakushi-no-kami** and Takami-musubi-no-kami. It dates, according to the mythology, to the time when the grandson of **Amaterasu-ōmikami** descended to the Japanese archipelago. The present building was erected in 1744 and stands 24 meters high. Its predecessor is said to have stood 48 meters and to have depicted palace life in ancient times. The **Nihon Shōki** (720) refers to an eight-fathom palace in Izumo, which would suggest a structure at least 48 meters tall. In April 2000, archaeologists digging near the present main building uncovered the base of a wooden pillar, estimated at three meters in diameter. A computer simulation by Obayashi Corporation, one of Japan's major construction companies, suggested that the probable height was equivalent to a modern 16-story building. Shrine records suggest that it was one of nine pillars, supporting what was then the world's largest known wooden building, one meter taller than the Todai-ji, the temple housing the Great Buddha of Nara, which was 47 meters tall. The tall structure appears to date to the late **Heian period** (794–1185).

Izumo Taisha is famous also for its **festival** known as the Kamiari-sai, held between October 11th and 17th, when the *kami* from all over Japan congregate to discuss their regional concerns. Since the 14th century, the Senge and Katajima families have served alternately as high priests. The Senge family has been in control since 1868.The shrine is also supported by a **Kyōha Shinto** (Sect Shinto) group, the **Izumo-ōyashiro-kyō**, that has an independent history but that has also become closely integrated with all other shrine believers.

– J –

JAPAN FEDERATION OF RELIGIONS. The federation, known in Japanese as the Nihon Shukyō Renmei, was formed in 1946. It consists of five independent religious federations: the Association of Shinto Shrines (**Jinja Honcho**); the Association of Sect Shinto (**Kyōha Shinto Rengokai**); the Japan Federation of Buddhists (Zen

Nihon Bukkyō Kai); the Japan Association of Christian Churches (Nihon Kirisutokyō Rengokai); and the Union of New Religious Organizations of Japan (Shin Nihon Shūkyō Dantai Rengōkai). Its goals are to maintain cordial relations among Japan's diverse religious groups, to maintain freedom of religion under the Constitution, and to ensure that religion and the state are kept separate. *See also* SHŪKYŌ DANTAI HŌ.

JIBA. The sacred spiritual capital of the former **Kyōha Shinto** (Sect Shinto) sect **Tenri-kyō**, designated by its foundress, **Nakayama Miki**. She is said to have passed away performing the salvation **dance**, the **Kagura Zutone**, at the Jiba.

JICHINSAI. Literally a "ground calming **festival**," it is a Shinto **ritual** of purification (**harai**). This is a traditional groundbreaking ceremony that precedes almost every building project, individual or communal, that entails turning over the soil. It follows a traditional pattern: a representative of the group or person erecting the building cuts some green leaves inserted in a sand mound with three symbolic cuts. The representative of the construction company symbolically breaks the top of a sand mound in response. The *kami* of the land are informed, and their understanding solicited.

In recent times, however, it has not been without controversy. In what some observers have referred to as a "landmark case," a citizens' group in the city of Tsu protested that use of public funds for a ceremony of jichinsai was illegal under terms of Article 89 of the Constitution guaranteeing freedom of religion and forbidding the use of public funds to support religious purposes. They went to court in 1965 and, after a long legal process, the Supreme Court ruled in 1977 that the action was not unconstitutional, which set off a frenzied reaction among those who believe that a conspiracy exists to reestablish **Kokka Shinto** (State Shinto), and that revived nationalism and militarism are on the rise. As always, the wording of court petitions and judgments often conceals the realities, especially in Japan. In terms of a strict understanding of the Constitution, money was not used to support any religious organization, but simply to pay for its services, which is perhaps the key legal point of interpretation.

If the same criteria were applied, the use of Buddhist priests at any public funerals could be classified in the same way. One underlying problem is that the Constitution was modeled on the U.S. separation of church and state, because of the politics of established churches' power in the West. However, as in the case of many other attempts to understand Japan, the Western model was not only inadequate, it was also misleading. Equally naive was the assumption that a Western-style solution would solve the problem. **Buddhism** and its political power in the Nara period (710–794) would be the closest analogy, and it should be remembered that the Nara court moved to Kyōto to escape the problem. State Shinto, whose revival was judged by the litigants to be the goal of the government action, in reality failed to achieve any of the goals the **Meiji** government set for it. At the end of the day, the Tsu case proved very little about anything.

JIGAMI. *Kami* of the land revered in regions west of the Kanto plain. The **soul (tama)** of the village founder is enshrined and revered as a community ancestor. In some areas, an individual becomes a jigami 33 years after death. In other areas, the jigami and the **ta-no-kami** (*kami* of the field) become identified. *See also* ANCESTRAL REVERENCE.

JIGOKU. A concept of hell found in popular **Buddhist** culture. The figure of **Jizō** is often associated with saving the souls of children who are trying to escape from Jigoku. The notion of punishment after death is alien to Shinto, but was used during the Edo period (1615–1868), in particular as tool of moral education. *See also* DEATH IN SHINTO.

JIKKŌ-KYŌ. Founded in the 16th century, it is a **Kyōha Shinto** (Sect Shinto) sect that practices **asceticism** through various **rituals**. Its origin is ascribed to **Hasegawa Kakugyō** (circa 1541–1646), who is also associated with the sect **Fusō-kyō**. His teachings were adopted and modified by Ito Jikigyo in the 18th century. Kotani Rokugyō (died 1841) expanded it into the concept of Moto-no-chichi-haha-kami, the divine father and mother of everything, who dwells on **Mount Fuji**. Tokudaiji Sangyō (died 1879), a former Buddhist priest, carried this a stage further after the **Meiji Restoration**. In cooperation with Shibata Hanamori (1809–1890), they successfully had it recognized by the Shinto Jimu-kyōku in 1873.

The goals originally set were to worship the three *kami* of creation, to worship "from afar" the **Kashikodokoro** in the Imperial Palace, to revere Mount Fuji, and to pray for the nation. Its goals were still to suppress human vanity, to eliminate academic controversies from religion, and to ensure or enforce these precepts, hence the name Jikkō (enforcement). The name Kakugyō, which means "block-discipline," is derived from the legend that Hasegawa stood on a block of wood for 2000 consecutive days seeking to attain the ability to release the spirit from the body (**ominuki**) so that the spirit could become united with, and receive the words of, the *kami*. Hence the strict image of the sect.

Jikkō-kyō's evolution through various leaders and periods is a complex piece of history, but after a schism, the mainline leadership went Tokudaiji Sangyo, who worked to make the sect compatible with the ideals of the Meiji government. He retired from the Buddhist priesthood and sent his colleague, Shibata Hanamori (who became the effectual founder of the modern version of the sect), to Tokyō to start Jikkō-Sha, which was to prepare Fuji-Do, as the sect had become known, to become a pure Shinto sect, stressing the virtues of loyalty and patriotism.

In 1872, the **Kyōbu-Sho** began its program of indoctrination and it was then that Tokudaiji and Shibata successfully sought recognition by the government for the sect. Jikkō-Sha was formally acknowledged in 1873 as a religious sect that could be supervised by the Shinto Jimu-kyōku. A headquarters was built in Tokyō in 1878. After Tokudaiji's death in 1879, the group became independent from the Jimu-kyōku in 1882 and was permitted to call itself Shinto Jikkō-kyō.

Shibata then became the first high priest, after which he structured Fuji-Do in such a way that it totally conformed to the ideology of the Meiji government. The headquarters are in Omiya City in Saitama Prefecture and its membership is around 100,000. Jikkō-kyō does not, however, have a shrine (**jinja**) either on or near Mount Fuji. It is a form of reverence from a distance. Members practice **divination**, spells, and invocations according to believers' requests, a clear reminder of its roots in the folk tradition. The sect is noted for its annual climb of Mount Fuji on August 3 by thousands of members attired in the white costume of **Heian period** pilgrims, shouting **Rokkon-shō-jō**, "purify the six organs of sense" (the eyes, ears, nose, tongue, body, and mind). *See also* MISOGI.

JIMMU TENNŌ. First legendary emperor and grandson of **Ninigi-no-mikoto** who reigned, according to the **mythology**, from 660 to

585 B.C.E. Narratives are recorded in the **Kojiki** (712) and the **Nihōn Shōki** (720). The honorific title Jimmu dates to the eighth century, prior to which he was referred to as Kamu-yamato-iware-hiko-no-mikoto, among other formal designations. Scholars have identified discrepancies in the two narratives of how he established control of the land of **Yamato**, leading in turn to Yamato hegemony over the entire Japanese archipelago.

Theories of Jimmu Tenno have a huge bearing on the understanding of the origin of both the **imperial household** and the Japanese race. One line of argument connects the **rice**-cultivating and metalworking Yayoi culture of Kyushū to its growth in the Kinai region, attributed partly to the work of a horse-riding race from Asia that settled in north Kyushū. It links also to the question of whether or not a kingdom called **Yamatai** actually existed independently of Yamato.

Other views suggest that Jimmu Tennō is a composite identity of Emperor Sujin, whose exploits resemble those of Jimmu Tenno, and Emperor Keitai (sixth century) who is said to have entered Yamato from Osaka and was enthroned in the Palace of Iware (Sakurai City, Nara Prefecture).

Under the strictures of **Kokka Shinto** (State Shinto), discussion of the origins of the imperial family was suppressed, as were discussions of the origin of the Japanese race. While the imperial household regulates all archaeological finds relating to such matters, there appears to be growing consensus that the imperial family most likely arrived in Yamato from Kyushū, Japan's link with the Asian mainland. Radical historians wish to affirm Asian origins of the imperial household. While historically this may set the records straight, it nevertheless has no material bearing upon the cult and culture that grew up around it as Japanese history unfolded, or how people of subsequent ages felt toward it. Origin and early development become less and less relevant to contemporary reality as institutions continue to evolve. *See also* EMPEROR SYSTEM.

JINGIHAKU. An office of the imperial court, traditionally held by the Yoshida and Shirakawa families, that bestowed authority to control shrines (**jinja**). They received the right to appoint shrines and priests in return for contributions received. The **Jingikan** absorbed these functions with the establishment of **Kokka Shinto** (State Shinto), and remained a titular position within the **imperial household** related to the imperial tutelary *kami.*

JINGI-IN (COLLEGE OF *KAMI*). Office of the Ministry of Home Affairs set up in 1940 to expand the **Jinja-Kyōku** in order to promote the use of **Kokka Shinto** (State Shinto) rituals for the enhancement of nationalism. It was abolished in 1945 through the **Shinto Directive** issued by the **Supreme Commander Allied Powers.**

JINGIKAN. The ancient government department of Shinto (*kami*) worship, which, along with the **Dajōkan**, formed the structure of government as defined by the **Taihō Ritsuryō**, the early code of practice and procedure issued in 701. It was restored in 1868 at the time of the **Meiji Restoration**, but became the **Jingishō** in 1871 and the **Kyōbushō** in 1872 before itself being abolished in 1877. *See also* KOKKA SHINTO.

JINGIRYŌ. Government budget for the support and upkeep of important shrines (**jinja**) as set up during the **Heian period** (794–1185).

JINGISHŌ. The Ministry of Shinto Affairs set up by the **Meiji Government** as part of the plan to establish **Kokka Shinto** (State Shinto), but which survived only from 1871 to 1872 before being replaced by other organs of state.

JINGŪ. Generic name for shrines (**jinja**) which have or had imperial connections. The character gu is also read as miya, which means palace. Famous on the list would be **Meiji Jingū** and Ise Jingū. It is sometimes used as a shortened way of referring to the **Grand Shrines of Ise** (Ise Jingū), known also as the **Kotai Jingū.**

JINGŪ BUNKO. The greatest library in Japan containing materials relating to the Shinto tradition. It includes holdings from the Inner and Outer of the **Grand Shrines of Ise** (Ise Jingū), and is now housed in its own building in Tokyō. The **Gekū** (Outer Shrine) Library (the Toyomiyazaki Bunko) was established in 1648, the collection having been assembled mostly by **Deguchi (Watarai) Nobuyoshi** (1615–1690). The **Naikū** (Inner Shrine) Library (the Hayashizaki Bunko) was set up in 1687.

The oldest records of emperors and deities go back to the eighth century. The Inner Shrine collection was consolidated in 1873 and placed under the supervision of the **Jingishō** (Ministry of Shinto Affairs), and thereafter under its successors. In 1906, a new building was erected and named the Jingū Bunko. The Outer Shrine collection was added in 1911.

The editorial office of the Koji Ruien moved its holdings there in 1914. Subsequent additions brought the collection up to 250,000 volumes. Authors who write on Shinto or related topics may send their works for the "pleasure of the *kami*." The library is open to the public.

JINGŪ HOSAIKAI. Society for offering gifts to the **Grand Shrines of Ise** (Ise Jingū), set up in 1889 to replace the dissolved sect **Jingū-kyō**, and predecessor of Tokyō Daijingu. It was one of the three organizations that merged to form the **Jinja Honcho** (the Association of Shinto Shrines) in 1945.

JINGU-JI. Joint shrines (**jinja**-temple) that grew out of the idea of the **assimilation of Buddhism and Shinto.** The idea started during the Nara period (710–794), reaching more concrete fulfillment in the early **Heian period** (794–1185). A document of the Tado-Jingū-ji records that, in 763, the *kami* known as Tado-no-kami (of the Tado Jinja in Tado-machi, Kuwana, Mie Prefecture) issued an oracle on this subject: "It is my fate to have been born a *kami* but I wish straightaway to practice the Buddhist oath, shed my *kami*-body and become a Buddha. But I am troubled without the ability to receive the necessary (good) karma. For this reason I desire that a place of (Buddhist) practice be established."

In response to this, a hall was erected for the purpose of training the *kami* in **Buddhism**, and this was the origin of the jingū-ji. The most well-known of the jingu-ji were Tado-jingu-ji, (already noted), the Kehi-jingū-ji in Echizen (Fukui Prefecture), the Nangu-jingu-ji in Mino (Gifu Prefecture), the **Atsuta-jingū-ji** (Nagoya city), and the **Kashima-jingū-ji** in Hitachi province (Ibaraki Prefecture). These were all separated by order of the Meiji government in 1868 on the principle of **Shinbutsu-bunri**, the separation of *kami* and Buddha.

JINGŪ KŌGŌ, JINGŪ (OR JINGO), EMPRESS. The empress (reigned 201–269) and widow of Emperor Chuai (reigned 192–200), who served as "regent" between Chuai and **Emperor Ōjin** (reigned 270–310) during a 56-year period when technically there was no emperor. She is identified as the daughter of Okinaga no Sukkune and Princess Katsuragi no Takanuka. After a vigorous campaign against the Kumaso clan of Kyushū, she set sail from Osaka, after worshipping at **Sumiyoshi Taisha**, to subjugate a rebellion in the Korean province of Silla. The fact of a fiefdom of Japan in Korea suggests that Japan had a stable form of government along with sufficient economic power and military capacity to mount the invasion. Her son and the future emperor, Ōjin, was born to her after her return to Japan, but she held power until her death.

Like **Jimmu Tennō** (reigned 660–585 B.C.E.), Japan's legendary first emperor, according to the **mythology**, her identity is subject to critical scrutiny and she is considered by some scholars to have a composite identity consisting of several shamanist rulers, such as **Himiko**. She is also linked to various Japanese campaigns in fourth-century Korea, much later than the legendary dates. Like many other doubted figures of history, most critics admit that even if she did not exist, someone like her must have existed in order to explain other material facts that defy any alternative interpretation. *See also* EMPEROR SYSTEM; WOMEN.

JINGŪ-KYŌ. A sect attached to the **Grand Shrines of Ise** (Ise Jingū), founded in 1872 by Urata Nagatami (1840–1893). It was never recognized as an official **Kyōha Shinto** (Sect Shinto) sect. It was involved in the **Taikyō Senpu Undō**, the great missionary drive of the early years after the **Meiji Restoration** between 1870 and 1874 but was dissolved in September 1899. It became first the **Jingū Hosai-kai**, a religious and educational organization that became a founding group of the **Jinja Honchō** (the Association of Shinto Shrines) after the **Pacific War** (World War II). It subsequently regained religious status and was transformed into Tokyō Daijingū.

JINJA. Generic name for the place where a *kami* is present and is revered. It is also read in older Japanese reading as yashiro. The word is made up of two characters: jin, a Chinese-influenced reading of the character read in old Japanese as *kami*; and sha, meaning place. Therefore it refers to a place that has the presence of a divine being within or around it. A jinja is territorially defined through the sphere of influence of the *kami* revered in it. **Buddhist** temples do not have territorial responsibility the way in which shrines and *kami* cover specific areas of land.

On such sites, various buildings (**Jinja Shaden**) came to be erected, using the appropriate style of **architecture** for the *kami*, for the purpose of revering the *kami* and performing appropriate **rituals** in a setting that is purified, clean, and well maintained. Generally, there are three main buildings, the **haiden** or worship hall, the **heiden** or hall of offerings, and the **honden** that is closed to all but the officiating priests (**kannushi**). The distinctive gate that marks entry to the shrine precincts, the **torii**, is a unique feature whose origins are uncertain.

Nothing impure may enter the shine grounds, and certainly nothing connected with death, the ultimate form of impurity, as **Izangi-no-mikoto** discovered when he visited the **Yomi-no-kuni** in search of his dead wife, **Izanami-no-mikoto**. Bones and remains may be brought to a Buddhist temple, but never within the grounds of a shrine. *See also* ARCHITECTURE IN SHINTO; FINANCE OF SHRINES; ICHI-NO-MIYA; JINJA FUKKYŪ; JINJA GAPPEI; JINJA HONCHŌ; JINJA KYOKU; JINJA SHINTO; JOINT SHRINES; KEGARE; MASSHA; MATSURI; MIKO; MIKOSHI; SAMPAI; SHAKAKU-SEIDO; SHIKINEN SENGŪ; TAMA-GAKI; TSUMI; UJIKO; YUISHO.

JINJA FUKKYŪ. A pre-**Pacific War** (World War II) **Kokka Shinto** (State Shinto) term meaning "Shrine Restoration," according to which, the *kami* of a shrine (**jinja**) was enshrined in another shrine with which it had been merged, thus "restoring it" by means of a verbal device. It was a cosmetic act to alleviate the misery caused by the forced merger of shrines under the **Jinja Gappei** (Jinja Seirei, shrine merger) campaign of the Meiji government, which sought to rid the country of all but the most prestigious-looking shrines. There was widespread local resistance to the practice, as there was to the entire movement to reduce the number of shrines nationwide. Postwar restoration of actual buildings took place where popular feeling remained strong and committed.

JINJA GAPPEI. The shrine (**jinja**) merger movement carried out from the early years of the **Kokka Shinto** (State Shinto) period in which mergers were forced in the interests of improving the image of Shinto as a national cult. The number of shrines was gradually reduced from over 170,000 to fewer than 70,000. In 1900, the Bureau of Shinto Affairs raised the status of shrines by declaring that Shinto was simply a patriotic institution. From 1906, the government began to escalate improvement programs for small shrines and **minsha**, which in turn raised the question of merging shrines.

The objective was simply to limit the number of shrines, making them impressive and fewer, easier to control, and more useful instruments of government policy. A set of rigorous and difficult standards was issued which had to be met if the shrine was to be permitted to continue its existence. Inspectors were dispatched nationwide, which led to the closure and abolition of many, with their *kami* being removed to new locations.

The movement was referred to by several names. There was the term goshi (joint enshrinement), jinja gappei (shrine merger), and jinja seirei (shrine consolidation). The latter was the official term, which concealed the severity of what was taking place. Gappei meant that the *kami* were being transferred to other shrines. Village shrines were thus consolidated into one, and traces of local shrines were mostly removed. The name of the consolidated shrine would reflect the community or town in order to strengthen the unity of Shinto and state. Between 1903 and 1920, the total number of shrines was reduced by 77,899. The movement created great resistance, reaching its zenith around 1911, after which it lost momentum. In fact, between 1903 and 1920, about 41 percent of village unranked shrines were abolished on the grounds that they had no recorded historical lineage (**yuishō**).

There was considerable hostility to the movement, on the grounds that it was weakening links between people and their communities and shrines, not making them stronger. It was argued further that filial piety was being ignored and the essence of the nation's life and history was being damaged in the process. Consequently, the mergers were damaging to patriotic feeling. Indeed, it was pointed out that the interference with the folk tradition might be damaging to the entire nation. The loss of local **festivals** was one tangible result, and it is recorded that many villages appeared depressed at traditional festival times. Some areas simply refused to cooperate. The government was forced to concede, and by the beginning of the Taisho period (after 1912), shrine mergers were not demanded, but prohibitions remained on their reconstitution. However, after the defeat of Japan in 1945 and the subsequent liberalization policy, many shrines were in fact reconstituted.

The entire episode helps to underline the degree of artificiality that existed even in the concept of State Shinto, and that the nation and its shrines were far from uniform in acknowledging its existence. It is best described as an extensive and highly controversial program that did serious, and in some cases, irreparable damage to the entire Shinto culture.

JINJA HONCHŌ. The Association of Shinto Shrines (as it is described in English) created after 1945 to replace the various bodies that administered shrine (**jinja**) business. When the Allied Occupation authorities decided to abolish the **Jingi-in**, leaders from the three major private groups, the Dai Nihon Jingikai (Great Japan Association for the *kami*), the Kōten Kokyu-shō (Center for Research on Imperial Rites) and the **Jingū-Hosaikai** (Grand Shrine Service Association), met and merged to form the Jinja Honchō.

Located originally near to **Kokugakuin University**, it moved in 1988 to a custom-designed building within the grounds of **Meiji Jingū**. Its principal tasks are centered on overseeing 80,000 shrines and their rank and status and that of the 20,000 priests (**kannushi**) who serve within them. While a priest may have a rank within a shrine, he or she will also have a rank (**Kai-i**) based on examinations supervised by the Jinja Honcho. These ranks are reflected in the color of robes (**saifuku**), particularly the hakama, that may be worn.

The Jinja Honchō espouses no particular form of Shinto, but merely sees itself supervising a nationwide network of shrines, supreme of which are the **Grand Shrines of Ise** (Ise Jingū). Each individual shrine is a **shūkyō hōjin** (a religious corporate person in law) in its own right, which is a reminder of the immense degree of local particularism that remains characteristic of Shinto. Only 80 percent of the nation's shrines are affiliated. Notable unaffiliated shrines are **Yasukuni Jinja**, the **Nikkō Tōshōgū**, the **Fushimi Inari Taisha**, and several regional networks that supervise their own affairs.

The modern organization is also responsible for ensuring that priests are properly qualified, and that unorthodox practices are contained. *See also* JINGIKAN; JINGISHŌ; JINJA-KYOKU; KYŌBUSHŌ.

JINJA KYOKU. Pre-war Ministry of Home Affairs (Naimusho) Department handling Shinto affairs after 1900, responsible for the regulation of shrines (**jinja**) and priests nationwide. The Ministry of Education's

Shukyō Kyōku dealt with all of Japan's religions except Shinto, which had been declared not to be a religion. Since the abolition of the Ministry of Religion (**Kyōbushō**) in 1877, the **Shaji Kyōku** had concerned itself with Shinto as well as the other religions.

The Jinja Kyōku has been viewed as the formal beginning of **Kokka Shinto** (State Shinto) as, in North American parlance, a "civic religion," which is understandable but inadequate. That view fails to grasp what its establishment represented, namely, the collapse of the entire State Shinto ideal and the transference of its ideological objectives out of the Ministry of Home Affairs to the Ministry of Education. This in turn was to enforce its role in the stimulation of militarism, a task totally under the control of that ministry. The Ministry of Home Affairs continued to administer shrines through the Jinja Kyōku, the highest ranked of its five bureaus.

JINJA SHADEN. Generic name for shrine (**jinja**) buildings, such as worship hall, **kagura** den, shrine offices (shamusho), and other buildings erected within shrine precincts for particular purposes. The principal buildings in most shrines are the **honden** (inner sanctuary), the **heiden** (hall of offerings), and the **haiden** (hall of worship). There may also be a noritoden (hall of ceremonies), and a **kagura** hall for ceremonial dances. *See also* ARCHITECTURE IN SHINTO.

JINJA SHINTO. Term used mostly by scholars as a classifier for mainstream Shrine Shinto as distinct from **Kyōha Shinto** (Sect Shinto) and **Kokka Shinto** (State Shinto). It is of postwar coinage, although the **Shinto Directive** of the **Supreme Commander Allied Powers** uses it in a rather inconsistent manner. There is also controversy about how the term Shinto itself should be understood.

JINNŌ SHŌTŌKI. **Kitabatake Chikafusa** (1293–1354) authored this work, the *Direct Descent of the Divine Sovereigns*, to chronicle the development of Japan from the age of the *kami* to the mid-14th century. It opens with the famous claim, "Dainippon wa *kami* no kuni" (Great Japan is the land of the *kami*), ever ruled by the descendants of **Amaterasu-ōmikami**. Unlike India and China, which had undergone major dynastic revolutions, Japan had remained a land of peace and tranquility under imperial benevolence, according to the author's understanding of history. The argument also claimed that when Amaterasu-ōmikami mandated the imperial family, other families were given privileged status to assist the imperial family. The **Nakatomi** clan (later the Fujiwara family) was authorized as the Shinto court ritualists.

The entire document was in fact a polemical tract that sought to legitimize the Southern Court's claims to legitimacy over the Northern Court, a legitimacy which Kitabatake himself took to be self-evident. Kitabatake's work was also extremely reactionary and his views on the military houses were most probably not well received. However, the text was hailed by succeeding generations as a classical study in imperial loyalty, and was praised by the **Kokugaku** (National Learning) scholars of the Edo period. The concept of Japan as a land of the *kami* was popularized, and certainly became the view of the **Kamakura Shogunate** after its establishment, and Kitabatake's famous sentence is still quoted. *See also* EMPEROR SYSTEM.

JISHA BUGYO. Edo period (1615–1868) magistrates in charge of shrines (**jinja**) and temples who were charged with the task of ensuring that the ownership of shrine lands was protected and the shrine buildings were periodically renewed. This was part of the Edo period management system for shrines and temples.

JISHA-HATSUIN-NO-GI. Ritual—one of many that comprise the funeral rites of a deceased emperor—that focuses on the transport of an imperial hearse to its funeral site. *See also* EMPEROR SYSTEM.

JISHUKU. Period of self-restraint, a term used in 1988 during the period leading up to the death of **Emperor Shōwa** (reigned 1926–1989), and during which all celebratory events, including weddings, year-end parties, and national days, were cancelled. The celebratory color red was removed from retail outlets. Even red beans became scarce. The impact on the economy of the cancellation of about 300,000 weddings created hardship for hotels and restaurant owners, for whom the year-end season and the ensuing New Year festivities were normally important sources of income. While the Japanese economy had been slipping toward recession, it has been argued that the period of jishūku acted as a trigger mechanism that speeded up the process. Criticism of the government and the Liberal Democratic

Party (LDP) was voiced on the grounds that the period of restraint was being manipulated in an attempt to restore emperor worship. True of false, no trace of emperor worship appeared to revive, and once all the obsequies were past, business and social life speedily returned to normal.

JIUN ONKŌ (OR SONJA, 1718–1804). A popular religious leader of the mid-Edo period (1615–1868) and a **Shingon Buddhist** monk who had a wide-ranging eclectic philosophy comprised of **Zen** meditation and Shingon esoteric practice. He developed an interest in the **Kokugaku** (National Learning) movement, which he began comparing with early Buddhist texts. He was eventually considered Japan's greatest Sanskrit scholar; his calligraphy is judged by some to have the style of Edo period (1615–1868) Zen.

Jiun spent most of his life as a priest of the Shingon Ritsu branch. He founded the Shingon sect known as Shingon Shoboritsu and a syncretistic sect known as Unden Shinto, which was a Shingon/Shinto union. Although never a pure Shinto believer, he was aware of its significance, and incorporated elements of the two traditions to which he seemed closest.

JIZŌ. Buddhist figure linked with Amida. It is also connected to the **ta-no-kami**, and frequently found in statues in temples at country road intersections. Various forms of Jizo are to be found, some in the presence of another important figure of Japanese **Buddhism**, the bodhisattva **Kannon**, a male figure in China but a female figure in Japan.

JŌE. Similar to the **kariginu**, it is worn both by priests (**kannushi**) and by lay people taking part in festivals (**matsuri**).

JOEI LAW (1232). The Council of State of the Kamakura period (1185–1333) issued the Joei ordinance requiring that shrines (**jinja**) were to be maintained in good order and used for showing reverence to the *kami*.

JOGAKU. The title given by scholars during the Edo period (1615–1868) to the study of the history and culture of the Nara period (710–794).

JŌGAN GISHIKI. A late ninth-century text which, along with the **Engishiki,** stylized imperial Shinto **rituals** and standardized shrine rituals and **Norito** (ritual invocations) for all related shrines (**jinja**).

JOINT SHRINES. A development among shrines (**jinja**) of the **Heian period** (794–1185) called sosha (meaning joint shrine), at which the worship of numerous *kami* could take place as **Aido-no-kami.** The *kami* of an entire province could be "invited" to a single provincial sosha and joint worship would be offered. In the same way, a large family would "invite" all the *kami* with which they had a relationship to a single clan sosha for special ceremonies. It also enabled government officials to offer worship in the most prominent shrine of the region.

JŌMON CULTURE. The food-gathering stage of Japanese civilization, from 7,000 to 250 B.C.E., named after cord-marked (jomon) pottery found in most Jomon sites. It was a nonmetal, but not totally a hunting and gathering, culture. Simple forms of agriculture appeared to have existed, along with other recognizable elements such as shamanistic practices, concepts of nature and the divine, and fishing and shellfish gathering, plus certain basic features of language.

The entire period can be subdivided into numerous phases. Generally speaking, the period corresponds to the pit-dwelling stage found in many civilizations prior to entry into the Bronze Age. Because of its agricultural activity, it represents the beginnings of a settled lifestyle, and consequently the birth of the communities whose self-understanding eventually found expression in the **rituals** of a **folk religion** that gradually evolved into Shinto.

JOTOSAI. When the ridgepoles of a new building are set in place on the roof, this ceremony of purification (**harai**) is performed for the safe completion of the project.

JUNPAI/JUNREI. A pilgrimage conducted by moving systematically and in order through a sequence of sacred places. While principally associated with **Shugendō,** many shrines (**jinja**) are also deeply involved. The **Kumano Junrei** is particularly famous. In **Buddhism,** people wearing the appropriate **Heian period** (794–1185) white costume, almost all adhering to **Shingon Buddhism,** are referred to as Henro as they traverse the Shikoku Junrei, a circuit of 88 temples.

– K –

KADA NO ARIMARO (1706–1751). Kokugaku (National Learning) scholar and poet. He was the nephew and adopted son of **Kada no Azumamaro** (1697–1736) and succeeded his father in the service of the shogunate. He was placed under arrest because a work of his describing the harvest **rituals** of emperors offended the government. He also clashed in opinions with **Kamo no Mabuchi** (1699–1769) over the quality of the **Man'yōshū** compared to the **Shin Kokinshū**, which he claimed was less refined than the latter. His most famous work on poetics was known as the *Kokka Hachiron* and was completed in 1742.

KADA NO AZUMAMARO (1699–1736). Early and important symbol of the **Kokugaku** (National Learning) movement, scholar, and poet whose family had served at the **Fushimi Inari Jinja** in Kyōto. He was educated in the writing of **waka** poems and in the culture of Shinto. After serving three years at the court of Emperor Reigen (reigned 1663–1687), he was summoned to Edo (now Tokyō) to work in the library of the shogun.

His work on the classics became widely recognized, and after having his son and successor **Kada no Arimaro** (1706–1751) assume his library duties, he presented a famous petition to the shogun, asking that he be permitted to found a school of national learning. He was mentor to **Kamo no Mabuchi** (1697–1769), who brought together Azumamaro's intuitive approach with the scholastic methods of **Keichū** (1640–1701).

KADOMATSU. A **New Year**'s decoration made of bamboo poles, varying in length but seldom over 1.5 meters long, decorated with the evergreen Japanese pine. Homes and businesses as well as schools, shrines (**jinja**), and temples usually display these, standing one on each side of the door or entrance. On account of the expense of making them, not infrequently a large sheet of paper bearing New Year Greetings and the picture of a kadomatsu replaces the real object.

KAEMPFER, ENGELBERT (1651–1716). German-born physician and historian who visited Japan between 1691 and 1692 as part of the Edo Sampu, the annual tribute visit by the Dutch factory (trading house) chief to the shogun in Edo. His careful accounts of his travels provide a large amount of accurate and valuable information about Edo period (1615–1868) Japan. In spite of his sharp insight, his best description of Shinto was as being merely Japan's ancient idol worship. As in the case of other likeminded criticism, Shinto proved it had a more profound dimension not readily accessible to a simplistic Western categorization.

KAGURA. Ceremonial dance to please the *kami* which, although having a clear Shinto origin and being related to **chinkon**, is now a recognized form of Japanese performing art in its own right. It refers to any performance involving masked dancing that is part of the annual **festival** of a shrine (**jinja**). It is one of three acknowledged categories of Japanese folk performing arts (minzoku geino).

Many of kagura's features indicate its roots in Shinto **rituals**. It is essentially an invocation of a *kami* followed by a dance and prayer for the betterment of human life. There are many forms of kagura, and there is a relation between kagura and **chinkon**. It dates from at least the ninth century, and has evolved into many forms. The paradigmatic dance was performed by **Ame-uzume-no-mikoto** when she enticed **Amaterasu-ōmikami** out of the **Ame-no-Iwato** in which she was hiding. Interesting forms of kagura include Shishi Kagura (Lion Kagura), using a lion mask, or Kojin Kagura, in which mediums enter trances while dancing. This is typified in the form of kagura found in the former **Kyōha Shinto** (Sect Shinto) sect **Tenri-kyō**, known as **Kagura Zutone** (salvation dance). Since dance forms relate to **shamanism** and **asceticism**, they have given rise to enormous varieties of ritual with deep religious meaning. *See also* MUSIC IN SHINTO; NOH.

KAGURA DEN. Traditionally, kagura was performed outside and in front of the shrine buildings, but for practical reasons it was moved indoors. The use of a staging area occurred also in the case of **Noh** and other performing arts.

KAGURA-UTA. Songs composed to accompany Shinto **ritual dances**. They were incorporated as part of the **Daijōsai** ceremonies from the ninth century, becoming an independent art form by the 11th century.

KAGURA ZUTONE. Salvation **dance** invented by the founder and performed by believers of the former **Kyōha Shinto** (Sect Shinto) sect **Tenri-kyō**, and considered by the government of the time to be subversive because it was created to be enjoyed by ordinary people.

KAIBARA EKKEN (1630–1714). Confucian scholar of the Edo period (1615–1868), born in Fukuoka, who became a ronin (masterless samurai) after a disagreement with his feudal lord. The next daimyo, Kuroda Mitsuyuki, restored his stipend, and he was sent to study in Kyōto. His knowledge of Chinese medicine was extensive and his sense of the natural equally profound, expressed in his book, *Yojokun*, a popular guide to keeping good health. His authorship of the *Onna Daigaku*, a manual for the moral training of **women**, has been called into question by some critical strands of scholarship. While not directly committed to any specific view of Shinto, his influence in social ethics, and the closeness to nature that is evident in his writing, places him in the mainstream of Edo period intellectual history.

KAI-I. Four ranks of quality or merit awarded to priests by the modern **Jinja Honchō** (Association of Shinto Shrines). The ranks are: first, Jōkai, or "Purity"; second, Meikai, "Brightness"; third, Seikai, "Righteousness"; fourth, Chokkai, "Uprightness." These are awarded on the basis of examination, experience, and recommendation. Other honors bearing greater status are given to highly ranked senior priests (**kannushi**) and high priests (**gūji**).

KAJIN MATSURI. The *kami* of seafaring and fishing is celebrated in seaports and similar areas: **Munakata Taisha** in Kyushū and **Sumiyoshi Taisha** in Osaka, from where **Empress Jingū** left for her Korean expedition, are famous for the festival celebrated annually.

KAKINOMOTO NO HITOMARU (CIRCA 685–705). The most important poet of the **Man'yōshū** anthology whose view of **nature** and the natural have been seen as the expression of the original, and by implication, Shinto spirituality of the ancient Japanese. Scholarship about him is complex, but he is universally ranked as one of Japan's three greatest poets, along with Saigyo and Basho, if not the greatest. When trying to develop a theory of Japanese culture, **Kokugaku** (National Learning) scholars often pointed back to the simple and direct sensitivities of the Man'yoshū as the finest expression of the Japanese spirit in ancient times.

KAKURIYO. Hidden world of the *kami* as against the visible world of ordinary life (**utsushiyo**), as taught in modern Shinto theology.

KAMADO-GAMI. *Kami* of the hearth, fire, and family protection. Although *kami* of fire, they are also linked to agriculture. Traditionally, they were known as Okitsuhiko and Okitsuhime. They are also known as Okamasama and Kojin.

KAME-URA. A form of **bokusen**, or **divination**, by tortoise shell, as practiced in the **Kyōha Shintō** (Sect Shinto) sect **Ontake-kyō**, and used also in the selection of the Yukiden and Sukiden, the two fields that must be selected for the performance of the imperial accession rite known as the **Daijōsai**.

KAMI. The object of reverence in Shinto culture, translated into English in a variety of ways, none completely adequate, but the most inappropriate of which is "god." Divinity, the divine, or the mysterious are better candidates because they are less specific in the imagery they generate, particularly to Western observers.

The etymology of the Japanese is unclear, but the term certainly came to refer to a unique force or power in nature, animals, or people that engendered attitudes of reverence, fear, or gratitude in those who perceived it. **Motoori Norinaga** (1730–1801), the **Kokugaku** (National Learning) scholar, made the statement that anything which filled a human being with wonder and awe might be referred to as a *kami*. His observation is reminiscent of what the neo-Kantian philosopher Rudolf Otto, in his phenomenological approach to the divine, called the *mysterium tremendum et fascinans*, in his pioneering work *Das Heilige* (*The Idea of the Holy*, 1917).

It can only be assumed that the ancient Japanese, living in a fascinating world of vast live volcanoes, surging rivers, powerful waterfalls, and other mysteries, felt that they were in an environment inhabited by *kami*. This too is probably the origin of the expression that opens the **Jinno Shōtōki** of **Kitabatake Chikafusa** (1293–1354): Japan was the "*kami* no kuni," the land of the *kami*, or a land filled with mysterious wonders.

Japanese civilization evolved with a perception of the *kami* as those who belonged to the **Kami of heaven**, head of whom became **Amaterasu-ōmikami**, and those of the **earthly** *kami*, head of whom became **Sarutahiko-ōkami**. It would be incorrect to say simply that the heavenly *kami* were **mythology**-based and politically more significant, while the earthly *kami* were clan-based tutelary figures. The overlap is complex, as is the concept itself, and the distinction is far from either clear or logical. Nevertheless, it is not completely unintelligible.

Kami are for the most part benign but, if distressed, can be troublesome, and unless pacified in some way—through **chinkon**, or by a propitious act—may wreak havoc. This is illustrated in the case of **Sugawara Michizane** (845–903), known subsequently as **Tenjin**, the *kami* of learning, and the great disasters that befell Kyōto when he was unjustly exiled. There is also the concept of the **nigimitama** (gentle), and **aramitama** (rough) aspects of the soul of a *kami*. **Empress Jingū** (reigned 201–269) embarked on her mission to the Korean peninsula, leaving the gentle soul behind. Finally, the Shinto ideal of spirituality is reunion of the human with the *kami* from which the human is derived.

To most Japanese, *kami* are local in their status and identity and derive their meaning from historical community rites. This fact lies behind the failure of **Suiga Shinto** and what came to be called **Kokka Shinto** (State Shinto) to introduce the idea of an all-embracing *kami* as a kind of divine cosmic principle. The Shinto *kami* remain localized and particular in their functions and in the **festivals** that celebrate them. *See also* ARAMITAMA; IKIGAMI; JICHINSAI; KAMI-ARISAI; KAMI-DANA; KAMI-KAKUSHI; KAMI-KAZE; KAMI-MUKAE; *KAMI* OF HEAVEN AND EARTH; KAMI-OKURI; KAMI-YO; NIGIMITAMA; SAMPAI; SHINJIN-GŌITSU; SHINJIN-KIITSU; SHOSHIN-NO-HI; ZŌKA-SANSHIN.

KAMI-ARISAI. **Festival** of the return of the *kami* to **Izumo Taisha**, held annually in October. Bonfires are lit on the beach to welcome the returning *kami*, which are then transported to the shrine (**jinja**) buildings in darkness, and order is restored in the land.

KAMI-DANA. Family altar (shelf) for reverencing tutelary and family *kami*. The offerings placed on it—water, **sake**, **rice**, and salt—are changed daily. These may be seen also in some traditional Japanese restaurants, especially sushi restaurants, **sumo** heya (stables) near the **dohyō**, and even in railway stations, police stations, and on company premises. Revering the appropriate *kami* is considered to afford protection to these activities and enterprises.

KAMI-KAKUSHI. Literally meaning "being hidden by a *kami*," kami-kakushi refers to the sudden and inexplicable disappearance of someone from his or her home, attributed normally to the work of a **tengu**, a mountain spirit capable of taking many forms, or **foxes**. Frequently, sick children disappeared in this way, and the child was expected to return after a period of time during which the child visited the **reikai**, the world of the spirits. Like belief in **kitsune-tsuki** (fox-possession), this belief still belongs to the folklore of rural communities, and still survives in some form. *See also* SHAMANISM IN SHINTO.

KAMI-KAZE. "Divine winds" that saved Japan twice, when the Mongols under Kublai Khan failed to invade in 1274 and in 1281. Japan was perceived to have been saved by the weather and the divine winds, the "kami-kaze," as **Nichiren** (1222–1282), the Kamakura period (1185–1333) Buddhist leader, designated them. The name was revived as an inspirational word for the young suicide pilots who tried to halt the American approach at the end of the **Pacific War** (World War II) by crashing explosive-loaded planes into U.S. ships. Most of the modern kami-kaze were barely out of high school when called upon to serve the nation. Their sacrificial death was one among many factors that had the effect of driving survivors to rebuild the nation, and which, at the same time, helped to create the prevalent postwar pacifist mood.

KAMI-MUKAE. The ritual invitation of the *kami* to alight on the evergreen **sakaki** in order to begin a Shinto ritual of purification (**harai**). *See also* KAMI-ARISAI; OKURI-BU.

KAMI **OF HEAVEN AND EARTH.** In **norito**, ritually intoned invocations of the *kami*, the formula "Amatsu kami, Kunitsu kami, Yao yorozu no kamitachi" is used, referring to the *kami* of heaven (headed by **Amaterasu-ōmikami**), the *kami* of earth (headed by **Sarutahiko-ōkami**), and the great myriad of *kami*. The distinction goes back to the **mythology**, but nowhere is there any consistent explanation of the meaning of the distinction. *See also* EARTHLY *KAMI.*

KAMI-OKURI. The ritual sending off of a *kami* after a purification ritual (**harai**) has been performed. It is the reverse of **kami-mukae**, when the priest in charge invites the *kami* by a vocalized sound known as keihitsu.

KAMI-YO. The age of the *kami*, the pre-historical age as recorded in the **mythology** of the **Kojiki** (712) and the **Nihon Shōki** (720).

KAMMU, EMPEROR. Fiftieth emperor according to the legendary count (born 737; reigned 781–806) whose reign was significant because during it, the capital was moved from Nara—first to Nagaokakyō, and finally to Heiankyō (Kyōto)—in order to prevent Buddhist monks from interfering in courtly matters. This ushered in the **Heian period** (794–1185). However, to both **Saichō** (767–822), founder of **Tendai Buddhism**, and to **Kūkai** (774–835), founder of **Shingon Buddhism**, he extended great largesse.

KAMO JINJA. Two important shrines (**jinja**) in Kyōto, linked in various ways, particularly by names. The one located in Kita Ward is the Kamo Wakeikazuchi Jinja, commonly referred to as Kami-Gamo Jinja (upper shrine), and is the place of reverence for Kamo-wakeikazuchi-no-kami. The other, located in Sakyō Ward, the Kamo Mioya Jinja, is known as Shimo-Gamo Jinja (lower shrine), and is the place of reverence for Tamayorihime-no-mikoto and Taketsunumi-no-mikoto, the parents of Tamayorihime.

One legend dates the shrines to 678, while others take them back to the legendary first emperor, **Emperor Jimmū** (reigned 660–585 B.C.E.). They are certainly old, and gained great prestige during the **Heian period** (794–1185), when they received endowments and other imperial benefits. The famous **Aoi Matsuri** (Hollyhock **Festival**) is one event for which they are well known, and is one of the major cultural events of the nation.

KAMO NO MABUCHI (1697–1769). Scholar of the **Kokugaku** (National Learning) movement and spiritual mentor to **Motoori Norinaga** (1730–1801). He was the son of a Shinto priest in Shizuoka, where he received training in composing **waka** (a form of Japanese poetry). Showing precocious talent, he grew to become very learned in **Confucianism**, Chinese learning, and in the Japanese classics. In 1733, he left his wife and his children and went to Kyōto to study under **Kada no Azumamaro** (1669–1736).

When Azumamaro died, Mabuchi moved to Edo (Tokyō) and began teaching the classics. Through reputation and introductions, he succeeded **Kada no Arimaro** (1706–1751), the nephew of Azumamaro, as Japanese literature tutor to Tayasu Munetake (1715–1771), son of Shogun Tokugawa Yoshimune (ruled 1716–1745). During this period, Mabuchi exerted an enormous influence on the revived study of the Japanese classics. His commentaries on the **Man'yōshū**, the eighth-century collection of Japanese verse and the oldest existing anthology of Japanese writings of its kind, dates to this period. The goal of his work was to combine the philological approach of **Keichū** (1640–1701) with the value approach of Kada no Azumamaro. He tried to revive a simple sense of what the Japanese felt about life and the world before **Buddhism** and Confucianism began defining it for them.

He understood Shinto as simplicity and spontaneity. As a poet in the classical mold, he tried to influence Japanese poetic style but failed to revive the long poem form; however, this was of little account since his main contribution to the National Learning movement was created through the way he tried to expound and interpret the mind of ancient poets. The expositions and explanations of the text of the Man'yōshū provided the linguistic, literary, and philological basis for the subsequent work of Motoori Norinaga (1730–1801), his most famous disciple and successor as the movement's leader.

KAMPEISHA. Highly ranked government shrines (**jinja**) of the **Kokka Shinto** (State Shinto) period distinguished by their receiving offerings from the **Jingikan**, in effect, from the **imperial household**. The title in the Meiji period (1868–1912) State Shinto system was linked to shrines (**jinja**) holding the title Taisha (great shrine).

KANADA TOKUMITSU (1863–1919). *See* P. L. KYŌDAN.

KANDOKORO. Shrine lands given as endowments to generate income, dating to the sixth century, for which the term kanbe is also used. The general meaning is in principle the same as **ando** and **hafuri**, other similar forms of shrine support.

KANJO. Invitation and proposal for the enshrinement of a *kami*.

KANKOKU-HEISHA. The official list of government and national shrines as designated under the **Kokka Shinto** (State Shinto) system of the Meiji period (1868–1912).

KANMURI. Special small black hat worn by priests (**kannushi**) in full vestments (such as ikan or **saifuku**) for important ceremonies. *See also* ASAGUTSU; HAKAMA; HŌ; KARIGINU.

KANNAGARA. Following the will and way of the *kami* is the root meaning, and was used as a linking concept in the form of kannagara-no-michi (the way of kannagara) to identify the formally organized system of shrines (**jinja**). The purpose was to distinguish them from the mass of **folk religion** that accompanies Shinto and shrines in different parts of the country. The **Jinja Honchō** (Association of Shinto Shrines) defines it as an "adverb modifying authoritative actions of a deity (*kami*) meaning divinely, solemnly, or sublimely." The intent is identical, namely to underline the distinction between **Jinja Shinto** and **Kyōha Shinto**.

KANNAGARA JINJA. In 1997, the Kannagara Dojo (a center for the practice of **aikido**) in Granite Falls, Seattle, Washington, was granted the status of **bunsha** of **Tsubaki Ōkami Yashiro** (Tsubaki Grand Shrine). The first honorary high priest was the late high priest of Tsubaki Grand Shrine, **Yukitaka**; he is now succeeded by his son, Yukiyasu. It was founded by the Rev. Koiichi Barrish, the first non-Japanese ever to be licensed as a **Jinja Shinto** priest to perform **rituals** and ceremonies.

Although some of its members and adherents are Japanese or of Japanese extraction, the majority are Americans of various backgrounds with an interest in the daily practice of **misogi** and **chinkon**. It is therefore the first clear instance of Shinto having found a congenial context in order to flourish in a non-Japanese, in this case, Western, setting. It also provides evidence for the proposition that Shinto has preserved many elements of ancient civilization that still have a universal appeal. The idea that a Japanese shrine (**jinja**) could have branches in a non-Japanese environment was argued by critics in Japan to be impossible and by critics outside of Japan to be undesirable. However, another shrine was established by a white American: Shinmei Jinja, in Vancouver, Canada, in 1999. *See also* SHINTO OUTSIDE JAPAN.

KANNAMESEI. *See* AKI MATSURI.

KANNARAU. A word seldom seen in modern writings, it refers to people who behave in a manner pleasing to the *kami*, and who in so doing, learn from them.

KANNON. A figure of popular **Buddhism**, known in India as Avalokitesvara (in Sanskrit) and in China as Guanyin, but with no specific sect affiliation. In combination with **Jizo**, Kannon is understood to be the personification of infinite compassion and capable of protecting anyone from any form of peril.

Originally revered in India and China as a bodhisattva, and therefore as male, Kannon in Japan became steadily feminized, transforming from the mustached figure of the Nara period statues to the Maria-Kannon invented by the "hidden Christians" of the 17th century. While not ever a part of the Shinto pantheon, Kannon and Jizo are often found together on Shinto-Buddhist sites, and the feminization suggests the steady cultural transformation of the deity from India and China into the Japanese paradigm of what the Japanese thought a *kami* should look like.

In addition, the ability of Kannon to appear in many forms and to perform miracles provided a natural bridgehead to Japanese **folk religion**. In the **Lotus Sutra**, one chapter explains 33 manifestations in which Kannon can appear. This seems to have added to the popularity of the figure. The most famous statues of Kannon are the seventh-century wooden figure in the Yumedono (Hall of Dreams) in the Horyu-ji, the temple in Nara, and the 1001 statues of the Thousand-armed Kannon in the Sanjusangendo, a 12th-century temple in Kyōto.

KANNUSHI. General term of reference to Shinto priests. Along with shinkan, meaning "servants of the *kami*," it is nowadays taken to refer to priests in general. However, it originally referred to those performing special priestly functions at a **festival**, standing between the people and the *kami*. At some large shrines (**jinja**) the title became institutionalized, for example, at shrines such as the two **Kamo**, the **Iwashimizu Hachiman**, or the **Kasuga** shrines during the **Heian period** (794–1185). These kannushi became the head priests, later (and still) known as **gūji**.

Once certain families had established themselves in office, the title of *kannushi* became hereditary. Thus certain families came to be closely associated with particular shrines. This is how the shake (major priestly clans) evolved. The best known are the **Nakatomi**, the Imbe, the Usa, the **Yoshida**, and the Aso families. This hereditary principle probably worked in favor of preserving the local character of shrines and **rituals**.

Neither the efforts of the Yoshida family in the 16th century to unify Shinto nor the clumsy efforts of the Meiji government to create **Kokka Shinto** (State Shinto) were able to break down this local character. The Yoshida movement did have a little success; however, this was undermined by the Meiji government, which had its own plan. Thousands of small shrines had no resident priests and were cared for by the **miya-za**, according to which lay people from principal families rotated as heads of major festivals and events.

While there are almost 100,000 shrines nationwide, the **Jinja Honchō** (Association of Shinto Shrines) has a list of less than 20,000 priests. Since some shrines may have as many as 20 or more priests, it is clear that many shrines may still be managed by lay families, although it is not uncommon for one priest to draw his living from serving up to 12 or more small shrines in various localities. *See also* SHINSHOKU.

KANRODAI-SEKAI. The perfect divine kingdom, as taught in the former **Kyōha Shinto** (Sect Shinto) sect **Tenri-kyō**.

KANSHA. The Japanese term for thanksgiving, used widely for appreciation of the kindness (**megumi**) of the *kami*.

KANYŌ. The spirit of toleration and peaceful co-existence of different religious traditions in Japan.

KANZUKASA. Central agency for selected ceremonies dating to the sixth century.

KARIGINU. Most of the liturgical vestments of modern Shinto clergy were developed in the **Heian period** (794–1185), modeled on the court dress of T'ang Dynasty China (618–907). The kariginu originated as a hunting garment worn by nobles and soldiers. The shaku, a flat wooden scepter, was used in the T'ang court as a memo pad, but is now carried by priests as a symbol of office. *See also* ASAGUTSU; EBOSHI; HAKAMA; HŌ; KANMURI; SAIFUKU.

KASHIKODOKORO. Literally "place of awe and reverence," it is the principal of the three main shrines within the Imperial Palace grounds that enshrine past emperors.

KASHIKOMU. Attitude of respect toward a *kami* and a term recurring in **norito** (liturgical invocations of the *kami*). It is followed by the word "maosu," the polite form of the verb "to address."

KASHIMA JINGŪ. Located in Ibaraki Prefecture, it enshrines Take-mikazuchi-no-mikoto, the *kami* recorded in the **Kojiki** (712) who pacified the country, making it possible for the *Kami* **of heaven** to take possession of the land. Along with **Katori Jingū**, it is one of the earliest **jingū-ji** (shrine-temple complex). While it is believed that its **Aidono** style of **architecture** goes back to the eighth century, the present shrine dates back only to 1619. There are records of regular rebuilding prior to that date.

KASHIWADE. Formal style of clapping when performing **sampai** (worship) at shrines (**jinja**) by raising both hands to chest level and then clapping the appropriate number of times. In the **New Religion**, **Kurozumi-kyō**, it is performed whenever the words of the founder, **Kurozumi Munetada** (1780–1850), are quoted.

KASUGA TAISHA. Nara-period (710–794) shrine (**jinja**), built in 709, dedicated to the ancestors of the Fujiwara clan that became in time the protective *kami* of the entire province of Yamato. It grew in prominence through its relationship with **Buddhist** culture, symbolized by the fact that its sacred symbol is the deer. It was one of the first shrines to be built under the influence of Chinese architecture. The present buildings were reconstructed in 1862. It received the title Taisha (Great Shrine) in 1946 from the **Jinja Honchō** (the Association of Shinto Shrines). *See also* HONJI-SUIJAKU-SETSU; ARCHITECTURE IN SHINTO.

KASUMI. Area of authority of leading **shūgenja**, or **yamabushi**, mountain ascetics, and practitioners of **shugendō** of the **Heian period** (794–1185).

KATO GENCHI (1873–1965). Distinguished scholar of Shinto, Katō Genchi is the author of numerous famous works, including a famous paper presented at Oxford in 1928 in which he explained the meaning and the significance of the concept of **ikigami** (living human *kami*) from extensive studies and research. He published numerous works on Shinto, offering particularly illuminating comparative observations concerning the Western classical tradition, in which he was well versed. *See also* HOLTOM, D. C.

KATORI JINGŪ. Located in Sawara City, Chiba Prefecture, it enshrines Futsunushi-no-kami, an ujigami of the Fujiwara family. This *kami*, along with Takemikazuchi-no-mikoto of **Kashima Jingū**, were both enshrined by the Fujiwara in Kasuga Jinja (**Kasuga Taisha** since 1946) in the eighth century. On 15 April, a **mikoshi** (portable shrine) is taken from Katori Jingū to Kashima Jingū and back up the Tonegawa River. The present **honden** (inner sanctuary) is constructed in the **Aido-no-kami** (joint enshrinement) style and dates to 1701.

KATORI NAHIKO (1723–1782). A poet and scholar of the **Kokugaku** (National Learning) movement who was a disciple of **Kamo no Mabuchi** (1697–1769). He published a dictionary of classical terms in 1765. He was also a scholar of the **Man'yōshū**.

KAWATE BUNJIRO (1814–1883). Founder of **Konkō-kyō** (Teaching of the Golden Light), a **healing** sect of **Kyōha Shinto** (Sect Shinto). He was born in Okayama as an Asakawa, but at the age of 11 was adopted into the Kawate family. In 1854, at the age of 40, he fell seriously ill. The powerful *kami* Konjin appeared to him and he recovered from his illness, pledging fidelity to Konjin. His younger brother also began to receive communications, and finally in 1859, Kawate was ordered to give up farming and transmit the words of

Konjin, whom he taught was a benevolent parent to humanity. This led to the expansion of his ideas, a growing following, and the birth of a new sect.

KEGARE. Ritual impurity or injury, one of the two basic concepts of Shinto, along with purification (**harai**) of defilements. It is understood by some scholars to imply the running down of virtue that needs to be re-energized through ritual purification. Traditionally, **death**, childbirth, or any occasion when blood is present become sources of pollution. While some of these taboos still hold, in modern times the concept has been linked more to spiritual than physical concerns. *See also* BACHI; DOHYO; SHINBATSU; TATARI; TSUMI.

KEHI JINGŪ. Located in Tsuruga in Fukui Prefecture, it enshrines Izasawake-no-mikoto and six other *kami*. Homudawake-no-mikoto, the Shinto name for **Emperor Ōjin** (reigned 270–310), revered this *kami* by order of his mother **Empress Jingū** (reigned 201–269) during a visit to the area after a successful campaign in Korea. Imperial offerings were first sent in 691. The shrine (**jinja**) is best known for its enormous four-posted entrance gate (**torii**) that dates to 1645.

KEIBA. Although now the normal word for commercial horseracing, the term referred originally to horse races as part of Shinto **rituals** that were a form of harvest **divination**. **Kamo Jinja** in Kyōto continues the practice.

KEICHŪ (1640–1701). A **Shingon** (esoteric Buddhist) priest and poet. He was born at Amagasaki (now in Hyogo Prefecture) into a family called Shimokawa. He showed great promise at an early age, and became a Buddhist priest at the age of 11. He also studied classical Chinese and Japanese writings and, although a priest most of his life, was able to devote many years to scholarly work in the fields of classical commentaries and language studies. He wrote with an independent critical style, quite out of character with the scholarship of his age. His research into Japanese language and literature can be understood as an attempt to get back to what was perceived as the wisdom and simplicity of classical times.

Keichu followed the **Ryōbu Shinto** tradition, which combined Buddhist and Shinto insights, and pursued his own search for spiritual truth. His most famous work remains his commentary on the **Man'yoshū**, undertaken at the behest of Tokugawa Mitsukuni of Mito and completed between 1683 and 1690. He is not always recognized as being among the more Shinto-based thinkers of the **Kokugaku** (National Learning) movement, but in reality his influence upon **Motoori Norinaga** (1730–1801) was profound, because of the latter's respect for the high quality of his scholarship.

KEIRAN JUYO SHU. Sacred text of the **Sannō Ichijitsu** tradition of **Tendai Shinto**, compiled sometime around 1347 and consisting of many of the narratives of the older oral tradition that was eventually transcribed for the sake of its preservation. The title means "Collection of Leaves Gathered in Stormy Waters." Analysis reveals the degree to which esoteric **Buddhism**, Shinto, and **Taoism** had become intricately integrated. This helped to give rise to the importance of Tendai Shinto. *See also* ASSIMILATION OF BUDDHISM AND SHINTO; HONJI-SUIJAKU-SETSU; TENDAI BUDDHISM.

KENKOKUSAI. National Founding Festival, established in 1966 to replace **Kigensetsu** (pre-war National Founding Day) which was instituted in 1872 by the Meiji government dating the founding of Japan to 11 February 660 B.C.E. and designating it as year 1. In 1951, Prime Minister Yoshida Shigeru wished to restore the traditional celebration of Kigensetsu, but was forced to bow to public pressure and abandon his plan.

KENPEISHI. In modern times, a messenger (usually from the **Jinja Honcho** (Association of Shinto Shrines) who delivers **heihaku**, an offering on the event of a major festival (**matsuri**).

KENZOKU. Minor *kami* or messengers subordinate to a major *kami*. Often found in **sessha** or **massha**, they become integrated with the local community *kami*.

KETSUEN-SHIN. This term refers to a *kami* revered by people of the same blood lineage. About 250 noble families claimed to be descended from *kami*, prominent among which was the imperial family.

The concept of descent from a *kami* also helps to explain the difference between Western and Japanese concepts of divinity. *See also* TENNŌ NO NINGEN SENGEN.

KI. The concept of energy that appears in many Japanese language compounds, such as ten-ki (heavenly energy, weather), gen-ki (good ki, meaning health), yaru-ki (energy to undertake something, motivation), and of course, **aikido**, meeting of energy points in the art of self-defense.

Although the same character is found in Chinese language and thought, the important difference in meaning should be noted. In Chinese, it is a more abstract and cosmic concept, a force in which people may participate. In Japanese, it is an energy form that can be generated by the self and from the self through the correct disciplines, and that can be used by individuals in many forms of activity.

KIBITSU JINJA. Place of enshrinement of Kibitsuhiko-no-mikoto, a legendary son of the seventh Emperor Korei (reigned 290–215 B.C.E.). Revered for defeating Korean invaders, he evolved into the children's folk hero Momotaro. The shrine, located in Okayama, was last rebuilt in 1390 and is famous for its massively large **honden** (inner sanctuary). *See also* ARCHITECTURE IN SHINTO.

KIBUKU. Mourning according to Shinto practice that entails remaining at home for a length of time, which varies depending upon rank and relationship. This has been perceived by some scholars as an instance of the influence of Chinese burial customs on Japan.

KIGENSETSU. The pre-war commemoration day of the mythical accession of the legendary first Emperor **Jimmū Tennō** (reigned 660–585 B.C.E.) in 660 B.C.E. It was part of the Meiji period (1868–1912) Ministry of Education indoctrination program created to stimulate nationalist fervor. *See also* KENKOKUSAI.

KIHAN-GAKU. Evaluative methodological study of ancient texts, as practiced and taught by **Motoori Norinaga** (1730–1801), central figure of the **Kokugaku** (National Learning) movement of the Edo period (1615–1868).

KIMOTOSAI. One of many ceremonies related to the 20-year rebuilding cycle of the **Grand Shrines of Ise** (Ise Jingū) known as **shikinen-sengū**.

KINRYŪ-DEN. Golden Dragon Pavilion, sacred place of the **Kyōha Shinto** (Sect Shinto) sect **Ōmoto-kyō**.

KISEI SHUKYO. Technical term for the older established religions (**Jinja Shinto, Buddhism**), in contrast to **New Religions** and **Kyōha Shinto** (Sect Shinto).

KISHITSU NO SEI. A philosophical term of neo-**Confucianism** created by **Chu Shi** (Zhu Xi, 1130–1200), referring to the physical nature of the universe. **Itō Jinsai** (1617–1705) was critical of the term because it suggested the natural evolution of values rather than their cultivation according to his understanding of the Confucian philosophical and ethical tradition.

KITABATAKE CHIKAFUSA (1293–1354). Born of a line of courtiers and imperial loyalists, he entered the Buddhist priesthood and commenced his career at court when the Northern and Southern Courts' confrontation (1332–1392) was in its early phase. From his base in **Ise**, he established an alternative court in Mount Yoshino in reply to self-styled Shogun Ashikaga Takauji, who set up the northern court in Kyōto.

His main work, the **Jinnō Shōtōki** (Records of the Legitimate Succession of the Divine Emperors, circa 1340) was written to offer guidance to Emperor Go-Murakami (reigned 1339–1368) at the time or his accession. The opening sentence of the Jinno Shotoki refers to Japan as the "*kami* no kuni," land of the *kami*, making Kitabatake the originator of this well-known expression. It also indicates the influence of **Watarai Ieyuki** (1293–1354), high priest of the **Gekū** (Outer Shrine) of the **Grand Shrines of Ise** (Ise Jingū), and a promoter of the **Shinto Gobusho**. Both Kitabatake and his son Akiie died for the imperial cause and were enshrined in the Abeno Jinja in Osaka. The fact that this shrine (**jinja**) was founded, and the enshrinement took place in 1883, 600 years after their death, speaks to the seriousness with which **ancestral reverence** and enshrinement are still taken in modern Japan. The inclination to preserve and use cultural heritage remains powerful.

KITAGAWA, JOSEPH (1915–1992). Greatly distinguished Chicago School of Religion professor of Japanese religious history. While being a comprehensive scholar with a realistic grasp of most features of Japan's religious culture, he was very sensitive to the power of Shinto.

In discussing the period of interaction between Shinto and Buddhist culture and in response to the claim made by some scholars that Shinto gave way to Buddhist influences, he questioned if the matter was quite so simple. He pointed out that it has been argued, on the other hand, that **Buddhism** compromised its essential character, its belief in reincarnation, and its moral principles in order to achieve that position. Kitagawa formulated the crucial question thus: "Is it not equally true that Buddhism surrendered to the ethos of that nebulous religion of Japan, which lay deeper than the visible religious structure, commonly referred to as Shinto?" His own Christian (Episcopalian) viewpoint probably served to strengthen his suspicion of any movement that eventually survives and becomes accepted in Japan.

KITANO TENJIN. The name of the *kami* of learning and scholarship, who was the vengeful ghost of courtier **Sugawara Michizane** (845–903) and whose story is recorded on the Kitano Tenjin Engi, a medieval narrative scroll that contains an account of the entire incident. *See also* ART IN SHINTO; EMAKIMONO.

KITSUNE. In Shinto thought, **foxes** have long been believed to possess supernatural powers that enabled them to bewitch people by changing their own form. They have also been considered to be messengers of **Inari** Myojin, the *kami* of cereals. Statues of them are found at Inari shrines, and offerings of fried bean curd are made to them. The famous *Konjaku Monogatari*, composed during the late **Heian period** (794–1185) contains narratives of foxes performing occult acts. The fox in Japanese folklore is intimately associated with bewitchment and possession of human souls. Foxes also frequently appear in folklore in the form of beautiful women who bewitched men but vanish in the morning. This phenomenon is perhaps less frequent in urban society, but one that still has credence in some rural areas. *See also* INARI; KITSUNE-MOCHI; KITSUNE-TSUKAI; KITSUNE-TSUKI.

KITSUNE-MOCHI. Possession of **fox** power by a human being.

KITSUNE-TSUKAI. Use of **fox** power by a human being.

KITSUNE-TSUKI. Being possessed by a **fox**, a serious condition requiring **yakubarai**, a purification ritual.

KIYOKI-NO-KOKORO. Purified heart, an expression found in the **Man'yoshū**. *See also* AKAKI KIYOKI KOKORO; ETHICS IN SHINTO.

KIYOME-NO-IKE. A pond for performing **misogi**, the purification (**harai**) **ritual.** One used by **Yamato-takeru-no-mikoto** is located near the **honden** (inner sanctuary) of the **Hodosan Jinja** in Saitama Prefecture.

KIYOSHI. Cleansed, a term originating in the **Man'yōshū**.

KŌBŌ DAISHI. Posthumous honorific name of **Kūkai** (773–835), founder of **Shingon Buddhism**, a Japanese version of Tibetan Buddhism imported from China.

KOBUNJIGAKU. Ancient Rhetoric School of **Ogyū Sorai** (1666–1728) that was part of the background to later developments that brought together **Confucianism and Shinto**.

KOCHOGAKU. Imperial learning, as described by **Kokugaku** (Ancient Learning) scholar **Motoori Norinaga** (1730–1801).

KODŌ. The ancient way, an old name for Shinto. Another term, **teido**, which means imperial way, was used to distinguish it from **folk Shinto**.

KOFUN. Protohistoric burial mounds built during the fourth to the seventh centuries for deceased members of the political elite, including the **imperial household**, ranging in size from 15 meters to 80 acres. They remain vital sources of information about Japanese culture and civilization of that period. *See also* HANIWA.

KOGAKU. The term for ancient Japanese learning, as described in the thought of **Kokugaku** (National Learning) scholar **Motoori Norinaga** (1730–1801).

KOGAKUKAN UNIVERSITY. One of two universities that include courses for the training of Shinto priests (**kannushi**). It was founded in 1882 by order of Prince Tomohiko as Jingū Kogakukan near the **Grand Shrines of Ise** (Ise Jingū) to train an orthodox priesthood and to provide education for the sons of Shinto priests. Originally located within the Hayashizaki Library in **Ise**, it was subsequently moved to Uji Yamada in 1903 and turned into a Ministry of Home Affairs (Naimusho) Shinto training institute. It closed down in 1945. It was reconstituted as a private university in 1952 and after intensive fundraising it was restored to its original site in Ise.

KOGIGAKU. The Ancient Meaning School of **Itō Jinsai** (1627–1705), a branch of Edo period (1615–1868) **Confucianism**.

KOGO-SHŪI. Meaning "Gleanings from Ancient Words," the text was presented by the Imbe family to Emperor Heizei in 807. It supplemented the **Kojiki** (712) and the **Nihon Shoki** (720) with material on words and practices not included in these texts. It also argues the case of the Imbe tradition of **ritual** in relation to the more dominant influence of the **Nakatomi** clan.

KOJIKI. Record of Ancient Matters, which is Japan's oldest surviving text narrating events from the **mythological** age of the **kami** to the reign of Empress Suiko (reigned 592–628). O no Yasumaro, the editor, claims that its presentation to Empress Gemmei (661–722; reigned 707–715) took place on 9 March 712. The political motivation for its creation is clear: It was said to have been compiled in response to a decree of **Emperor Temmu** (reigned 673–686), which stated that the *Teiki* (the genealogy of the imperial line) and the *Kyuji* (myths and legends of the imperial family and other leading families in the country) had become corrupted and were in need of clarification and correction. A court member called Jieda no Are was to memorize these two sets of traditions, but on 3 November 711, Empress Gemmei ordered O no Yasumaro to write down the contents of the oral tradition, and so the Kojiki (712) was created. Along with the **Nihon Shōki** (720), it provides the scholastic materials for the research of Japan's mythology and early history.

The contents break into three parts. The first deals with the myths of the creation of heaven and earth and the creation of the Japanese archipelago, and is referred to as the *Jindai no maki*, the book of the age of the *kami*. It narrates the descent of **Ninigi-no-mikoto**, grandson of **Amaterasu-ōmikami** and ancestor of the imperial line, to a mountain in Kyushū called Takachihonomine. It refers to Um-isachihiko, ancestor of the Hayato of southern Kyushū, who pledged their loyalty to Hohodemi-no-mikoto, grandfather of **Jimmū Tennō** (reigned 660–585 B.C.E.), Japan's first emperor.

Part two begins with the reign of Emperor Jimmu and narrates events and people through to the late fourth-century reign (270–31) of **Emperor Ōjin**. Part three takes up the narrative with the reign (313–399) of **Emperor Nintoku** and concludes with the reign (582–628) of Empress Suiko in the early seventh century. In sharp contrast to the Nihon Shoki, in which accounts of the imperial line after the mid-fifth century become more detailed, the Kojiki accounts become less detailed. This fact has given rise to speculation about its authenticity as a document of that period. Nevertheless, it found acceptance as a source of the ancient tradition, and as such was duly respected.

Scholarly research on it began in the Edo period (1615–1868) with the writing of the Kojikiden by **Motoori Norinaga** (1730–1801), who viewed it as both historical and as a fruitful source of information about Japanese mythology, religious roots, and traditional beliefs, as well as being a work of literature. His interest was in separating the Chinese elements—since it was written in Hentai Kambun, a form of Japanese writing heavily Chinese in style—from the Japanese core, which he judged to be the narratives of Amaterasu-ōmikami.

KOJIN. Generally used to refer to a less sophisticated *kami*, identified in some areas with the **jigami** of the land or yama-no-kami of the mountains, both of which are enshrined outdoors.

KOKINKAKU. Sacred place of enshrinement of the founder of the Shinto-based **New Religion Shinrei-kyō**.

KOKINSHŪ. Literally "Collection from Ancient and Modern Times," the complete title is the Kokin Wakashū. It was commissioned by **Emperor Daigo** (reigned 897–930) and completed about 905. Aside from the historical and literary merits of the collection, it mirrors sentiments of the period, and in relation to Shinto, it reflects the mood and tone of the aesthetic and spiritual values of the eras it covers.

Like the **Man'yōshū**, it is a record of the feelings of the people of the period, and, because of its style and structure, suggests a move into formalism that caused spontaneous feeling to be less common than in the earlier classical period.

KOKKA SHINTO. State Shinto of the Meiji period (1868–1912), as subsequently described in English by the 1945 Allied Occupation of Japan and by scholars of Japanese history dealing with the period 1868 to 1945. It was abolished under the provisions of the **Shinto Directive** of 1945, which banned all government support for not only shrines (**jinja**), but for all religious bodies. The directive elides State Shinto (Kokka Shinto), National Shinto, and Shrine Shinto (Jinja Shinto), as opposed to **Kyōha Shinto** (Sect Shinto).

What in reality was being abolished was the government enforcement of Shinto-style **rituals** in public places designed to promote the ideal of emperor worship, a concept that the Meiji government felt central to its ideological program intended to promote national unity in the interests of speedy **modernization**. While concepts such as **saisei-itchi**, the unity of worship and government, go far back into Japanese history, the shrines themselves took no initiative whatsoever in promoting State Shinto. It was primarily the work of bureaucrats who decided to classify shrines and rank them, with the **Grand Shrines of Ise** (Ise Jingū) at the pinnacle, down to small local village shrines, thousands of which were closed down or destroyed in a program referred to as **jinja gappei**, or jinja seirei, shrine mergers or shrine consolidation. This program was criticized by thousands of villages nationwide, but with the backing of the military police, it was enforced until about 1911, when it ran out of momentum.

One critical incident, which had enormous significance for how the claims of State Shinto were represented, occurred in 1932 when some Roman Catholic students refused to pay homage at **Yasukuni Jinja**. The Ministry of Education then issued a statement that Shinto was not a religion and that attending shrines was a patriotic duty and nothing else. Although shrines at that time were under the Ministry of Home Affairs, it was the Ministry of Education that took the initiative in pressuring people to attend these rituals.

Also, while the rituals of Shinto were employed for the reasons stated, the entire **emperor system** itself was tacitly accepted by all religious groups, including most Christian sects. Much postwar Christian critique of the emperor system was retrospective redefinition of positions derived from confidence acquired from the perception that it was the "Christian" nations, particularly the United States, that were victorious in the **Pacific War** (World War II). Therefore, all references to State Shinto by Christian groups should be evaluated with reference to this basic understanding. Other groups created their own accommodations at the time, and have said little about them since.

Since the 1960s, there have been numerous attempts to justify conspiracy theories about the restoration of State Shinto. In 1982, Dr. Ernest Lokowandt of the German East Asia Society in Tokyō gave a lecture to the Asiatic Society of Japan on the revival of State Shinto. Others have followed, but there has been little evidence to suggest that such theories are anything other than mere speculation.

KOKORO. Meaning heart, this concept, of great importance for popular religious movements past and present, gained special prominence in the **Shingaku** (Heart Learning) movement created by the Edo period (1615–1868) scholar **Ishida Baigan** (1685–1744).

KOKU-BUNGAKU. National (Japanese) literature as described by **Kokugaku** (National Learning) scholar **Motoori Norinaga** (1730–1801), and still used as a term of reference to the study of literature in modern Japanese education.

KOKUGAKUIN UNIVERSITY. A **Kokugaku** (National Learning)-approved research institute founded in 1882 as a university derived from the Koten Kokyusho. The first director was Prince Arigusawa Takahito. It received senmon gakko (specialized training college) status in 1904 and status as a private university in 1906. A department of Shinto Studies was added in 1927. While the Koten Kokyusho was abolished in 1946, the university was incorporated under postwar law.

The university expanded into various areas and added night studies because of its convenient location in the Shibuya area of Tokyō. The Institute of Japanese Culture and Classics is internationally respected, publishes much valuable research material, and is an indispensible source of contemporary information about the academic study of Shinto and Shinto self-understanding. It still continues its two-year program for the training of Shinto priests (**kannushi**). Along with **Kogakukan University** it is one of Japan's two official Shinto academic institutions.

KOKUGAKU SHINTO. National Learning, referring to Shinto studies of the Edo period (1615–1868), based on the textual and exegetical studies of the Japanese classical texts that began in the 17th century, not dissimilar to the German textual reevaluation of the same period of the Christian biblical writings, known as *Formgeschichte*. The goal was to try to discover the original meaning and intention of the sacred writings.

Kokugaku is best understood as the philological and hermeneutical study of writings of the Japanese classical period. The early scholarship of **Kamo no Mabuchi** (1697–1769), followed by that of **Motoori Norinaga** (1730–1801) was the foundation, with Motoori Norinaga's *Kojiden*, his commentary on the **Kojiki** (712), considered the greatest text of the movement. Motoori referred to his work as **Kogaku** (study of antiquity), which was concerned with the better understanding of the Japanese tradition. After this work was completed and its influence had begun to spread, the emphasis shifted from the discernment of the ancient ideas to the notion of Japan before the introduction of alien ideas such as **Buddhism** or Christianity. This, however, was never part of the original Kokugaku agenda, and as such belonged to the pre-Meiji and Meiji (1868–1912) periods' fascination with, on the one hand, importing Western skills, but, on the other hand, trying to define what was authentically Japanese.

It is generally acknowledged that the influence of **Hirata Atsutane** (1776–1843) led the tradition into the support of the ultranationalism which arose during the late Edo period (1615–1868) when Japan was facing external threats, and thereafter again when the government of the **Meiji Restoration** required an ideology to help unify national consciousness during the period of intense **modernization**. It then became transformed into Shinto studies with little real appreciation of the meaning of Shinto per se, and was eventually rejected by a disgruntled populace that had a greater experience and understanding of diversity than the government had common sense. The movement is seen most easily through the development of its central themes through each individual scholar's contribution to the thought and ideals at different periods.

Western critics of Kokugaku's later phase would do well to remember that saber-rattling nationalism was no prerogative of the Japanese, nor was it necessarily a major contributor to Japan's later militaristic phase. The record of the European colonial nations, particularly the British, in Africa—to name but one theater of activity— was driven by almost precisely the same kind of ideology of superiority. Kokugaku was only one contributory source to a movement that was modeling itself quite self-consciously on the British and European colonial systems.

KOKUHEISHA. National shrines (**jinja**) as defined under the provisions of **Kokka Shinto** (State Shinto).

KOKUMIN-DŌTOKU-RON. A term meaning national morality created and used by **Kokugaku** (National Learning) scholar **Motoori Norinaga** (1730–1801).

KOKU-SHI. National (Japanese) history, as referred to by **Kokugaku** (National Learning) scholar **Motoori Norinaga** (1730–1801).

KOKUTAI-NO-HONGI. A controversial text produced in 1937 by the Ministry of Education on the theme of the "Foundation Principles of the Body Politic." It was designed to be used as a textbook of moral education expounding the **emperor system** and how it was the foundation of the state. It was to be taught in schools and colleges, read and discussed at all levels, and be the text against which deviant thinking was to be tested. It also included some themes, such as the virtue of patriotism as expounded in the **Kyōiku Chokugo** (the **Imperial Rescript** on Education) of 1890.

It opens with a section expounding the national founding **mythology** and placing the imperial line in its descent from **Amaterasu-ōmikami**. Although referring to the classic texts, it used the work of the **Kokugaku** (National Learning) movement to explain the meaning of the mythology. The virtue of the emperor system was extolled as the reality that united ritual, government, education, and patriotism. Filial piety is also praised in the section that deals with the duties of subjects.

The uniquely virtuous history of the Japanese nation is the subject of the second part of the text, which deals with "The Manifestation of our Nation in History." The harmonious co-operation of Japan's religious culture in its many forms is held up as an ideal that stands in sharp contrast to the individualistic egoism of Western civilization.

The text, which was used until 1945, had many critics such as the father of former Governor Minobe of Tokyō, **Minobe Tatsukichi** (1873–1948), when he was a professor at the University of Tokyō. His father's published work on the subject was condemned for his "irreverent" discussion of the text. Its use remained in force until 1945.

KOKUTAI-NO-KODŌ. Way of the body politic, a term used by **Kokugaku** (National Learning) scholar **Motoori Norinaga** (1730–1801).

KOMA-INU. A pair of sculptured animals resembling a cross between a lion and a dog. They are placed facing outwards at the entrance of shrine (**jinja**) avenues (**sando**) that lead toward the main buildings, as protective symbols. The sculptures are thought to have originated in Korea, or perhaps before that, in China. Similar figures can be seen in both countries. Usually in Japan, one stands with its mouth open, and the other with its mouth closed. They are also known as shishi-koma-inu.

KONKŌ DAIJIN. The principal deity of the **Kyōha Shinto** (Sect Shinto) sect **Konkō-kyō**.

KONKŌ-KYŌ. A **Kyōha Shinto** (Sect Shinto) sect, meaning the Teaching of the Golden Light. It dates to 1859 and was the creation of **Kawate Bunjiro** (1814–1883), who was born in Okayama Prefecture. He was a hard-working and spiritually conscientious farmer who was overtaken by a series of crises, and at the age of 42, was struck down by a serious illness. He recovered, believing that his disrespect for daily prayer was the reason for his illness. He received a revelation from **Konkō Daijin** (Great Deity of Golden Light), who taught him that life was to be lived in harmony with nature and earth, recognizing the power of spirituality. He took the name of the *kami*, calling himself Konkō Daijin, transformed his farmhouse into a shrine, and began teaching. He spent many hours each day listening to the teachings of the *kami* and then passing these on to his disciples.

The initial appeal was to the middle-class farmers of the Inland Sea area, and eventually churches had formed that appealed to all the strata of Edo period (1615–1868) society: peasants, merchants, crafts-men, and farmers. By the beginning of the **Meiji Restoration**, Konkō-kyō had spread and, in spite of brief reversals of fortune, had found favor in the eyes of the Shirakawa family, ministers of Shinto affairs (**Jingihaku**) in 1864. In 1867, Konkō Daijin himself was licensed as a priest of the Konjin Shrine. The movement had received government acknowledgement. However, his license was partly revoked in 1871, and in 1873 he was ordered to dismantle the Konjin Shrine under the Meiji government policy of religious consolidation.

In spite of suppression, by 1875 Konkō-kyō had spread to Osaka, shifting its focus from the early rejection of superstition to an em-phasis upon the power of the *kami* and upon the ideal of prosperity. Konkō himself opposed subordination to the state control of shrines (**jinja**), but his staff found ways of compromise and, led by Sato No-rio (1856–1942), doctrines were developed that led to the movement becoming Konkō Church in 1885. By 1900, its recognition as a Kyōha Shinto (Sect Shinto) sect had been achieved. Under the slogan "faith, loyalty, and filial piety are one," it was integrated into the national ideology. After 1945, it returned to its origins, and along with other branches of Sect Shinto, began a painful process of redefinition.

The sect, which claims around 500,000 members, is headquartered in Okayama Prefecture. The basic teaching asserts that Konjin is the parent *kami* **of heaven and earth**, and refers to him as Tenchi Kane no Kami, a deity of love. All human beings are children of the divine and are equal, and therefore should work together in harmony. Al-though not offering any systematic teaching, Konkō-kyō's message is summed up in the words of Konkō's Tenchi Kakitsuke, addressed to the Gracious Living *kami* of heaven and earth, Konkō: "Pray with one mind! Your blessings are in my mind. Entrust yourself now!" He believed that people should enjoy happiness and prosperity and that they can glorify God through this enjoyment. The highest human ideal of participating in the glory of God can be realized by living one's everyday life to the fullest.

The mediator helps to solve the problems of everyday life so that people can live more effectively and freely. Although the mediator bases his advice on the life of the founder and his teachings, he deals with the problems individually so that flexibility is possible and the doctrine can be chosen according to the particular problem. Reward after death is not as important as effort within life. In this way,

Konkō-kyō mirrors the outlook of Shinto, although other elements are clearly present. It is a liberal religion that sometimes prefers to speak of itself as a way of life. Believers may carry out wedding and funeral ceremonies at different religious organizations with no impediment. Indeed, there is no definite doctrine that everybody should follow regardless of circumstances. Since human nature is considered to be basically good (in line with the general Shinto outlook), ascetic practices or ecclesiastical rituals are not considered to be replacements for benevolent and unselfish acts in daily life. As a consequence of its beliefs, the movement is also very active in social issues. One of the main branches of the movement is the Konkō-kyō Church of Izuo, led by the internationally known Miyake family.

It has also developed a following in the United States, where it first established a presence in 1938. It developed into the Konkō Churches of America (KCA) in 1954, and became the Konkō Churches of North America (KCNA) in 1961. The KCNA is a supportive organization for its believers and churches, and currently consists of twelve churches and one propagation hall. The churches are located in Toronto, Ontario, and Vancouver, British Columbia, in Canada; Fresno, Gardena, Los Angeles, Sacramento, San Diego, San Francisco, San Jose, and Whittier in California; Portland, Oregon; and Seattle, Washington.

KŌNO SEIZŌ (1883–1963). Commentator on Shinto who described it as the Japanese people's principle of life, rooted in their fundamental character. He placed the emperor at the center of his thought, arguing that only by people showing proper reverence would the nation find happiness and peace. In this he was echoing the pre-war view in its more idealistic form.

KŌREIDEN. Sacred pavilion within the Imperial Palace in which certain **rituals** of the **imperial household (Kōshitsu Saishi)** are performed throughout the year. *See also* EMPEROR SYSTEM.

KŌSHIN-NO-GI. Alighting of a *kami* on a **sakaki** branch at the beginning of a Shinto **ritual**. *See also* KAMI-OKURI.

KŌSHITSU-SAISHI. Collective name for Shinto ceremonies and **rituals** of the **imperial household**, such as the **Daijōsai** and other special

festivals. On some occasions, the emperor himself acts as the high priest (**guji**); on other occasions, he delegates the tasks to a deputy.

KŌSHITSU-SAISHIEREI. Ordinance issued by the government in 1900 governing **imperial household** ceremonies. In the absence of newer regulations, the provisions of these were followed in the accession rites of Emperor **Heisei** in 1989.

KŌTAI JINGŪ. Another name for the **imperial household**-linked **Grand Shrines of Ise** (Ise Jingū).

KOTO-DAMA. Pleasant sounding words thought to please the *kami*, which also have a power similar to the sense of the power of words found in many religious traditions, but particularly in Shinto and in **norito** (liturgical invocations) of the *kami*. Linked to this idea is that of Koto-damashii, the power of the soul of words. *See also* YAMATO-DAMASHII.

KOTOHIRA JINGŪ. Better known in popular parlance as "Kompi-rasan," located in Sanuki Province (now Kagawa Prefecture on the island of Shikoku) and enshrines Omononushi-no-kami along with Emperor Sutoku (reigned 1123–1142), who died in Sanuki Province in exile, highly devoted to the shrine (**jinja**). It dates to the 11th century, and was originally the place of enshrinement of Kompira Daigongen, a **Buddhist**/Shinto deity that appears to have its origins in a crocodile deity of the Ganges in India known as Kumbhira. Being close to the sea, the link with the protection of sailors and fishermen became natural.

The shrine's prominence peaked in the Muromachi (1333–1568) and again in the Edo period (1615–1868), during which time, many **bunsha** (branch shrines) were established. After the enforced separation (**Shinbutsu-bunri**) of Buddhism and Shinto in 1868 by order of the Meiji government, Kompira Daigongen was renamed Omononushi-no-kami, referred to in the **Kojiki** (712) as the *kami* who illumines the ocean. *See also* ASSIMILATION OF BUDDHISM AND SHINTO; HONJI-SUIJAKU-SETSU.

KŌTSŪ ANZEN HARAI. Purification (**harai**) of (usually new) automobiles for road safety.

KUGATACHI-SHIKI. Subduing hot elements, **fire calming rituals**, demonstrated by pouring or sprinkling boiling water on the body without harm, practiced by the **Kyōha Shinto** (Sect Shinto) sects **Ontake-kyō** (Mitake-kyō) and **Shinshū-kyō**. *See also* SHUGENDO; YAMABUSHI.

KUJI, KUJIKI. Shortened version of the full name of the *Nihon Sendai Kuji Hongi*, thought to have been compiled during the reign of Empress Suiko (reigned 592–628). It documents Japan's historical and cultural development from early times to her reign. While it runs parallel with the **Kojiki** (712) and the **Nihon Shōki** (720), it contains material not found in either. Authorship is not certain, but it is thought by some scholars to date to the late ninth century.

KUJO. Lowest rank of priest (**kannushi**), below gon-negi. *See also* GŪJI; SHINSHOKU.

KUKAI (774–835). Founder of Tibetan-style esoteric **Buddhism** that became **Shingon Buddhism**, which he introduced into Japan from China during the **Heian period** (794–1185). He received the posthumous title **Kōbō Daishi**.

KUMANO JUNREI. A mountain pilgrimage practiced by the Kumano **Shugendō** ascetics since the **Heian period** (794–1185). After being abolished in 1868, it was revived in the 20th century, demonstrating the vitality of the Japanese love of pilgrimages. Kumano had long been a sacred place, and pilgrimages to Kumano became so popular that later literature referred to the "pilgrimage of ants to Kumano."

Many of these were led by retired **Emperor Shirakawa** (reigned 1072–1086) who made the first of 23 pilgrimages there in 1091 after he became a "retired emperor" (**insei**) in 1086. The details of the pilgrimage, its route, and rituals are depicted on the most famous of the Shinto/Buddhist relics of the age, namely the Kumano **Mandala**, a systematically assembled piece of syncretistic cosmological art. *See also* ART IN SHINTO.

KUMANO SANJA. The three shrines (**jinja**)—the Hongū, the Shingū, and the Nachi—in Kumano that are close to the great waterfall, the

Nachi-no-Taki. They are central to the activities of the cult of **Kumano Shinto**.

KUMANO SHINTO. The name given to an assortment of cults that grew up during the **Heian period** (794–1185) around the great waterfall at Nachi. From ancient times, Kumano, a mountainous region overlooking the ocean, was known as the "kami no kuni," the land of the *kami*, and was thought to be the dwelling place of myriad *kami*. Mountain ascetics known as **shūgenja** may be dated much earlier, but it was during the Heian period that the beginnings of those cults, which came to flower during the Kamakura period (1185–1333), could be traced.

Certain **Buddhist** concepts became widespread and popular, such as the idea of the final age of the Buddhist Dharma law, in the form of the widely influential concept of **Mappō**, an eschatological doctrine. The Pure Land faith at this time became popularly associated with the Bodhisattva **Kannon**. This developed naturally in the Kumano region, since Kumano was to the south of the capital and Kannon's place of dwelling was also to the south. This kind of development was typical of **Honji-Suijaku-Setsu**, the Buddhist/Shinto syncretism of the Heian period. Three religious centers—the Hongu, the Shingu, and the Nachi—developed in Kumano close by the great waterfall. These became known as the Kumano Sanja.

From a Buddhist perspective, the three shrines (**jinja**) were known as the Kumano Sansho Gongen, and were linked with Amida, the popular deity of Pure Land Buddhism. Popular with the Heian court, many **Junpai** or Junrei (pilgrimages) were made to Kumano. The cult also became a center for **Shugendō**, mountain asceticism. The teachings and rituals of the cult were spread by **hijiri** (holy men), **miko** (shrine maidens), and Shugendō practitioners known as **yamabushi** (mountain ascetics).

KUMAZAWA BANZAN (1619–1691). An influential **Confucian** thinker of the early Edo period (1615–1868), who was born the son of a ronin (a masterless samurai) in Kyōto. He entered the service of the daimyo of Bizen Province (now part of Okayama Prefecture), Ikeda Mitsumasa (1609–1682), in 1634, but resigned in 1639. He studied under Nakae Toju (1608–1648), founder of the Wang Yang-ming School of neo-Confucianism.

He rejoined the administration of Ikeda Mitsumasa in 1645 but resigned again in 1656. After moving to Kyōto, he set up as a teacher but was forced to leave in 1667, living in different provinces in a semi-exiled condition. During this latter period, he preoccupied himself with questions of moral philosophy, social and political issues, and writing a commentary on the *Genji Monogatari.* His eclectic ideas led him to a kind of moral intuitionism, close to the Western 18th-century idea of a "moral sense." This arose from his own form of philosophical empiricism. His general views exerted an influence on later Edo period (1615–1868) thought, particularly upon the **Kogaku School** (Ancient Learning) that ultimately fed into the mainstream of **Fukko Shinto** (Restoration Shinto). *See also* HIRATA ATSUTANE.

KUMOTSU. Offerings to a *kami. See also* SHINSEN.

KUNI-NO-MIYATSUKO. Local ruling families whose powers slowly collapsed under Yamato clan hegemony. Hereditary priestly families such as the Senge of **Izumo Taisha** or the Aso of **Aso Jinja** are modern survivors of that tradition.

KUNI-TOKOTACHI-NO-MIKOTO. The everlasting *kami* of the land, and the first *kami* to appear at creation. This *kami* was revered in the tradition of the **Gekū** (Outer Shrine) of the **Grand Shrines of Ise** (Ise Jingū).

KUNITSU-KAMI. The earthly *kami*, head of which is **Sarutahiko-ōkami**. The expression appears in all Shinto **ritual** formulae (**norito**). *See also KAMI* OF HEAVEN AND EARTH.

KUROZUMI-KYŌ. A healing cult of **Kyōha Shinto** (Sect Shinto) founded by **Kurozumi Munetada** (1780–1850) in the late Edo period (1615–1868); it was headquartered in Okayama City at Munetada Jinja. Kurozumi's father was a priest at the Amaterasu Jinja. He regarded filial piety as the highest good and resolved at the age of 19 to honor his parents by becoming a *kami* in his lifetime. When his parents died in 1812, he felt devastated, since his purpose in life had been to please them. As death came near, he was moved to the veranda (engawa) of the house to revere the sun for the last time.

Miraculously, he recovered, and two months later, he revered the sun again and was completely healed.

In November 1814 he received a divine revelation while performing another act of reverence toward the sun. When he faced the east, he inhaled the sun's rays and felt transformed. This experience of unity with the divine came to be known as the Tenmei Jikiju, the Direct Receipt of the Heavenly Mission. It was at this point that his new life as a religious teacher began. He started a program of charismatic teaching and healing which spread among the urbane commoners of southwest Honshū to Kyushū. He was enshrined in **Munetada Jinja** as Munetada Daimyōjin in 1872. In 1876, the sect was recognized by the Bureau of Shinto Affairs as an independent sect, with authorization to seek members and to teach and conduct rituals.

A basic part of the activities of Kurozumi-kyō includes sermons and preaching that are not normally part of **Jinja Shinto** activities. Sermons tend to stress that problems arise from lack of harmony with the divine and teach that the solution to all problems lies in restoring the harmony between man and the *kami*. Sermons make use of loud claps (kashiwade) and believers also clap twice (in the manner of saluting a *kami* at a shrine) whenever the words of the founder are quoted.

Counseling and healing are practiced, but these are considered to be subordinate to the source of all problems, namely the heart (**kokoro**) that is out of harmony with the divine. Once that harmony is restored, all will be well. Medicine is not ignored, but it is regarded as useless because problems of a medical nature are merely symptoms of deeper problems, and removing the symptoms is only half a cure. **Majinai** is used as a form of healing in which a minister transfers from his or her own **nippai**, the energy of the sun, to the diseased person. In nippai, a believer sits and faces the sun and inhales the yoki, the essence of the deity, and this can be transferred to the sick. Like the groups already discussed, Kurozumi-kyō offers a full range of services and rituals. These, however, are recognizable both as **folk Shinto** and as common to many other traditional religious movements. At the end of the 20th century, it had fewer than 200,000 members.

KUROZUMI MUNETADA (1780–1850). Founder of the **Kurozumi-kyō** sect of **Kyōha Shinto** (Sect Shinto).

KYŌBUSHŌ. Ministry of Religious Instruction of the Meiji period (1868–1912), established in April 1872. It was to replace the **Jingishō** (Ministry of Shinto Affairs), which had mixed results. To use Shinto as a unifying ideology, the government had revived the ancient **Jingikan**, the Office of the Divinities, and in 1868 created the Senkyōkai, the Board of Mission.

The Jingikan was replaced by the Jingishō, which in turn was replaced by the Kyōbusho. It took over the administration of all religions, the care of imperial tombs, and the missionaries of the Senkyōkai. The Kyōbusho itself was abolished in 1877 when it was realized that public cooperation was minimal. This paved the way for the final rearrangement under which shrines (**jinja**) were administered by the Ministry of the Interior (Naimushō), while all other religious groups were placed under the supervision of the Ministry of Education.

KYŌDŌSHOKU. System of Shinto Missionary Instructors of the Meiji period (1868–1912) appointed under the plan to spread **Kokka Shinto** (State Shinto) as a national ideology.

KYOGEN. A performing art, along with **Noh**, that was stylized during the Muromachi period (1333–1573) that came to be thought of together as Nogaku (Noh and Kyōgen). Unlike the more elegant Noh, Kyōgen is spoken and based upon comedy taken from the everyday life of the common people in feudal society or from folk tales It has been suggested that Noh pursues ideal beauty while Kyōgen expresses a more down-to-earth and realistic essence of human nature. *See also* DRAMATIC ARTS IN SHINTO.

KYŌHA SHINTO. Sect Shinto, specifically the 13 sects approved by the government during the late Edo (1615–1868) and early Meiji (1868–1912) periods. They were formally listed between 1876 and 1908 as follows: the Pure Shinto Sects, **Shinto Taikyō** and **Shinri-kyō**; the Confucian Sects, **Shusei-ha** and **Taisei-kyō**; the Mountain Sects, **Jikkō-kyō**, **Fusō-kyō**, and **Mitake-kyō**; the Purification Sects, **Shinshū-kyō** and **Misogi-kyō**; and the Healing Sects, **Kurozumi-kyō**, **Konkō-kyō**, and **Tenri-kyō** (no longer a member of the group). After the **Pacific War** (World War II), the group came to include a larger number of sects, all claiming ancestry from the original 13.

If the **New Religions** derived from Sect Shinto, groups are added; the number comes to over 130 sects. *See also* KYŌHA SHINTO RENGŌKAI.

KYŌHA SHINTO RENGŌGKAI. The Association of Sect Shinto groups comprising 11 sects and led by a rotating directorate that represents Sect Shinto where required. It was set up in 1946 as part of the **Nihon Shūkyō Renmei** (The Japan Federation of Religions). **Shinshū-kyō**, **Taisei-kyō**, and **Tenri-kyō** do not belong to the association, but **Ōmoto-kyō** gained admission after 1945. Originally the group had 13 sects as members, but the resignation of three and the admission of Ōmoto-kyō left 11 members in the group.

KYŌIKU CHOKUGO (1890). The **Imperial Rescript** on Education is a mature document of Meiji ideology that speaks of the moral relationship between emperor and people. It was frequently memorized, in English, by late Meiji-period (1868–1912) students. It is a heavily **Confucian**-style document, stressing the ideals of virtue, filial piety, benevolence, and loyalty in the way these concepts had been interpreted during the Tokugawa period (Edo period, 1615–1868). It also speaks of the beauty of the Empire, hinting at the value that gives the rest meaning and context.

It is not a text that explicitly calls for emperor reverence, but it does draw its power from the **mythology**, and when a reverent attitude toward it was called for in schools, it provoked considerable controversy when some people refused to show the degree of respect that the government required. In the case of Mori Arinori, the early Minister of Education, it led to his assassination. In full, the official English text of the edict issued on 30 October 1890 reads as follows:

Know ye, Our Subjects:

Our Imperial Ancestors have founded Our Empire on a basis broad and everlasting and have deeply and firmly implanted virtue; Our subjects are ever united in loyalty and filial piety and have from generation to generation illustrated the beauty thereof. This is the glory of the fundamental character of Our Empire and herein also lies the source of Our Education. Ye, Our Subjects, be filial to your parents, affectionate to your brothers and sisters; as husbands and wives be harmonious; bear yourselves in modesty and moderation; extend your benevolence to all; pursue learning and cultivate arts, and thereby develop intellectual faculties and perfect moral powers; furthermore, advance public good and promote common interests; always respect the Constitution and observe the laws; should emergency arise, offer yourselves courageously to the State; and thus guard and maintain the prosperity of Our Imperial Throne coeval with heaven and earth. So shall ye not only be Our good and faithful subjects, but render illustrious the best traditions of your forefathers. The Way here set forth is indeed the teaching bequeathed by Our Imperial Ancestors to be observed alike by the Descendants and the subjects, infallible for all ages and true in all places. It is Our wish to lay it to heart in all reverence in common with you, Our subjects, that we may all attain to the same virtue.

It remains a key document for the study of the ideology that was developed to support the process of **modernization.**

KYŌKU. Administrative ward in the **Kyōha Shinto** (Sect Shinto) sect **Kurozumi-kyō.**

KYŌSOSAMA. Founder of a religion used especially of **New Religions** in Japan as well as of non-Japanese religious historical figures, such as Mohammed or Moses.

KYŪCHŪ SANDEN. Three principal shrines (**jinja**) within the grounds of the Imperial Palace in Tōkyō used by the imperial family for ceremonies and **rituals** of the **imperial household (Koshitsu Saishi).**

KYUDO. The name for Japanese archery as a martial art, the way of the bow, but which also features in Shinto and Shinto-related rituals and ceremonies. The bow itself is unique, measuring about two meters, and is the longest of its type in the world. While the form of the activity and its manner of execution of the art is based on **Zen** stylization, it appears in modified form in **yabusame, omato-shinji** (acts of **divination**), and in the **sumo dohyo,** where it used to perform symbolic circular sweep of **purification** of the ring by a figure known as the dew sweeper.

– L –

LOTUS SUTRA. The Hokke-kyō is a sutra of early Mahayana **Buddhism,** by Kumarajiva (Sanskrit: *Saddarmapundarika-sutra*), translated into Chinese in 406. Because of its all-embracing philosophy, it was highly regarded by the T'ian T'ai patriarch Zhiyi (Chuh-i, 583–597) who used it to emphasize the universality of the Buddhist nature, and declared its teaching to be the continued existence of the Buddha in the world after his final extinction.

The Lotus Sutra was known in Japan in the time of **Shotoku Taishi** (574–622), but came to real prominence when **Saicho** (767–822) introduced the Tendai tradition of Zhiyi into Japan during the **Heian period** (794–1185). The Lotus Sutra began to gain general popularity, and during the Kamakura period (1185–1333), under the influence of **Nichiren** (122–1282) and **Dogen** (1200–1253), it rose to prominence in popular religion and in philosophy. Nichiren taught the merit of chanting the Daimoku (its title) in the invocation "Namu Myoho Renge Kyō" as the ultimate act of devotion.

The Lotus Sutra remains the most influential sutra in Japanese Buddhism and, because of its philosophy, has made possible spiritual transactions between some Buddhist and Shinto groups. **Tendai Buddhism** itself became closely associated with the Lotus Sutra and with **Shugendō**. **New Religions**—for example, movements such as Soka Gakkai, Reiyukai, and the more liberal Rissho Koseikai—all derive their inspiration from Nichiren and from the Lotus Sutra.

LOWELL, PERCIVAL (1855–1916). American-born scientist and author. After graduating from Harvard in 1876, he became an international businessman and traveled extensively in Asia between 1883 and 1893. His book *The Soul of the Far East* (1888) was highly regarded by **Lafcadio Hearn** (1850–1904) because it contained valuable insights into the cultures of Asia. *Occult Japan*, published in 1895 contained descriptions of various rites of Shinto as a result of following a pilgrimage to **Mount Ontake**, home of the **Mitake-kyō** of **Kyōha Shinto** (Sect Shinto). Lowell later became known as an astronomer, and finally was appointed a non-resident professor at the Massachusetts Institute of Technology.

– M –

MAGATSUHI-NO-KAMI. These are *kami* who in some way bring pollution or disaster to the world. They are thought to come from **Yomi-**

no-kuni, the land of pollution referred to in **mythology**. The etymological root of maga means complication, confusion, or even distortion of life; maga-goto refers to confusing or impure things. *See also* AKU; BACHI; ETHICS IN SHINTO; KEGARE; SHINBATSU; TSUMI.

MAGOKORO. Magokoro is identical in meaning to the **Man'yōshū** expression **makoto no kokoro**—sincerity of heart.

MAHIKARI. A **New Religion** with Shinto rather than Buddhist roots, and that grew out of another sect, the **Seikai Kyūsei-Kyō** (the Church of World Messianity). Sukyō Mahikari was founded by Okada Kotama (1901–1974), formerly a soldier and a businessman whose body was occupied by Su-no-Kamisama in 1959 when he received a revelation to become Sukuinushi-sama (Master of Salvation) for the world.

As a young man, his back was injured in a horse-riding accident that resulted in an incurable disease. After dedicating himself to religion, his disease miraculously vanished. When his business failed in 1945 with the end of the **Pacific War** (World War II), he joined Seikai Kyūsei-Shuyo. Working hard to pay off his debts and in the course of his struggles, on 27 February 1959 at 5:00 A.M., he received his first revelation that his mission was to "purify" the world through the power of the True Light, which radiated through his hands. He had also the task of unifying world religions and building the World Shrine in order to enshrine the Almighty Creator God and to awaken people to the reality of human spirituality. Until his death, he travelled internationally and met various world religious leaders including (at that time) Pope Paul VI.

On 13 June 1974, 10 days before his death, Okada officially handed over his divinely commissioned mission to his daughter Sachiko, now known as Oshienushi-sama (Master of Teaching). The sacred text from which the teachings are drawn is the Goseigen, interpreted by Okada's idea of genreigaku (the science of interpreting words by spirit). The practice of radiating light from the hands is called **Mahikari no Waza**. The Shinto dimension is found in the emphasis on purification (**harai**) and on light, along with the titles of the *kami* of the sect.

The chief deity of Mahikari is Su-no-kami, or Mi-oyamoto-su-mahikari-o-mikami, the creator of the whole world who sends out a supernatural light, Mahikari, which is the secret of the power of the religion. This *kami* is the source of all the gods of other faiths, **Amaterasu-ōmikami** in Shinto, Jehovah in Judaism and Christianity, Allah in Islam. These are all forms that are appropriate to their own historic situation. Mahikari claims that there is only one origin of religions and one origin of all human races. The theme may have a universal sound, but there is implicit ethnocentrism in the claim that the origins of all races and religions are to be found in Japan.

The headquarters is located in Takayama City in Gifu Prefecture, and claims 500,000 members. It has branches in North America, and considers itself capable of being a world religion. The sect under Okada Keishū (the founder's adopted daughter) was forced to separate in 1978 from the original Seikai Mahikari Bunmei Kyōdan, led thereafter by Sekiguchi Sakae after a court battle for leadership occasioned by Okada's death in 1974. The court awarded the succession to Sekiguchi, whose group numbered at the time just over 80,000. This was a difficult period in the history of the sect.

There is also the breakaway Shinyugen Kyusei Mahikari Kyōdan, founded by Yoda Kuniyoshi, and the Subikari Koha Seikai Shindan, founded by Kuroda Minoru in 1980. The latter listed 4,500 members at the time. The common feature is that all the groups practice Okada's Mahikari no Waza. The two major groups have active overseas branches. Sukyō Mahikari has 150 in Europe and Africa, 30 in North America, 70 in South America, and 50 in the Pacific Region. Sekai Mahikari Bunmei Kyōdan has only18 overseas missions. *See also* SEKAI-KYŪSEI-KYŌ.

MAHIKARI NO WAZA. Light radiating from the hand as a healing power, as practiced by followers of the sect **Mahikari**.

MAJINAI. Healing through infusion of **Nippai** (inhaling the sun) as practiced by followers of the **Kyōha Shinto** (Sect Shinto) sect **Kurozumi-kyō**.

MAKOTO NO KOKORO. An expression meaning sincerity of heart (**kokoro**) as found in the **Man'yōshū**.

MAKOTO SHINJUSUI. Sincere piety, as taught by the former **Kyōha Shinto** (Sect Shinto) sect **Tenri-kyō**.

MANDALA. Symmetrically laid out symbolic cosmograms found in Indian and esoteric **Buddhism**. During the **assimilation of Buddhism and Shinto** in Japan, Shinto/Buddhist mandalas were created, the most famous of which is found in the three shrines (**jinja**) of **Kumano**.

MANDOKORO. The name given to administrative offices of estates during the **Heian period** (794–1185). Originally, these were offices designated to administer private estates (shoen). The extensive estates of the Fujiwara were administered by a Mandokoro that was virtually a government inside the state. It included the official offices of kumonjo (department of documents) and kurodo-dokoro (secretariat). **Minamoto Yoritomo** (1147–1199) established a Mandokoro in Kamakura at the beginning of the Kamakura period (1185–1333), and subsequently integrated the kumonjo into his government. The Muromachi government (1338–1573) followed suit and established a Mandokoro along the same lines. The administrative model of the great families and shogunal governments was followed by the large shrines (**jinja**) and temples, particularly those granted estates from which supporting revenue could be drawn. *See also* ANDO; HAFURI.

MAN'YŌSHŪ. Literally "Collection of Ten Thousand Leaves," this is the oldest anthology of Japanese poetry, dating to the eighth century; the last items are dated **New Year** 759. It probably spans the preceding century, and consists of 4,515 numbered, and mostly author-identified poems. There are 4,200 in the **tanka** (short) style, 240 in choka (long) style, and other assorted forms, including some Chinese poems. The content of the verses cover the entire gambit of human and social experience, from courtiers to observations about human life, making it a valuable research document.

As a significant literary work, the collection has remarkable merits, as scholars have pointed out. With regard to Shinto, it was identified by **Kokugaku** (National Learning) scholars in particular as the only extant account of the way of life and the spirit of the ancient Japanese. Critics considered that the classical spirit went into decline after this period, losing its spontaneity and becoming more formalized and stylized. Themes such as purification (**harai**), sincerity of heart (**kokoro**), purity of heart, and the basic moral values usually associated with Shinto are found in abundance, along with expressions of the Japanese sense of awe at perceived theophanies such as the fiery volcanic activity of **Mount Fuji**. It is perhaps this phenomenological awareness that most impressed the Shinto scholars of later ages, such as **Kamo no Mabuchi** (1697–1769) and **Motoori Norinaga** (1732–1800), the Kokugaku scholars of the Edo period (1615–1868).

While the study of the history and composition of the text of the Man'yoshū is the work of literary scholars and philologists, its significance for students of Japanese culture is beyond doubt immense.

MAPPŌ. The doctrine of an apocalyptic evil age in **Buddhism** that was popular during the Kamakura period (1185–1333), and which influenced the thinking of people such as the radical Buddhist leader **Nichiren** (1222–1282).

MAREBITO. Visiting *kami* in disguise who fulfill certain community functions at various times of year, especially **New Year** in rural areas. In some villages, the idea has been stylized into **namahage**, masked figures wearing straw capes, who visit village homes. They ask children about their school examinations and their behavior, and admonish entire families for various reasons. The meeting with these special guests represents a cosmology where the vertical dimension (human-*kami*) and the horizontal dimension (community-*kami*) intersect. While belonging to the realm of **folk religion** and **folk Shinto**, they nevertheless offer pointers to an older perception of the nature of the relationship between human and divine that underlies **mythology in Shinto**.

Folklorists have noted that they are also referred to as marodo, and have traced them to ancestral spirits. The argument was that in old and isolated communities, **ancestral reverence** was a prime source of spiritual energy. When new *kami* were introduced, it was natural that older ones would be displaced to the status of occasional visitors. Either way, the marebito concept opens yet another intriguing window on the development of Shinto from being merely a form of folk religion to what it subsequently became.

MARTIAL ARTS. While Shinto per se did not create any martial arts of its own similar to those developed in Chinese temples such as the Shao-lin-ji, Shinto thought about nature and life helped to inspire the creation of distinctively Japanese approaches to the martial arts such as **aikido**, which has its own protective *kami*.

The distinctive approach of the Japanese martial arts lies in their understanding of the role of **ki**. The character for ki is read chi in Chinese as in Tai-chi, the exercise program that is the underlying foundation of the Chinese martial arts. Chi is the energy of the cosmos upon which the individual can draw by participating in its flow. For the Japanese, ki arises from within through disciplines designed to stimulate and release it. Terms such as yaru-ki express this idea that determination and resolve within the framework of discipline and effort will yield the sought-after energy. Both, however, share the basic insight of **Taoism** as expressed in the concept of the virtue of non-action found in the *Daodejing*, the classic text of the Taoist tradition. aikido uses this concept in the underlying passivity and non-aggression of what is presented as essentially a form of self-defense.

Unlike other martial arts such as kickboxing or karate that have become global sports because they can be competitive, there are no aikido tournaments, contests, or world championships. In the dojo, aikido practitioners work at their skills in order to heighten them but not in a competitive context. **Ueshiba Morihei** (1883–1969) began as a student of jujitsu, a popular style of martial arts, at the end of the 19th century. He had a vision in which he claimed to have seen the truth that the purpose of the martial arts is universal love rather than combat. His principles of harmony and gentleness were embodied in his new art called aikido and employed in the first dojo he opened in Tokyō in 1927. Unlike jujitsu and judo, where the opponent waits for a strike, in aikido, the opponent is absent, in the sense of being passive. There are no offensive strikes, only locks and holds that protect. Ueshiba was revered after his death at Aiki Jinja in Ibaraki Prefecture.

The art/sport known as **sumo**, the imperial sport, was very much part of the entertainment culture of the city of Edo (Tokyō) during the Edo period (1615–1868). However, its roots lie in Japanese agriculture and in divining harvest prospects. Even in its modern form, sumo remains steeped in the culture of Shinto and the shrines of Japan. The modern **dohyō** (wrestling ring) is a 15-foot-diameter raised dirt ring modeled on similar rings in many rural areas. Among the symbols of Shinto are the great canopy which resembles the roof of the **Grand Shrines of Ise**. It formerly stood on four posts that were removed in the interests of televising tournaments. The dohyō itself is purified (**harai**) in a special ceremony before each tournament. Each wrestler upon entering the dohyō, after ritual salutation, moves from his side to the center to face his opponent, taking and throwing a handful of salt, also an agent of purification. This can continue for up to four minutes, until the officiating referee (gunbai) indicates that the bout should commence. Officials are licensed Shino priests, and until the tournament has ended, only such purified persons may step up into the dohyo. Individual sumo stables (heya) purify the dohyo and after each day's training, it is brushed and symbols of Shinto are placed in the center with **gohei**, zigzag paper strips that hang from a thick rope (**shimenawa**). The elaborate costume of the Yokozuna, the highest rank of champion (tsuna), includes both shimenawa and gohei. Yokuna, upon reaching the rank, received their license at the **Meiji Jingū** (Meiji Shrine) in Tokyō. Yokuzuna daily perform the dohyo-iri, or entrance ceremony to the ring before the highest level of contests begins. The first performance of this ritual takes place also at the Meiji Shrine at the time of receiving the Yokozuna's license. Yokozuna are not always the largest competitors. Use of weight and balance is important, a version of the virtue of non-action, the positive value of passivity in the context of precise timing.

Most other Japanese martial arts are directly or indirectly linked to **Zen Buddhism**, as it developed in Japan. **Kyudo**, the way of the bow, Japanese **archery** makes use of the Zen concept of mushin (the emptied mind). Kendo, the way of the sword, was the basic skill of the warrior (bushi) class and has features derived from both Zen Buddhism and Shinto. Before engaging in battle, the warrior would celebrate the Zen tea ceremony in order to empty his mind of all distractions. The Japanese sword itself was treated with reverence, and its purity depended, among other factors, on being the possession of one person.

Distinct from the martial arts in general is the unique Japanese tradition of **Ninjutsu**, the art of the Ninja. The Ninja is the result of the evolutionary meeting of the **yamabushi**, the Shinto/Buddhist mountain ascetic, with the practitioner of the martial arts that produced some of the deadliest and most efficient warrior assassins that history has ever seen. Because of their familiarity with the mountain ranges where they lived, yamabushi were frequently asked to act as couriers for local lords or for the government. In order to protect themselves, they began to learn the arts of concealment and devised costumes that could protect them at night because they were black but that could be reversed to be white against a background of snow. Gradually they developed defensive skills and, once the government had recognized their value, Ninja became an independent institutionalized profession. They developed and mastered a range of techniques to cope with almost any situation. As spies and assassins, they formed a vital surveillance network that protected and supported the Tokugawa Shogunate until its collapse in 1868. While having no direct relationship to either Buddhism or Shinto, the emergence of the Ninja provides a good illustration of the way in which eclectic principles worked in the evolution of many distinctive phenomena in Japanese cultural history. *See also* SHUGENDŌ; TOKUGAWA IEYASU; USHIBA MORIHEI.

MARUYAMA SAKURA (1840–1899). A scholar of the **Kokugaku** (National Learning) movement, in particular of the thought of **Hirata Atsutane** (1776–1843). He was imprisoned for advocating anti-shogunate propaganda before the **Meiji Restoration**, but subsequently became a member of the Meiji government and was a supporter of the re-established **Jingikan** (Office of the *Kami*), which was abolished in 1871.

MASKS. From as early as the seventh century, masks for use in Japanese **dance**, **rituals**, and religious ceremony have been preserved in shrines (**jinja**) and temples. Very early clay masks date to the **Jomon** period (circa 7,000 to 250 B.C.E.). Later masks are carved from wood, sometimes lacquered. They reflect both the influence of Asian cultures in Japan and the local tradition. Apart from early masks of Chinese origin, two in particular are identifiable as Japanese; among the best known are masks worn at **festivals**, or in honor of figures such as **Tengu**, or at the **Shishi-mae** (Lion dance). Shinto rituals and ceremonies gave birth to **Noh** and **Kyōgen**, famous for their use of masks. Although these had folk roots, they grew into sophisticated art forms in which various types of human beings and *kami* are depicted. *See also* DRAMATIC ARTS IN SHINTO.

MASON, JOHN WARREN TEETS (1879–1941). American journalist and writer about Shinto in the pre-war period who approached it from the viewpoint of creativity. Heavily criticized for romanticizing the tradition, particularly by more conventional Western scholars, his intuitive approach enabled him to make observations that narrower and more rigid approaches would never have disclosed. He was highly regarded by a number of prominent Shinto scholars who had serious reservations about both the **Pacific War** (World War II) and **Kokka Shinto** (State Shinto).

MASSHA. A subordinate shrine (**jinja**) located within the grounds of a major shrine, of very basic construction and accorded less reverential treatment because it may enshrine *kami* of minor status.

MASUHO ZANKO (1655–1742). A Pure Land Buddhist who was converted to the **Nichiren** tradition and who became a well-known street orator on behalf of an early type of Japanism that stressed the superiority of the Japanese Way over that of other Asian nations. He designated it as wa no michi (the way of harmony), makoto no michi (way of sincerity), and kodo (the imperial way). His views were a mixture of many elements, including **Watarai Shinto, Suiga Shinto**, and **Yuiitsu Shinto**. Although rejecting the basic tenets of **Confucianism**, he nevertheless taught people to bow to their destiny and fulfill their obligations in a traditional manner.

MATOI. Archery practiced within shrine (**jinja**) precincts as a form of **divination** at **New Year**, relating to harvest intended to predict the outcome. In some part of the country, the Chinese character for oni (demon) is written on the target. In Chiba and Ibaraki prefectures to the West of the Kanto Plain, the ritual is known as obisha. *See also* ARCHERY IN SHINTO; BOKUSEN; OMATO-SHINJI; YABUSAME.

MATSURI. The generic term in Japanese for **festivals in Shinto**, namely the **rituals** surrounding the celebration of a *kami* in a community. While many modern "matsuri" are celebrated which have no religious background whatsoever, the oldest remain rooted in, or linked to, Shinto. They begin with a solemn ritual involving presentation of **shinsen** (offerings) to the *kami*. A **norito** is recited and **sake** is drunk as an act of communion. Thereafter, the event becomes one of celebration that might entail a procession through the village or town, **music** and **dance, sumo** wrestling, and a lot of eating from vendors who provide food and beer or sake during the day and well into the evening.

MATSURI-GOTO. The unity of reverence for the *kami* and political order were united in ancient times such that matsuri-goto, the normal term for a **festival**, also carried the nuance of government. This constitutes further evidence that ancient Japan was a sacral society in which the functions of cult and government were combined, as expressed in the system of **saisei-itchi**, the unity of worship and government that the Meiji period (1868–1912) government tried to revive.

MEGUMI. Bestowing of grace by a *kami* or ranked person upon a believer or worshipper.

MEIJI, EMPEROR (1852–1912). The symbol of Japan's **modernization** and entry into the modern world, Emperor Meiji (who became Crown Prince Mutsuhito in 1862) was the son of Emperor Kōmei (reigned 1874–1866), the 122nd emperor according to the traditional list and last emperor to be subordinate to the Tokugawa Shogunate. He became emperor at the age of 14.

While therefore not himself part of the revolutionary movement against the Tokugawa government, his pivotal role soon became apparent as the government transformed him into a Western-style constitutional monarch who was also the centerpiece of the government's modernization project. His image was affected by both the government's desire to promote him as a modernizing figure to bring Japan into the modern world, while other factions invoked his name for the opposite purpose in the **Sonnō Joi** (revere the emperor—expel the barbarians) slogan. Hence the historical controversy about Emperor Meiji and his successors, principally **Emperor Shōwa**.

The Charter Oath, issued, as with all subsequent **imperial rescripts**, in the emperor's name, contained the goals and vision of the new government. The first act was to remove the capital to Edo, which was renamed on the Chinese model, Tokyō, the eastern capital. A constitution was drawn up, the National Diet established, and, after wars against Russia and China to prove her international standing, Japan and the United Kingdom formed their famous Nichi-Ei Domei, the Anglo-Japanese Alliance, in 1902.

Although the entire system was apparently designed to concentrate power into the emperor's hands, in reality it is quite unlikely that he actually exercised these powers. He was surrounded by strong-willed and powerful men, rebels from the old regime, whose agenda was fundamentally to make Japan militarily and economically strong. This included using the emperor, in any way considered appropriate, to achieve that end. In a way, his grandson, Hirohito, Emperor Showa, faced the same issues when confronted by the militarism of the first part of the 20th century.

It is recorded that Emperor Meiji composed a poem that implicitly criticized the government decision to go to war with Russia. Of interest is the fact that Emperor Showa quoted it at the imperial conference of 6 September 1941, when Japan-United States relations had broken down. In a sense they were like classic tragic heroes facing similar circumstances that were beyond their control and against which they could make only token gestures.

Well-educated in the Chinese classics and Japanese tradition, Emperor Meiji was the ideal of the "enlightened monarch." As such, he deeply revered the Japanese tradition, and cared little for the European-style practices being introduced. He accepted them only as necessities and thought that a sense of proportion should be maintained in which only justifiable imitation was acceptable.

An enigmatic, intriguing, and key figure at a decisive juncture of Japanese history, he stands as a bridgehead between the feudal age and the era of modernization. Committed to the cause of Japan's successful entry into the modern world, he appears to have been quite an intense person who internalized many of the issues of the day, a factor that contributed to the breakdown of health that in turn led to his premature death at the age of 60 in 1912.

MEIJI JINGŪ. Large central Tokyō shrine **(jinja)** that celebrates the **soul** of **Emperor Meiji** (reigned 1868–1912) and his empress, Empress Shoken. It was constructed between 1920 and 1921 and involved the voluntary labor of thousands as well as official government support. It certainly reflected the deep respect and affection felt for Emperor Meiji. It was destroyed during the Tokyō air raids on 14 April 1945 and reconstructed in 1968 by public subscription.

All modern **sumo** (the imperial sport) tournaments are dedicated to the **soul (tama)** of Emperor Meiji, and all new Grand Champions (Yokozuna) receive their certification of status from the shrine and perform their first ring-entering ritual (dezu-iri) at Meiji Jingū. It still attracts hundreds of thousands of worshippers at **New Year** and other times of the Shinto calendar. *See also* KOKKA SHINTO; MEIJI RESTORATION; MODERNIZATION.

MEIJI RESTORATION (MEIJI ISSHIN). The Meiji Restoration was so designated because it was the represented as the "restoration" of direct imperial rule, enacted in 1868. It was in fact a revolution of **modernization**, typical of the stage in the evolution of a civilization when industry begins to take precedence over agriculture. This would place the Meiji Restoration on a par with the American Civil War, or even the Bolshevik Revolution in Russia. In spite of apparent and obvious differences, the basic agendas were identical, namely, the creation of a powerful, modernized, industrial state. It ushered in the Meiji period that ended in 1912 with the death of **Emperor Meiji**. It marked the dramatic commencement of Japan's process of modernization. The shogunate stood down in favor of new leadership surrounding Emperor Meiji, thus bringing to an end almost 300 years of feudal government.

The factors leading up to the Meiji Restoration can be classified broadly into internal and external ones. Internally, a spate of serious famines between 1833 and 1836 of the Tempō era (1830–1844) began to create economic disorder and consequently, social disorder which the Edo Shogunate seemed incapable of responding to either appropriately or effectively. The gradual escalation of social unrest and disgruntlement produced various reactions (such as the Eejanaika movement) that resulted in the loss of government credibility among the masses of the people. These factors generated the conditions that made revolutionary change appealing.

Externally, the power of modernized industrial nation states in the West and their predatorial activities within Asia had alarmed elements within the nation's leadership that judged the shogunate to have failed in its task of taking steps to ensure the safety of the nation against such potential foes. Hence slogans such as **fukoku-kyōhei** (rich country/ strong army) became the ideals of the day. **Wakon-yōsai** (Japanese spirit/Western techniques) was another that stressed the selective way in which Western ideas were to be adopted and adapted.

While the process was in effect a revolutionary way forward, it was presented as a restoration of an older tradition. In this regard, it was argued that it had roots that go deep into the Edo period (1615–1868), centering on the work of the **Kokugaku** (National Learning) scholars and the movement known as **Fukko Shinto** (Restoration Shinto), advocated by thinkers such as **Hirata Atsutane** (1776–1843), who urged the return to a society ruled by the emperor. Thus, in reality, it was a combination of both revolution and reversal. The people were still nurtured in the virtues of **Confucianism** such as loyalty, filial piety and respect for the emperor, but in addition were encouraged to think of themselves as replacing the samurai of the past, particularly those who entered the service of the new imperial army.

The various stages of evolution of the Meiji period (1868–1912) are marked by **imperial rescripts** on different themes, along with constitutional issues that were debated in the National Diet. In keeping with most modernizing nations, the centralized Meiji government desired a common ideology to unite the nation, and tried to create one through using the concept of **Kokka Shinto** (State Shinto) and the **emperor system**. The rise and fall of State Shinto is one feature of the Meiji period, although it was not formally abolished until the **Supreme Commander Allied Powers** issued the **Shinto Directive** of 1945.

The Meiji Restoration opened Japan to the world. Apart from the 1933–1945 period, when Japan left the League of Nations and joined the Berlin-Rome (and Tokyō) Axis, the nation has enjoyed good relations in general with Western nations, and as a result of the intense efforts that began in the Meiji period and continued in the postwar reconstruction, Japan rose to being, statistically, the world's second economy after the United States. As yet, however, in the view of many critics, the government is overdue in transferring some of the benefits of the nation's efforts to the people themselves who struggled to achieve them.

MICHI. The term means "way" (the character is also read as dō) in both the sense of an actual road and of a systematic discipline with rules for the cultivation of the art and the self at the same time. Almost all martial arts and aesthetic arts in Japan are suffixed by the term do: sado (tea ceremony), shodo (calligraphy), and judo are among the best known. It is also used for references to Shinto as the **Kodō**, which means ancient way, and **Teidō**, which means imperial way. *See also* AIKIDO.

MICHI NO KAMI. *Kami* of the road, acknowledged especially during the Edo period (1615–1868), that protected travellers who journeyed on foot.

MICHIZURE. Followers of the teachings of the **Kyōha Shinto** (Sect Shinto) sect **Kurozumi-kyō** are called Michizure.

MIFUNE-NO-IWAKURA. A rocky crag or crevice considered to be the seat of a *kami*. The Mifune-no-iwakura is also the sacred landing place of **Ninigi-no-mikoto**, when he descended from the Plain of High Heaven (**Takama-no-hara**) to the Japanese islands. It is located within the grounds of **Tsubaki Ōkami Yashiro** (Tsubaki Grand Shrine) in Mie Prefecture. Counter-claims locate the descent of Ninigi-no-mikoto to a site in Kyushū. However, in view of the fact that Tsubaki Ōkami Yashiro is the officially recognized head shrine of **Sarutahiko-ōkami**, and in view also of its proximity to the **Grand Shrines of Ise** (Ise Jingū), Kyushū seems less likely than central Honshū, in terms of the status of Ise and the *kami* of the sun, **Amaterasu-ōmikami**.

MI-ITSU. The august dignity of a *kami*. It is sometimes interchangeable with shintoku, the divine virtue of a *kami*.

MIKAGURAUTA. Along with the **Ofudesaki**, it forms the two sacred writings composed by founder of the former **Kyōha Shinto** (Sect Shinto) sect **Tenri-kyō**.

MIKI. Rice wine offered to a *kami* as part of the three items—water, salt, and sake—that are placed on altars where reverence is offered.

MIKI TOKUCHIKA (1900–1983). Founder of a **New Religion** known as Hito no Michi (The People's Way) which grew from the **Kyōha Shinto** (Sect Shinto) mountain movement **Mitake-kyō** and a second group which grew from it, Tokumiktsu-kyō. The movement had varying fortunes, and was criticized by pre-war government officials as reverencing the sun rather than the *kami* of the sun. The post-1945 period saw it renamed as **P. L. Kyōdan** (P.L. meaning Perfect Liberty).

"Life as art" became its principal theme, along with the capacity of human beings to realize divinity in themselves. The sect owns a high school that is famous for its baseball team, which in turn gives it national profile at the annual national high school tournament. The tournament in many of its features continues to reflect the moral values of the past, another dimension of its wide appeal.

MIKO. Shrine (**jinja**) maiden or supplementary priestess, originally most likely a shamanistic person, but in modern times, institutionalized into daily shrine life to perform various tasks ranging from cleaning to **kagura,** sacred dance. Miko may be seen at shrines in their distinctive white kimono top with the lower half covered by a scarlet **hakama,** split trousers that look like a wide skirt. On **festival** (**matsuri**) days, they may be seen selling souvenirs, talismans, **ema,** and **omikuji, divination** papers at the shrine office (**shamusho**). *See also* KANNUSHI; SHINSHOKU.

MIKOSHI. *See* OMIKOSHI.

MIKOTO. The command of a *kami*, or a title of respect.

MIKUNIMANABI. The **Kokugaku** (National Learning) scholar **Motoori Norinaga** (1730–1801) used this term to describe imperial country learning.

MIKURIYA. Estates granted by Minamoto no Yoritomo (1147–1199) to assist in the upkeep of shrines (**jinja**). *See also* ANDO; HAFURI.

MINAMOTO YORITOMO (1147–1199). First shogun of the Kamakura period (1185–1333), he established his military government (bakufu) in Kamakura, and moved the nation's capital to that city. The imperial court remained in Kyōto until the **Meiji Restoration** (1868). This sequence of events began Japan's Kamakura period (1185–1333).

Minamoto no Yoritomo's earlier life was quite dramatic. He was captured after the Heiji uprising (the Heiji no ran of 1160) and was sent in exile to Izu where he spent 20 years, until he was 34 years old, when he began raising troops to challenge the government of the day. He seems to have developed a personal devotional faith in **Kannon** through those years. When he began formally raising an army, he turned his devotions to the *kami* Hachiman, visiting, particularly, the **Tsurugaoka Hachiman-gū** in Kamakura. The Hachiman cult consequently grew widely due to its popularity with Yoritomo, although it had a previous history. However, he also maintained a reverential attitude toward the **Grand Shrines of Ise** (Ise Jingū). As a mark of respect, he donated estates known as **mikuriya** to shrines along with land ownership rights known as **ando.**

There is a reference, in a text known as the *Gyokuyo*, to Yoritomo presenting a general report to the emperor in 1183 which referred to the promotion of shrines (**jinja**) and temples in the land of the *kami* (shinkoku in Japanese). He actively cultivated this theme and appeared to be quite serious in his religious commitments. He is remembered for establishing Japan's first military warrior government, the basic structure of which lasted almost 700 years, until the **Meiji Restoration** (1868), when the modern state was ushered in and a form of democracy was introduced.

His brother, Yoshitsune (1159–1189), who was highly regarded by retired Emperor Go-Shirakawa, in 1185, requested (and was given) a decree from the emperor to attack Yoritomo. With poor support, rather than face his brother, he went into hiding and finally sought the protection of Fujiwara no Hidehira, who died in 1187. Hidehira's son was pressurized by Yoritomo to attack Yoshitsune, who in turn was forced to commit suicide along with his wife and daughter.

Yoritomo's image thus remains that of an uncompromising and brutal feudal lord. This stands in stark contrast to his brother ,who is still depicted romantically as a tragic hero, principally because he was only 30 years old at the time when he died under such sad circumstances at his brother's behest. The story remains a popular classic of Japanese history and there have been both books written and television dramas made about it.

MINKAN SHINTO. Folk Shinto rituals and beliefs, found mainly in rural and mountain areas. Anthropologists of religion in Japan use this academic classification used by to discuss, for example, religion in Okinawa, or obscure community rituals that are considered in danger of disappearing. *See also* MAREBITO; NAMAHAGE; SHAMANISM IN SHINTO; YANAGITA KUNIO.

MINOBE TATSUKICHI (1873–1948). Professor at the University of Tokyō who expressed opinions critical of the concepts presented in the **Kokutai no Hongi**, the text produced and used by the Ministry of Education to explain the basis of national identity. He advocated the theory of "emperor as organ of the state" (Tenno kikan setsu). He faced serious charges from the authorities of treason, and was dealt with very severely. He was forced to resign from the House of Peers, and his books were suppressed. His son, Ryokichi (1904–1984), became the progressive party governor of Tokyō in 1967, and again in 1971 and 1975. *See also* EMPEROR SYSTEM.

MINSHA. The Meiji government destroyed over 70,000 minsha, or folk shrines (**jinja**), during **Jinja Gappei** (or Jinja Seirei, shrine consolidation) in the early 20th century. It was part of the program to impose **Kokka Shinto** (State Shinto), according to which poor-looking shrines would be eliminated to enhance the image of Shinto as a national cult.

MIROKU-ŌKAMI. The name of the *kami* revealed to the founder of the sect **Sekai Kyusei-kyō**.

MISASAGI. Mausolea for members of the imperial family. **Emperor Hirohito** (Shōwa) was entombed in Hachioji near Tokyō. When an emperor passes away, it is customary not to use the term shinu (even in its honorific forms) in reference to his death, but rather to use **hōgyo**, which refers to the passing of a *kami*. *See also* KOFUN.

MISOGI. The practice of misogi as a discipline undertaken with specific goals in mind, such as purification (**harai**) in preparation for special events or for spiritual enlightenment. The origin of misogi is recorded in Shinto **mythology** as being the act of purification performed by **Izanagi-no-mikoto** when he washed himself in the River Tachibana after visiting his deceased wife in the land of pollution (**Yomi no kuni**). It has become a paradigmatic aspect of Japanese culture, with misogi performed not only in Shinto rituals, but also in rituals of **Shugendō** practitioners. The following is a rough guide as to how it is generally practiced. The model in this entry refers to misogi practiced under a free-standing waterfall. However, the sequence is almost identical for misogi performed in the sea, in a river, or in a special pond (**kiyome-no-ike**).

Participants first enter the shrine grounds and purify themselves (hands and mouth) in the te-mizuya-no-gi, at a large trough on which small ladles (sendatsu) are to be found. The te-mizuya usually stands at the entrance to the shrine precincts. This is followed by a formal **oharai** ceremony to purify the participants before they proceed toward the fall, because the waterfall itself is a *kami*. This takes place in a building adjacent to the area where the waterfall is located, and follows the normal practice using a **harai-gushi**.

Male participants don a loincloth (fundoshi) and a headband (hachimaki), while female participants wear a long white kimono and headband. Next, they perform a series of calisthenic exercises, beginning with a ritual in which the hands are held in front of the body, clasped as if holding a golf ball and shaken. This is called furitama, or **soul** shaking. Other exercises entail shouting, invoking the *kami* who will be a party to the purification, and a dramatic movement of the hand from a kind of boy scout salute forward and down to the left to represent the cutting away of impurities. A breathing exercise (**ibuki**) completes the sequence. Participants bow twice toward the waterfall, clap their hands twice, and bow again to the waterfall before moving toward the water itself.

A fire is usually lit in a brazier and candles set around the fall. Participants receive a small ladle containing Japanese sake and salt. This is disposed of in three mouthfuls, each blown out of the mouth into the running water below the fall. The leader (michihiko) throws salt over the participants and shakes the remainder of a large bottle of sake into the water, invoking the *kami*.

The leader performs a number of secret hand signs, borrowed from esoteric **Buddhism**, and symbolically cuts all impurities from the nine squares of existence. He then goes forward first and covers loins, chest, and face in water, claps twice, makes the cutting sign as described earlier. He then gives a loud shout of "Ie!" and moves under the fall, right shoulder first and turns around completely. With hands clasped and middle fingers alone pointing out, he repeats the incantation "Harae tamae kiyome tamae, rokkonshō-jō," an invocation for the purification of the soul and the washing away of impurities (**tsumi**). Each participant performs the same sequence of movements and chants the same invocation. This continues until all participants have been under the fall.

The final action after getting dressed is to move to the haiden, the worship hall of the shrine for the ceremony of **chinkon**, the calming of the soul. This is followed by **naorai**, or drinking sake with the *kami*, a ritual of human/divine communion that may also extend after leaving the worship hall into an informal atmosphere. Misogi is normally performed late at night, but sometimes early in the morning. When misogi is referred to in a **norito**, it is spoken of as misogi harai.

When spoken of as a discipline, it is referred to as **misogi shūho**. *See also* MISOGI-KYŌ; SHUGENDŌ.

MISOGI-KYO. One of the **Kyōha Shinto** (Sect Shinto) groups that practices **misogi**, founded by Inoue Masakane (1790–1849), whose real name was Ando Kisaburo, descended from a distinguished samurai family. The sect's breathing discipline breathing is based upon the idea that the origin of this world is the breath of the *kami*, and consequently, through controlled breathing, it is possible to be in communion with the divine. Other sects also practice controlled breathing for religious purposes. The sect also holds the doctrine of **Anshin Ritsumei**, the belief that people should not worry about daily concerns, but rather be concerned with their own long-term personal and spiritual development. *Kami* reverenced by the sect include the three *kami* of creation (**Zōka-sanshin**), **Amaterasu-ōmikami**, and other select *kami*, including Misogi-oshie-no-okami.

Misogi-kyō was officially recognized in 1894 as a sect. However, owing to the Meiji government's attitude toward such activities, the performance of misogi as a discipline was not encouraged. Misogi Jinja is located in Yatsugatake, after being renamed (from Inoue Jinja) and relocated from the old Taito Ward in Tokyō. The headquarters remains in Setagaya Ward in Tokyō. The sect ruptured in 1989, when the Misogi-kyō Shin-ba was set up in Tochigi City. It lists around 20,000 members.

MISOGI-SHUHŌ. The technical term used to describe the practice of **misogi** as a discipline, performed on a regular basis to develop the purity that enables people to return to their *kami* nature.

MITAKE-KYŌ. Also known as **Ontake-kyō**, this movement within **Kyōha Shinto** (Sect Shinto) practices mountain **asceticism**, including **misogi**.

MITAMA-NO-FUYU. Similar in meaning to **megumi**, it refers to divine blessing

MITARASHI. Water provided for ablution upon entering shrine precincts found in the **te-mizuya**.

MITEGURA. Alternative name for **gohei**, paper streamers used as part of the markings to identify the perimeter of a sacred space.

MITOGAKU. Tokugawa Mitsukuni (1628–1700), the second daimyo of Mito, founded this Edo period school of **Confucian Shinto** that was founded in the Mito domain that gave it its name. Tokugawa's goals were to provide a basis for loyalty and reverence for the **imperial household**, even though he was a branch family member of the ruling Tokugawa House. In this way, Mitogaku helped to provide an intellectual basis for concern with the emperor, distinct from the later scholarly **Kokugaku** (National Learning) movement, that later helped to pave the way for the **Meiji Restoration** (1868). Particularly debilitating to Tokugawa government ideology was the concept of the nation as a "family," with the emperor as a father figure. This also had a greater appeal than the secretive type of intimidating rule preferred by the Tokugawa Shogunate. *See also* EMPEROR SYSTEM.

MITSUMINE JINJA. A large and historically famous shrine (**jinja**) located in Chichibu National Park in Saitama Prefecture, north of Tōkyō. It was a favorite shrine of the 20th-century **Emperor Shōwa**'s brother, Prince Chichibu. Along with Hodosan Jinja and Chichibu Jinja, it comprises a group of three **gongen** style shrines, all of which bear influence of **Shingon Shinto** from the era of **Kūkai** (773–835), who is said to have visited many mountain shrines, including these, to teach the ideas he learned in China. It enshrines the souls of wild dogs or wolves who lived in the mountain, referred to as O-inu-sama.

MIYABIKA. This term, meaning "refined elegance," was used by **Kamo no Mabuchi** (1697–1769) in referring to the classical age of Japanese history, an integral part of the historical views of the **Kokugaku** (National Learning) scholars, that the model age of Japanese culture was that of the early emperors.

MIYA-ZA. Traditional community organization that oversees shrine (**jinja**) affairs planning ceremonies and **festivals** in the absence of official priests, and communing (**naorai**) with the *kami*.

MIYAZAKI JINGŪ. Shrine (**jinja**) established by grandson Takei-watatsu-no-mikoto, a grandson of Japan's legendary first emperor,

Jimmū Tennō (660–585 B.C.E.), to honor the emperor, the emperor's father, his father, Ugayafukiaezu-no-mikoto, and the emperor's mother, Tamayorihime-no-mikoto. It is located in the city of Miyazaki in Miyazaki Prefecture, Kyushū, reportedly on the site of Jimmu's first palace.

The buildings are said to have been erected during the reign of Empress Keiko (reigned 71–130 C.E.). Although of such seeming importance, the shrine was maintained primarily by local effort, and did not receive imperial recognition until the **Meiji Restoration** (1868), when even tenuous connections with Japanese **mythology** were nurtured and propagated by those advocating state control of Shinto shrines. This may also have been related to later counter-claims by the **Yamato** line that there never existed any older independent **Yamatai** kingdom in Kyushū.

MODERNIZATION AND SHINTO. While expressions such as Westernization or industrialization have been used to describe the development of Asia and other regions of the world in the late 19th and early 20th centuries, the consensus of scholarship prefers to use the term modernization became it is comprehensive and includes themes such as industrialization along with political and social change. The modernization of Japan is therefore an academic field in its own right, one which combines history with politics, economics, and other related disciples, including religious studies. One question that remains controversial within that study is of the relationship between Shinto and the modernization process focusing specifically on the status of **Kokka Shinto** (State Shinto) with that process and beyond, until its abolition by the **Supreme Commander Allied Powers** in the **Shinto Directive** of December 1945. The historical background is as interesting as it is complex.

For any nation to modernize effectively, three conditions usually must be met: First is that a strong military should be established for defense; second is that economic growth must be promoted; and third is the creation of a unifying ideology. This pattern can be observed in the process by which most nations join the modern world. In some cases these occur over a long period of time, and not necessarily in the same order. There is also usually an armed conflict that forces the old system to give place to the new. The Meiji Restoration in Japan entailed a comparatively brief conflict that brought down the shogunate. The necessary elements of change developed simultaneously, which is one reason Japan was able to move quickly from being a feudal to being a modern state.

Since fear of invasion was a prime motivator for change, the early Meiji period (1868–1912) Japanese slogan **fukoku-kyōhei**, "a rich country and a powerful military," was speedily implemented. To create an ideology that would add emotional drive to the process, and the appearance of political enlightenment, the Meiji government promulgated a new constitution on 11 February 1889 that included the following sentences:

> Having, by virtue of the glories of Our Ancestors, ascended the Throne of a lineal succession unbroken for ages eternal (note: since 661 B.C.E. according to the mythology); desiring to promote the welfare of, and to give development to the moral and intellectual faculties of Our beloved subjects. . . . We hereby promulgate. . . . a fundamental law of State . . .

The law is enumerated by clauses, the relevant of which read:

> I. The Empire of Japan shall be reigned over and governed by a line of **emperors** unbroken for ages eternal.
> II. The Emperor is sacred and inviolable.
> XXVIII. Japanese subjects shall, within limits not prejudicial to peace and order, and not antagonistic to their duties as subjects, enjoy freedom of religious belief.

Prior to the Article XXVIII declaration of toleration, the government had tried to create a national ideology in **Kokka Shinto** by linking it to reverence for the emperor. Shrines (**jinja**) were ranked in a hierarchy with the Grand Shrines of Ise (**Ise Jingū**) at the pinnacle. A movement to reduce the number of shrines, especially poorly maintained ones, and the idea of centralizing worship in more impressive-looking locations produced the movement of shrine consolidation, known officially as jinja, and goshi (joint enshrinement) but in popular critical parlance called **jinja gappei** (shrine mergers). While the movement was resisted and lost its impetus after 1911, over 77,000 small local shrines had been eliminated and the goals of the program had been partly realized.

Other questions have been raised about the relationship between Japan's modernization and the Shinto tradition. Was there a Shinto work ethic, similar to the Protestant work ethic that Max

Weber (1864–1920) defined and argued was one fundamental element in the rise of Western capitalism? Similarly, the rational element in Confucianism has been proposed as a candidate. It could be justifiably argued that the **nenchū-gyōji**, the agricultural cycle celebrated throughout the year at shrines, helped to create a rational and disciplined state of mind that kept all activities moving forward in order. Shinto was very much the religion of life in the sense that **Buddhism** became the religion of the funeral. Such positive influences cannot be overlooked. **Confucianism** undoubtedly left its mark on the "vertical society," as the sociologist Nakane Chie called it. It also remains visible in many aspects of business organization and management. Perhaps, however, the **Hōtoku** principles of **Ninomiya Sontoku** were the closest to a Shinto work ethic. They instilled into people the virtue of hard work and the merit of saving, two fundamental elements of a modern economy.

MONO NO AWARE. Kokugaku (National Learning) scholar **Motooori Norinaga** (1730–1801) used this term in his writings, of the meaning "the pathos of life," or sometimes translated less meaningfully as "the pity of things." It refers in broad terms to aesthetic sensitivity, in all its dimensions, as the basic outlook that reveals the richness and diversity of life, with the beauty of its sadness as a distinguishing character.

MONO-IMI-HO. Abstinence from food and drink for religious reasons as practiced by followers of the **Sect Shinto** sect **Shinshū-kyō**.

MOTOORI NORINAGA (1730–1801). Born during the rule of the eighth shogun, Yoshimune, the son of a cotton wholesaler who worked in Matsuzaka City in the province of **Ise**, Motoori Norinaga received a classical literary education typical of the social class into which he was born. He subsequently studied in Kyōto to become a physician and a Confucian scholar, eventually becoming the pivotal scholar of the **Kokugaku** (National Learning) movement of the Edo period (1615–1868).

At age 28, he returned to Matsuzaka and worked as a physician as well as a teacher. At the age of 34, he met **Kamo no Mabuchi** in Matsuzaka, and while he never had the opportunity to meet him again, he remained profoundly under the influence of his scholarship. He turned his attention to the pre-**Heian period** (794–1185) writings, particularly the **Man'yōshū**, where he claimed to have found the purest form of the Japanese spirit preserved and expressed.

Motoori's methodology of exegetical or philological study (setsumeigaku) and normative study (kihangaku) were central to the discovery of his findings. It enabled him to bypass and see beyond the layers of influence of Chinese thought, helping to reveal the original thought of the Japanese, which he took to be centered on the doctrine of **Amaterasu-ōmikami**, *kami* of the sun.

MOUNTAIN WORSHIP. Known also as **Sangaku Shinko** (mountain cults) this is considered to be the oldest form of Japanese religious worship. Mountains were perceived to be the residence of local community ancestors, and consequently natural places where **ancestral reverence** should take place. Some of Japan's oldest shrines are located in mountain areas, which made natural meeting points with Shinto for **Shingon Buddhism** and **Tendai Buddhism**, introduced from China during the **Heian period** (794–1185). *See also* FOLK RELIGION; MINKAN SHINKO; MOUNT FUJI; MOUNT ONTAKE; SEN-NICHI-KAI-HŌ-GYŌ; YAMABUSHI.

MOUNT FUJI. At 3,776 meters Japan's highest mountain, an object of religious veneration throughout the ages, lies between Shizuoka and Yamanashi Prefectures. Its magnificent conical form is known worldwide as a symbol of Japan. Its crater has a 500 meter diameter and a depth of 250 meters and its diameter at the base is around 50 kilometers. Although it has not erupted since 1707, it is still classified as a live volcano.

Climbing Mount Fuji has been practiced as a religious discipline for centuries, and the mountain is also the center of legends and cults. One narrative explains that Mount Fuji was once visited by a *kami* called Miogi-no-mikoto, who requested lodging for the night. Mount Fuji refused and so the visiting *kami* went instead to Mount Tsukuba. In retaliation for the inhospitality, he decreed that Mount Fuji would always be covered with snow so that she would become isolated.

The early collection of Japanese poetry called the **Man'yōshū** depicts Mount Fuji with awe and splendor, as a *kami*:

Lo, there towers the lofty peak of Fuji
The clouds of heaven dare not cross it.
Nor the birds of the air soar above it.
It is a *kami*, mysterious...
It is our treasure, our tutelary *kami*
The snow that crowns the peak of Fuji
melts on the mid day of June
And that night it snows again.

To calm the volcano, shrines (**jinja**), particularly **Sengen Jinja**, were built to revere Sengen-okami. Mount Fuji was then an object of prayer and reverence rather than the place of **asceticism**, it later came to be. By the 12th century, shrines and temples began to appear on and around Mount Fuji. Matsudai Shonin, also known as Fuji-Shonin, built the first known temple, Dainichi-ji (Great Sun Temple). He was also an associate and friend of the cloistered Emperor Go-Toba (reigned 1183–1198), who retired to become a Buddhist priest. The Buddhist symbol for Mount Fuji was male (a Bodhisattva) while the Shinto *kami*, Sengen-okami, was considered female.

Reverence of Mount Fuji was developed by the numerous mountain cults of **Sangaku Shinko** already in existence around Japan, and different groups grew up around the Fuji cult. Believers of the **Kyōha Shinto** (Sect Shinto) group **Fusō-kyō** climb annually following a route that divides the mountain into ten stations referred to as gome. Perambulating the eight rocky peaks that encircle the crater is known as ohachimeguri, while to walk around the mountain at the level of the fifth station is called ochudo.

In earlier literature Mount Fuji is referred to as a *kami*, but in subsequent eras, while considered a sacred place, it is spoken of more as the dwelling place of *kami*. Mount Fuji is widely depicted in art and has been the subject of countless poems.

MOUNT ONTAKE. Locally referred to honorifically as Ontakesan, it is a 3,063-meter-high mountain in the Japan Alps between Nagano and Gifu Prefectures long associated with mountain **asceticism** and the **folk religion** of **Sangaku Shinko** (mountain worship). It also gives its name to **Ontake-kyō**, one of the 13 **Kyōha Shinto** (Sect Shinto) sects.

MUNABETSUSEN. A household tax imposed during the Kamakura period (1185–1333) and continued into the Muromachi period

(1333–1568), known variously as munebetsusen, munabechisen, and muneyaku, and imposed for the purpose of raising revenue for court, shrine, and temple expenses. Like most taxes imposed for a specific purpose, it became essential to support a bloated bureaucracy with excessive ambitions. It disappeared in the early Edo period (1615–1868) when various national taxes were systematically devised and strictly imposed on the populace by a most uncompromising government.

MUNAKATA SHINKŌ. This early cult flourished in northern Kyushū between the fifth and ninth centuries C.E., when the imperial court of the day exchanged formal emissaries with China and Korea. The three principal shrines (**jinja**) are located in the city of Genkai, 30 kilometers north of Fukuoka, and on two islands in the Genkai Sea, namely, **Okinoshima** and Oshima. They enshrine three female sea *kami*, and were the site of purification (**harai**) rituals designed to guarantee the safety of the diplomatic missions dispatched to the Asian mainland. The cult spread nationwide, creating 9,000 branch shrines.

The **Kojiki** (712) and the **Nihon Shōki** (720) make reference to the Munakata Shrines. The three *kami* of the sea are identified as daughters of **Amaterasu-ōmikami**, and consequently commanded respect from the members of the **Yamato** Court. The principal shrine (Hetsumiya) is located on the mainland of Kyushū and reverences Ichikishimahime. The Nakatsumiya enshrines Takitsuhime (also read as Tagitsuhime), and the Okitsumiya enshrines Tagorihime on Okinoshima, some 50 kilometers off the Kyushū coast. While the two island shrines, as befits their antiquity, are simple and classic in style, the main shrine was regularly reconstructed. The present buildings were erected between 1578 and 1590 under the direction of Kobakawa Takakage, and are considered national treasures.

The islands, themselves considered *kami*, are still visited, and priests must perform **misogi** in the sea before setting foot on the islands to renew the offerings. The sites themselves are of great antiquity, exhibiting remains of **Jōmon** artifacts (circa 7,000 to 250 B.C.E.). Research on the cultic remains of Okitsumiya on Okinoshima has yielded a large number of relics used in rituals and ceremonies. Bronze mirrors, musical instruments, jewelry, and ceramics have been uncovered, some dating to the first century C.E. (Yayoi period). It appears that Japanese emissaries en route to Korea or China left these as offerings for their safe passage to their various destinations.

Since 1954, many have been deposited in a museum within the Het-sumiya complex.

MURAOKA TSUNETSUGU (1884–1946). Distinguished scholar of classical Japanese culture and Shinto and author of numerous works. His most famous book was *Studies in Shinto*, which found its way into English translation through the work of two equally famous North American scholars, Dr. Delmer Brown and James T. Araki.

MUSIC IN SHINTO. Shinto liturgies (**norito**) are vocalized in a special way that has musical properties. Frequently performed ceremonies entail a number of performing arts particularly at **wedding rituals**, but also at festival (**matsuri**) times and other important events of the **nenchū-gyōji**, the annual cycle of shrine events. Music and **dance** are basic components. The traditional Japanese flute and the classic drum are the most widely used. Each has three variants. The sankan means "three reeds" and refers to the Fue, a six-holed flute; the Hichikiri, a nine-holed flageolet; and the Sho, a 17-holed bamboo instrument. The sanko are three drums that vary in size. The kakko, or small drum, is for time-keeping; the shoko is a larger accompanying drum; and the **taiko** is the large drum used in most rituals, struck with heavy wooden sticks. There is also the odaiko, the great drum that can produce enormous sounds that can he heard within most shrine (**jinja**) precincts when rituals are being conducted. *See also* GAGAKU; MYTHOLOGY IN SHINTO; NOH; RITUAL AND DRAMA IN SHINTO.

MUSUBI. The spirit of binding, becoming, growth, harmonization, and completeness as understood in the context of the Japanese **mythology**. Several *kami* are concerned with musubi: Takamimusubi-no-kami (Great musubi *kami*), Kamimusubi-no-kani (Divine musubi *kami*), Homusubi-no-kami (Fire musubi *kami*), Wakamusubi-no-kami (Young musubi *kami*), Ikumusubi-no-kami (Life musubi *kami*) and Tarumusubi-no-kami (Plentiful musubi *kami*).

Two of the *kami* linked with musubi, Takamimusubi-no-kami (High *kami* of musubi, related to the heavenly *kami*), and Kamimusubi-no-kami (*kami* of musubi, related to the **earthly** *kami*) along with Ameno-minakushi-no-kami (*kami* of central heaven) form the **Zōka-sanshin**, the three *kami* believed to be responsible for all creation.

MYTHOLOGY IN SHINTO. The core of the ancient beliefs of Shinto derive from the mythology recorded in the **Kojiki** (712) and the **Nihon Shōki** (720), the section in particular referring to the *kami-yo*, the age of the *kami*. Scholars have identified two sets of narratives, identified by some as the **Yamato** myths, which were interpreted to support the claims of the Yamato clan to be descended from the *kami* of the sun, **Amaterasu-ōmikami**.

According to this tradition, the **Zōka-sanshin** (three central *kami* of creation) in **Takama-no-hara** (the Plain of High Heaven) produced other *kami*. A complex pattern of *kami* emerges after which **Izanagi-no-mikoto** and **Izanami-no-mikoto** set about procreating the Japanese islands. Izanami dies after giving birth to the *kami* of fire, and she goes to **Yomi-no-kuni**, the land of the dead, which is one of the few concrete concepts related to the idea of **death in Shinto** thought.

Izanagi-no-mikoto visits her and finds a land of decay and pollution from which he escapes, and immediately purifies himself by performing **misogi harai** in the River Tachibana. Various *kami* continue to be born. Principally from his nose emerges **Susano-o-no-mikoto**, who becomes a key figure for the understanding of subsequent narratives. His sister is Amaterasu-ōmikami who is born from his left eye. Susano-o-no-mikoto creates havoc in the palace of Amaterasu, and eventually, Amaterasu is so distressed, she hides in the **Ame-no-iwato**. A ribald dance by **Ame-uzume-no-mikoto** entices her out because of the noise of the other *kami* laughing, and the world, darkened by her absence, is again filled with light. As a result of his indiscretions and tempestuous behavior, Susano is finally banished from the Plain of High Heaven.

The other strand, designated by some the Izumo myths, focus on Susano-no-mikoto after he is banished from the Plain of High Heaven, when he settled near **Izumo**. His descendant, **Okuninushi-no-mikoto** (Master of the Great Country), features in numerous Japanese legends, such as the Hare of Inaba, a skinned rabbit that is advised by his brothers to bathe in salt water, and that Okuninushi saves. His brothers try in vain to kill him, having once succeeded only to find that his mother had brought him back to life. He has many adventures, the outcome of which is that he effectively conquers much of the land of reed plains, and finally agrees to hand over the country to the *kami* of heaven, in particular to **Ninigi-no-mikoto**, child of Amaterasu-ōmikami, who is guided by **Sarutahiko-ōkami** to where he will settle, assisted by Ame-uzume-no-mikoto, who subdues the fish of the sea.

This brings the narratives to the third phase, the principal feature of which is the descent of Ninigi-no-mikoto. Before he is able to complete the descent, Ame-uzume-no-mikoto is dispatched to meet a huge earthly *kami*, Sarutahiko-okami, who guards the crossroads of heaven and earth. He is perceived as fearsome, and that is why she was sent. However, she charms and pacifies him, and the descent is thus facilitated. The mythological narrative continues through various imperial reigns into the more clearly evidenced historical period.

Other aspects of mythology in Shinto include the **Shichi-fuku-jin** (Seven *kami* of Good Fortune), tradition surrounding **foxes**, the mountain spirit known as the **Tengu**, strange seasonal visitors known as **marebito**, or **namahage**, and troublesome fierce spirits known as **oni**. Some of these are closer to **folk Shinto** than mythology, but they all possess some kind of mythological character. *See also* EMPEROR SYSTEM; MODERNIZATION AND SHINTO.

– N –

NACHI NO HI MATSURI. At this famous **festival** of the Nachi Taisha at **Kumano**, fire-filled buckets are carried up flights of steps inside the shrine (**jinja**) precincts to welcome Buddhist incarnations. They are borne from the Hiryu Jinja (Flying Dragon of the Waterfall) Shrine.

NAIKŪ. This is the term for the Inner of the **Grand Shrines of Ise** (Ise Jingū), as opposed to the **Gekū**, the Outer Shrine. It enshrines **Amterasu-ōmikami**, ancestor of the imperial family and principal *kami* of heaven. All major events and activities of the **imperial household** are reported at the Inner Shrine, and all new government cabinets are inaugurated by a visit to **Ise**. The **Sumo** Association also visits the Inner Shrine grounds once a year on its provincial tour, as do many invited visiting heads of state. *See also* EMPEROR SYSTEM.

NAISHOTEN. Dedicated priestesses who perform ceremonies in the Imperial Palace and who are under direction of the Board of Ceremonies of the **Imperial Household** Agency (Kunaichō).

NAKAE TŌJU (1608–1648). Confucian scholar drawn to **Taoism** and to neo-**Confucianism**, and who became teacher to **Kumazawa Banzan** (1619–1691). He taught inner spirituality and self-criticism before the divine.

NAKAIMA. The Shinto concept that the middle of the present is the best possible configuration of circumstances, and that human beings should learn to co-operate with these circumstances.

NAKAMURA HAJIME (1912–1999). Internationally famous Japanese intellectual historian and scholar of **Buddhism**, professor emeritus of the University of Tokyō, and director of the Eastern Institute, which he founded. Although best known for his work on Buddhism, particularly Indian Buddhist thought, he was profoundly aware of the importance of Shinto, whose influence in the formation of Japanese culture is explained in numerous of his works. He was also deeply sensitive to comparative issues, made possible by the enormous breadth of his learning.

NAKATOMI. Members of this family were among the first assigned to perform Shinto rituals in the **imperial household** and within the offices of government, and many became hereditary liturgists. The name of the Nakatomi appears in the texts of the **Engishiki** of the **Heian period** (794–1185). *See also* KANNUSHI; NORITO; OBARAE NO KOTOBA.

NAKAYAMA MIKI (1798–1887). Founder, a female shaman, of what was an original **Kyōha Shinto** (Sect Shinto) sect, **Tenri-kyō**, meaning "Teaching of Heavenly Reason." Using a very simple doctrine, she encouraged people to seek the kanrodai sekai (Perfect Divine Kingdom).

Nakayama received a revelation from Tenri-o-no-mikoto, the heavenly divinity known as Oyagami, "Parent God." After the revelation, she became known as the Kami no Yashiro, the living shrine (**jinja**) of the *kami*. She was the eldest daughter of Maekawa Masanobu, who lived in the province of Yamato at Sanmaiden (Nara Prefecture). She showed early signs of being charismatic and began as a devout member of Pure Land Buddhism. Although she had wanted to become a nun, she was married in 1810 to Nakayama

Zembei. In 1838, she had a vision that transformed her life and to which she devoted herself wholly and totally, neglecting her family, which eventually fell into poverty. She began performing healing miracles and teaching that divine protection was attainable through a life of sincere piety. She developed a form of worship characterized by ecstatic dancing and shamanistic practices.

In 1853, Nakayama was widowed, and Kokan, her youngest daughter, went to Osaka to teach the new ideas. During the time she was in Osaka, a fire destroyed the Nakayama house and over the next 10 years, the family had extreme financial problems. During this time, she wrote her books, *Mikagurauta* and *Ofudesaki*, which became the basic manuals of Tenri-kyō.

In September 1875, Nakayama was forced to report to the prefectural government and she was arrested for ignoring religious ordinances. She was eventually released, but was arrested again in 1882 and charged with confusing Shinto and **Buddhism**, which had become a crime in the Meiji period (1868–1912). Tenri-kyō was officially recognized in 1885, and on 26 January 1887, Nakayama began advocating the **Kagura Zutone**, salvation dance, which was subsequently banned by the police. Deciding that the laws of God were more important than the laws of man, Nakayama performed the dance at the **Jiba**, the spiritual headquarters of the sect, and reportedly died.

NAMAHAGE. A figure of **folk religion**, a **marebito**, a strange visitor who come in the form of a frightening creature covered in straw who visits the homes of village people at **New Year**. It is particularly famous in Akita Prefecture in the Oga Peninsula. The Namahage was understood as a *kami* who came from far away to visit the community in order to reprimand errors and encourage effort.

NAOBI-NO-KAMI. Literally "Rectifying *kami*," these are recorded in the **Kojiki** (712) and the **Nihon Shōki** (720). The names are sometimes read Naohi rather than Naobi. The two *kami* are Namu-naohi-no-kami and Onaohi-no-kami who appear after **Izanagi-no-mikoto** has escaped from the land of pollution (**Yomi-no-Kuni**) where he visited his dead wife, Izanami-no-mikoto.

Among the *kami* to which he gave birth when he had purified himself were the two "rectifying *kami*," whose status has been the subject of great controversy within Shinto thought. Basically *kami* are good, although some may be troublesome. The idea that there could be an evil *kami* was suggested by the **Kokugaku** (National Learning) scholar **Motoori Norinaga** (1730–1801), but rejected by **Hirata Atsutane** (1776–1843), who defended a monistic view of the nature of *kami*. The existence of these *kami* came to be explained as arising from the desire of Izanagi-no-mikoto to rid the world of pollution (**tsumi**) for the benefit of humanity.

NAORAI. The act of communion with a *kami* after performance of **sampai** (formal worship) or **misogi** (purification under a waterfall, in a river or in the sea). It consists in the ritual drinking of Japanese rice wine (sake). It marks the return to ordinary life after a period of **imi** (abstinence), and is usually celebrated away from the sacred area in a separate place set apart for the purpose.

NATIONAL LEARNING. *See* KOKUGAKU.

NATURE IN SHINTO. Before Western influences entered Japan, there was no separate term for nature, which of course does not imply that religious appreciation of the natural did not exist. The term chosen to mean "nature," shizen, is a Japanese reading of the Chinese *ziran* as found in the *Daodejing* (*Tao de Ching*), the classic text of **Taoism** (Chapter 25 line 12). It has the connotation of something that operates according to its own principles, that is to say, something that is sui generis, spontaneous.

Early Japanese appear to have believed that nature was the realm in which *kami* or divine beings lived, manifested themselves and interacted between heaven and earth, and between the divine and the human. The Japanese **mythological** accounts of creation in both the **Kojiki** (712) and the **Nihon Shōki** (720), while heavily Chinese in style, clearly express these distinctively Japanese concepts. As Shinto rituals developed around the cycle of the rice production year, these ideas again came into focus as the conceptual framework for the understanding of the life of the people. When the imperial institution came into being, accession rites, principally the **Daijōsai** were timed to coincide with the rice harvest.

Japanese thinkers of different eras had different approaches to nature. During the Edo period (1615–1868), under the influence of neo-**Confucian cosmology**, attempts were made to understand nature according to laws. **Yamaga Sokō** (1622–1685) wrote of cosmic inevitability, portraying the idea of a universe governed by necessity. Miura Baien (1723–1789) and Ando Shoeki (1703?–1762) attempted to discuss nature in holistic terms.

However, it was not until the Meiji period (1868–1912), when Western thought was introduced, that the term shizen came to be used in the Greek sense from which the idea of natural science was derived. One point upon which a large number of commentators agree is that the religious celebration of natural events and the demonstration of respect for the power of those events was also closely associated with a deeply aesthetic appreciation of nature. From an early work such as the **Man'yōshū** to the great landscape paintings of the **Zen Buddhist** tradition, the sacred beauty and the power of nature is consistently extolled. Shinto uses natural sites and forces, such as rivers, waterfalls in sacred mountains and the ocean to perform exercises of purification (**harai**). The importance of sacred mountains and **mountain worship** in Japanese religious culture is universally acknowledged.

The Japanese view of nature is clearly distinguishable from the Western idea of nature and humanity in a contest for power on at least three basic grounds. Firstly, nature is sacred in and by itself, and not as a derivative factor arising from having been created by a deity. In a highly empirical and phenomenological sense, sacred spaces and places form the basis of this reverence. Hence shrines (**jinja**) are located at places of natural beauty or perceived power.

A second point is that to the Japanese, human beings and *kami* alike live within the natural order, an idea that contrasts sharply with the Western concept of transcendence. Therefore in **festivals**, people and *kami* celebrate together. The **omikoshi** bouncing around the streets is the *kami* among the people.

Finally, while nature also can produce disasters as well as sights of beauty, not even this has prevented the Japanese from taking a positive attitude toward nature. While there are *kami* who may work mischief, there is nothing approaching evil, and there is no inclination whatsoever toward a dualistic understanding of the cosmos.

Critics (mostly Western) have written frequently about the decline of this awareness among modern Japanese, and about toleration of pollution, as if the existence of Shinto should provide a solution to such problems. The Oriens Institute of Tokyō found, in a survey conducted in the 1980s, that sacred places still exerted their charms and their power and that the traditional aesthetic perception of nature was very much alive. The Japanese view of nature has had its impact, as for example when the Tokyō Municipal government enacted in 1999 that 20 percent of all high-rise roof areas be planted with bushes and trees to provide more oxygen. Awareness of nature and nature's importance for life seems still to exist. Although Tokyō failed in its bid for the 2016 Olympic Games, the goal of becoming an environmentally friendly "green city" remains on the municipal government agenda.

NENCHŪ-GYŌJI. The annual cycle of events that constitute the agricultural calendar as it proceeds through the rice cultivation year. While it varies from region to region in detail because of weather and climate, it was commonly based on the lunar year. This was replaced in 1872 by the Western solar calendar. While various methods are used to fix official dates, there is a general consensus concerning the order of events. The Autumn **Festival**, the **Niinamesai**, is the most significant of the year, elevated in status when it becomes the accession rite of a new emperor, and is known as the **Daijōsai**.

NENGO. The custom of naming imperial eras using titles drawn from the Chinese classics. *See also* EMPEROR SYSTEM; TENNŌSEI.

NEO-CONFUCIANISM. *See also* CONFUCIANISM AND SHINTO.

NEW RELIGIONS. The New Religions of Japan, the Shin Shūkyō or Shinko Shūkyō, as they are termed (in contrast to the older established religions known as Kisei Shūkyō), are a well-known feature of Japan's postwar religious and cultural landscape. The Ministry of Education statistics on religious groups list over 2,000, ranging in size from small groups with as few as a hundred followers and one spiritual leader, to vast denominations like the Nichiren thought-based Buddhist movement Sōka Gakkai, which claimed at its peak to have had 16 million followers.

With the exception of the Unification Church, which originated in Korea, and one or two foreign Christian groups, all of these movements have developed indigenously. They support the fact that religion does continue to play a role in Japanese society; they continue to represent certain traits within Japanese religious life that seem to be present in all periods of Japanese history. This is one way in which patterns of continuity in Japanese society and values have been preserved in the midst of change. Apart from a few large ones that are derived from Buddhist origins, there are movements that are based upon and influenced by ideas that can be derived from the Shinto tradition in one form or another. There may not be overt Shinto connections, but the central ideas and practices are closer to Shinto than to any other tradition in Japan. Many of the new groups make striking parallels when considered alongside the various **Kyōha Shinto** (Sect Shinto) sects. It could be argued that in their essentials, they are similar and that it is only time that separates them.

The **Kyōha Shinto Rengōkai** (Association of Sect Shinto) originally included only the 13 officially recognized sects. After 1949, many new groups emerged, increasing the number of Shinto-based sects to 82 by 1980. A further 48 appeared claiming lineage from the new stream of Shinto. At that point also, some of the non-Shinto New Religions joined the great stream of the evolution of Japanese religion. The religious liberation of 1946 enabled hitherto suppressed movements to flourish, simultaneously encouraging them to be less nationalistic and to think again, as they had in the Meiji period (1868–1912), in terms of the wider world. Many of these groups became involved in movements such as the World Conference for Religion and Peace (WCRP) and the International Association for Religious Freedom (IARF) while others undertake charitable work, nationally and internationally.

Only the principal Shinto-based New Religions with large memberships have been listed in the this volume: **Mahikari**, **Ōmoto-kyō**, **P. L. Kyōdan**, **Seicho-no-Ie**, **Shinrei-kyō**, and **Seikai-Kyūsei-kyō**. The following other groups claim over 10,000 but less than 100,000 members each, which indicates the power of continuing growth within the life of Shinto: Nenbyō-Shinkyō, Oyama-Nezu-no-Mikoto-Shinji-Kyōkai, Shizen-no-Izumi, **Byakkō-Shinkōkai**, Kedatsu-kai, Kyō-sei-shū-kyō, **Annanai-kyō**, Sekai-Mahikari-Bunmei-Kyōdan, Shinsei-kai, Daiwa-Kyōkai, Shōroku-Shinto-Yamatoyama, Nippon-Sei-Dō-Kyōkai, Shin-mei-ai-shin-kai, Shizen-Kai, Shizen-sha, Shizen-Shin-Dō, Makoto-no-Ie, Sumera-kyō, Maruyama-kyō, Komyo-kai, Heiwa-Kyōkai, Ichi-gen-no-Miya, Kami-Ichi-Jo-Kyō, Dai-Shin-Kyō-kai, and Tenrei-Shinrei-Kenkyu-Jo.

The most recent wave of New Religions, known as the New-New Religions (Shin Shin Shūkyō), presents a different spectacle. These tend to be rather postmodern in the sense that they clearly do not belong to any single older tradition. They are syncretistic in a global sense, mixing ideas from many sources, often in an inconsistent and, to the outsider, an unintelligible fashion. The notorious acts of Aum Shinrikyō seem to suggest an entirely different agenda, and have caused, with justification, considerable social criticism along with a corresponding degree of concern, forcing the Japanese National Diet to implement laws in the interests of public safety to deal with the potential danger that may arise from any more such radical movements. Prominent among and typical of other eccentric and highly postmodern but benign groups would be Kofuku no Kagaku (The Science of Human Happiness) whose founder has published 400 books, several of which claim that he embodies the teaching of all the great religious leaders of all ages. In all, several hundred new religions have emerged between 1945 and the beginning of the 21st century. *See also* BUDDHISM; DEGUCHI NAO; LOTUS SUTRA; NICHIREN; TANIGUCHI MASAHARU.

NEW YEAR IN SHINTO. The New Year is the major public event of the cycle of rituals. Apart from being the commencement of the Solar Year, it is the one other time apart from **Obon**, in the summer, when people make their way back to their hometowns.

Hatsu-mōde, the first New Year visit to a shrine (**jinja**) or temple, is performed usually by over 90 million people. Other activities accompany New Year, including eating of special foods, parties, and many public New Year gatherings. The imperial household poetry reading takes place then, as does the Hatsu Basho, the first **sumo** tournament of the year. There is also hatsu-hi-node, sitting outside waiting for the first sunrise of the New Year.

NICHIREN (1222–1282). Founder of a new Japanese form of **Buddhism** developed during the Kamakura period (1185–1333), Nichiren became spiritual father to a great tradition of Buddhism based on the **Lotus Sutra** that gave rise to many **New Religions** even in the 20th century. He was born in Kominato (now within Chiba Prefecture), and he claimed to find enlightenment at sunrise. His name is a combination of the characters for "sun" and "lotus," suggesting that the Shinto roots of his thought were not merely imagined.

When the Mongol invasions failed, he referred to the winds as **kami-kaze**, divine winds that saved the nation, although he himself thought that the invasion was to be a kind of eschatological judgment on the government for supporting impure Buddhism. Early in his career, in 1260, he produced his famous *Risshō Ankoku Ron* (A Discourse on Protecting the Nation by Means of Righteousness), which provoked a government response that led to his exile. Nichiren became a romantic figure to later observers, such as the Christian Uchimura Kanzo (1861–1930), who saw him as a defiant figure, like one of the eighth-century B.C.E. reform prophets of the Hebrew tradition.

Modern movements claiming his ancestry range from Sōka Gakkai (founded in 1930), which is perhaps the most extreme, to the more liberal Risshō Kōseikai (founded in 1938). In spite of controversy over the character of Nichirenism, it will doubtless continue to grow and develop new forms. One legacy has been the peace orientation of most branches after 1945 and the positive steps taken to engage in peace work.

NIGIMITAMA. The spirit of integrating power in a *kami*, usually considered the calm and peaceful aspect of a *kami* in contrast to the **arami-tama** (the "rough" or powerful aspect). *See also* SOUL IN SHINTO.

NIHONGI. *See* NIHON SHŌKI.

NIHON MINZOKU BUNKA EIZO KENKYUJYO. The Audio-Visual Research Institute of Japanese Folk Culture, located in Shinjuku, in Tokyō. This organization films and records rituals and ceremonies nationwide that may be in danger of dying out. One such cycle filmed in Hiroshima took seven years to complete.

NIHON SENDAI KUJI HONGI. *See* KUJI; KUJIKI.

NIHON SHŌKI. Chronicles of Japan, 720, the second oldest set of historical records that commence with the age of the *kami* to the reign (686–697) of Empress Jito. Its sequel volume, the **Shoku Nihōngi** (797), dates it to Yoro 4.5.21 (1 July, 720). It states also that by order of **Emperor Temmu** (reigned 672–686), his son, Prince Toneri, created the Nihon Shōki, and that he compiled 31 volumes, one of which was a set of genealogical tables. The official name of the text was the Nihongi; the eighth-century **Man'yōshū**, and the Koki, an eighth-century commentary on the **Taihō Ritsuryō**, use the term Nihon Shoki when referring to it.

Volumes one and two deal with the mythological age from creation to the descent of **Ninigi-no-Mikoto**. Volumes three to 30 deal with the emperors from **Jimmu Tennō** (reigned 660–585) the first to that of Empress Jito (reigned 690–697) in the seventh century. One significant point of difference between the earlier **Kojiki** (712) and the Nihon Shōki is that the influence and presence of Chinese and Korean elements is explicit and apparent. The Chinese *Wei Zhi* is quoted, and a the entire text is written in classical Chinese. Use of varied Chinese characters and words in different chapters has been cited as evidence that the text was a composite work assembled by a large number of researchers. Numerous historical points are noted with interest, such as the reference to Princess Abe (later Empress Gemmei (reigned 707–715), who is recorded as having established a capital in Nara.

The constant reference to "Nihon" (Japan) in discussions of Japan's relations with Asian regions suggests also a great desire to establish a national identity within Asia. While obviously respecting China, it tends to represent Korea (Silla, as it was called) as a tribute-paying land of savages, which was hardly true of any countries under the hegemony of China.

It became an important reference text that was lectured on, studied, and analyzed in commentaries over the centuries. First was the **Shaku Nihongi**, compiled in the 13th century. During the Kamakura period (1185–1333), it was perceived to have an aura of divinity about it, in keeping with the *kami* no kuni (land of the *kami*) self-understanding of Japan at the time, and commentaries tended to be ethnocentric and divine-country oriented, with special respect for the imperial institution. **Ichijō Kaneyoshi**'s *Nihon Shoki Sanso* is a well-known example. During the Edo period (1615–1868), studies became more academic, and the **Kokugaku** (National Learning) movement drew much from the classical writings.

NIHON SHŪKYŌ RENMEI. *See* JAPAN FEDERATION OF RELIGIONS.

NIINAMESAI. Annual autumn **festival** celebrating the harvesting of the first cuttings of rice. Traditionally, it occurred in the 11th month and became fixed on 23 November in more recent times. During the accession of a new emperor, it is referred to as the **Daijōsai** and replaces the regular Niinamesai. According to the **Nihon Shōki** (720) it is referred to also as the Shinjosai, and is traced back to the first rice crop harvested by **Amaterasu-ōmikami** in the rice fields of the Plain of High Heaven (**Takama-no-hara**).

The Niinamesai was not observed from the beginning of the Onin War (1467–1477), and was not formally reinstituted until around 1739, according to the majority historical judgment. The ritual itself takes place within the Shinkaden, a special hall erected within the Imperial Palace grounds, on 23 November and again on the next morning. The ritual is followed by a **naorai** feast, known as the Toyo no Akari no Sechie. Offerings are also made at the **Grand Shrines of Ise** (Ise Jingū) and prominent provincial shrines (**jinja**), usually in October.

Since 1948, the national identity of the festival has lost prominence because of the establishment of a national holiday on the same date, namely Labor Thanksgiving Day (Kinro Kansha no Hi). However, the Autumn Festival is celebrated nationwide on different dates, and remains the major and the most solemn festival of the year at most shrines. *See also* AKI MATSURI; EMPEROR SYSTEM; ENGISHIKI.

NIJŪ-NI-SHA. The principal 22 shrines (**jinja**) as listed during the **Heian period** (794–1185), including shrines in Ise, Kyōto, and Nara areas that received special acknowledgement and donations from the imperial court. The "upper seven" were **Ise, Iwashimizu**, both **Kamo** shrines, Matsuno, **Hirano**, and **Kasauga**. The "middle seven" included Oharano, Omiwa, Isonokami, Yamato, Hirose, **Tatsuta**, and **Sumiyoshi**. The "lower eight" were **Hie**, Umenomiya, **Yoshida**, Hirota, Gion, **Kitano**, Niukawakami, and Kifune. *See also* ICHI-NO-MIYA.

NIKKŌ TOSHŌGŪ. Tendai-Shinto shrine (**jinja**) created to revere the **soul** of **Tokugawa Ieyasu** (1543–1616), founder of the Tokugawa Shogunate. It is famous for its architectural style, which is richly filled with Chinese imagery, and is in the **gongen**, or "incarnation" style, reflecting the Shinto/Buddhist synthesis of the **Heian period** (794–1185).

The name means literally "Palace of the Eastern Incarnation of the Light of the Sun," which all but confers divinity on Ieyasu, but is quite in line with his obvious desire to rule from the grave, which, through his successors, he did successfully for almost three hundred years. It also reflects the Edo government's liking for religious **syncretism** and for blurring the lines of distinction between **Buddhism** and Shinto to pre-empt any religious challenges to governmental authority.

NINGEN-SHIN. Human beings whose spirits are worshipped as *kami*. **Sugawara Michizane** (845–903) is the most famous, but unlike in his case, where he was worshipped after he died, some people are worshipped during their lifetimes. *See also* IKIBOTOKE; IKIGAMI; KATŌ GENCHI.

NINIGI-NO-MIKOTO. Grandson of Takamusubi-no-kami; his father was Ame-no-oshihomimi-no-mikoto and his mother was Takukata-chijihime. Ame-no-oshihomimi-no-Mikoto was the son of **Amaterasu-ōmikami**, making **Ninigi-no-mikoto**, the grandson of Amaterasu-ōmikami. It is from here that the imperial family traditionally claimed its lineage of divine descent. Amaterasu-ōmikami dispatched him to the land of reed plains to pacify it and create civilization.

As symbols of his authority he was given the mirror, jewel, and sword, the **sanshū-no-shinki**, the **imperial regalia**. Various accounts of his descent exist. According to one, he landed on Takachihonom-ine, claimed by some to be located in Kyushū, which would naturally support arguments about an older civilization in Kyushū.

There is also the site of the **Mifune-no-Iwakura**, located at **Tsub-aki Ōkami Yashiro** in Mie Prefecture where **Sarutahiko-ōkami** assisted him upon his landing to find the land of Ise. He married Konohana-no-sakuyahime (symbol of a blooming flower) rather than Iwanagahime (symbol of the timelessness of rocks), contradicting the will of the father of both female divinities, Oyama-atsumi-no-kami. The net result was to be that future emperors were not to be permitted to live long lives, as were the *kami*.

The great grandson of **Ninigi-no-mikoto** became the first emperor, the legendary **Jimmu Tennō** (reigned 660–585). Ninigi-no-mikoto is enshrined at Kirishima Jinja in Kagoshima Prefecture, and Kono-hana-no-sakuyahime, associated with **Mount Fuji,** is enshrined in the **Sengen Jinja** in Shizuoka.

NINJA. Martial Arts specialist who evolved out of the culture and activities of the **yamabushi**, who became spies and assassins working for the Tokugawa government until its collapse in 1868. They were famous for their many skills, including the art of making themselves seem invisible. *See also* NINJUTSU.

NINJOMAI. Dance of the leader of a **kagura** orchestra. The head of the **imperial household** guard of the Heian period (794–1185) traditionally performed this master of ceremonies role carrying a branch of **sakaki**, the Japanese evergreen in his hand.

NINJŌ SHUGI. Kokugaku (National Learning) scholar **Motoori Norinaga** (1730–1801) defined this concept as the principle of human feeling that constitutes the essence of humanity.

NINJUTSU. The arts of the **ninja**, especially the art of making themselves appear invisible through a variety of methods and devices including small explosions to extensive training in stealth movements.

NINOMIYA SONTOKU (1787–1856). A peasant sage of the Edo period (1615–1868) who was an outstanding leader in the field of agricultural science and philosophy. He created the concept of **Hōtoku**, repayment of virtue, meaning that by repayment of benefits received from heaven and earth and other people, society would be peaceful and prosperous. Sincerity, diligence, thrift, and co-operation were the key values he preached, and these accorded well with both the Tokugawa government's thinking and that of the Meiji government after 1868.

The consistency of his ideas with Shinto was pointed out by his disciple Fukuzuki Masae (1824–1892), who was one of the founders of the Hotokusha (Society for the Repayment of Virtue). One of the physical remains of his thinking was in the statues of a mythical figure, Ninomiya Kinjiro, a little boy who is depicted carrying a sack of wood on his back and who is, at the same time, reading a book. This became a symbol of the moral value of hard work to overcome hardship that became popular during the Meiji period (1868–1912). Statues were placed in all elementary school playgrounds to encourage children to emulate the efforts of Ninomiya Kinjiro. They were removed by a **Supreme Commander Allied Powers** order in 1945, presumably because they were considered to be part of pre-war moral education. The confusion of this with militarism was an illustration of how little the occupation understood Japanese culture. Many were removed to local shrine grounds. Many vanished, but some still remain.

In the early 1990s, it was suggested within the Ministry of Education that the statues might be replaced, itself an interesting idea, demonstrative of the importance of the role of symbols in Asian moral education.

NINTOKU, EMPEROR (REIGNED 313–399). The 16th emperor who dates to the last half of the fourth century and who is buried in the largest tomb found in Japan, in the city of Sakai in Osaka Prefecture. It is a keyhole-shaped burial mound (**kofun**), 486 meters long, surrounded by three moats, and occupies 80 acres of land. Under the protection of the **Imperial Household** Agency, it has never been excavated. A landslide in 1872 revealed numerous artifacts, including iron armor, bronze ornaments, a glass bowl of Persian origin, and a stone coffin. However, these have been considered peripheral grave artifacts.

Nintoku is depicted as a highly enlightened and benevolent emperor who reigned, according to the **Nihon Shōki** (720) from 313 to 399. These dates are unacceptable to many historians for a variety of reasons, not least of all the legendary length of his reign. The **Kojiki** (712) records him as the fourth son of **Emperor Ōjin** (reigned 296–313), who succeeded his father because of the death of his younger half-brother.

On the basis that Nintoku was one of the five kings of Wa referred to in the records of the Chinese Liu-Song Dynasty (420–479), by the name of Zan (San in Japanese), it has been suggested that he probably did rule over a court in Naniwa (now Osaka), and that he actively pursued trade and diplomatic policies relating Japan to Korea and southern China. The enlightened policies attributed to him suggest the strong influence of Chinese humanism, and would help also to account for the scale of the monument created to honor him after his death. *See also* EMPEROR SYSTEM.

NIPPAI. Inhaling the sun for healing, a doctrine of the **Kyōha Shinto** sect **Kurozumi-kyō**. *See also* MAJINAI.

NITTA KUNIMITSU (1829–1902). Founder of the Confucian **Kyōha Shinto** (Sect Shinto) sect **Shusei-Ha**. He claimed decent from Nitta

Yoshisada, an early 14th-century warrior famed for his belief in the virtue of loyalty.

Nitta was born in Awa (in modern Tokushima Prefecture). His Confucian and warrior backgrounds inspired him to try to master the arts of both pen and sword. Although the samurai class was in decline by the early 19th century, in the old tradition, he studied the Chinese classics and the way of the bushi (warrior), trying to discover the proper bearing for a warrior and a gentleman scholar.

At age 20 he began to promote the teachings of Shinto as he understood them for the enlightenment of his fellow countrymen. Members of the Oshi clan opposed his activities, and began successful slander campaigns after which he was imprisoned. His imprisonment, however, had the effect of inducing "enlightenment" as often happens in such cases. His writings before and after the imprisonment period indicated the nature and depth of his conversion experience. After his release, he became extremely determined to work for the improvement of public morality as understood in its meaning as derived from **Confucianism**.

With a show of public spirit, Nitta and his companions tried to bring Shinto to greater prominence, stressing moral obligations, patriotism, and its own status as a great way. He wished to teach people to become good citizens, to serve in the military if required and, above all, to make Japan's economy prosperous by whatever sacrifice was required. These themes found favor with the Meiji government and he finally was vindicated when the sect was formally recognized in 1876. He eventually received 10 citations and honors from the **imperial household** for his good influence on society.

His teachings, although extremely Confucian in character claimed to be drawn from the classic texts, particularly the **Kojiki** (712) and the **Nihon Shōki** (720) as well as the **Kogo Shūi** (Mythological Annals of Japan, [801]) and the *Shi sho go kyō*. There is also the influence of the *Chu kun ai koku* and this implied that in his thought the imperial tradition was to be revered above all other institutions. He belonged to the **Sonnō-Joi** faction (revere the emperor—expel the barbarians) that tried to exclude all foreign influences from the developing nation. He reflected very much the ideology of the period, which called for people to act morally, meaning simply being loyal to the Meiji government, to work and support their families, serve the country, and make Japan great. *See also* MODERNIZATION AND SHINTO.

NOGI JINJA. Located in the Akasaka district of Tokyō, it enshrines General Nogi Maresuke (1849–1912), veteran of the **Meiji Restoration** struggle who became famous for his military exploits particularly in the Sino-Japanese War of 1902 and the Russo-Japanese War of 1904–1905. Although a nationally revered figure, his life was not without controversy, partly because he lost the imperial standard during an early campaign, and partly because elements within the army would not conform to his Prussian values of discipline and order. He left the army and returned to it more than once during a tempestuous career that saw him move from the military to farming and finally to become a professor in what is now Gakushūin University.

Nogi committed suicide by performing seppuku, the classical method of disembowelment, accompanied by his wife, on the day of the funeral of **Emperor Meiji** (reigned 1868–1912). It was referred to as junshi, following one's master in death. He was enshrined in 1919 as a national hero, perhaps even a tragic hero, on account of his contribution to the development of Japan, on an international level, during the Meiji period (1868–1912). While this happened during the relatively liberal Taisho democracy period, as it came to be known, political motivation was probably minimal. Nogi became classified as a private religious corporate person after 1945. However, the shrine (**jinja**) came to be an integral part of the **Kokka Shinto** (State Shinto) system, although never being a rallying point for either nationalism or militarism. Nogi Kaikan, the adjacent building containing restaurants and reception facilities, is a popular location for weddings and parties. *See also* MODERNIZATION AND SHINTO.

NOH. Religious drama that evolved from Shinto rituals that in turn expressed themes from Japanese **mythology**. It arose from lengthy rituals that were performed initially by priests, but subsequently by actors, who performed only the early parts of the total sequences as separate artistic modules.

Although it is performed in a secular context in modern times, many performances still take place at shrines. Even when they do not, the actors, chorus, orchestra and stage assistants as well as costumes and **masks** all receive ritual purification (**harai**) before performances commence.

The oldest deal directly with themes from the age of the *kami* (**kami-yo**) as recorded in the classical texts, the **Kojiki** (712) and the **Nihon Shōki** (720). As the art form developed, new themes were introduced from time to time, but in spite of its evolution, many of the ancient features remain highly visible. *See also* DENGAKU; DRAMATIC ARTS IN SHINTO; FOLK CULTURE; NOH; KYOGEN; SARUGAKU.

NORITO. Ritual invocations of the *kami,* first compiled in the **Engishiki** during the **Heian period** (794–1185). Most famous is the **Ōbarae no Kotoba.** The Engishiki contains numerous liturgical forms that are associated with **festivals** and shrines (**jinja**). The manner of celebrating these events is detailed along with the form of words to be used at the time.

Norito have certain common characteristics that seem to be the key to how they were created. Firstly, they are normally addressed to the *kami* of heaven, earth, and the myriad *kami.* Secondly, they invariably go into great descriptive detail. This is still the case when farmers are reporting their rice crop or other harvested goods at their tutelary shrine. Thirdly, they specify a date on which the offerings were made, when the purification (**harai**) takes place, and when the norito was recited. This is the pattern shown by analytically examining norito listed in the Engishiki, and is yet another continuing facet of Shinto rituals.

Reading norito in translation is not of great value as means toward their understanding. The theology they imply is simple, if articulated in propositions derived from the study of the content. However, the ritual acts which surround the occasion on which they are intoned, the liturgical appliances, the apparel of the priests and the atmosphere which these generate are designed to create an aesthetically pleasing offering to the *kami.* This is the total context of the idea of **kotodama,** sounds that are pleasing to the *kami.* The idea of an informal Shinto ritual, with the priest wearing a lounge suit instead of robes is as unthinkable as it would be improper. This in itself tells a great deal about the meaning, role, and function of ritual in Japanese society as a whole.

– O –

OAGATA JINJA. Famous shrine (**jinja**) in Inuyama city near Nagoya City that celebrates the **Ososo Matsuri,** or Vagina Festival. It is intended to protect crops, cure sterility and impotence, and to guarantee business success and fertility. The clam, a symbol of the vagina, is believed to guarantee marital harmony, pregnancy, and the cure of sexual diseases in addition to a good harvest. *See also* FERTILITY RITES IN SHINTO; HENOKO MATSURI; SEX IN SHINTO; TAGATA JINJA.

ŌBARAE NO KOTOBA. The most famous of all **norito** (liturgical addresses to the *kami*) is the Obarae no Kotoba, which appears in the **Engishiki**, Book VIII as norito number 10. It was traditionally recited by the Ōnakatomi, the head of the **Nakatomi** family who specialized in Shinto rituals, and was initiated by imperial command to be performed twice a year, at the end of June and at the end of December.

The great purification (Ōbarae) is still performed symbolically on behalf of the nation at the **Meiji Jingū** in Tokyō. The words of the Obarae, however, are also used at many shrines (**jinja**) simply as an act of worship in the normal course of shrine rituals, and at morning assemblies of the shrine staff. The interpretation of its archaic words and concepts first became controversial during the Edo period (1615–1868), when various schools of scholarship began to dispute its meaning. **Motoori Norinaga** (1730–1801), the **Kokugaku** (National Learning) scholar, argued that it should be taken literally, at face value, as an account of how things were in ancient times. Others preferred to read it in symbolic or allegorical terms.

It can be read as referring exclusively to Japan and as an article of national faith. The first English translation may be found in W. G. Aston's *Shinto: The Way of the Gods*, London, 1901, 296–302). Subsequent translations have rendered it less obscure, but approaches to how it should be understood still vary. Apart from Motoori's approach, it can also be read in a wider sense as deriving from a solar myth of creation from which broader implications may be drawn from its meaning.

Its central position as the definitive form of the norito guarantees its continued uses irrespective of how it is understood, partly on account of its kotodamashii, the natural energy that arises from its words, along with its **kotodama**, the sounds that please the *kami.*

OBOE. This term is used for things to be learned and remembered by believers in the teachings of the **Kyōha Shinto** (Sect Shinto) sect **Shinri-kyō**.

ODA NOBUNAGA (1534–1582). After the century of civil wars, the **Sengoku Jidai** (1467–1568), Oda Nobunaga began the process of national reunification. Although he was finally forced to commit seppuku (the classical method of disembowelment), he advanced the cause of unification by various means, including the ruthless destruction of many religious houses which he considered dangerous to his ambitions, including the temples of Mount Hiei that housed several thousand warrior monks and their families. His religious policy was rather more ad hoc than that of his successors, **Toyotomi Hideyoshi** (1536–1598) and **Ieyasu Tokugawa** (1543–1616), who took clear and calculated steps to effect control over all religious institutions.

OFUDA. An amulet bearing the name of a *kami* and kept by believers as an **omamori**, a symbol of the protective power of the *kami* whose name it bears. They are normally taken home and placed on the household **kamidana**. *See also* OMAMORI.

OFUDESAKI. The sacred scriptures of the former **Kyōha Shinto** (Sect Shinto) sect **Tenri-kyō**. *See also* MIKAGURAUTA.

OHARAI. Polite and formal way of referring to ritual purification (**harai**). *See also* MISOGI.

OHIRUME-MUCHI. Yamazaki Ansai (1618–1682), founder of **Suiga Shinto**, used this term to define the way of **Amaterasu-ōmikami**. Suiga Shinto, the Shinto of divine blessing, placed Amaterasu-ōmikami at its center.

OHYAKUDO-MAIRI. The practice of going back and forth one hundred times between a shrine building and a place in the precincts, praying for help in cases of sickness and disaster. The term sengori means to do this one thousand times. *See also* OKAGEMARI.

ŌJIN, EMPEROR. According to the **Nihon Shōki** (720) Emperor Ojin reigned from 270–310, but the dates have been disputed. He was represented as being the fourth son of Emperor Chūai (reigned 192–200) and **Empress Jingū** (reigned 201–269). He was born after Empress Jingū had successfully subdued a rebellion on the Korean peninsula.

The fact that both Japanese and Chinese dynastic records refer to Korean immigrants entering Japan during his reign, many known by name such as Yuzuki no Kimi, has meant some scholars have preferred to date him to the late fourth- to early fifth-century period. It would appear that one source of his success was in the use of technology and the introduction of the material culture of China and Korea. One other feature of his reign was the successful conquest of Kyushū by Takenouchi no Sukune, strengthening further the hegemony of the **Yamato** court. This may be why Ojin's image was used to depict the *kami* **Hachiman** in **mandalas** that were created to express the unity of Buddha and *kami* (according to the principle of **honji-suijaku-setsu**), since Hachiman was the principal tribal *kami* of Kyushū.

Ojin shares two features in common with **Emperor Nintoku** (reigned 313–399). Firstly, he is thought to be one of the five kings of Wa, according to the records of the Liu-Song Dynasty of China (420–479). Also like Nintoku, he was interred in a **kofun** burial mound in the city of Habikino in Osaka Prefecture. Ojin's tomb is second in size only to that of Nintoku, measuring 415 meters in length. Like that of Emperor Nintoku, it is also a keyhole-shaped mound. Considering the scale of the two burials, it has been taken to suggest that the Middle Kofun period was a time of general prosperity and of growing political centralization. The period also seems to have been one in which political power had come clearly into the hands of the Yamato clan. *See also* EMPEROR SYSTEM.

OKADA KOTAMA (1901–1974). *See* MAHIKARI.

OKADA MOKICHI (1882–1955). *See* SEKAI-KYŪSEI-KYŌ.

OKAGEMAIRI. Thanksgiving visits to the **Grand Shrines of Ise** (Ise Jingū) undertaken at approximately 60-year intervals during the Edo period (1615–1868) in 1650, 1705, 1771, and in 1830. The largest recorded number of pilgrims—3.62 million—was recorded in 1705, according to **Motoori Norinaga** (1730–1801), the **Kokugaku** (National Learning) scholar. A local official reported that the 1830 pilgrimage was attended by 2.28 million over a one-month period.

By the end of the Muromachi period (1333–1568), the imperial association with Ise Jingū had become accompanied by popular belief that every Japanese should visit Ise once in his of her lifetime.

Following each 20 year reconstruction of the Grand Shrines of Ise (**shikinen sengū**), there was a thanksgiving year (okage-doshi) during which, it was believed, a visit to Ise would bring special benefits, specifically the protection of **Amaterasu-ōmikami**.

Invariably, these rather spontaneous events were precipitated by rumor, in one instance that sacred amulets (gofu) were falling from heaven. On hearing this, people simply dropped everything and set off for **Ise**, without proper government permission to travel and without any other preparation. The tone ranged from serious spiritual concern on the part of some to carnival antics on the part of others. On the way, a journey of many weeks, okage dori, wild dances, were performed. Tea-houses, open-air baths, and even brothels appeared on the way. Wealthy families on the road were often prevailed upon to help pilgrims, partly to gain merit from their visit to Ise, and partly to keep public order.

From a conventional sociological point of view, the entire phenomenon could be interpreted as representing a clear mood of defiance within the entire culture, not unlike the Eejanaika public protest movement of the latter stages of the Edo period (1615–1868), which was an overt demonstration of anti-shogunate feeling. The growing attitude of defiance on the part of ordinary people against the Tokugawa government suggested that the end of an era was at hand.

OKINOSHIMA. A sacred island 50 kilometers off the north coast of Kyushū on which one of the three **Munakata** shrines (**jinja**) is located, the Okitsumiya, shrine of Tagorehime. Its strategic location on the trade route between Kyushū and the Asian mainland has been confirmed by many significant archaeological discoveries.

Women have always been strictly prohibited from worshipping there. Since it was an important stopping point on the trade route between Japan and the Asian mainland, it can only be assumed that the mariner's normal superstition about women and ships ensured that the protective *kami* of their journey was in no way offended by any possible impurities on the island, some of which are considered attached to normal female functions such as menstruation and childbirth.

OKUMOTSU. Sacred food offerings in the rituals of the Shinto-based **New Religion, Shinrei-kyō**, that are charged with divine power and that believers take home.

OKUNINUSHI-NO-MIKOTO. Early *kami* of creation, the Master of the Great Country and son of Susano-o-no-mikoto, enshrined at **Izumo Taisha** in a building thought to be referred to in the mythology as an eight-fathom palace, and located in Taishamachi in Shimane Prefecture. He is represented in the mythology as a benevolent figure who imparts civilization and who is unswervingly committed to his work. He is remembered especially because he helped a hare that was being tortured by his brothers in the Hare of Inaba story. This afforded him an oracle that predicted he would marry the beautiful Yagamihime, which he did, to the great chagrin of his brothers. In revenge, they burned him to death.

By intervention of his mother, **Kamimusubi-no-kami** agreed to heal him, and he returned to life. He endured many tribulations, but finally received power to banish his troublesome brothers. In Izumo, he met Sakunahikona-no-kami who helped him to subdue the country which he and his son Kotoshironushi-no-kami presented to the emissaries of **Amaterasu-ōmikami**. The **Kojiki** (712) and the **Nihon Shōki** (720) suggested that he was a powerful regional *kami*. The Izumo no Kuni **Fudoki** (a record of the Izumo Province), in 733 stated that he was also viewed as the creator of the world. He was also considered a *kami* of rice. At **Omiwa Jinja** in Nara Prefecture, he is enshrined under the name Omononshi-no-kami. In popular culture, or **folk Shinto**, he was also known as **Daikokuten**, the Buddhist guardian figure, and therefore as one of the **Shichi-fuku-jin** (the seven *kami* of good fortune).

ŌKUNI TAKAMASA (1792–1871). A **Kokugaku** (National Learning) scholar of the late Edo period (1615–1868) and disciple of **Hirata Atsutane** (1776–1843). He also studied **Confucianism** under Koga Seiri (1750–1817) and became familiar with Western learning and with Christianity while in Nagasaki. He grew up in the Tsuwano, a feudal domain in what is now Shimane Prefecture.

Okuni developed his own philosophy of Shinto that he called Honkyō (basic teaching) or Hongaku (basic learning), according to which people should follow the path set out for them. The world and its choices for what people should do was the work of **Amaterasu-ōmikami**. In his Amatsu-norito no futo-norito ko, a work on Shinto liturgies, he declared that Shinto established the foundation, aided the kingdom, and saved humankind. It was, in its totality, no more than these three things.

He was deeply concerned about the influence of Western civilization, and particularly about the impact of Christianity upon Japanese culture. Hence his vision of a powerful Shinto culture to counteract this. He worked for the government after the **Meiji Restoration** with that vision in mind, but found that even using the Great Teaching issued in the name of **Emperor Meiji (Taikyō Senpu Undō)**, he was unable to create the movement he saw as necessary to save the country. The idea of a Shinto as a religion for daily life was swept aside by the **Hirata** Shinto faction that was principally concerned about the performance of imperial rituals at the **Grand Shrines of Ise** (Ise Jingū). *See also* KOKKA SHINTO; MODERNIZATION AND SHINTO.

OKURA. Classic term for National Treasury or repository for valued artifacts, which survives in the title of the modern Ministry of Finance.

OKURI-BI. Sacred fire lit to send off the *kami* who assemble at Izumo for the festival (**matsuri**) of **Kami-aisai**. It is also used when sending off the **souls** of the dead after Obon, the **Bon-matsuri**, held in summer.

OMAIRI. The technical term that refers to visiting a shrine (**jinja**) in order to perform **sampai** (to offer worship).

OMAMORI. Protective talisman from a shrine that may be for travel, health, road safety, or simply good fortune. Shrines (**jinja**) and temples nationwide provide many of these to cover almost all the possibilities within life. They offer protective elements which **ofuda**, another type of talisman, cannot normally provide, although in practice their roles are virtually interchangeable.

OMATO-SHINJI. Divination by firing an arrow, performed at different times, but frequently as the commencement of the Setsubun festival at the end of winter. *See also* ARCHERY IN SHINTO; SUMO; YABUSAME.

OMI JINJA. Located in the city of Otsu, Shiga Prefecture, it enshrines Emperor Tenji (626–672, reigned 661–672), who was the force behind the **Taika Reform**. He was also instrumental in moving the capital from Asuka to Nara in 667, assisted by Prince Naka no Oe.

The first proposal for a shrine (**jinja**) to honor him was presented in the Imperial Diet of 1908. The decision to proceed was made in 1937 and the construction of the buildings was completed in 1940. This fact speaks to the issues of both **ancestral reverence** and its expression in the Shinto concept of enshrinement. *See also* EMPEROR SYSTEM.

OMIKOSHI. Portable shrine for carrying a *kami* through the community at the time of a **festival**, called a mikoshi, normally referred to in honorific terms as omikoshi, honorable palanquin.

OMIKUJI. Divination in which printed fortune papers are chosen by lot. Subscribers receive small printed papers with fortunes written on them. If they are favorable, they can be taken home. If they are unfavorable, they are often left tied to tree branches within the shrine (**jinja**) grounds as an act of protection.

OMINUKI. Release of spirit from body to receive the words of the *kami*, according to the teachings of the **Kyōha Shinto** (Sect Shinto) sect **Jikko-kyō**.

OMIWA JINJA. Located in the city of Sakurai, it enshrines **Okuni-nushi-no-mikoto** under the name of Omononushi-no-kami. It is the oldest shrine (**jinja**) in the **Yamato** region, and probably one of the oldest in the country. Several very old shrines do not have a **honden** (inner sanctuary) in which the symbol of the *kami* (the **go-shintai**) is kept. In the case of Omiwa Jinja, Mount Miwa is the go-shintai, and between it and the worship hall (**haiden**), stands a gateway (**torii**), in the unique Miwa style, which is in reality three gateways combined. Between the 13th and the 16th centuries, the shrine was the center of the Miwa cult, which was a Shinto-**Shingon Buddhist** syncretic mixture. Healing powers are associated with the shrine; as an odd mixture, makers of sake (Japanese rice wine) considered it their tutelary shine. Sake is used extensively in all Shinto rituals.

OMONONUSHI-NO-KAMI. *See* OKUNINUSHI-NO-MIKOTO

ŌMOTO-KYŌ. A Shinto-based **New Religion**, but not one of the original 13 **Kyōha Shinto** (Sect Shinto) sects. The name of the movement means "The Teaching of the Great Origin." This expression, according to sect records, was invented by the foundress, **Deguchi Nao** (1836–1918), in 1892 when she planted a flower, the *Rhodea Japonica* (Omoto in Japanese), and in a *kami*-possessed state uttered the words "This is the Omoto, the Great Foundation of the World: the teachings of the Great Beginning, the First Cause, shall be preached."

After this revelation, the life of Deguchi became the history of the movement. Although poor, she was by nature pious, hardworking, and sincere, and after her husband Deguchi Masagoro died, she began to have visions and experiences of being the medium of a *kami*. After a series of these in which her late husband appeared, she asked for the name of the spirit seeking to make contact with her in response to which it identified itself as Ushitora-no-Konjin. Her strange behavior drew the attention of the police and she was imprisoned. She scratched her ideas on the walls of her cell with a nail and these became the beginnings of the sacred book of Omoto, the *Ofudesaki*. She also predicted the coming of a fellow-believer whom she called the Master.

In 1898, a young man called Ueda Kisaburo visited her, claiming that he too was a believer in Konjin, and he married into the Deguchi family. He then became **Deguchi Onisaburō** (1871–1948) and from his efforts, the real expansion of Omoto-kyō began. He too had come from a poor family and had experienced a severe depression when his father died. To find relief, he began practicing various forms of **asceticism** in the mountains of Takuma. He came to believe that his mission was to save the world by improving human society. His own revelations thus matched those of Deguchi Nao and this became the basis of the expansion of the Omoto-kyō teaching.

Government recognition of the movement was withheld for a number of reasons, partly because the teaching was heavily monotheistic and partly because of its innate suspicion of any new movements which implicitly criticized then contemporary society by proposing programs of "reform." Police action against Omoto-kyō was brutal and repressive. On charges of treason, the headquarters were destroyed and large numbers of members arrested, charged with violations of the Maintenance of the Public Order Act and imprisoned, in 1921 and again in 1935. It took until 1942 for Deguchi to be released after six years and eight months in prison.

Deguchi Onisaburo's own life was equally full of dramatic incidents, especially his return in chains from an aborted mission to

China in the company of **Aikido** founder and master **Ueshiba Mori-hei** (1883–1969), with whom he maintained a close relationship all his life. After the war, the movement gained fresh momentum and became active in defending the postwar peace constitution.

Ōmoto-kyō also developed a strong interfaith approach to religious dialog, particularly with Episcopal Christians in the United States, with which it has conducted numerous joint religious services in various locations. The movement is administered from a headquarters in Kameoka City in Kyōto-fu. Its holy place is the Miroku-Den and the Kinryu-Den (Pavilion of the Golden Dragon) in Ayabe, which is near Moto-Ise.

The island of Meshima in the Japan Sea is sacred because Deguchi Nao went there in 1905 to pray and receive revelations. Hitsujisaru no Konjin is enshrined Kamishima in the Sea of Japan. In 2001, the fifth head, Kurenai Deguchi, took office succeeding Deguchi Kyōtaro, a great-grandson of Deguchi Nao. It claims a membership of 200,000 and is one of the larger of the Shinto-based new religious movements.

ŌNAKATOMI. Family of imperial Shinto liturgists, tracing its origins to at least the Nara period (710–794), if not earlier, and active in development of Shinto through the centuries. **Shinshū-kyō**, a **Kyōha Shinto** (Sect Shinto) sect, was founded by a member of the Onakatomi family. *See also* NAKATOMI; ŌNAKATOMI NO YOSHINOBU.

ŌNAKATOMI NO YOSHINOBU (921–991). A courtier and Shinto liturgist who compiled the second imperial classical **mythology**, the *Gosen Wakashū (Gosenshū)* of 955 to 966. He served also as chief priest (**saishū**) of the **Naikū** (Inner Shrine) of the **Grand Shrines of Ise** (Ise Jingū), although he resided in Kyōto. His poetic writings were considered the model of elegance, gracefulness, and good taste, and were carefully prepared for special events at court or at important **festivals**. The name **Ōnakatomi** continued to be linked with Shinto rituals, and appears in the **Engishiki** of the **Heian period** (794–1185). *See also* NORITO.

ONI. Near human form of a spirit with frightening appearance that belongs to the realm of **folk religion**, along with figures such as **Tengu**, **marebito**, **namahage**, and other mythical characters.

ONOGOROJIMA. The concept of a self-moving mass which has been identified as either Japan or the planet Earth in the **mythology**, depending upon the meaning given to the concept of **Takama-no-hara**, the Plain of High Heaven.

ONRYŌ. Angry and unpacified spirits that can become vengeful. Belief in such spirits was very strong during the **Heian period** (794–1185), when elaborate pacification rites known as **chinkon** were devised. The posthumous enshrinement of **Sugawara Michizane** (845–903) as the *kami* of learning, **Tenjin**, is perhaps the best known and most often quoted historical example. Concern about the three million souls in **Yasukuni Jinja** remains strong in the minds of many Japanese, not least of all those whose relatives are enshrined there, and who they believe died for a just cause or were victims of the politics of the day. Either way, the tradition of **ancestral reverence** sustains grief. This is one feature of the Yasukuni Shrine controversy that Western and Asian critics too readily ignore when discussing other aspects of the problem.

ONTAKE-KYŌ. Also known as Mitake-kyō, this is one of the officially recognized 13 **Kyōha Shinto** (Sect Shinto) sects, and one that the three sects linked to mountains. It was founded by Shimoyama Osuke, an oil merchant in the city of Edo who became a mountain ascetic (**gyōja**) of Mount Mitake (3,063 meters) in the Japan Alps between Nagano and Gifu Prefectures. Mount Mitake has been revered from time immemorial by local residents who still refer to it as Ontakesan, which means simply Honorable Great Mountain; this is the reason that the sect is known as Ontake-kyō.

Its roots are deeply embedded in the folk tradition and in the beliefs of **sangaku shinko** (mountain worship). Shimoyama researched to identify the *kami* revered on Mount Mitake. Mitake Okami was the only known name until Shimoyama claimed that it was a collective name for **Kunitokotachi-no-mikoto**, Onamuchi-no-kami, and Sakuna-Hikona-no-kami. To these he added Tenshinchigi, Rekidai-korei, and Ubusuna-no-kami. The sect was early on closely related to Tosei Kyōkai, but was given government recognition as an independent sect in 1882. Since the Meiji government was very reluctant to license new groups, Ontake-kyō carefully included strong sentiments of patriotism, teaching its followers to reverence the *kami*, love their country, honor and obey the emperor, conform to the decrees of the state, and by constant diligence in business to lay the foundation of a prosperous land and a strong military (**fukoku kyōhei**).

The principal act of reverence is climbing Mount Mitake chanting **Rokkon-shō-jō**, for the **purification** (oharai) of the body and senses, which takes place on August 8 every year. This is similar to other mountain groups. The three shrines (**jinja**) on the mountain are the Omiya (great shrine), the Wakamiya (young shrine), and the Yamamiya (mountain shrine) which is located on the summit. In addition, believers also practice **chinki-shiki**, a fire calming ceremony performed by walking barefoot over red-hot charcoal. and **kugatachi-shiki**, a ritual in which boiling water is sprinkled on the body after the heat has been subdued. Besides these spectacular rites, there is also meigen-shiki (ritual use of a bow string), shimbu-shiki (sacred dance), **ibuki**-ho (deep breathing), and kame-ura (**divination** using a tortoise shell).

The rituals reflect two strong **folk religion** aspects of Ontake-kyō. First is its interest in **healing** and medicine that developed as a basis for belief in other of the Kyōha sects that focus on healing. Second, the secrets of the quasi-magical rites are also transmitted by the *kami* of Mount Mitake to believers. **Shamanistic** group leaders can become *kami* possessed and can teach special revelations to believers who may find themselves in an ecstatic state. Such groups assemble and roam the mountain from time to time seeking to induce similar states of consciousness.

The ceremonies are designed not only to heighten spirituality, but also to secure the power and blessing of the *kami*, prosperity, longevity, guidance for the future through special revelations, and happiness after death. It is these elements of universal appeal that have doubtless enabled Ontake-kyō to retain its attraction in the midst of the many **New Religions** that Japanese society has produced particularly since the **Pacific War** (World War II) ended in 1945. The membership is estimated at just over 500,000.

ORIGUCHI SHINOBU (1887–1953). A scholar and imperial extremist in his views. According to his theory, the one single and eternal imperial **soul** is forever transmitted from emperor to emperor at the time of the **Daijōsai**. There was no basis in **imperial household** literature or Shinto theory for this position, and it was therefore never publicly acceptable. However, it illustrates the lengths to which some ultranationalists were prepared to go in the invention of their own ideas, which created misunderstandings about what the imperial household actually believed about itself.

OSAZUKE. Gift of the divine to an aspiring teacher of the former **Kyōha Shinto** (Sect Shinto) sect **Tenri-kyō**.

OSHI. A highly ranked **Shugendō** master of the **Heian period** (794–1185). The etymology is thought to be an abbreviated version of oki-toshi, a reciter of prayers. The **Grand Shrines of Ise** (Ise Jingū) and the **Kumano Sanja** employed them to maintain a close relationship with the shrine (**jinja**) support groups. They traveled around the country, visiting groups and giving out various talismans from the shrine.

OSHOKU. Leading master guide in **Shugendō** of the **Heian period** (794–1185).

OSOSO MATSURI. The famous Vagina Festival (**matsuri**) is celebrated annually at the **Oagata Jinja**, a well-known shrine in Inuyama City. The clam, a symbol of the vagina, is believed to guarantee marital harmony, pregnancy, and the cure of sexual diseases in addition to a good harvest. *See also* FERTILITY AND SEX IN SHINTO; HENOKO MATSURI; TAGATA JINJA.

OTOME-MAI. Dances performed by shrine (**jinja**) maidens (**miko**), probably originating in the original dance of **Ame-uzeme-no-mikoto**. They are the precursor of **Noh** dramaturgy, but historically linked to an experience of Emperor **Temmu** (reigned 672–686) when a divine emanation danced before him as he played the koto at his Yoshino palace. There are many forms and various dances, all of which have some imperial connection. *See also* DANCE; DRAMATIC ARTS IN SHINTO; MUSIC IN SHINTO; MYTHOLOGY.

OTSUKA KAN'ICHI (1891–1972). *See* SHINREI-KYŌ.

OYAGAMI. Meaning parent *kami*, it is the principal deity in the teaching of the former **Kyōha Shinto** (Sect Shinto) sect **Tenri-kyō**.

– P –

PACIFIC WAR. Japan customarily uses the Term Pacific War
(Taiheiyo-senso) when referring to the Pacific theater of World War
II (1939–1945), which commenced with the Japanese assault on
Pearl Harbor in November 1941 and ended with the Japanese surren-
der signed on the deck of the U.S.S. *Missouri* in August 1945.

The role of State Shinto in the Japanese war drive was strongly
emphasized by American propaganda movies made for the purpose.
They attributed Japan's aggression to belief in the emperor's divinity and in the power of the **Yamato-damashii**, the unique fighting
spirit of the Japanese race. These claims were underlined by the
scale of the Pacific theater that covered the whole of Southeast Asia,
except Thailand: Indonesia and Borneo, the Philippines, Singapore
and Malaysia, Korea, and large areas of mainland China, along with
Taiwan and Hong Kong. These were all listed as part of Japan's
Great East Asia Co-prosperity Sphere. Controversy still rages as to
why Japan began such a massive program of colonization, beginning
with the Korean peninsula in 1910, and whether there was any merit
in what was achieved. Substantial armies were deployed to keep
order, and state (**Kokka Shinto**) shrines (**shōkonsha**), for soldiers
who died in action were established. Local people were expected to
pay homage to the emperor at these shrines and education contained
large doses of propaganda.

The gradual defeat of Japan began as the army was forced to
retreat from one island after another. How long Japan would have
persisted is also a matter of debate, but the nation's fate was sealed
by the detonation of two atomic bombs, one over Hiroshima and the
other over Nagasaki. Post 1945, Japan moved into a mode of pacifism that has prevailed ever since. Japan has only self-defense forces
and holds to its anti-nuclear policy. Every so often the question of
constitutional reform arises, but even 60 years after the war, the issue
remains unresolved.

P. L. KYŌDAN. A **New Religion** that can be traced to Hitonomichi
Kyōdan, a 1931 pre-war movement and even further back as the successor to Tokumitsu-Kyō founded in 1912 by **Kanada Tokumitsu
(1863–1919)**. Kanada had a childhood interest in religion, particularly **Shingon Buddhism**, and he was a devotee of its founder, **Kōbō**

Daishi (774–835). Like his ideal, he jumped off a cliff, injuring himself but finding illumination in the prowess of his act. When he married into the Kanada family, he changed his name to Tokumitsu. He established a successful cutlery shop business and, although not able to devote himself fully to religion, he became a teacher of the **Kyōha Shinto** sect **Mitake-Kyō**. His Tokumitsu-kyō was originally a group within Mitake-Kyō.

When news of Kanada's miraculous powers began to spread, followers began to increase. It found great acceptance, among the merchants of Osaka who were experiencing the business boom of World War I. It died, however, with its founder, which enabled Miki Tokuchika, one of his disciples, to create a new movement in the mid-1920s, whose main emphasis was humanistic, with stress on husband-wife and parent-child relations. In 1936, the leadership passed to Tokuchika, and thereafter persecution began. The name Hitonomichi was adopted in 1931. The movement was forcibly disbanded; however, Hitonomichi believers continued their faith in secret through Tokuchika, who was also imprisoned, and remained so until 1945. When religious freedom was proclaimed after the **Pacific War** (World War II), the believers wished for the religion to be restarted. With some hesitation, he organized the Perfect Liberty Club, but after the constitutional guarantee of religious freedom on 29 September 1946, he established the P. L. Kyōdan in Tosu in Saga Prefecture. Tokuchika is referred to as Oshieoya (teaching-parent) and his father became the official founder of P. L. Kyōdan.

He described the persecution his father faced as the "egoism of state power." Although in principle religious toleration appeared in Japan with the revoking of the ban on Christianity and was included in Article 28 of the Meiji Constitution, it did not in fact confer total freedom of religious practice. Therefore even when Hitonomichi tried to accommodate itself to **Kokka Shinto** (State Shinto), it was still considered to be subversive. Consequently, the basis for the name Perfect Liberty appears to be a statement of a point of view in relation to the absence of freedom that was characteristic of pre-World War II Japanese society.

P. L. Kyōdan is monotheistic and believes in a parent God called Mioya-Okami. It is claimed that, by himself, man can do nothing, and that the power of **nature** controls everything one does. Daishizen also controls the progress of all creation. There is a great power in the uni-

238 • P. L. KYODAN

verse which human beings can receive if they live in accordance with the power and flow of Great Nature. This is God, the great power, the spiritual power that controls life and every human activity. God manifests himself in man and man therefore makes self-expressions with the knowledge that God is his sustenance to lead to a perfect artistic life. God is also working for the betterment and improvement of man. However, there is also a sense in which man and God are quite different: "Man is God manifested as a human being, but Man is not God Himself and remains man, but possesses the essential qualities of God." This is close to one implicit tenet of Shinto thought, that in some sense, humans are children of the *kami*.

According to the book *Perfect Liberty: How to Lead a Happy Life*, an artist is said to be someone who devotes himself completely to his work without thinking of anything else. Thus is an object of art created. The reward of such creativity is spiritual pleasure or religious exaltation: The artistic life brings about happiness, the joy of the artist. Thus, if the purpose in life is to create art, that is, to express oneself, there can be nothing but happiness in life, and unhappiness cannot exist. However, if people forget God, life ceases to be artistic and such individuals will meet various reversals of fate. The environment does not develop favorably, nothing happens as desired, and finally, illness may occur. Sufferings and misfortunes are **gasho**, warnings from God. If the events are recognized as a warning, then there is hope. The believer goes to the Master (Miki) or a consultant to ask for a kokoroe (prescription). The problem is diagnosed and a treatment for the misfortune is proposed. If time is too short, the Master saves the believer by vicariously accepting his sufferings.

The ultimate goal of P. L. Kyōdan is world peace on the basis that as more people embrace it and live artistic lives, the more evils will vanish and the world will become a world of perfect liberty. The membership is listed as over 1 million worldwide in 500 churches, under the direction of over 28,000 teachers, and in ten countries. It is administered from its headquarters in Osaka-fu. Active missionary work in the 1960s enabled P. L. Kyōdan to establish a presence in South America and the United States. It also has a presence in Canada, Brazil, Argentina, Paraguay, and Peru. Its Oceania headquarters, founded in the 1990s in Brisbane, Australia. It has a modest presence in Europe as well, especially in France, Portugal, and Hungary. The third patriarch, Miki Takahito, took office in 1983, succeeding Tokuchika after his death.

PONSONBY-FANE, RICHARD (1878–1937). Eccentric but intriguing Englishman who was a scholar and Kyōto resident and a devotee of the Japanese **emperor system**. He also wrote in enormous detail about many of Japan's shrines (**jinja**), especially in shipping magazines. He is commemorated by a society named after him, which still exists in Kyōto.

PRIESTHOOD. *See* GŪJI; KAI-I; KANNUSHI; SHINSHOKU.

PRIESTLY DRESS. *See* SAIFUKU.

PURIFICATION. *See* HARAI; MISOGI.

– R –

RAIJIN. The *kami* of thunder, known as Kamowakeikazuchi-no-kami. The associations and roots are unclear.

REIJIN. Gagaku musicians who perform at major shrines.

REIKAI. The spiritual realm that is believed to exist in the teachings of **Sekai Kyūsei-kyō** (the Church of World Messianity), a **New Religion**.

REISAI. The principal **festival** of any shrine (**jinja**) performed once or twice a year, depending on local custom.

REISEI. A general term referring to human spirituality.

REITAI. The spiritual part of human beings, as believed in the teachings of the **New Religion**, known most commonly as **Mahikari**.

RENSO-TŌJITSU-HINKUYSAI. Imperial household funerary **rituals** preceding the burial of a deceased emperor.

RESTORATION SHINTO. English name of **Fukko Shinto**, of which **Hirata Atsutane** (1776–1843) was a leading exponent, the movement which helped to create the intellectual mood that brought about the **Meiji Restoration** in 1868. *See also* MODERNIZATION AND SHINTO.

RETIRED EMPERORS. It was not unknown in the **Heian period** (794–1185) for an emperor to retire from the center stage to become a Buddhist monk. These retired emperors often devoted themselves to pilgrimages, although others preferred to continue meddling in court affairs, giving rise to the expression **insei**, referring to government by a cloistered emperor.

RICE IN JAPANESE CULTURE. Not only the traditional staple diet of the Japanese, but also the foundation of the agricultural system from which the cycle of year's events (**Nenchū-gyōji**) are derived. The oldest strains have been traced to the Shanghai region of China and researchers consider it has a 2,000 history in Japan.

Rice should be considered not only as food, but also as a sacred object used in all major rituals. Rice, salt, and water are the three universal elements found on all Shinto altars, whether in shrines, offices, or homes (**kami-dana**). It is of course the basic ingredient in the manufacture of **sake**, the popular rice wine also found used at all Shinto shrines as a sacred drink, drunk usually after performing the ceremony of purification (**harai**). Much of the distinctive character of Japanese society comes from the culture of rice, which requires cooperation with others to both plant and harvest. The modern Japanese open-plan office is often likened to the rice paddy.

The importance of rice as a religious symbol was highlighted in an unusual way when the governments of Japan and the United States were engaged in their discussions known as the **Structural Impediments Initiative (SII)** in the early 1990s, aimed at opening up Japanese markets to more imports. The question of importing California rice was raised. Enormous pressure was exerted on Japan to import rice. However, it took no account of the central place of rice in Japan's religious culture and that rice grown in Japan had virtually a sacred aura because of the rituals preceding the planting of rice (**ta-asobi**) and the festivals that follow its harvesting (**aki-matsuri**). The issue was further complicated by the fact that the terms of the General Agreements on Trade and Tariffs (GAAT) required Japan to import rice from other countries as well. Japanese rice has a slightly sticky texture, as compared to the dry species of rice found in most other Asian countries. These proved unpopular, and in spite of blending various types, the attempt to import alien rice proved unsuccessful. Shrines would use only locally grown rice, and the Japanese public did not take to the imported types of rice.

RIGAKU SHINTO. A branch of Confucian Shinto attributed to **Yoshikawa Koretari** (1616–1694). *See also* CONFUCIANISM AND SHINTO; YOSHIKAWA SHINTO.

RIKKYO SHINDEN. The divine call to **Akazawa Bunji** in 1859, according to the followers of the **Kyōha Shinto** (Sect Shinto) sect **Konkō-kyō**.

RITSURYŌ SEIDO (RITSURYŌ SYSTEM). The systematic reform of government begun in the seventh century and completed in the eighth century. It covers the period when the imperial institution first began to create a rational bureaucratic system which lasted until 967, when a regency government replaced bureaucratic control with prerogatives of status and law based on custom.

It was the threat of an expansionist T'ang dynasty (618–907) in China that compelled the Japanese to modernize their government. The only way it was thought possible to compete with Chinese power was to emulate it. It was basically a continuation of the implementation of Chinese moral and political values begun by **Shōtoku Taishi** (574–622) in the early seventh century. The extension of the power of central government was achieved through the creation of detailed laws and regulations that reduced local discretionary powers to a minimum.

The **emperor system** and the court were to be moral exemplars to the people, and the laws, issued as an expression of the imperial will, were to be morally educative. The importance of Shinto **rituals** fitted into this Confucian logic quite effectively. The basic moral stance survived the death of the system, and indeed, were continued through the Edo period (1615–1868), revived in the Meiji period (1868–1812), and still have a clear presence in the educational philosophy of present day Japan. *See also* CONFUCIANISM AND SHINTO.

RITUAL AND DRAMA IN SHINTO. One interesting aspect of Shinto mythology is the way in which it was presented in **rituals** and later stylized more formally in **drama**. Indeed, it provides support for the view that drama was a performing art that evolved from liturgical rituals. There is a great deal of literature on the relationship between ritual and drama in the evolution of cultural forms not only in Japan, but also in the West. The music/drama art form known as **Noh** appears to have its origins in the dramatic presentation of themes from the ancient mythology of Japan that narrated the great stories of the origin of the country and the role of **Amaterasu-ōmikami**, ancestor of the imperial family. These in turn derived from the mythological texts, the **Kojiki** (712) and the **Nihon Shoki** (720) and the liturgical formulae that grew out of them recorded in the later work known as the **Engishiki**. *See also* DRAMATIC ARTS IN SHINTO; GAGAKU; IMPERIAL HOUSEHOLD; MUSIC IN SHINTO; MYTHOLOGY IN SHINTO.

RITUALS IN SHINTO. Shinto is frequently assailed by critics as having no theology, in the Western sense of the term. While this is true, note should be taken of the fact that Shinto has survived in ritual rather than through doctrine. Indeed, the entire social framework of Japanese culture is formed by rituals of many kinds, performed at the correct time and in a proper manner. Shinto in particular should be studied through its extensive rituals. Principal among these are the following:

Highest in rank are the **imperial household** rituals, performed by the emperor himself or someone appointed by him, on behalf of the nation and in deference to the imperial tradition. These are referred to as the Kōshitsu Saishi, and include events such as the coming of age of members of the household, the annual poetry reading ceremony at **New Year**, ceremonies held to mark the passing of previous emperors, the rituals accompanying accession, such as the **Daijosai**, and others relating to the seasons of the year.

Below these in rank would be rituals and ceremonies involving the **Grand Shrines of Ise** (Ise Jingū), which include visits by members of the imperial household to announce important events such as trips abroad, births, or marriages. The **Sumo** Association makes visits annually as well as all new cabinets to mark their inauguration. The **Shikinen-sengū** ritual to reconstruct the Grand Shrines every 20 years is perhaps the best known of all the rituals of the **Ise** tradition.

The **nenchū-gyōji**, the cycle of annual events is observed at all shrines (**jinja**) nationwide. The various major **festivals** such as the **Haru-matsuri** (Spring Festival) and the **Aki-matsuri** (Autumn Festival) are the two principal events of the year. Festivals are held at other times, such as summer, and many shrines have their own special and famous ones, such as the **Aoi matsuri** in Kyōto. Other rituals performed by people at shrines include **misogi**, purification in a river, under a waterfall, or in the sea. **Divination** events such as **Yabusame** (mounted archery), **Omato-shinji** (individual archery), or **Ta-asobi** (also known as otaue-sai), all concerned with harvest, are widely practiced.

At the popular level, there are events such as **hatsu-mode**, the first shrine visit of the New Year, **hatsu-miya-mairi**, the first visit of a new baby to his or her tutelary shrine, or requested performance of ritual purification (**harai**) on occasions such as the building of a new home, the opening of a new business, for the safety of a new car, or for success in examinations, to name but a few.

Finally, within individual households, there may be **kamidana**, household altars, whose offerings of water, salt, sake, and rice will require to be replaced with fresh offerings every day.

At every level, Shinto rituals and their meanings have an impact on Japanese life, giving it meaning, order, and purpose. Not only are the rituals important, but so also is the quality of the performance, something which is for the pleasure of the *kami*. *See also* ENGISHIKI; KOTODAMA; NORITO; RITUAL AND DRAMA IN SHINTO.

ROKKON-SHŌ-JŌ. Purification (**harai**) of the six elements of existence, an objective of the **misogi** ritual and of mountain climbing as an act of **asceticism**. Participants shout the expression "Rokkon-shō-jō" in unison as they climb the mountain or stand under the waterfall or in the river. *See also* ONTAKE-KYŌ; SHUGENDŌ.

RUIJU JINGI HONGEN. This famous collection of Shinto thought and information whose title means "Compendium of the Origins of the *Kami*," compiled by Watarai Ieyuki (1255–1351) in 15 volumes. It systematically expound the themes of **Watarai Shinto**, beginning with creation and going on to the secret inner meanings of Shinto, containing most of the wisdom and understanding of medieval

Shinto. It was made public in 1320, and its deep and awesome level of scholarship gave it status as the basic textbook and summary of all Shinto knowledge of the time. It was studied by the Southern Court (1336–1392) and had a profound influence on **Kitabatake Chikafusa** (1293–1354) as he was working on his *Tokahiden* and other works that became part of the movement that led to Shinto's revival.

RYOBŪ SHINTO. Shinto of the two parts (Dual Shinto), often mistakenly taken to mean Shinto and **Buddhism** but actually referring to two famous **mandalas**, the Kongokai Mandala, known as the Diamond Mandala, and the Taizokai Mandala, known as the Womb Mandala of **Shingon Buddhism**. In this Dual Shinto, the **Naikū** (Inner shrine) of the **Grand Shrines of Ise** (Ise Jingū) was associated with the Dainichi Nyorai (Mahavairocana) of the Womb Realm and the **Gekū** (Outer Shrine) was considered the equivalent to Dainichi Nyorai of the Diamond Realm. In addition to mandalas, Ryobu Shinto also made use of mudras (secret hand signs), dharani (mystical incantations), and yoga (concentration), all of which found their way into aspects of Shinto rituals. The secret rituals were one way to achieve Buddhahood in the flesh, and consequently to attain superior powers through severe and demanding spiritual exercises that are the core of the **asceticism** practiced in **Shugendō**. Although neo-magical, this aspect has had great appeal even in modern times. **Heian period** (794–1185) priests performed kaji-kito, a ritual for the **healing** of the sick, calming the **souls** of ghosts, and for safe delivery at childbirth. Traces of these are to be found surviving in extant groups of **Kyōha Shinto** (Sect Shinto) and in the Shinto-based **New Religions**. *See also* ART IN SHINTO.

RYŌSHŌ-NO-GI. The ceremony of entombment of a deceased emperor. *See also* EMPEROR SYSTEM.

RYŪJIN. A dragon *kami* associated with water, most probably introduced to Japan from southern China. This *kami* is revered at numerous shrines (**jinja**) which are associated with water, the sea, or fishing. Although the origins are Chinese and most likely Buddhist, once a protective role had been introduced it became part of **folk religion**, and eventually of **folk Shinto**. The seaport culture of Nagasaki, on account of its use by the Edo period (1615–1868) government as a source of information about the outside world, contains relics of

Dutch and Roman Catholic presence as well as featuring prominent use of the dragon cult in festivals and boat races.

– S –

SACREDNESS IN SHINTO. In Western culture, the sacred is usually juxtaposed with the profane, following the philosophical lines of a metaphysical dualism, a characteristic of its intellectual history and a byproduct of Judeo-Christian thought. In Shinto, the entire world is the dwelling place of *kami*, in which some locations are more clearly "sacred" than others. What differentiates them is purity. Impurities such as **kegare** (defilement) or **tsumi** (impurity) may be removed by **ritual** purification (**harai**). Once purified, sacred spaces are marked with ropes (**shimenawa**), and if they are to be used for a ceremony to welcoming a *kami*, a wooden altar is set up.

Studies have shown that Japanese religiosity is tied firmly to the idea of sacred places—such as mountain tops, crags, and waterfalls—as residences of *kami*. Mountains may be treated as sacred, such as **Ontakesan**, the mountain where the **Kyōha Shinto** (Sect Shinto) sect **Mitake-kyō** conducts its ceremonies. Trees may be regarded as sacred (shimboku) and will have a shimenawa tied round the trunk like a belt. Even the top rank of Yokozuna (in **sumo**) wears a shimenawa around his waist, with **gohei** attached, designating him as a being of special quality, and sacred bearing.

Shrines (**jinja**) were traditionally created as places to revere *kami* in a sacred environment. **Festivals** (matsuri) are conducted at these as both purification and community reverence for the *kami*. The Shinto scholar Fujita Tomio argues that the sociological approach of Emil Durkheim to the sacred is inappropriate, and that in Japan, rather than the bipolar structure of sacred and profane, Shinto has a tripolar structure of **ki** (ordinary energy in life), which is made impure by kegare, and then by purification it returns to its original state. Purified energy is thus obtained, but it slowly acquires impurity and therefore one year later, the festival takes place again to restore purity. It is thus also a cyclical process. *See also* IWASAKA; SANGAKU SHINKO.

SADAIJIN. Highly ranked official of the **Heian period** (794–1185) imperial court.

SAICHŌ (762–822). Also known posthumously as Dengyō Daishi (767–822), he was the founder of **Tendai Buddhism**. He visited China as part of a special delegation in 804 and returned in 805 with a solid understanding of the principles of the esoteric **Buddhism** of Mount T'ien-T'ai, which included various **rituals**, meditation techniques, and rules for monastic life.

Saicho established his headquarters at the Enryaku-ji, a temple complex on Mount Hiei outside of Kyōto. The various doctrines of Tendai are derived from the **Lotus Sutra** (Hokke-kyō), a text that came to be central for the development of Buddhism in Japan, mainly because of its flexible approach to spiritual enlightenment. **Sannō Ichijitsu Shinto** grew from this tradition, and spread throughout the country. The nature of the cult made fusion with Shinto quite natural, and hence the evolution of Tendai Shinto during later historical periods. *See also* BUDDHISM; NIKKŌ TŌSHŌGŪ.

SAIFUKU. Dress worn by priests (**kannushi**) at the performance of all **rituals**. Modeled on Chinese T'ang Dynasty (618–907) court dress, **Yoshida Kanetomo** (1435–1511) formalized the wearing of the various items. They remain in use at the present. *See also* ASAGUTSU; EBOSHI; HAKAMA; HŌ; JŌE; KANMURI; KARIGINU; YOSHIDA SHINTO.

SAIGŪ. Young **priestesses** dispatched to the **Grand Shrines of Ise** (Ise Jingū) to perform specified rituals on behalf of the emperor were called saigu (also saio). Details of the saigu's duties are listed in the **Engishiki**, the record of rituals and ceremonies of the **Heian period** (794–1185).

SAIJIN RONSŌ. A Meiji period (1868–1912) debate over the inclusion of **Okuninushi-no-mikoto** along with **Amaterasu-ōmikami** and the **Zōka-sanshin**, three *kami* of creation, as outlined in the **Taikyō Sempu Undō** promulgated by **Emperor Meiji**. From 1875, the campaign was in the hands of the priests at the **Grand Shrines of Ise** (Ise Jingū). Because of this fact, **Senge Takatomi** (1845–1918), high priest (**gūji**) of **Izumo Taisha** challenged the hegemony of the Ise shrines on this matter.

The effect was to bring a doctrinal issue to the center of the campaign of weakening the campaign completely because it was forcing people to take sides on an abstract issue. It merely added strength to the cause of **Hirata Shinto**, which focused on rituals and liturgies rather than on doctrines.

SAIJITSU. Meaning literally "**festival**-day," it is the formal expression that refers to the day on which a festival is being held.

SAIKAI. Known also as **bekka**, it is the required period of abstinence (from, for example, sex, eating meat, or alcohol) before and immediately after the celebration of a ceremony. Seclusion in a building called an imiya is common, along with the performance of **misogi**, and meditation on serious themes. The lower level of abstinence is called araimi, meaning basic abstinence. Total abstinence is called maimi. *See also* SHUBATSU.

SAIKIGU. Technical collective name for a variety of artifacts used in purification (**harai**) ceremonies. Basic is the hassoku-an, an eight-legged table normally set up where the ceremony is to take place. Two or more sambo may be placed upon it bearing various offerings (heihaku) including salt, water, and sake. Food offerings (shinsen) along with other offerings and are placed onto a tray called an oshiki, which is then set on the sambo. Other utensils used for caring offerings are kaku-takatsuki (square) and maru-takatsuki (round) trays. Almost all of these are made of Japanese cypress (**hinoki**).

SAIMOTSU. Offerings made to a *kami* when visiting a shrine (**jinja**) for worship. Money or sometimes sake is placed in the altar area of the worship hall. *See also* FINANCES OF SHRINES.

SAISEI-ITCHI. The classical ideal of the unity of worship and government, a concept formally defined as part of the **Taika Reform** in 645. It was revived after the **Meiji Restoration** (1868) as part of the project to create a **Kokka Shinto** (State Shinto) system.

SAISEN. Money offered during shrine visits, and formally to shrine officials in presentation envelopes. *See also* FINANCES OF SHRINES.

SAISHU. The highest priestly office at the **Grand Shrines of Ise** (Ise Jingū). From the **Heian period** (794–1185) to the beginning of the

Meiji period (1868–1912), a priest from the **Jingikan**, the Office of the Divinities, held the post. Thereafter until 1945, it was occupied by a male member of the imperial family, after which it became occupied by a female. This kept the practice close to the older tradition of **saigu**, the unmarried princess who served at the shrine known as a mitsue-shiro.

SAKAKI. A distinctive Japanese evergreen (*cleyera ochnacea* or *theacea japonica*) used in Shinto rituals to permit the invoked **kami** to alight.

SAKE IN SHINTO RITUALS. Japan's **rice** wine, the nation's traditional alcoholic beverage has a long history. It is drunk not only when dining, but is used also in **Shinto** rituals because it comes from rice. A lot of sake is drunk at celebratory events, especially **festivals** once the serious formalities of the **aki-matsuri**, for example, are completed.

The 2,000 member Sake Brewer's Association claims that it has a history of 2,000 years, a long time within which to develop and refine the product. Over 10,000 brands are on sale in Japan, all coming from areas of the country where differences in soil, water, rice, and in manufacturing technique are reflected in taste and texture. While popular proprietary brands such as Ozeki exist, the higher-graded varieties tend to be produced, like rice, regionally and in smaller amounts. Shrine festivals also make use of taru-zake, sake in large barrels (taru), still fermenting, making it less refined, but rich in taste. It is drunk from a small square wooden cup called a masu, made of **hinoki** (Japanese cypress), with its distinctive fragrance.

The unique character of sake culture can be experienced at New Year, or at celebratory events such as an anniversary or the beginning of a special event. Major undertakings may begin with breaking open a taru and everyone involved drinking from it. Ground-breaking ceremonies (**jichinsai**), the opening of large department store promotions, or the beginning of construction projects are typical occasions. *See also* RITUALS IN SHINTO.

SAKITAMA. One of the four aspects of the **tama** (or **soul**), especially of a **kami**. It refers to the aspect that produces **megumi**, gracious blessings.

SAKOKU JIDAI. The Edo period (1615–1868) during which the country was closed to foreign visitors from shortly after 1600 until the **Meiji Restoration** in 1868.

SAKURA JINJA. Located in Setagaya Ward, Tōkyō, the chief priest, the Rev. Yoshimura Masanori established the first Virtual Shrine (**jinja**) site to attract communication from people of the Internet generation in 1998.

SAMPAI. The official term that means formal offering of worship at a shrine (**jinja**).

SANGAKU SHINKŌ. Folk Shinto beliefs associated with reverence for mountains and the spirits who reside on them. Mountains were believed to be the residence of spirits, principally the spirits of the dead who watched over and assisted the living. Mountains themselves were often considered to be *kami* and were accorded special reverence.

Ancient Japanese religion was based largely on a fascination with mountains, the roots of Sangaku Shinkō. Climbing mountains and living in mountains seems always to have been associated with the search for a natural expression of human spirituality. Many old Shinto shrines (**jinja**) and Buddhist temples are located on the peaks of mountains, which in modern times require railways, paved roads, and cable cars to become conveniently accessible. How they were built and how people lived there in the past can only be a matter of speculation.

Kūkai (773–835) chose Mount Kōya in Wakayama Prefecture as the site of the Kongobu-ji, the head temple of **Shingon Buddhism**. **Saicho** (767–822) chose Mount Hiei near Kyōto as the site of the Enryaku-ji, the head temple of **Tendai Buddhism**. The Kamakura period (1185–1333) Buddhist leader **Nichiren** (1222–1282) received his spiritual enlightenment on a mountain. Climbing **Mount Fuji** has been a religious act for centuries, usually an act of purification. In some rural areas, boys reaching puberty still purify themselves by climbing a local mountain. The **Kumano Junrei**, the pilgrimage related to the **Kumano Sanja**, the three great shrines of Kumano, is basically an exercise in mountaineering by people dressed in **Heian period** (794–1185) costume.

The fundamental role of mountains in Shinto in particular, and in Japanese religion in general, has lent a distinctive character to the style of Japanese **asceticism**. If an ascetic is defined as someone who lives at the center of his or her spiritual energy, then the manner in which that energy is channeled toward achieving a particular state of mind or body depends upon the perception of the self that the ascetic holds. If the self is viewed as evil, then it may merit punishment, as in the case of medieval Western asceticism. If the self is capable of divinity, the purpose of the discipline correspondingly becomes positive, which is the dynamic behind Japanese asceticism. Buddhists speak of the soku-shin-jo-butsu, meaning literally "one who becomes a Buddha in the flesh." Shinto similarly aims at transforming a human being into a living *kami*. In the mountain tradition of the Buddhist/Shinto amalgam known as **Shugendō**, the full flowering of these ideals can best be seen. *See also* HONJI-SUIJAKU-SETSU; MOUNTAIN WORSHIP; NATURE IN SHINTO.

SANJA MATSURI. A **festival** of the Sanja Myojin, popular name for the Asakusa Jinja (**jinja**) in Taito Ward, Tokyō. The three great festivals of Edo (modern Tokyō) were the Kanda Matsuri, honoring the **Kanda Myōjin**, the **Sannō Matsuri** and the Sanja Matsuri. Over one hundred **mikoshi**, portable shrines, are vigorously paraded through the streets and, because Asakusa was traditionally an entertainment district, are followed by dances performed by geisha.

SANJA-TAKUSEN. Collective name for famous oracles delivered from **Amaterasu-ōmikami**, the great *kami* **Hachiman**, and the **Kasuga** Daimyōjin. According to legend, they appeared in the pond at the Tōdai-ji, the temple of the Great Buddha of Nara during the era of Shōō (1288–1293) during the reign (1288–1298) of Emperor Fushimi. These came to be the basis of moral thinking about purity, honesty, and benevolence as the natural foundation of Shinto teaching.

SANJO NO KYŌSOKU. Term for the three great teachings of the **Taikyō Senpu Undō**, the Great Promulgation issued by **Emperor Meiji** during the period 1870 to 1874. The great teachings were: people should love their country and revere the *kami* **of heaven and earth**; people should have a sound understanding of the Way of Heaven and the way of man under it; everyone should display reverence for the emperor and obedience to the orders of the imperial court.

Kyōdōshoku, Shinto evangelists, were appointed and charged with teaching the people the meaning of these ideals. Many of the meritorious concepts of the **modernization** program were also included, such as the notion of compulsory education and the industrial and scientific development of the nation. However, it was all comprehended with the more limited goals of a narrow nationalism, which guided government policy thereafter.

One byproduct of this was the creation of **Kokka Shinto** (State Shinto) as a national ideology that was intended to unite the nation in its support of the ideals of the Great Teaching. Another was the **Jinja Gappei** (shrine consolidation) movement that targeted the elimination of small or untidy shrines (**jinja**) as part of the process of making all shrines nationally controlled symbols of the emperor and the state. The disastrous failure of both of these movements displayed how little an understanding the Meiji period (1868–1912) leadership had of its own culture and traditions, and how deeply embedded these traditions remained in the national psyche.

SANJŪBAN-SHIN. The 30 specified *kami* of the **Heian period** (794–1185) used to name the days of the month, a practice developed within **Tendai Buddhism**.

SANKU. Custom of scattering offerings at the four corners and the center of a ritual site. These include **rice**, **sake**, pieces of cloth, or money as gifts to the *kami*.

SANNŌ ICHIJITSU SHINTO. *See* TENDAI SHINTO.

SANNŌ MATSURI. Major **festival** of the **Hie Jinja** in the Akasaka district of Tokyō, dating to the Edo period (1615–1868), when it was one of the three main city festivals known as the **Sanja Matsuri**. The Sannō Gongen, the *kami* of the shrine (**jinja**), was one of the tutelary deities of the Tokugawa family, and therefore the shrine received government patronage.

The name refers also to the lesser known but much older festival of the original Hie Jinja, (now Hiyoshi Taisha) in Otsu, Shiga Prefecture. It is famous for its floating **mikoshi** that transports the enshrined *kami* on Lake Biwa.

SANSHU-NO-SHINKI. Sometimes known as the sanshū-no-jingi, they are the three sacred emblems of the **imperial regalia**—the mirror, jewel, and sword—that symbolize the imperial throne and its legitimacy as an institution. The mirror, known as the **yata-no-kagami**, is kept in Ise Jingū (the **Grand Shrines of Ise**). The sword, the kusanagi-no-tsurugi is kept at **Atsuta Jingū** in Nagoya. The jewels, known as the **yasakani-no-magatama**, are kept in the imperial palace. Together, they stand for wisdom, courage, and benevolence. Each new emperor receives them immediately following the decease of the previous emperor. *See also* JINNŌ SHŌTŌKI.

SARUGAKU. Also called Sangaku, this was a form of performing art in ancient Japan that was the precursor of **Noh**, and in fact from which Noh was derived. At **festival** times, Sarugaku players would provide side-shows in the form of **dances** and other arts depicting narratives from the classical **mythology** or comic tales based on **folk culture**. By the 14th century, this had evolved into the more stylized forms of Noh and **Kyōgen**. *See also* DRAMATIC ARTS IN SHINTO.

SARUTAHIKŌ-OKAMI. Head of the **earthly** *kami*, referred to in the **Kojiki** (712) and in the **Nihon Shōki** (720) as standing at the crossroads of heaven and earth. After **Ame-uzume-no-mikoto** had been sent down to prepare for the descent of **Ninigi-no-mikoto**, she encountered a huge *kami* whom she pacified and who eventually became her husband. He is enshrined in many places but principally at the head shrine, **Tsubaki Ōkami Yashiro** in Suzuka City, Mie Prefecture. He is the *kami* of guidance and pioneering, who taught the culture of rice and the basis of civilization. *See also* ICHI-NO-MIYA.

SATOMIYA. A village shrine that is part of a pair, the other of which is usually located in or on a mountain that is not easily accessible. Worship at the satomiya can be counted as worship at the less accessible shrine.

SATOW, SIR ERNEST MASON (1843–1929). British diplomat, scholar, and authority on Japan and China, he served in the British diplomatic mission from 1862 to 1882, covering the end of the Tokugawa Shogunate and the early period after the **Meiji Restoration** in 1868. He spoke both Japanese and Chinese and served successively as minister plenipotentiary (ambassador) to Japan from 1895 to 1900, and to China from 1900 to 1906.

During his retirement, he devoted the last years of his life to work on varied academic subjects. His writings and reports remain a valuable source of insight derived from an inside understanding of Japan. He compiled *An English-Japanese Dictionary of the Spoken Language* that was published in 1878. His numerous contributions to the *Transactions of the Asiatic Society of Japan* are the principal source of his general writings on Japan, which include insights on contemporary Shinto in his day.

SECT SHINTO. *See* KYŌHA SHINTO.

SEI-AKU-SETSU. Doctrine of inherent evil in human nature derived from the less optimistic tradition of early **Confucianism**, from the teachings of Hsun Tzu (298–238 B.C.E.) This doctrine had very little influence upon Japanese Confucian thought, and therefore equally little impact upon the meeting of **Confucianism and Shinto.** *See also* ETHICS IN SHINTO.

SEICHO-NO-IE. A **New Religion** whose name means "house of growth," the title given by its founder, **Taniguchi Masaharu** (1893–1985) to a cultural magazine he first published in March 1940, and out of which the movement emerged. The life of Taniguchi is the key to how the movement developed, something which is true of many of the New Religions.

The basic ideas of the sect are in its name. Ie refers not to a house, but to the Great Universe. The term seicho means "to grow," that is, to create as the universe is creating and growing infinitely. The great universe is the House of Growth and members study the rules of life and teach people the rules that make it work. Taniguchi calls the true state of life (Jisso-no-Sekai) the Seicho-no-Ie. The Buddhist notion of Nirvana, particularly in Mahayana **Buddhism,** may be similar to this, but Taniguchi thought this was too negative. He thought that paradise should have a more joyful and lively image; therefore, to him, Seicho-no-Ie means "always growing and infinitely young." It is also regarded as a kind of paradise on earth.

Seicho-no-Ie claims to be a guide for people who seek the true meaning of their own religion. Therefore, members of any religion can also be members of Seicho-no-Ie, although the rituals of Seicho-no-Ie are fundamentally Shinto because Taniguchi felt that Japanese would be most at home with these. The movement has three main rituals. One is a memorial service for the dead, performed three times a year, in spring, summer, and autumn. Seicho-no-Ie supports the idea of the government becoming responsible for the **Yasukuni Jinja**, the shrine for the war dead. A second ceremony, this one for the living, is for healing and enlightenment. The third is a ceremony of purification (**harai**). Members write on sheets of paper about things that are troubling them, and the sheets are burned in a ritual rather like **goma**, the fire ceremony of purification performed in esoteric Buddhism and at some Shinto shrines.

Believing that negative feelings cause unhappiness, believers avoid using negative words following the Shinto taboo of **imi no kotoba**, words to be avoided. Instead they must concentrate on the idea that the knowledge, love, life abundance, happiness, and harmony of the *kami* is flowing through the body and enabling them to leave the world of senses to enter the world of "truth."

Seicho-no-Ie claimed to have about 800,000 members including branches in North and South America. Dr. Taniguchi Seicho (born 1919) succeeded to the leadership on the death of the founder in 1985. The present leader is Masanobu Taniguchi, who became the third president in 2008. Its headquarters are located in Harajuku, Jingū-mae, Shibuya Ward, in Tokyō near **Meiji Jingū**.

SEIKYŌ-BUNRI. Separation of government and religion, a policy of the Meiji period (1868–1912) government announced in 1882 after it was clear that the idea of Shinto as a national religion was not going to be workable. By classifying "religions" in a manner that excluded Shinto, the path was open to declare Shinto a "way" but not a "religion."

The secularization of Shinto around its ritual functions enabled subsequent governments to insist that it could be a patriotic duty to visit a shrine (**jinja**), but that this did not constitute a religious activity, thus ostensibly guarding the constitutionally guaranteed freedom of religion. This position was, of course, challenged, and led to serious controversy over the status of shrines and the requirement of attendance at shrines as a patriotic duty. *See also* KOKKA SHINTO; MODERNIZATION AND SHINTO.

SEIKYO SHINTO. Yamaga Soko (1622–1685) established this neo-Confucian tradition of Shinto during the Edo period (1615–1868).

SEI-MEI-SHIN. The concepts of "purity" and "brightness" are central to **ethics in Shinto**, and have the identical meaning (and characters) as akaki in **akaki kiyoki kokoro.** Important also is shojiki (honesty).

SEI-ZEN-SETSU. Doctrine of the inherent goodness of human nature, derived from the more optimistic tradition of **Confucianism** that came through Mo-Tzu (371–289 B.C.E.). Because it accorded well with the basic insights of Shinto, it was integrated into **ethics in Shinto.**

SEKAI-KYŪSEI-KYŌ. The Church of World Messianity, a **New Religion** with a Shinto background, founded in 1928 by Okada Mokichi (1882–1955). His family lost everything in the great Tōkyō earthquake of September 1923, at which time he was exposed to **Ōmoto-kyō** whose ideas of spiritual healing attracted him. Okada claims to have been instructed by God in 1926 to build a heaven on earth and to prophesy concerning the last judgment to the Japan of the 1920s and 1930s.

Although very much a Japanese movement, it tried to take on the image of a world religion. It followed the recurring pattern of being created in Japan for the Japanese, who then felt the need to spread it for the salvation of the world. Its first name was Dainihon-kannonkai (Great Japan Association for the Worship of **Kannon**) and was founded in February 1928 with two objectives: the goal of communion with the divine, and the ideal of the healing of disease through the laying on of hands.

In 1931, Okada received another message, this one telling him that the spiritual world had been transformed from dark and painful to bright and pleasurable. He believed that he was to perform the mission of saving the world. "Heaven on earth," he declared, was a world without illness, poverty, and conflict; it was a utopian society of health, wealth, and happiness, as well as truth, justice, and beauty, all in perfect harmony. The government ordered him to limit himself to one purpose, and **faith healing** was chosen.

In 1934, Okada changed the group's name to Nihon-Jyoka-Ryoho (Japan Association for Therapy through Purification). During the **Pacific War** (World War II) the movement was suppressed but was revived in 1947 as the Nihon-Kannon-Kyōdan (Japan Society for the Worship of Kannon). In 1950, it split and Okada formed the Sekai-Meshiya-Kyō, the World Messianic movement. The final name of Sekai-Kyusei-Kyō was determined just after that.

In June 1980, the Mokichi Okada Association (MOA) was formed to engage in activities that would not be affected by Okada's teachings. A great deal of doctrine had been acquired from Omoto-kyō. Okada believed that the *kami* of creation, Sozo-shūshin wished to establish paradise on earth, so the organization laid stress on two themes: faith healing and utopianism. Okada was referred to as Meishūsama (enlightened master) and is believed to have ascended to heaven, where he is still directing the affairs of this world. After his death, his widow, Yoshiko, assumed the leadership role as Nidaisama (second master) until she died in 1962. Their daughter, Fujita Itsuki, became Sandaisama (third master) after her mother had died.

The MOA aims at overcoming racial, religious, and cultural barriers by means of art, education, agriculture, and environmental sciences. It seeks to deepen people's awareness of their cultural heritage and its beauty and so increase international understanding. The worldwide campaign began in July 1980 following Okada's ideas that the religion could save even America. In one of his speeches he declared, "no other nation besides America is today equal to the task of maintaining peace in the world. It is one of the most urgent tasks of the day to help America to improve the health conditions of her people. I therefore want to stop the spread of diseases there and eradicate all existing disease."

The MOA has used International Exchange Programs on Contemporary Art in order to enable one culture to see others, a window to spiritual heritage. Since 1973, a Japan-Brazil Art Exhibition has been an annual event and others are held in the United States. Scientific Research being conducted includes the idea of natural agricultural techniques that promote proper and healthy growth of vegetables without chemicals that damage the soil and threaten human life. In 1982, a Natural Agriculture International Research and Development Center was established in a 50-hectare farm in Izu. Farms now exist in Hokkaido, Okinawa, and Nagano, as well as in Hawaii, Brazil, and Thailand. The movement is also politically active, supporting the Liberal Democratic Party through its own Jiyu-minshū-to-Kyusei Rengokai to actualize their ideals.

The headquarters is located at Gora near Hakone, where there is a model of the miroku-ōmikami (heaven on earth), called Saichi, on display. It is said to be reflected in the Reikai, which in turn will be reflected in all the corners of the earth, thus making the miroku-ōmikami a reality. The church has three gardens in Japan, which depict the three elements of the universe and are meant to symbolize the links between nature and humanity. There is an oriental-style garden in Hakone that symbolizes fire, and a Western garden in Atami symbolizing water. There is also a flat garden in Kyōto symbolizing the earth.

Atami Shoji was set up in 1948, and was replaced in 1983 by the The MOA Trading Company to provide natural foods for a healthy and peaceful society and to operate hotels and restaurants for the welfare of followers. It also provides travel services, and produces art goods, books, newspapers, and magazines. Kamei Kanichiro founded the Economic and Industrial Research Association in 1947, and that became a member of the MOA in 1973. It provides the economic input to the concepts of progress necessary to construct the "ideal" society. The MOA reports 800,000 registered believers in Japan and beyond. Brazil has been extremely fertile soul even among Brazilians not of Japanese extraction. It underwent some factional strife in the late 1980s that Fujita Itsuki had some trouble in ending.

While apparently the movement was reconstituted, its image remains somewhat confusing because of the complex relationship with other movements whose leaders originally belonged to Okada's movement, and because of the court cases that arose to determine the succession. Sekai Mahikari Bunmei Kyōdan founder Yoshikazu Okada (1901–1974) and Sukyō Mahikari founder Okada Kotama (1901–1974) were both members of the Church of World Messianity. According to some scholars, all of the groups including the Mahikari groups all follow the same **healing** rituals.

SENDAI KUJI HONGI. *See* KUJI.

SENDATSU. The formal title of the Shugenja (practitioners of **Shugendō**) in the **Kumano Shinto** tradition during the **Heian period**

(794–1185). It subsequently came into use as a title for guides who led groups of people on these pilgrimages. *See also* OSHI.

SENGOKU JIDAI. Era of the civil wars that saw the introduction of Roman Catholicism into Japan, first by the Jesuits, who took a cautious approach, but later by the Franciscans, whose conquest of the Philippines inspired them to encourage the burning of shrines (**jinja**) and temples, initially to the anguish of local people, and subsequently to the anger of the emerging feudal leadership. **Toyotomi Hideyoshi** (1536–1598) clearly perceived the incursions as a threat to social order and ordered the execution of a group of 26 Christian believers in Nagasaki. This led eventually to **Tokugawa Ieyasu** (1543–1616) issuing a ban on Roman Catholicism and to the expulsion of all missionaries.

This period of Japanese history appears to have been known in Europe, and is referred to by Immanuel Kant (1724–1804) in his *Essay on Perpetual Peace* (1786), in which he commends the Tokugawa government for its actions, on the grounds that movements subversive to social order and peace should be contained.

SEN-NICHI-KAI-HŌ-GYŌ. Practiced on Mount Hiei near Kyōto, it is a **mountain** ascetic discipline of **Tendai Buddhism** which takes 1,000 days to complete, divided up over a period of seven years.

The nightly cycle includes **rituals** of both Shinto and **Buddhism**. **Misogi** at midnight, for example, is the first act performed by the gyoja, the practitioner, before he commences the circuit of holy places for that night. Purified, he goes through the dark vastnesses of the mountain, praying at designated sites, and returns in the morning light to prepare for the day's chores.

Those who successfully complete the **gyo,** or discipline, receive certification of merit as living Buddhas (**ikibotoke**), the Buddhist equivalent of **ikigami** (living human *kami*), at the Imperial Palace in Kyōto. In keeping with the narrow understanding of religion associated with the Meiji period (1868–1912) government, the discipline was banned after 1868. It was revived after 1945, but between then and the year 2010, fewer than a dozen people had successfully completed the discipline.

SEN NO RIKKYU (1522–1591). Founder of the Sen School of Tea Ceremony, and aesthete who stylized the ritual, blending elements of Shinto purification and **Zen** contemplation. He was forced by **Toyotomi Hideyoshi** (1536–1598) to commit ritual suicide in 1591 for reasons that remain obscure.

SESSHA. A subordinate shrine (**jinja**) within the grounds of a major one. For example, sessha dedicated to **Inari** are found within the precincts of many old shrines, because of their general popularity during the Edo period (1615–1868).

SETSUBUN-SAI. This period, which coincides with the lunar **New Year**, marks the transition from one season to another. Beans are thrown from wooden boxes to force out misfortune and usher in good news and prosperity. The words "**Oni** wa soto, fuku wa uchi" (literally, "demons out, good fortune in"). At major shrines (**jinja**), celebrity figures born in that year often scatter packages of beans from a large platform into assembled crowds of people, who collect them as good luck charms.

SEX IN SHINTO. According to Japanese **mythology**, the Japanese archipelago comes about as a result of the procreative act of **Izanagi-no-mikoto** and **Izanami-no-mikoto**, an act described in great detail. It so distressed the 19th-century translator of the **Kojiki** (720), **Basil Hall Chamberlain**, that he rendered the passage into Latin. He did the same when translating the passage in which **Susano-o-no-mikoto** so frightened some workers in the palace when he threw a flayed horse through the roof that one young **woman** struck her genitals against a loom and died. Shinto, in its worldview, was quite open in its treatment of fertility and sexuality, and shows no sign of either the prudery or the narrow moralism associated with the Western tradition.

At the level of **folk Shinto**, in spite of pressure to the contrary, much of the traditional **fertility** culture survived the enormous purges conducted, often at the behest of Western critics, during the **Meiji Restoration**. In popular entertainment at village **festivals**, overt sexual themes were frequently depicted. Normally after a major project had been completed, banquets at which people ate and drank freely and entertained each other with song and dance of a ribald nature were normal practice. Festival times in general were occasions when promiscuous sex was openly tolerated.

While the agricultural background of Japanese culture may have weakened, the tradition continues into the kind of drinking gatherings of various groups, social or corporate, where language and behavior is tolerated that would be regarded as improper if judged by politically correct Western standards. In some shrine rites, at certain festivals, phallic symbols are displayed as part of the celebrations.

The famous **Henoko Matsuri** or Phallus Festival of the **Tagata Jinja** in Komaki, near Nagoya Airport in Aiichi Prefecture is one of the best known. Nearby Inuyama city's **Oagata Jinja** hosts the **Ososo Matsuri** (Vagina Festival). These festivals are intended to protect crops, cure sterility and impotence, and to guarantee business success and fertility. The touching of the sacred objects, the phallus at the Tagata Jinja Matsuri, by women assures pregnancy, while at the Oagata Jinja, the clam, a symbol of the vagina, guarantees marital harmony, conception, and the cure of sexual diseases, in addition to a good harvest.

The very survival of these festivals indicates how deeply rooted in agricultural concerns and motifs Japanese culture remains. They may not have as much relevance to the present as they did in the past, but they open another window to the understanding of the evolution of Japanese culture.

SHAGO. Titles of ranks of shrines with dai-jingu at the top (for example the **Grand Shrines of Ise**), jingu (for example **Katori Jingū**), taisha (for example **Izumo Taisha**) and sha or jinja (for example, **Yasaka Jinja**). *See also* SHAKAKU-SEIDO.

SHAJI-KYOKU. The **Meiji Restoration** government Bureau of Shrines (**jinja**) and Temples, set up in 1877 to take the place of the **Kyōbusho** (the Ministry of Religious Instruction) which had been incorporated into the **Jingisho** (Ministry of the *Kami*). *See also* JINGIKAN; KOKKA SHINTO.

SHAKAKU-SEIDO. The system of ranking shrines (**jinja**) that was instituted from the period of the **Engishiki** (905–922) until 1945. Various categories existed, such as National Shrines (Kampeisha); Provincial Shrines (Kokuheisha); local shrines; the **niju-ni-sha**, the 22 special shrines in the Kyōto area; and the **ichinomiya**, the first shrines of the regions nationwide. Under **Kokka Shinto** (State Shinto), the classification became stricter and more complicated. Since 1945, no official ranking system has existed under the Religious Juridical Persons Law (**Shūkyō Hojin Hō**) of 1951.

SHAKU. Wooden baton carried by priests since the Heian period (794–1185). Originating from the T'ang Dynasty (618–907) court dress, it was used to carry notes or used as a prompt during special ceremonies.

SHAKU NIHONGI. This oldest known commentary on the text of the **Nihon Shōki** (720) was written by Urabe Kanekata (late 13th–early 14th century), a member of the priestly Urabe family. It consists of 28 volumes. It consists of a compilation of materials derived from lectures on the Nihon Shōki, given at the imperial court during the **Heian period** (794–1185), where his father, Kanefumi, had also been a lecturer. *See also* HIRANO JINJA; YOSHIDA SHINTO.

SHAMANISM IN SHINTO. Shamanism is a strong feature of Japanese religion since earliest times. Most of the **New Religions** that have emerged since the early 18th century have been the work of people with clear charismatic or shamanistic traits. The same may probably be said of religious movements that date to earlier periods and of those that were established in the post-1945 period.

Speculation exists that many of Japan's early empresses were shamans, and that at least some power of the **emperor system** arose from that source, which would account for the cultic nature of various aspects of the imperial institution. Certainly oracular mediums and oracles were very much part of court life in the sixth and seventh centuries.

Beyond the New Religions, in the mainstream of Shinto, two traditions of shamanism remain. One is associated with **miko**, or female mediums who speak the words of *kami* while in a trance. These shamanistic oracles have a long history. The blind women shamans, the itako of Osorezan in Aomori Prefecture, are the best-known surviving example. The other variety is that of **Shugendō**, the activity of **shūgenja**, mountain ascetics (**yamabushi**) who practice fasting, **misogi**, a form of purification (**harai**) in cold water, and other stern rites in order to enhance their spirituality and their powers.

Healing powers and the ability to calm troublesome *kami* should be the result of the discipline. Gyoja, or shūgenja, are also capable of unusual feats such as fire walking, or being unhurt by boiling water, as in **Ontake-kyō**. Rather than being seen as a special phenomenon in its own right, it can also be understood as part of the expression of Japanese religious culture in general.

SHAMUSHO. The administrative center of a shrine. It is referred to differently in older shrines. In the **Grand Shrines of Ise** it is known as the Jingū shichō. In Atsuta Jingū it is known as the Guchō.

SHICHI-FUKU-JIN. Seven folk *kami* of good fortune and commercial prosperity. The group consists of **Ebisu**, Daikoku-ten (the folk name of **Okuninushi-no-mikoto**), Bishamon-ten, Fukuroku-ju, Jurojin, Ben-ten (or Benzai-ten), and Hotei. They are frequently depicted in pictures or models as sitting in a boat filled with treasure. Their origin is obscure, but was certainly linked with the merchant classes in the city of Edo (Tokyō).

SHICHI-GO-SAN. The festival in which girls of three and seven years of age, and boys of five years of age visit the family shrine (**jinja**) to mark a rite of passage. Children normally wear kimonos for the occasion and formal photographs are usually taken.

SHIKINAISHA. A list of shrines contained in volumes nine and ten of the **Engishiki**, known as the Jinmyocho. There were 2861 shrines (**jinja**) enshrining 3,122 *kami*, all of which were entitled to state offerings at their **festivals**. The **Jingikan** (Office of the *Kami*) was responsible for offerings to the Kampeisha (National Shrines) and the kokushi (local shrines), while the government presented offerings to the Kokuheisha (Provincial Shrines), according to the hierarchy of the **Shakaku-Seido**, the **Heian period** (794–1185) system of shrine rankings.

SHIKINEN SENGŪ. Periodic reconstruction of shrine (**jinja**) buildings, followed by removal of the enshrined *kami* to the new building. In the case of the **Grand Shrines of Ise** (Ise Jingū), the period is 20 years. Other shrines where this occurs have varying times, and some, only when the economy permits. The 66th reconstruction of the Grand Shrines of Ise was completed with due ceremony in 1993. The 67th reconstruction will be completed in 2013.

SHIMENAWA. Twisted rope, sometimes white, and sometimes brown straw, used to denote a sacred space. Most famous and frequently photographed is the great Shimenawa that hangs in front of the main worship hall (**haiden**) of **Izumo Taisha** in Shimane Prefecture. The shimenawa is also part of the formal costume of a **sumo** grand champion (Yokozuna), and may also be seen on old and venerable trees (**shimboku**) within shrine (**jinja**) precincts.

SHINBATSU. Punishment by a *kami* of someone who acts in a disrespectful, unbelieving, or impure manner and who commits any of the wrongful acts listed in the famous **norito**, the **Ōbarae-no-kotoba**. *See also* BACHI; ETHICS IN SHINTO; HARAI; KEGARAE; TATARI; TSUMI.

SHINBOKU. A sacred tree of grove within shrine (**jinja**) precincts thought to be a place where a *kami* had descended. These will often have a twisted rope (**shimenawa**) tied around them for identification. This draws attention to them and encourages worshippers to show respect toward them.

SHINBUTSU-BUNRI. Also referred to as Shinbutsu-hanzen, it was the Meiji period (1868–1912) formal and legal separation of Shinto and **Buddhism** as a step toward the creation of **Kokka Shinto** (State Shinto). The order was issued formally by the **Dajōkan** (Council of State) of the new Meiji government on 28 March, one of its earliest acts of the new era.

Shrines (**jinja**) were ordered to submit copies of their history, including any Buddhist associations. Such associations had to be renounced through the removal of any Buddhist artifacts, such as statues, bells, or art. This was followed by a further order in April of the same year, requiring Buddhist-ordained clergy to leave the service of the shrines or be re-ordained as Shinto priests if they wished to continue. They were required, however, to let their hair grow back as evidence of having ceased to be Buddhist.

The government also placed a ban on aristocratic families becoming Shinto priests as part of a coordinated drive to break hereditary control of shrines by major families. The 1872 ban on the concept that the Buddhas were the true essence and the *kami* were the incarnation provoked movements of protest from Buddhist groups that seriously impeded the implementation of the originally planned pure Shinto order.

The haibatsu-kishaku (destroy the Buddha, kill Shakyamuni) slogan even resulted in anti-Buddhist mob violence against some temples particularly where they were close to famous shrines. The government ban also affected the centers of **Shugendō**, because they combined Buddhist and Shinto rituals. It was not until the post-1945 period, with the effective implementation of religious freedom, that Shugendō was able to recover and restore itself. *See also* ASSIMILATION OF BUDDHISM AND SHINTO; SYNCRETISM IN SHINTO.

SHINBUTSU-SHUGŌ. Integration of *kami* and Buddha that began during the Nara period (710–794) and developed significantly during the **Heian period** (794–1185). This was one form of the system of ideas used to maintain harmony between Shinto and **Buddhism** in the process of the **assimilation of Buddhism and Shinto**.

It can be traced back to as early as 698, when the Taki Daijingu was moved. This is recorded in the *Zoku Nihongi* as having taken place during the second year of the reign of Emperor Mommu (reigned 697–707). It is probably safe to say that it was a policy that had been in existence since the earliest encounter between Buddhism and Shinto, as a way of avoiding conflict and gradually effecting harmony over the centuries.

SHINGAKU. The name of this popular movement means "Heart Learning." It was founded by **Ishida Baigan** (1685–1746) and usually classified as a type of popular Shinto. The central ideas were both religious and ethical with strong moral teaching, combining elements of **Buddhism** with some of the virtues of **Confucianism**. It had a strong foundation in Shinto, particularly stressing the worship of **Amaterasu-ōmikami** and of the family *kami*, Oruji-gami.

However, it also included features of Chinese neo-Confucian cosmology that were combined into simple precepts for the daily life of ordinary people. It first gained popularity when Ishida gave a series of public lectures in Kyōto in 1729, after which it quickly spread. It stressed the improvement of the heart (**kokoro**), a central concept which continues to play a very important part in the teachings of the **New Religions**), hence the name shin-gaku, "heart-learning." The concept of "heart" in Ishida's thought encompasses the seat of the emotions and the source of actions. By purifying it, moral actions are thought to ensue.

Ishida's followers expanded his ideas into a philosophy that taught the integration of all the feudal classes into a world of harmony and peace. The movement was one which widely influenced ordinary people and which was easily combined with whatever local shrines (**jinja**) or temples they were affiliated. Later followers, who were deeply concerned about human nature, took up the issue of social and moral education and became involved in the Terakoya (temple schools of the Edo period, 1615–1868).

While as a movement it no longer exists, its ideas survive in various indirect forms and continues to be in the background of many New Religious movements, in the same way as it lay in the background of **Kyōha Shinto** (Sect Shinto).

SHINGAKU. Meaning *"kami* learning," this is the modern Japanese way to translate the academic term "theology." It can also refer to Shinto studies in general.

SHINGON BUDDHISM. Esoteric sect of Japanese **Buddhism** derived from Tibetan Buddhism and introduced into Japan by **Kūkai** (773–835) in the ninth century. Its principal temple is the Kongobu-ji on Mount Kōya in Wakayama Prefecture. Unlike **Tendai Buddhism**, which is partly esoteric, Shingon is completely esoteric, using mudras, mandalas, and hand movements introduced from Chinese and Tibetan Buddhism. Many of these found their way into the practices of **Shugendō** practitioners (gyoja) and even Shinto rituals such as **misogi**.

Kūkai visited many mountain shrines and introduced aspects of Shingon rituals, which resulted in many shrines incorporating Shingon features into their **architecture** and rituals. **Mitsumine Jinja** in Saitama Prefecture is an example of a shrine (**jinja**) visited by Kūkai and whose architecture is in the **gongen** (incarnation) style, with intricate symbolic painting inside the roof. While it is **Jinja Shinto** (Shrine Shinto) in its affiliation, its history is complex and typical of Shinto-style **syncretism**. Many other **Jingū-ji** (shrine-temples) were created to unite Shinto and esoteric Buddhism, which in the form of **Watarai Shinto** was even found within the **Gekū** (Outer Shrine) of the **Grand Shrines of Ise** (Ise Jingū) and those shrines influenced by it.

SHINGON SHINTO. *See* SHINGON BUDDHISM.

SHINJIN-GŌITSU. Organic spiritual unity of human and *kami*, a doctrine basic to the Shinto ideal that human beings are in some way descended from *kami* but are also distanced from them by impurities (**tsumi**), which must be removed.

SHINJIN-KIITSU. Restoration of the divine within the human, or the return of the purified human nature to the *kami* status from which it has fallen because of its impurities (**tsumi**).

SHINJI-NOH. **Noh** plays performed as part of Shinto ceremonies. One of the origins of Noh may be found in the activities of the **za**, the shrine guilds that cared for shrines. The great shrines **Kasuga Taisha** and **Hie Jinja** are particularly famous, but there are many nationwide. *See also* DRAMATIC ARTS IN SHINTO.

SHINKAI. Ancient term of rank assigned by the imperial court to the *kami* of a shrine (**jinja**). The practice was first noted in a text of the Todai-ji, referring to the temple of the Great Buddha of Nara about 1134. The *kami* **Hachiman** was given third rank as a prayer for the emperor's illness. It is a valuable research resource on the status and prestige of various *kami* of that period.

SHIN KOKINSHŪ. Also known as the Shin Koko Waka Shū, this collection of court poetry, later than that of the **Kokinshū**, dating to 1205 and the eighth and final anthology to be completed in the style of Hitomaro. The battle of **Dannoura** led to the destruction of the Heike family by the Minamoto that in turn established a new shogunate at Kamakura in 1192. Cloistered Emperor (**insei**) Gotoba (reigned 1183–1198) initiated the work and entrusted a group of editors to complete it. The authors were priests, aristocrats, or courtiers, so they did not necessarily represent the mood of ordinary people of the time in the same manner as did the **Man'yōshū**.

However, as the people responsible for religious ordinances, some of those writers did express ideas and feelings relevant to this study. The selection reflects these points. As with the Man'yoshū and the Kokinshū, these poems are signed by their authors. They likewise cover the spectrum of human feelings about life, love, and death, set against the seasons of the year and the corresponding beauty of **nature**. It is interesting also to read poetic descriptions of **Mount Fuji** emitting volcanic smoke. Here is an instance of direct continuity with the Man'yoshū, and indeed of the continuity that is a profound characteristic of Japanese culture throughout the ages.

SHINKŌ (SHIN) SHŪKYŌ. *See* NEW RELIGIONS.

SHINOHAI. In this **ritual**, reverence toward **nature** is shown by bowing to the north, south, east, and west.

SHINREI-KYŌ. A Shinto-based **New Religion** founded by Otsuka Kan'ichi (1891–1972), the son of a wealthy merchant in Tokushima who showed prodigious capacities in the activity of fortune-telling. At age 16, he went to various famous centers of mountain religion in Japan, not to learn about **Buddhism** or **Shugendō**, but to confirm his own spiritual powers.

The name combines *kami*, spirit, and teaching, giving the meaning "teaching of the *kami* spirit." The miracles that *kami* power made possible to its founder are what believers claim differentiate it from other faiths. It claims, first, that miracles do take place, and ,second, that these are without parallel in any other religion. Consequently, its basic approach to explaining itself is through case studies that demonstrate how its principles work. Miracles are the authenticating proof of Shinrei-kyō beliefs, evidence of a new coming world order. Through a process of skull expansion (which happens to every follower), brain cells are activated and the mind is calmed. Thus through being able to make sound judgments, believers are enabled to develop themselves to the fullest.

Shinrei-kyō believers claim to die a natural death in such a way that their bodies will not experience rigor mortis, death spots, or putrid odors. This enables the sublime transmigration to take place from death to a new life which follows. Otsuka first published a pamphlet entitled *Dainippon-seishin* (The Spirit of Great Japan) in 1911 after extensive travels in Korea, Manchuria and Mongolia. He argued that the focus of international religions was shifting from West to East and that the core of human existence was rejecting materialism for what he called seishinteki bunmei (spiritual civilization). The idea itself is not clearly defined, but is suggestive of a type of society rather different from that of modern Japan where, according to Otsuka's views, material things had become dominant.

He founded a second movement that was called Nippon Seishin Fukko Sokushin-Kai (Society to Promote the Restoration of the Soul of Japan), aimed at restoring the true Japanese spirit that had been lost in the midst of the great economic changes of the postwar world. It was intended to stress Japan's role in international relations as a creator of world peace. Otsuka's widow (Kyōbosama) succeeded him as leader after his death in 1972.

SHINRI-KYŌ. A **Kyōha Shinto** (Sect Shinto) sect founded by Kannagibe (later Sano) Tsunehiko, (1837–1910) who claimed to be the 77th descendant of a *kami* called Nigi-hayahi-no-mikoto. This *kami*, he argued had served **Amaterasu-ōmikami**. The Kannagibe family was originally one of practitioners of medicine, but because of the influences of foreign learning upon medicine, their activities became confused with Christianity. Sano himself wished to go into medicine, but for fear of being mistaken for a Christian believer, he decided to propagate the family teaching instead. Between 1882 and 1886, he claimed to have received *kami* revelations in his dreams which gave him confidence in both his *kami* mission and his *kami* ancestry.

The sect was given government recognition in 1894, became a part of **Ontake-kyō** initially, but separated in 1908 and became an independent sect. Sano's brother, Takane, and his son Izuhiko became the principal exponents after Sano died in Kyushū in 1910. Groups gradually began to emerge, initially in northern Kyushū. The tradition is maintained by direct descendants who use either Sano or Kannagibe as a family name.

The name Shinri-kyō includes the basic character, kyō, which means teaching. Shin is the same character as *kami*. Ri (principle or reason) is a **Confucian** concept that refers to the principles of order within the universe. The name Shinri-kyō thus means "teaching of the *kami* order." The sect sought to promote the national language and, like **Shinto Taikyō**, the writing of poetry, **kagura** (sacred dance), and flower arrangement.

The *kami* revered include the three central *kami* of creation (the **Zōka-sanshin**) and the principal *kami* of the **kami-yo**. The basic doctrines make use of the idea of the spirit of words (**kotodama**), indicating that the concepts are grounded in the classic ideas of Shinto. The fundamental ideas do not depart far from traditional **Jinja Shinto** (Shrine Shinto) in that the *kami* are revered and proximity to the *kami* remains the basic condition for human happiness. To achieve this, believers must purify their own hearts and then their surroundings. With blessings from one's ancestors, happiness will come about through these improvements.

Shinri-kyō claims that people are reincarnations of their ancestors, and that if there is unhappiness or misery, the essential cause lies with displeased ancestors. The basic root of unhappiness is due either to the fact that either some ancestor did not rise to divinity, or that individuals are not paying adequate respect to their ancestors. Ancestors must be properly served in order to bring about the best possible conditions in the present. This in turn becomes the power to protect one's own offspring and to guarantee survival to posterity.

The headquarters of the sect is in Kokura, in Kita-Kyushū. The fourth-generation head of the organization was Kannagibe Takehiko (born in 1948). It claims 1.5 million members.

SHINSEN. The various kinds of offerings made to *kami*, either regularly or at times of **festivals** at shrines (**jinja**) or on a daily basis in domestic **kamidana**. There are many varieties of these; at major shrines they may be prepared in a special hall (shinsen-den), after which they are borne ceremonially and placed in the altar area of the main hall of worship (**haiden**).

SHINSHOKU. A general term for the Shinto priesthood. The highest shrine (**jinja**) rank is **guji**, beneath which is a gon-gu ji. The next rank is negi, below which is a gon-negi, a junior priest. *See also* KANNUSHI.

SHINSHŪ-KYŌ. According to this **Kyōha Shinto** (Sect Shinto) sect, the idea of purification (**harai**) itself, the sole and central concern of its activities and beliefs. It was founded by Yoshimura Masamochi (1839–1916) a member of the great Shinto family of **Onakatomi**. After the **Meiji Restoration** (1868) and the **Shinbutsu-bunri** edict promulgated by the government, he was able to advance his ideas, which were purged of all elements of **Buddhism** whatsoever, going back to the era before the Nara period (710–794). It received formal recognition from the government in 1880.

Yoshimura himself became the first head priest of the movement. He declared as its goals: to learn the way of the *kami* in silence; to master the national rites; and to pray for the imperial family's eternal wellbeing, the emperor's health, the nation's prosperity, and world peace, along with an abundant harvest of grains and cereals. Much **folk religion** remained in it in spite of all declarations of purity. Basic to Shinshū-kyō are the ideas of harmony of yu (the unseen world of the *kami*) and gen (the world that human beings inhabit and that is seen). The sect's teaching emphasizes that it is by good actions that people become *kami*.

This is the basis for the various ascetic rituals practiced by the group. In April and in September, believers practice two ascetic semi-magical rituals, the fire calming ceremony, **chinka shiki** and the sprinkling of boiling water on the body, **kugatachi-shiki.** These are considered to be forms of purification, and according to the traditions of the sect, no one has ever been injured or harmed in any way by performing them. Four other rituals are also performed, often in conjunction with the above: **misogi**-hō, in which cold water is poured over the believers for purification; batsujo-hō, which is a form of meditation which claims to rid the personality of bad attitudes such as anger and selfishness; mono-imi-ho, abstinence from certain foods and drinks; and shinji-ho, a procedure designed to lead to "*kami* possession" of the believers, a ritual that testifies to the **shamanism** that is a characteristic of the sect.

One feature of the sect that is most explicitly Shinto is the idea that religious truth is set forth, grasped, and experienced primarily in ritual and ceremonies. By purification of the spirit, it is possible to come to know the *kami*, and consequently to heighten human spirituality. This is the reason why the sect is also known as Mugon-no-oshie (teaching without words) because it believes that it is by actions and rites such as those described above that human beings can become *kami*. The membership hovers around 300,000, and the headquarters is located in Setagaya Ward in Tokyō. The leader remains a member of the Yoshimura family.

SHINTAI. *See* GO-SHINTAI.

SHINTAI-ZEN. A mountain revered as the home of a *kami*, which means that the shrine may not have **honden**, or main worship hall. Kanasana Jinja in Saitama Prefecture is a well-known example.

SHINTO-BASED NEW RELIGIONS. *See* NEW RELIGIONS.

SHINTO DIRECTIVE. The office of the **Supreme Commander Allied Forces (SCAP)** issued this short text on 15 December 1945, which banned all government funding or support for any Shinto rituals or all religious activity, especially any that was militaristic, ultranationalistic, and that claimed the superiority of the emperor or the people of Japan over all other nations. **Jinja Shinto** (Shrine Shinto) and **Kyōha Shinto** (Sect Shinto) thus came under the same general heading of "religions of Japan." It also had the effect of enabling many amalgamated shrines to be re-established, because it was in fact also a proclamation of religious freedom, with each group becoming an independent religious legal person (shūkyō hojin) in its own right, according to the Religious Juridical Persons Law of 1951. *See also* SHŪKYŌ HŌJIN HŌ.

SHINTO GOBUSHO. The Five-fold Shinto Canon was the title given to the collected works of 13th-century Shinto priestly and scholarly family **Watarai**, of the **Gekū** (Outer) of the **Grand Shrines of Ise** (Ise Jingū). These are the texts of what came to be called Early Ise Shinto, as against the Later Ise Shinto of the Edo period (1615–1868). It was originally believed to have been authored by legendary figures, such as Yamatohime-no-mikoto, who was the founder of the Grand Shrines of Ise in the year 4 B.C.E.

They were part of an ambitious campaign to promote the interests of the Gekū against the **Naikū** (Inner) of the Grand Shrines of Ise. One of the main claims in the Gobusho is that the principal *kami* of the Outer Shrine, Toyouke no Okami, is to be identified with **Kunitokotachi-no-mikoto**, the *kami* who preceded the *kami* of the sun, **Amaterasu-ōmikami**, and who therefore should be given precedence over Amaterasu.

The texts were speculative and practical, and contained the philosophy of a Shinto tradition that is independent of Buddhism. They were entitled: *Amaterashimasu Ise ni-sho kōtaijingū gochinza denki* (Records of the Enshrinement of the Two Imperial *Kami* at Ise); *Amaterashimasu Ise ni-sho kōtaijingū shiidaiki* (Ceremony of the Enshrinement of the Two Imperial *Kami* at Ise); *Toyoke kōtaijingū gochinza hongi* (Authentic Records of the Enshrinement of the Toyoke Imperial *Kami*), *Zō-Ise ni-sho Daijingū hōkihon-gi* (Treasure of the original Records of the Founding of the Two Grand Shrines of Ise); *Yamatohime-no-mikoto no seiki* (Chronicles of Princess Yamato). The texts also pressed the claims of the Outer Shrine and its *kami*, Kunitokotachi-no-mikoto, which led to rivalry with the Inner Shrine.

The texts were used by **Watarai Nobuyoshi** (1615–1691) to expound an academic version of Shinto which was also linked into **Confucian** ideas. As well as being designed to establish the lineage of the Outer Shrine, its status as a source of the ancient way gave it precedence within the world of Shinto and equality with the immigrant cults. This marks a stage in the long process through which Shinto regained its identity from the initially overwhelming power of the culture of **Buddhism**.

SHINTO HONKYOKU. The government office for administration of shrines (**jinja**) during the Meiji period (1868–1912) that replaced the Shinto Jimukyōku.

SHINTO INTERNATIONAL FOUNDATION. *See* SHINTO KOKUSAI GAKKAI.

SHINTO KAIGA. Paintings of Shinto *kami* in various forms modeled on the idea of the **Buddhist mandala**. The *kami* **Hachiman** was traditionally depicted as the emperor **Ōjin** (reigned 270–310).

SHINTO KOKUSAI GAKKAI. Umeda Yoshimi founded this organization on 31 May 1994. He became and continues to be director general; Nakanishi Akira is chairman of the Board of Trustees. It was created with the object of promoting interest and understanding of Shinto around the world. It is not affiliated to any particular shrine or tradition, and functions quite independently of even the **Jinja Honchō**. It was responsible for the establishment of the first chair of Shinto Studies in the University of California at Santa Barbara in 1997, occupied by the distinguished scholar Professor **Allan G. Grapard**. Its most recent activities include its 15 January 2010 14th Seminar on Shinto and the Martial Arts. It also published its *Shinto Forum* 31 at the same time. It has an extensive publishing program about various aspects of Shinto, and produces DVDs of its major events for international circulation. Its offices are in Edogawa-ku, Tōkyō.

SHINTO MEIBEN. This famous text of the **Watarai** School, which means "A Clear Explanation of Shinto," was composed by Watarai Tsuneakira (1675–1752), the last of the great Watarai thinkers to offer an exposition and defense of Ise Shinto. Tsuneakira was the second son of Kawasaki Nobusada, a priest of the **Gekū** (Outer) of the **Grand Shrines of Ise** (Ise Jingū).

He composed his principal work in 1737, and in it offered a powerful argument to the effect that Japanese history proves that Shinto is the original basis of government and order in Japan. He speaks of the Way as a form of universality, a concept that bears a distant resemblance to Plato's theory of forms (*eidos* in classical Greek). While it is not pure philosophical speculation as such, it is nevertheless very close to metaphysical speculation in the context of evolving a philosophy of culture. His views justify the claim that the Watarai school of thought on Shinto is the closest to evolving a Shinto philosophy, and further encourages the view that there is justification for greater Western interest in Watarai Shinto as an academic exposition of Shinto that might be analyzed in terms of Western thought.

The view has been expressed that the use of the term "way" (dō) in the name of Shinto, could be taken as Tao in Chinese, suggesting the influence of **Taoism**. That would cast the interpretation into a totally different perspective. However, the first reference to the name in the **Nihongi** (720) is introduced to distinguish the native cult from Butsu-do, the way of the Buddha. In any event, the philosophically speculative nature of Watarai Shinto places it in a special category within the history of Japanese thought. It has recently attracted the interest of younger Western scholars.

SHINTO OUTSIDE JAPAN. The first Shinto shrines (**jinja**) to be created outside of Japan were in Hawaii and in Brazil. These were the work of Japanese immigrants of the **Meiji period** (1868–1912) who left Japan in poverty looking for alternatives to the struggling economy of the early **modernization** period. Many also were former soldiers who had been demobilized after the Sino-Japan War (1894–1895) and the Russo-Japan War (1904–1905). They settled from 1885 onward in Hawaii as contract workers in sugar cane and pineapple plantations. Hawaii Daijungu and several other shrines were eventually established to remind Japanese of their identity and to seek the protection of the *kami.*

From 1908, Brazil coffee plantations attracted workers from Japan as the industry grew. There was a labor shortage due to Brazil's abolition of slavery in 1888. As early as 1920, the Bugre Shrine was built at the Japanese colony of Uetsuka, in the present city of Promissao, Sao Paulo state. The Kaminoya Daijingu is one of 11 major shrines (jinja) that remain. The immigrants in both countries grew into large communities that continued to revere ancestors, and once it was clear that most would not return to Japan, they created Buddhist temples to perform funeral and ancestral rites. National identity was asserted by the creation of shrines. Robert J. Smith, whose work on **ancestral reverence** has been discussed, also conducted valuable research on the ethnic Japanese in Brazil in the *Journal of Japanese Studies* 5, no. 1 (Winter, 1979).

A second phase of overseas shrine building began during the time when Japan was actively colonizing areas of East Asia. These were the result of **Kokka Shinto** (State Shinto, the creation of the Meiji government as a uniting national ideology that was abolished in 1945). Shrines were built in China, Korea, and in Taiwan (**Taiwan Jinja**) all of which had come under Japanese rule. Local people were required to attend these shrines as evidence of respect for the emperor and the Japanese Empire. These shrines were also heavily patronized by the Japanese military.

The postwar period from 1945 onward saw the dismantling of the State Shinto shrine buildings by the liberated governments, but did not mark the complete end of Shinto outside Japan. The main Brazil and Hawaii shrines remained, and it appeared that Shinto, now liberated from state control, had returned to being the indigenous cult of the Japanese people, and as such was not suitable either for export abroad or even for foreign or domestic research at home. Indeed, Shinto faced a stigma that lasted well into the 1970s. Publications were few, and only one major book appeared between 1945 and 1970: Jean Herbert's *Shinto: The Fountainhead of Japan*. The book was very much influenced by the State Shinto ideal and, while factually accurate in most details, failed to convey much about the richness and complexity of the tradition as it had evolved over the centuries.

The first postwar shrine outside Japan was established in the United States, in Stockton, California in 1987 as a branch shrine (**bunsha**) of **Tsubaki Ōkami Yashiro** (in Mie Prefecture) as Tsubaki Grand Shrine of America. It was removed to the site of **Kannagara Jinja** in Granite Falls, Washington State, in 1997 that in turn became a branch shrine of Tsubaki Grand Shrine in Japan. The head priest is the Rev. Koiichi Barrish, the first white American to have been licensed as a Shinto priest, an appointment not without controversy at the time.

The **Shinto Kokusai Gakkai** (Shinto International Foundation) was formed in 1994 to promote the international understanding of Shinto. It is unaffiliated to any shrines or to the **Jinja Honchō**, the Voluntary Association of Shinto Shrines, and creates its own agenda.

SHINTO TAIKYŌ. A **Kyōha Shinto** (Sect Shinto) sect founded in 1873 as the Taikyō-in, intended to be the central organization of the domestic missionary activity of Shinto, following the **Taikyō Senpu Undo**, the instruction to promote the "Great Teaching" issued in the name of **Emperor Meiji**. The Taikyō-in was dissolved after factional struggles and instead the Shinto Jimukyōku, the office of Shinto, was established. After the separation of religion from politics (**seikyō-bunri**) had been declared in 1882, the Shinto Jimukyōku was renamed Shinto Honkyōku and Viscount Masakuni Inaba was elected as the first president (kanchō). He defined the basic doctrines of Shinto Taikyō in response to which the Ministry of Home Affairs recognized it as a sect, distinguishing for the first time between Kyōha Shinto and **Kokka Shinto** (State Shinto). Inaba can be given credit for both forming the Shinto Taikyō as it is now known and for making space within the government system for other forms of Sect Shinto.

The history of the movement can most simply be described by referring to the influence that each kancho had on its development. Viscount Inaba was followed by Inaba Masayoshi (appointed in 1898), whose main work was the organization of both teaching and teachers. Sect Shinto began to rise in popularity because it was seen to be in harmony with Japan as a land of the *kami*, an ideal which had been revived for ideological purposes during the Sino-Japanese War

(1894–1895). The next president, Honda Kojo, took up office just before the Russo-Japanese War (1904–1905). He meticulously observed government injunctions to stimulate nationalism. The Shinto Honkyōku, along with **Buddhism** and Christianity, encouraged the nation to confront Russia, and was merely acting in common with all other religious movements of the time.

The sixth kancho, Hayashi Gosuke, decided to replace the name Shinto Honkyōku with Shinto Taikyō, in an effort to establish some independence from government pressure. Thus it continued to promote the great teaching until the end of the **Pacific War** (World War II), when its status came up for review. In 1951, it was recognized by the Ministry of Education as a religious corporate person (shūkyō hojin) and received the formal identity of Shinto Taikyō, the name by which it is still known.

Like the other movements in the group, Shinto Taikyō underwent a transformation after the war that resulted in the emphasis of its teaching ceasing to be upon **kannagara** (the way of the *kami*) as a way to unite the nation but rather upon kannagara as a way of peace and harmony. The new ideals were to be achieved by the composition of waka poems, the practice of calligraphy, the way of tea, and **martial arts** such as **aikido**. By means of these, people would become closer to the *kami*, a doctrine that became the focus of Shinto Taikyō.

Shinto Taikyō drew up plans for expansion in 1965, but its plans were not carried out because of lack of resources. The development of Shinto Taikyō explains not only the various steps in the recognition of the Kyōha movement but also how Kyōha Shinto in general and Shinto Taikyō in particular played a significant role in the rise of Japanese nationalism alongside Kokka Shinto. Its teachings are centered on four ideas: Tentoku (heaven-virtue), which refers to Ame-no-minakushi-no-kami, the source of human virtue; Chi-on (earth-benefit), referring to the **Zoka-sanshin**, the three *kami* of creation, Shōjō (purity); and Kōmyō (light-bright), all familiar Shinto themes. It claims a support base of 45,000, but may face an uncertain future in view of the somewhat limited goals that brought it into being.

SHINZA. Tatami-matted reclining throne used in the **Daijōsai** ritual, when the new emperor spends a night in the Yuki and Suki Pavilions.

SHINZEN KEKKON. Formal title for a Shinto wedding. *See also* FINANCES OF SHRINES.

SHINZO. Sculpture of a *kami* in which its **tama** or **soul** is thought to reside. Shinto did not favor depicting *kami*, but popular pressure from **Buddhism** led to the practice.

SHIRAKAWA, EMPEROR (REIGNED 1072–1086). He is reported to have completed the **Kumano Junrei** (pilgrimage) at last 23 times after he had retired as emperor to become a monk. *See also* EMPEROR SYSTEM; INSEI.

SHIROKI. Light colored **sake** presented as **shinsen** (offerings to the *kami*) at the time of the **aki matsuri** (autumn festival). The dark colored **sake** is called kuroki.

SHISHI-MAI. Ritual **dance** derived from Gigaku (masked dance) using the mask of a lion (or a deer in some regions), introduced from China into Japan toward the end of the seventh century, as a form of ritual purification (**harai**), known as **yakubarai**, intended to calm troublesome *kami*. Shishi-mai using two or more dancers to create the lion form becomes a species of **kagura** (sacred ritual dance) and is usually accompanied by musical instruments such as the shamisen or those used in Nagauta. *See also* DRAMATIC ARTS IN SHINTO.

SHIZEN. A Meiji period (1868–1912) term borrowed from Chinese classic the *Daodejing*, and used to express the concept of nature as in "Natural Science," but which also carried more cosmological nuances. It is used in expressions such as Dai-shizen (Great Nature) and **kannagara** (following the way of the *kami*). *See also* NATURE IN SHINTO.

SHOJIKI. The Shinto virtue of honesty. *See also* ETHICS IN SHINTO; MAKOTO NO KOKORO; SEI-MEI SHIN.

SHŌKONSHA. Shrines (**jinja**) built for the war dead at which their **souls** are invoked and through reverence are believed to be calmed. The purpose was originally to honor those who loyally served the emperor. The first and most famous was the **Yasukuni Jinja**, which was followed by a further group. By the turn of the century, the number had risen to around 138, all of which were redesignated Gokoku Jinja (Shrines for the Protection of the Nation) in 1939. Under the **Shinto Directive**, many non-shrine war memorials were removed from schools and other public places, although some remain as they were.

SHOKU NIHONGI (797). A compilation of Japanese history following on from the **Nihon Shōki** (720), and a major source of information about seventh- and eighth-century Japan.

SHOMU, EMPEROR (701–756, REIGNED 724–729). The first Japanese emperor to become a Buddhist priest, but within a **Buddhism** designed to ensure the protection and prosperity of the state. The creation of a network of provincial temples called kokubunji (with convents called kokubunniji) was one aspect of this policy, as was the building of the great bronze Buddha to protect the nation. The building of the Todai-ji was conducted under the protection of the *kami* **Hachiman**, which had long associations with the early **imperial household**. *See also* EMPEROR SYSTEM.

SHŌSHIN-NO-GI. Ascent of a *kami* as the closing act of a **ritual**.

SHŌTOKU TAISHI (PRINCE SHŌTOKU, 574–622). Political leader and statesman of the Asuka period (552–710) and second son of Emperor Yomei (reigned 585–587). He is associated with the early promotion of **Buddhism** in Japan and with the structuring of Japan's early social and political system. A version of his life is recorded in the **Nihon Shōki** (720). Legend has it that he was born in a stable, and that he was named Umayado-no-miko (Prince of the Horse Shed). After various struggles, Empress Suiko (reigned 592–628) appointed him as regent, giving him virtually absolute power.

Shotoku Taishi created a bureaucratic system and then added a Seventeen Clause "Constitution"—in reality not so much a constitution as a set of moral guidelines—in 604. It was a composite system of Buddhist, **Confucian**, and Chinese values that served to give the country a political system and a set of social goals.

Shōtoku Taishi is also associated with the introduction of the word **tennō** (heavenly sovereign, emperor) in preference to the older **daio** (great king). In this sense he placed the imperial institution at the center of the nation's political system. He is also recorded as having sent an envoy to China bearing greetings from the Ruler of the Land of the Rising Sun, which is one of the early uses of the name of Japan (Nippon) in the international arena. He dispatched a large number of monks and scholars, many of whom did not return until after his death, but whose collective research contributed to the **Taika no Kaishin** (Taika Reform) of 645.

Toward the end of his life, he is said to have declared, "The world is a lie. Only the Buddha is true." This is normally interpreted as implying his disillusionment with politics. While not referring to Shinto directly, there is no record of him having interfered with **festivals** or **rituals** in the **imperial household**. Indeed, it is likely that he viewed Shinto as part of the **emperor system** and Buddhism as something to be promoted in the interests of social control. At any rate, his important role in Japanese history and the high regard in which he was held are beyond doubt.

SHŌWA, EMPEROR (1901–1989). Third emperor (reigned 1926–1989) of the modern period that began with **Emperor Meiji** (reigned 1868–1912) and the **Meiji Restoration** of 1868. Showa was 124th in the legendary and historical line. His personal name was Hirohito, but the name of his imperial reign was Showa. He became crown prince (kotaishi) in 1912 on the death of Emperor Meiji, his grandfather, and emperor on 25 December 1926, on the death of Emperor Taisho. His reign was the longest on record, spanning 63 years.

In spite of various accusations and criticisms about war responsibility, he appears to have been quite liberal-minded, and a moderate man in his thinking on most matters who performed the role of a constitutional monarch through difficult times in the history of modern Japan. He was also the first emperor to address the nation on the radio when he made his famous speech that ended the **Pacific War** (World War II) in 1945; the first to be interviewed by a foreign journalist; and the first reigning emperor ever to have traveled outside of Japan.

He has left numerous writings about his research as a marine biologist, using his personal name "Hirohito, Emperor of Japan," when he wrote. However, his most famous legacy may be the **Tennō no Ningen Sengen** of 1 January 1946 (known in the West as the renunciation of his alleged divinity), when he declared that the links between the emperor and people were not based on myth, but on other more solid and historical foundations.

When Emperor Hirohito died in January 1989, the issue of religion and state came up again on the questions of who should pay for the funeral and what kind of funeral should take place. The **Taiso no Rei** was held on 24 February 1989 in Shinjuku Gyoen, in central Tokyō, attended by heads of state from all over the world, including the Duke of Edinburgh representing the British monarchy. The late emperor was interred at the site of the imperial mausoleum in Hachioji.

Controversy centered on the erection of a white **torii**, the gate entrance to shrine (**jinja**) grounds, in front of the pavilion where the rites were conducted according to the Shinto tradition. The argument was whether the **imperial household** should use Shinto **rituals** as their own personal right, or that the national funeral should be free of religious ritual. A white torii was erected for the imperial family's part of the ceremony, but removed for the public part, at which the heads of state from around the world were present. *See also* EMPEROR SYSTEM.

SHOZOKU. Another form term for robes worn by priests (**kannushi**) when performing ceremonies derived from Heian period (794–1185) costumes worn by the nobility whose original meaning was something ornamental. *See also* ASAGUTSU; EBOSHI; HŌ; KARIGINU; SAIFUKU.

SHRINE. *See* JINJA.

SHRINE SHINTO. *See* JINJA SHINTO.

SHUBATSU. Ritual of self-purification by priests before the performance of a ceremony of purification (**harai**).

SHUGENDŌ. The unique **syncretism** produced by the **assimilation of Buddhism and Shinto** which began during the **Heian period** (794–1185) as the outcome of the concept of **Honji-suijaku-setsu** but which developed even more extensively during the Kamakura period (1185–1333).

With the growth of ascetic religious practice in esoteric **Buddhism** under the influence of both **Saichō** (767–822) and **Kūkai** (773–835), many Buddhist temples came to be built in mountains, some in areas where shrines (**jinja**) as far back as the sixth century had already been established. Two key terms were introduced to describe these practitioners of **asceticism**: shūgen, to acquire spiritual powers through special discipline; and **shūgenja**, someone who is in the process of acquiring or has acquired such powers. They were also called **yamabushi** (literally, those who lie down and sleep in **mountains**) because they lived there for long periods of time.

The goals of Shugendō were apparently, very simply, to find ways of drawing spiritual energy from sacred places. The roots of the popularity of these mountain cults were strengthened by the natural reverence the Japanese had for mountains. In addition, shrines of ancient origin could be found in many mountain areas that were thought to possess such power spots.

Because of the prestige and the mystical imagery of esoteric Buddhism in all its exotic manifestations, some of these developed as centers of mountain ascetic activities between the Nara and the Kamakura periods, and in spite of reversals of fortune, managed to continue the tradition down to modern times. Not a few of these claim a lineage in Shugendō practices that can be traced back to a visit (real or alleged) by Kukai, who was said to have initiated those there into the secrets of esoteric practices after his return from China. *See also* SANGAKU SHINKO; SHINGON SHINTO; TENDAI SHINTO.

SHUGENJA. Name for someone who practices **Shugendō**.

SHUIN-RYŌ. Literally "vermilion seal money," referring to shrine (**jinja**) grants made by the government during the Edo period (1615–1868).

SHUKI KOREISAI. Spring Equinox **festival** observed in the rituals of the **imperial household**.

SHŪKYŌ DANTAI HŌ. The law enacted on 8 April 1939 in an attempt by the Ministry of Education to bring all religious organizations under state control. Numerous provisions required an official leader to be appointed who was responsible to the government for ensuring that the religious group conformed to all the requirements of law. It distinguished between Shinto rites as a patriotic duty, and religious activities. It was abolished in 1945 and replaced with the **Shukyō Hojin Ho** (the Religious Juridical Persons Law).

SHŪKYŌ HŌJIN HŌ. Religious Juridical Persons Law enacted in 1951 creating each group or individual shrine (**jinja**), temple, or church as a legally incorporated religious body. Registration is required in order to apply for tax exemption and all documentation and records are kept by the Ministry of Education. The Ministry has a list of 183,000 registered persons. The Ministry explains the policy as follows:

> In order to ensure the freedom and autonomy of activities by religious groups on the basis of freedom of religion and principle of the separation of religion and government guaranteed by the Constitution, the religious juridical persons system aims to secure a foundation for the administration of the property and organized structure of religious associations by granting them the status of corporate entities.

See also SHINTO DIRECTIVE.

SHUNKI SHINDENSAI. Major Spring **festival** observed in the rituals of the **imperial household**. *See also* RITUALS IN SHINTO.

SHUSEI-HA. Confucian **Kyōha Shinto** (Sect Shinto) sect organized by Nitta Kunimitsu (1829–1902), who claimed descent from Nitta Yoshisada, an early 14th-century warrior famed for his belief in the virtue of loyalty. He wished to teach people to become good citizens, to serve in the military if required and, above all, to make Japan's economy prosperous by whatever sacrifice was required. These themes found favor with the Meiji government and he finally was vindicated when the sect was formally recognized in 1876. He eventually received 10 citations and honors from the **imperial household** for his good influence on society.

Shusei-ha exemplified the blending of Confucian influences with Shinto to generate the social ethics which promoted ideals such as loyalty, filial piety, and respect for government authority. It does however, quite explicitly make use of fundamental Shinto concepts such as *kami* but combines them with elements of the **cosmology** of neo-Confucian thought and other syncretistic elements. He taught that **Izanagi-no-mikoto** and **Izanami-no-mikoto**, at the command of the *kami* of heaven, improved and consolidated the country and everything in it. The name Shusei consists of the first half of shūri (to repair) and the second half of kosei (to consolidate), both terms coming from the Kojiki in relation to the work of Izanagi and Izanami.

Thus in shūri-kosei lies the fundamental law of the evolution of the universe, and in truth, the progress of humanity and the advancement of society are due to the effective operation of this principle. It is also the process of observing faithfully the moral law and the means by which the affairs of family and society are administered. The purpose is brought to realization through the glorious and radiant virtue of **Amaterasu-ōmikami**. The sect also reveres the three central *kami* of creation, the **Zōka-sanshin**. Together with Izanagi-no-mikoto and Amaterasu-ōmikami, they are known as the Go-chu-no-Amatsu-Kami; in combination with the myriad of *kami* (yao yorozu no *kami*), they are revered under the general name of Shu Sei Tai Shin, the Great *Kami* of Shu Sei, Tai Shin being the Chinese style of reading of Okami.

The center of its religious activities is in Shizuoka Prefecture on a mountain where the worshippers revere Shinto Shusei Ha Tai Gen Shi. The original Head Office was in Saitama Prefecture, but was moved to Suginami Ward in Tokyō. Membership totals around 46,000. The fourth generation of the Nitta family, Kunio (born 1972), is leader.

SŌJŌDEN-NO-GI. Funeral hall ceremony observed at the passing of an emperor in the **rituals** of the **imperial household**.

SOKAREN. Palanquin bearing an imperial coffin to its place of interment.

SOKUI-KANJŌ. Traditional Buddhist element in imperial accession rites that date back to the **Heian period** (794–1185), but which was purged in the early Meiji period (1868–1912), when the plan to create **Kokka Shinto** (State Shinto) was being implemented.

SOKUI NŌ REI. Imperial accession proclamation ceremony, last performed by Emperor **Heisei** in 1990.

SONNŌ-JOI. Meiji period (1868–1912) ideological slogan of anti-foreign groups, meaning "revere the emperor—expel the barbarians."

SONNŌ SHUGI. Principle of reverence for the emperor, as taught by Yamazaki Ansai (1618–1682). *See also* SUIGA SHINTO.

SOSHA. *See* JOINT SHRINES.

SOUL IN SHINTO. Various Shinto ideas exist about the basic elements of human beings, the soul, **tama** or tamashii, and in the case of a *kami*, mitama. According to the teaching of ichi-rei-shi-kon, four aspects of the soul or four types of soul are seen as co-existing under the control of one spirit. These are usually identified as the **aramitama**, the wilder and more primal aspects of the soul; the **nigimitama**, the more peaceful and refined aspects of the soul, the sakimitama, the happy and creative aspects of the soul; and the kushimitama, the mysterious and concealed aspects of the soul. These are known as the shi-kon.

The significance of these aspects is also reflected in the fact that in different shrines, different aspects of the same mitama may be enshrined. According to one theory, in the **Grand Shrines of Ise** (Ise Jingū), there is an ara-matsuri-no-miya in enshrined the aramitama of **Amaterasu-ōmikami**, while in the **Gekū** (the Outer Shrine), her nigimitama is enshrined.

When **Empress Jingū** (reigned 201–269) invaded Korea, she was accompanied by the protective aramitama of the *kami* she invoked for her defense, while the nigimitama remained in Japan. There is no doubt that the aramitama was considered to possess special powers and that these were not infrequently associated with the military spirit. **Motoori Norinaga** (1730–1801), the **Kokugaku** (National Learning) scholar, identified the sakimitama and the kushimitama in his studies, and this is usually taken to be reflected in the use of the mitsu-domoe, the circle consisting of three equally shaped loops which narrow at one end to meet in the middle.

Closely associated with tama is its power or energy, known as tamashii. This too has special overtones, such as in the expression kotodamashii, the power of the spirit of words or **Yamato-damashii**, the unique spirit of the Japanese. **Kokoro** (mind or heart) is also a basic part of the human structure referring to the heart or the seat of the will and the source of volition and motivation. The kokoro was singled out by **Ishida Baigan** (1685–1744) as the place where the training of the spirit can begin and has become a central concept of the **New Religions**.

STATE SHINTO. *See* KOKKA SHINTO.

SUGAWARA MICHIZANE (845–903). Confucian scholar of the **Heian period** (794–1185) who rose to prominence at court, only to become the victim of slander by a brother of the empress because one of his daughters married the emperor's younger brother. He was exiled and went to live in Daifazu, devoting himself to composing poems. He protested his innocence until he died, having lost his rank and status.

Kyōto was subsequently hit by a series of disasters, by a plague, by floods, and by some mysterious deaths, including those of Fujiwara no Sugane, Fujiwara no Tokuhira, Minamoto no Akira, and Yasuakira, an imperial prince. It was concluded that the **aramitama** of Sugawara was seeking revenge. Following the contemporary practice of **chinkon**, acts designed to pacify an angry soul, Emperor Daigo (reigned 897–930) lifted the ban of exile in 923, and restored his court rank.

Various accounts are given of how his shrine came into being, but the initiative seems to have come from the local people, first with a girl who claimed to have heard his voice in 943. She built a little shrine (**jinja**) near her home to honor him, and called it **Tenmangū**. The seven-year-old son of a Shinto priest also claimed to have heard a voice. Bit by bit, the legend grew, and Sugawara's image developed as a teacher of the young and as a patron of learning. At any rate, momentum grew, and by 959, at the behest of the Fujiwara family that had destroyed him, he was accorded full enshrinement as **Tenjin**, the "heavenly *kami*."

The court ordered a **festival** to be held for him in 987, and by 990, the shrine was listed among the nation's top 19 shrines. In 1005, a little over a century after his death, the shrine received an imperial visit: truly a remarkable process, but one in keeping with the highly superstitious character of the Heian period. The origins of the names Tenjin and Tenmangu are not certain.

SUIGA SHINTO. Confucian-style Shinto of "divine blessing" developed in the Edo period (1615–1868), and formed by **Yamazaki Ansai** (1618–1682). His was the "Shinto of Divine Revelation and Blessing," known as **Suiga Shinto**, perhaps the strongest form of anti-Buddhist Shinto outlook. Having studied the ideas of **Yoshikawa Shinto** and **Watarai Shinto**, Yamazaki claimed that there was but one Way, that of Ohirumemuchi (**Amaterasu-ōmikami**, the *kami* of the sun). There was only one Teaching, namely that of **Sarutahiko-ōkami**, who had guided the heavenly grandson from the Plain of Heaven to the land of Japan.

The term Shinto meant the study of the sun-virtue (nittoku) of Amaterasu, who Ansai claimed was united with the sun in the heavens, amatsuhi. He also added to this the concept of the absolute sovereignty of the emperor as direct descendant of Amaterasu. The greatest political reality on earth thus became not only identified with, but ultimately united with, the greatest celestial power of the heavens. Later disciples of Ansai, such as Ogimachi Kinmichi and Izumoji Keichoku, provided some solid academic support for the imperial loyalists and anti-government movements of the late Edo period. *See* EMPEROR SYSTEM.

SUIJIN. *Kami* of water worshipped at irrigation systems, lakes, rivers, and wells. Suijin is variously depicted as an eel, a serpent, a fish, or a kappa, a water fairy.

SUMIYOSHI TAISHA. Located in Sumiyoshi Ward in Osaka, it enshrines four *kami*. Three of them were born of **Susano-o-no-mikoto**, and are known collectively as the Suminoe-no-Okami (the *kami* of Sumiyoshi, Suminoe being an older version of Sumiyoshi). They are Uwatsutsuno-o-no-mikoto, Nakatsutsuno-o-no-mikoto, and Sokutsutsuno-o-no-mikoto. The fourth *kami* is Okina-gatarashime-no-mikoto, who in fact is **Empress Jingū** (reigned 201–269). Legend has it that she founded Sumiyoshi Taisha upon her return from her successful campaign in Korea, recorded in the **Nihon Shōki** (720). She wished to express gratitude to the three *kami* who protected her during the campaign. Sumiyoshi Jinja, enshrining the same three *kami*, are found also in Fukuoka and Shimonoseki, as well as in 2,000 other centers.

Proximity to Kyōto may have served the interests of the Osaka shrine (**jinja**), according to some skeptics. Nevertheless, the shrine and its antiquity are beyond doubt, and it is referred to frequently in poetic and other literature. Taisha simply means "Great Shrine."

SUMO. Japanese style wrestling that originated as a form of harvest divination and became later a popular sport, and eventually the imperial sport. With a history of 2,000 years, it is probably one of the oldest continually practiced ceremonial sports in any country. It became professional during the Edo period (1615–1868), and its form has altered little to the present.

It is steeped in the culture of Shinto. The **Dohyō Matsuri** is performed as each ring is set up for a new tournament. Yokuzuna, the highest rank, receive their certification from **Meiji Jingū**, where they perform their first ring entering ceremony (dezu iri). The throwing of salt and the clapping of the hands are all part of Shinto ceremony. All tournaments in modern times are dedicated to the soul of **Emperor Meiji** (reigned 1868–1912). *See also* MARTIAL ARTS; WOMEN.

SUPREME COMMANDER ALLIED POWERS (SCAP). Title of the head of the mainly U.S.-staffed postwar occupation administration that controlled the country from 1945 to 1951. The Religious Division of the Civil Information and Education Section of the Supreme Commander Allied Powers under director William K. Bunce produced the **Shinto Directive** that abolished **Kokka Shinto** (State Shinto) and gave all religious organizations equal status under the law.

The Constitution, which was written under the direction of the Supreme Commander Allied Powers, guaranteed religious freedom and implemented a U.S.-constitutional-style separation of "church" and state. This was followed in 1946 by the imperial declaration that renounced the concept of a divine emperor (**Tennō no Ningen Sengen**).

The education system was demilitarized, democratized, and (theoretically) decentralized, and all traces of ideology and nationalism were removed. The actual damage sustained by the central institutions of Japan was minimal. The emperor remained in place and, externally, the symbols of the past and the great shrines (**jinja**) were preserved. The liberation of **Jinja Shinto** (Shrine Shinto) from 70 years of state control was in many cases welcomed, because shrines were allowed to return to the concerns for which they had first been created, in many cases centuries before. Many that had been destroyed during the Shrine Merger (**Jinja Gappei**) movement were restored.

SUSANO-O-NO-MIKOTO. According to many scholars, a composite figure generated from myth and legend. In the **mythology**, he was a brother of **Amaterasu-ōmikami**, born from the nose of **Izanagi-no-mikoto** after his escape from the land of pollution, **Yomi-no-kuni**. His antisocial behavior drove Amaterasu into hiding in the **Ame-no-**

iwato, which caused the light in the world to be extinguished. **Ame-uzume-no-mikoto** performed a ribald dance which made the *kami* laugh in order to entice Amaterasu back into the world.

Susano-o-no-mikoto was consequently driven out of the High Plain of Heaven (**Takama-no-hara**), and descended to **Izumo**, where he became a hero, slaying the eight-headed, eight-tailed serpent known as Yamata-no-orochi. He rescued a young woman and acquired the sword known as the kusanagi, one of the three pieces of the **imperial regalia**.

In spite of his impetuous and stormy character, he is still revered as a *kami* of protection, particularly at the **Yasaka Jinja** in Kyōto, although there are other shrines (**jinja**) to him under various names around the country.

SUWA TAISHA. A shrine (**jinja**) in Nagano Prefecture which combines two shrines, the Upper Shrine (Kami Sha) and the Lower Shrine (Shimo Sha). The former is located in Suwa City, while the latter is in the town of Shimo Suwa, some 10 kilometers away.

Enshrined are Takaminakatatomi-no-kami, Yasakatome-no-kami, and Kotoshironushi-no-kami. Takaminakatatomi-no-kami was the son of **Okuninushi-no-mikoto**, who came to that part of the country to subdue it in preparation for the arrival of the descendants of **Amaterasu-ōmikami**. The Suwa clan, hereditary priests of the shrine, claimed descent from him, and therefore enshrined him. The shrine is famous for its Ombashira Matsuri, held in each year of the monkey and the tiger, in which tall fir trees are transported by 1,000 men and set up to mark the sacred precincts in which the *kami* are believed to reside.

SYNCRETISM IN SHINTO. Shinto has engaged in syncretistic relationships with numerous imported thought and belief systems, such as **Buddhism**, **Taoism**, **Confucianism**, and even Christianity. It has been a long tradition within Japanese culture to import and adapt from many alien sources with the goal of enriching the original and indigenous underlying layer of culture. Some scholars, both Japanese and non-Japanese, have argued that the underlying layer itself is syncretistic and therefore defies precise definition or exact characterization.

Various characterizations of this have been made. It has been called a "bricolage culture" (La Fleur) and a "multiplex system" (Picken), and described as a feature of all phases of Japanese culture

(Miyaji). It has been particularly influential in religion from where it has spread to all levels of popular and sophisticated culture. The **assimilation of Buddhism and Shinto** through the concepts of **Shinbutsu Shugō, Honji-suijaku-setsu**, the role of **Confucianism in Shinto**, as well as the integration of many isolated features of imported ideas have resulted in the creation of a highly complex religious culture which has never formed a coherent system and which defies simple cause-effect types of analysis. **Shugendō** is one of the finest flowerings of this process that is still ongoing in all forms of religious development in Japan, especially in the **New Religions**. Indeed, if there is any central core that is influential in the selection and rejection process involved in importing new ideas, it is aesthetic rather than ethical or rational. But even that would be an oversimplification to attribute everything, per se, to that criterion. It is one pervasive theme of all Japanese culture which, in the view of many, has never been thoroughly researched or analyzed. It is also one vital reason why most Western sociological analyses of Japanese religious culture do not achieve much: because they were theories generated to examine Western phenomena that had, from its beginnings, firmly set its face against any kind of syncretism.

– T –

TA-ASOBI. A **ritual** pantomime of the year's **rice** cycle (**nenchū-gyōji**) performed at the first full moon of the **New Year** for the **divination** a good harvest. The actual date may vary from region to region, but the underlying idea is basically the same. It is also referred to as otaue-sai if it coincides with the planting of rice seedlings. At the **Grand Shrines of Ise** (Ise Jingū), the same ritual is called otaue-shinji and it takes place in mid-June.

TAGATA JINJA. A shrine (**jinja**) in Komaki, near Nagoya City Airport in Aiichi Prefecture, famous for its **henoko matsuri**, or Phallus Festival, is one of the finest examples of this kind of **fertility** cult celebrations in the country. *See also* OAGATA JINJA; SEX IN SHINTO.

TAIHŌ RITSURYŌ. The Code of the Taiho period was promulgated in 701, entailing, within a plan for restructuring the government, numerous major provisions for both **Buddhism** and Shinto. It set up a Council of State known as the **Dajokan** and an office of Shinto affairs known as the **Jingikan** (office of *kami*). The authorization was contained in the **Jingiryo**, the part of the code that dealt with all matters relating to Shinto.

Its chief official was entrusted with the responsibility of ensuring that the *kami* were properly worshipped. His work included also the supervision of priestly families with fund-raising powers (**hafuri**) and the divine estates (**kanbe**) which had been given to very privileged shrines (**jinja**). The Jingiryo also classified shrine **festivals** into three ranks. Firstly were major festivals (taishi). This title was given exclusively to the Oname Matsuri, which is also known as the **Daijōsai**, the first celebration of the harvest festival by a new emperor. Secondly there were middle-ranked festivals (chushi) which included the Toshigoi (the Spring Festival), Tsukinami (acts of thanksgiving performed on appointed days) and the Kanname or **Niiname** (the Autumn Festival). Thirdly were minor festivals (shoshi) which included all other festivals anywhere in the country.

All shrines nationwide were officially ranked and records of the important ones began to be kept in registers (Kanshacho). These were to be the responsibility of the Jingikan, which also presented offerings to these shrines on the occasion of the Toshigoi and Niiname festivals. The establishment of regular rituals under government supervision, plus the erection of buildings to house these, gave to Shinto much of its ordered and nationwide character, and led to the ranking and regulating of these facilities. In this way, Shinto grew in close relationship with the government and its supervision of national life, while, at the same time, still maintaining good relations with Buddhist institutions.

TAIKA NO KAISHIN (TAIKA REFORM 645–646). An early attempt to organize the emerging nation into a hierarchical order. A system of provincial districts was organized during the work of governmental restructuring known as the Great Reform (**Taika Reform**). The two districts of Taki and Watarai in the province of Ise were gifted to the **Grand Shrines of Ise** (Ise Jingū) as divine estates (**ando**) and similar grant land endowments were made to shrines (**jinja**) such as **Izumo Taisha** and **Kashima Jingū**. During the reign (673–686) of **Emperor Temmu**, the sacred office of the highest priestess (itsuki no hime miko) at Ise, also known as the **saigū** (saio), was again filled. The last occupant had been Sukate-hime-no-hime-miko, who died in the 29th year of the reign (592–628) of Empress Suiko. The office of saiguryo, the government official at Ise responsible for the saio, was also created.

The practice of removing the Inner and Outer Ise shrines to alternate sites (**shikinen sengū**) was also decreed by the emperor, a tradition that has continued in almost unbroken cycles of 20 years. The annual cycle of **festivals** and other gyoji, or events, for major shrines was stylized and implemented on a nationwide scale. The identity and recognizable pattern of Shinto activities dates largely to the era of Emperor Temmu.

The ancient clan histories were corrected at this time to conform to "official," meaning government-approved accounts of history. These histories included texts such as the *Teiki* and the *Kyuji* (neither of which now exist), which contained legends of the powerful clans. This provided the formal basis for the traditions of the nation, both legend and myth as well as history, to be recorded and made publicly available. These activities indicate the work of a powerful central authority with an acute political consciousness and a sense of the importance of controlling historical perspectives.

TAIKO. Distinctive style of Japanese ritual drumming that accompanies the celebration of festivals (**matsuri**) in the streets and that has now become a form of entertainment in its own right. Different types and sizes of drum are used, from smaller drums that keep time to the huge odaiko (great taiko drum) at the apex, found in all shrines (**jinja**) where regular **rituals** are held. Outside Japan, the term Taiko is often used to refer to any of the various Japanese drums (wa-daiko, literally Japanese drum) and to the popular art form of ensemble taiko drumming (sometimes called kumi-daiko). Taiko drumming groups that train in **dojo** exist now outside of Japan and, because of its popularity, it has become a cultural exercise in schools as well as clubs internationally. *See also* MUSIC IN SHINTO.

TAIKYŌ SENPU UNDŌ. The Promulgation of the Great Teaching, issued in the name of **Emperor Meiji** (reigned 1868–1912), was the first step by the Meiji government between 1870 and 1884 to create a state religion around Shinto, subsequently referred to as **Kokka Shinto** (State Shinto). A renewed interest in Shinto had been part of the background to the **Meiji Restoration** of imperial power; consequently, the concept of **saisei-itchi**, the unity of worship and government, came to be revived.

The objective of the exercise was to affirm unambiguously that the way of the *kami* was the true guiding principle for the state. The Taikyō-in was established in Tokyō from which missionary/teachers were dispatched nationwide. After heavy criticism, the Office of Shinto Worship (**Jingikan**), which was ranked above the Council of State (**Dajōkan**), was renamed the Ministry of the *kami* (**Jingishō**). The Ministry of Religion (**Kyōbushō**) in turn replaced it in 1872, and the Kyōbushō was absorbed into the Ministry of the Interior (Naimusho) in 1877. *See also* HIRATA ATSUTANE; SANJO NO KYOSOKU; SHINTO TAIKYO.

TAISEI-KYŌ. A **Confucian Shinto** sect of **Kyōha Shinto** (Sect Shinto), founded by Hirayama Shosai (1815–1890), who was born as Kuroda Katsuensai, adopted as a Hirayama, and who in time became a foreign affairs official of the Edo government. He was a loyal follower of the Tokugawa regime and served it as a samurai in several capacities, including being a member of the Council of the Shogun. He was deeply concerned to use Shinto forms to promote neo-Confucian values. Because of his loyalty to the Edo Shogunate, he was confined in 1870 by the Meiji government to Shizuoka, where he studied Taidokokugaku Shinto under Munihide Honso, after which he became a priest of the Hikawa Nichie Jinja.

The new sect was approved on 19 September 1879 under the name Taisei-Kyōkai. In 1882 it became Shinto Taisei-Kyō. It professes, like other Kyōha Shinto sects, to worship **Amaterasu-ōmikami** and the three central *kami* of creation (**Zōka-sanshin**). The sect reveres seven other *kami*, Amano-onchu-no-kami, Koho-sanrei-no-kami, Shinko-sanrei-no-kami, Tensho-kodai-o-kami, **Izanagi-no-mikoto**, **Susano-o-no-mikoto**, and **Okuninushi-no-mikoto**.

The name combines tai (great) sei (achievement) and kyō (Teaching). The root term taisei also carries the nuance of successfully completing a task. One of these was listed as continuing religious rites and ceremonies after the manner of successive generations of imperial courts. It also teaches the doctrine of improving human instincts by means of the Twelve Oriental Zodiac Signs. The current head shrine is Tensho-San-Jinja in Shibuya-ku near Harajuku Station in Tokyō. The movement claims over 60,000 adherents organized into 19 churches. The 15th generation leader and superintendent, Iida Kingo, trained as both Shinto priest and **yamabushi**, and his personal philosophy centers on the ideas of *kami*, great nature (**daishizen**), and gratitude (**kansha**), which he sees as a virtue on a par with love in the Judeo-Christian tradition.

TAISHI RYŪ SHINTO. The Shinto of **Shotoku Taishi** (573–621), as identified by Urabe Kanetomo or **Yoshida Kanetomo** (1435–1511), principal scholar of the **Urabe Shinto** tradition. The roots of **Ryōbu Shinto**, he claimed, could be traced to the rapport between **Buddhism** and Shinto that existed in the thought of Shotoku Taishi, the statesman and imperial regent of the Asuka period (522–710). The use of Prince Shotoku was probably symbolic more than substantial, unless documents existed in the lifetime of Kanetomo that were subsequently destroyed. It was probably intended to show that, even from the very beginning of the introduction of Buddhism to the imperial court, there was an accommodation to Shinto.

TAISO NO REI. State funeral for a deceased emperor conducted according to the **rituals** and procedures of the **imperial household**.

TAIWAN JINJA. **Kokka Shinto** (State Shinto) shrine (**jinja**) established in 1901, under the leadership and direction of General Nogi, governor of Taiwan, enshrined Okuni-tama-no-mikoto, Onakuji-no-mikoto, Sakunahikona-no-mikoto and Kitashirakawa-no-miya, whose real name was Yoshihisa Shinno. It brought the total number of shrines in Taiwan to 30. These were part of wider network in Korea and in China that were created wherever Japanese troops were stationed. *See also* SHINTO OUTSIDE JAPAN.

TAKAKUYA. Primitive "High House" shrine (**jinja**) building style of **architecture**, originating possibly in the raised floor dwellings and storehouses of southeast Asia where houses were built on stilts to cope with flood conditions. These can still be seen in New Guinea, Sumatra, and even in Okinawa.

TAKAMA-NO-HARA. Also known as takama-ga-hara, this is the Plain of High Heaven referred to in the **Kojiki** (712) and in the **Ni-**

hon Shōki (720) where the three *kami* of creation (**Zoka-sanshin**) began their work, and from where eventually, **Ninigi-no-mikoto**, son of **Amaterasu-ōmikami**, descended to bring the land under control for his son, **Jimmu Tennō**, Japan's first emperor (reigned 660–585 B.C.E.), according to the traditional lineage.

TAKENOUCHI SHIKIBU (1712–1767). Shinto scholar and devotee of the imperial line who deeply influenced **Yamazaki Ansai** (1618–1682) and the development of his thought. Takenouchi was arrested and executed for appearing to express anti-shogunate sentiments.

TAKUSEN. Term for an oracle delivered through a medium, normally a woman or child. *See also* DIVINATION; SHAMANISM IN SHINTO.

TAMA. Also referred to as tamashii, rei, or kon, tama is the human **soul**, or the soul of a valued object such as a ningyo (Japanese doll), as understood in Japanese culture. The term appears in compounds such as **yamato-damashii**, the unique spiritual quality of the Yamato people, or in **kotodamashii**, the soul or energy of words.

TAMA-GAKI. Fence surrounding the buildings of a shrine (**jinja**), which marks off the area into which ordinary worshippers may not enter. At the **Grand Shrines of Ise** (Ise Jingū), **sampai** (reverence) performed inside the fence is referred to as uchi-gaki sampai, and is usually reserved for special guests, the imperial family, new cabinet members, ranking **sumo** wrestlers, or visiting heads of state.

TAMAGUSHI. A branch of **sakaki** with strips of paper (shide) attached that is presented with the number of bows and claps appropriate to the shrine (**jinja**), most frequently two bows, two claps and a single bow, as the final act of **sampai** (reverence).

TANABATA. Festival of Chinese origins first introduced in the eighth century. Its official name refers to the seventh day of the seventh month, the only day that a mythological star-crossed and forlorn couple could successfully meet according to the legend, but the link with stars in the story gave it the image of a star festival. It received official recognition in 755. It is still observed in some parts of Japan, particularly in the northeast. It lost status after the **Meiji Restoration** (1868), when it gave way, along with much **folk religion** and folk culture, to government-sponsored events and institutions.

TANAKA YOSHITO (1872–1946). Scholar of Shinto whose major work *Shinto Gairon* (Introduction to Shinto) claimed that Shinto was the reality created by the ancient *kami*, which has enriched the spirit of the people of Japan. Although writing in support of the ideal of a form of **Kokka Shinto** (State Shinto), he was in reality offering a somewhat spiritual interpretation.

TANIGUCHI MASAHARU (1893–1985). Founder of the Shinto-influenced **New Religion, Seicho-no-ie,** which means "house of growth," the title given by Taniguchi Masaharu to a cultural magazine he first published in March 1940 and out of which the movement emerged.

He was born the son of a Karasukara-mura farmer in Hyogo Prefecture on 22 November 1893. His parents were poor and he was given up for adoption at the age of four. He states in his autobiography that he considered himself in some way different from his brothers, believing that he had been selected by the *kami* for some special work. While an able student, he appeared very self-possessed, and subsequently became a university dropout during his third year at Waseda University in Tokyō.

While trying to find a meaning in life, he became interested in **Omoto-kyō**, at that time a new and controversial religion that attracted Taniguchi. He was fascinated by the Omoto-kyō teaching that the world would soon be rid of all evil and that the present age would be followed by a new age of purity. Although critical of some aspects of the movement, he joined it, and became editor of two publications of the sect, *Ayabe Shimbun* and *Shinreikai*.

He then began to develop his own disciplines, including wearing an inexpensive robe tied with a rope and calling himself the "St. Francis of the Ōmoto-kyō." He also fasted for days on end, and performed the Shinto ritual of river **misogi** in order to purify himself.

After the great Kanto earthquake of 1 September 1923 Taniguchi and his wife went to Kobe, where their parents helped them. He thereafter worked for various organizations, finally, publishing his magazine called *Seicho-no-Ie* in March 1940, which expounded his views of the world and started his movement.

TANKA. Poetic form with the syllabic pattern is 5-7-5-7-7, first found in the **Man'yōshū**, in contrast to the haiku form of 5-7-5-7. It is considered a short poetic form and was one of Japan's earliest classical forms of composition, considered by some scholars to be a Japanese response to more elaborate Chinese styles which the ancient Japanese respected, but which did not convey their own attitudes or express their experiences. *See also* WAKA.

TA-NO-KAMI. *Kami* of the rice fields, identified by various names in different regions of the country (such as **Ebisu** in the Kanto region and **Daikoku** in the Izumo area), but with the common link being rice cultivation.

TANRITSU-JINJA. Technical name for one of the small number of shrines (**jinja**) that are not affiliated to the **Jinja Honcho** (Association of Shinto Shrines) or any other regional association. The **Yasukuni Jinja** and the **Nikko Toshogu** are two such shrines.

TAOISM. Taoism, attributed to the work of Lao Tzu, who is thought to have lived in the fourth century B.C.E., is considered a great cultural system of Chinese thought along with **Confucianism**. Two main strands developed. Philosophical Taoism, as in the *Daodejing*, was aimed at achieving union with the Tao through the utility of non-action and the virtue of non-being. This is a concept used in the **martial arts**. Popular Taoism also emerged, which encouraged the belief in the idea of material immortality, achieved by certain tried means, including special nourishment of the body and nourishment of the spirit by meditation and by a better understanding of the human body as identical with the world, as a microcosm within a macrocosm. Although some traces of Taoism can be found in Japanese culture before the ninth century, it never seems to have succeeded in establishing a separate identity, although it undoubtedly did exert some influence on the evolution of Japanese thought, at least through its presence within Chinese **Buddhism**.

TATARI. Misfortune that comes as a punishment or warning from a *kami* angered by some human word or action. *See also* HARAI; KEGARE; TSUMI.

TATSUTA JINJA. Located in Ikoma District, Nara Prefecture, it enshrines Ameno-mihashira-no-mikoto and Kunino-mihashira-no-mikoto. Its historical beginnings are traced to a legend that Emperor Sujin was told by an oracle that only by enshrining these *kami* would be able to end a series of natural disasters that had befallen the people of that region. The shrine (**jinja**) came to be associated with the power to calm strong winds, and is often linked with **Hirose Jinja**, which is believed to have the power to prevent water-related natural disasters.

TEIDŌ. The imperial way, an old name for Shinto associated with **Hayashi Razan** (1583–1687), Confucian thinker and advisor to the Tokugawa government at the beginning of the Edo period (1600–1868).

TEMIZU. Water used in the purification of hand and mouth upon entering shrine (**jinja**) precincts.

TEMMU, EMPEROR (REIGNED 673–686). Remembered for issuing an edict ordering the rebuilding (**shikinen sengu**) of the **Grand Shrines of Ise** (Ise Jingū) every 20 years to keep them eternally new and fresh. *See also* TAIKA NO KAISHIN.

TEMPON. Japanese readings of the **Man'yōshū** created by the **Kokugaku** (National Learning) scholar **Kamo no Mabuchi** (1697–1769).

TENCHI-GONGEN. Primitive style of shrine (**jinja**) building that possibly evolved from the sloped roof covering of ancient Japanese pit dwellings. The name means "heaven-earth origin." *See also* ARCHITECTURE IN SHINTO.

TENCHI-REIKI-KI. Text (translated as Notes on the Numinous Energy of Heaven and Earth) compiled during the Kamakura period (1185–1333). It supported the idea of **Ryōbu Shinto** and was attributed, probably incorrectly, to **Kūkai** (774–835), founder of **Shingon Buddhism**. It was the most important text in the tradition that argued for the association of the Buddha Dainichi Nyorai and **Amaterasu-ōmikami**. *See also* ASSIMILATION OF BUDDHISM AND SHINTO; SYNCRETISM IN SHINTO.

TENDAI BUDDHISM. A **Heian period** (794–1185) branch of **Buddhism** brought from China by **Saicho** (767–835), posthumously known as **Dengyō Daishi**, modeled on the Buddhism found on Mount T'ien T'ai in China. Unlike **Shingon Buddhism**, which is totally esoteric, Tendai Buddhism is only partly esoteric. Its mountain associations made it easy to forge links with Shinto.

The famous discipline of Mount Hiei, **Sen-nichi-kai-hō-gyō**, a thousand days of running around the peaks of the mountain over a period of seven years, and totaling in miles the circumference of the earth, is a traditional practice of ascetic Tendai monks. *See also* IKIBOTOKE; IKIGAMI.

TENDAI SHINTO. Tendai Shinto was developed by **Saichō** (767–822), founder of **Tendai Buddhism**. When he established his head temple, the Enryakuji on Mount Hiei near Kyōto, he chose Oyamakui-no-kami, protector of Mount Hiei, as protector of the temple. The *kami* was renamed Sannō (Mountain King) after the guardian of Mount T'ien T'ai in China, where Saicho had learned the secrets of semi-esoteric **Buddhism**. The **honji** of this *kami* was considered to be Yakushi, and the honji of Omiwa-no-kami was identified with Shaka, the historical Buddha. These relationships were explained through the Tendai concept of isshin sangan (one mind, three insights). The name **Sannō-Ichijitsu**, which refers to this style of Shinto, means "Three Mountain Kings: One Truth." It was one outcome of the **Honji-Suijaku** principle of the **assimilation of Buddhism and Shinto** that Shinto *kami* were considered manifestations of Buddhist divinities. Elaborate tables of equivalents were drawn up at the time. The Sanno Buddhist deities were said to correspond with the *kami* of the **Grand Shrines of Ise** (Ise Jingū). The **Lotus Sutra** became the principal text of the sect, with the claim that Sanno was the Japanese incarnation of Shaka, the Buddha of the Lotus Sutra.

A subsequent leading monk of the Edo period, Tenkai (1536–1643), and an adviser to **Tokugawa Ieyasu** (1543–1616), proposed the doctrine of Sanno Ichijitsu Shinto (the One Truth of Sanno Shinto) that **Amaterasu-ōmikami**, while being the counterpart of Dainichi Nyorai, was the source of all divine beings. The **syncretism** appealed to the Tokugawa mind, as did the power conferred by Amaterasu-ōmikami. Hence the creation of the **Nikkō Tōshōgū** to enshrine Tokugawa Ieyasu. Loss of patronage after the **Meiji Restoration** (1868) hurt the Sanno Shrines, although the Enryakuji remains symbolically perhaps the most important Buddhist temple in Japan.

TENGU. A complex figure of Japanese **folk culture** in the form of a mountain spirit usually depicted with a long nose, wings, a human body, glittering eyes, and often carrying a feather fan. He is considered often as a transformation of a Yama-no-kami, guardian of mountains and trees. In literature, he is often depicted as hostile to **Buddhism** and Buddhist priests and as an abductor of children, because of his ability to transform himself into many forms. He is also depicted wearing parts of the costume of the **yamabushi**, so there is a great range in his imagery. He is also depicted as a benevolent transmitter of esoteric skills.

TENJIN. The **soul (tama)** of **Sugawara Michizane** (845–903), the **Heian period** (794–1185) courtier and scholar who became the *kami* of learning after his enshrinement.

TENMANGŪ. Shrines **(jinja)** dedicated to the soul of **Sugawara Michizane** (845–902), the **Heian** period (794–1185) courtier who was deposed from office but subsequently restored posthumously and finally enshrined as the *kami* of learning and scholarship.

TENMEI. Japanese reading of Tiang Ming, the Mandate of Heaven, as understood in traditional Chinese **Confucian** thought. While in Chinese thought, the concept of heaven (Tiang, read in Japanese as Ten) possesses a cosmic dimension, the Japanese version related the idea more specifically to the destiny of the Japanese people, the Yamato minzoku.

TENNŌ. Formal title in Japanese for the emperor, who is normally referred to as Tennō Heika (His Majesty the Emperor). *See also* EMPEROR SYSTEM.

TENNŌ NO NINGEN SENGEN. The declaration made on 1 January 1946 at the request of the **Supreme Commander Allied Forces (SCAP)** by **Emperor Showa** (reigned 1926–1989) that he should not be considered in a superstitious way as in any sense "divine" in accordance with **mythology** or legend. This was a concession to

Western perceptions of the meaning of the word *kami* translated as "divinity." The general opinion of scholars is that this step was taken for the benefit of Western observers who did not fully understand the concept of "divine" entailed in the nature of a *kami*.

TENNŌSEI. Term for the imperial lineage from **Jimmu Tennō**, Japan's legendary first emperor (reigned 660–585 B.C.E.) to the current incumbent emperor. *See also* EMPEROR SYSTEM.

TENRI-KYŌ. Meaning "Teaching of Heavenly Reason," originally a **Kyōha Shinto** (Sect Shinto) sect founded by a female shaman called Nakayama Miki (1798–1887). Using a very simple doctrine, she encouraged people to seek the kanrodai sekai (Perfect Divine Kingdom). The movement was first considered to be a branch of **Yoshida Shinto**, but in 1880, it changed its affiliation and was then recognized as one of the official 13 sects of Kyōha Shinto. The founding date is usually given as 12 December 1838. Its distinctive feature is that it is considered to be genuinely monotheistic in the Western sense.

Nakayama received a revelation from Tenri-o-no-mikoto, the heavenly divinity known as Oyagami, "Parent God." After the revelation, she became known as the Kami no Yashiro, the living shrine (**jinja**) of the *kami*. After a vision in 1838, she developed a form of worship characterized by ecstatic **dancing** and **shamanistic** practices.

The first worship hall was built in December 1864, which became the first Tenri-kyō Church. After the **Meiji Restoration**, the Japanese government classified Tenri-kyō as a Kyōha Shinto sect and in this way, it slowly began to gain formal recognition. However in 1872, a department of the imperial government was set up to examine the main doctrines of all the religious bodies in Japan. In July 1874, a formal notice was sent to prefectural governors and head priests concerning a prohibition on selling protective charms and offering prayers. This was the beginning of a period of intense police interference that resulted in some of Tenri-kyō's religious artifacts being seized in October 1874. In September 1875, Nakayama was arrested for ignoring religious ordinances. She was eventually released, but was arrested again in 1882 and charged with confusing Shinto and **Buddhism**, which had become a crime in the Meiji period (1868–1912).

It was not until 1885 that official authorization of Tenri-kyō was given by the Central Office of Shinto and after formal recognition the head church of Tenri-kyō was moved from Tokyō to Jiba. On 26 January 1887, Nakayama began advocating the **Kagura Zutone**, salvation dance, which was subsequently banned by the police. The dance was performed at Jiba, during which Nakayama reportedly died.

On August 1899, the head priest applied for independent status from Shinto, but this was denied. In 1901, the school of Tenri-kyō was established and a second application for independence was made. This was refused again on the grounds that the church doctrines were not clear. Three applications and seven years later, the Home Ministry licensed Tenri-kyō on 27 November 1908.

In spite of domestic reversals, Nakayama's teachings began to spread outside of Japan, in the United States, Taiwan, Korea, and China. After 1945, the Fukugen movement undertook the purification of Tenri-kyō teaching because it had been influenced by State Shinto (**Kokka Shinto**) and nationalism. This movement redefined Tenri-kyō and chose to separate it from Kyōha-Shinto. On 30 April 1970, Tenri-kyō withdrew from the **Kyōha-Shinto Rengōkai** (Alliance of Kyōha Shinto sects).

At least part of the appeal of Tenri-kyō seems to lie in the idea of Oyagami, the Parent God, as psychologically reassuring since the Parent is everywhere, an image accord with Japanese spirituality, its reverence for **nature**, and its pursuit of harmony and peace. Social service is prominent and includes children's homes, homes for the mentally handicapped, day care centers and kindergartens, crisis centers, and homes for the aged. With at least 2 million registered members it can be considered the most successful and the largest of the modern developments in Kyōha Shinto, although it now disclaims that identity.

TENSHŌ KŌTAI JINGŪ-KYŌ. A **New Religion** with Shinto roots founded in 1945 by Kitamura Sayo (1900–1967). Tensho refers to **Amaterasu-ōmikami** and Kotai Jingū is another way of referring to the **Grand Shrines of Ise** (Ise Jingū). Therefore the name means sect of the Amaterasu-Grand Shrines of Ise. After a miserable marriage, Kitamura had a revelatory experience in which she was possessed by a wise snake-*kami* who subsequently turned out to be Tenshō. From this she began various kinds of ascetic rituals, including **misogi** (purification ritual) after which she commenced her mission with a stern critique of Japanese society.

Her eccentric image, such as being dressed as a man, and her claims to have performed miracles of **healing** gave her considerable profile and identity in religious circles. Not unlike other female **shamanistic** religious leaders, she also advocated a special **dance**, known, in her case, as muga-no-mai (a no-self dance). The use of the **Buddhist** concept of "no self" illustrates the principle of syncretism found so widely in the groups that emerged after the 13 **Kyōha Shinto** (Sect Shinto) sects had been defined. At least, however, they remained within the Shinto/Buddhist framework, unlike the New-New Religions that are much more diffuse both in their eclecticism and in their conceptualization.

TOKOYO-NO-KUNI. The world in which the purified spirits of the dead reside; a land of eternal youth, not to be confused with **Yomi-no-kuni**, the land of pollution where the deceased **Izanami-no-mikoto** went after she died. Probably a by-product of the concept of the Western paradise of Amida, it never grew to anything more than a shadowy concept that housed the *kami* and hotoke (Buddhas), who were the ancestral deities.

TOKUGAWA IEYASU (1543–1616). Civil war feudal lord and founder of the Tokugawa Shogunate who united Japan finally and created a dictatorial system that survived from 1600, when he defeated his rivals, until the **Meiji Restoration** which brought it to an end in 1868. Having dealt with the disruptive presence of Roman Catholic missionaries, whom he expelled, he made part of his basic policy the exercise of strict controls over all religious institutions. He commanded **Buddhist** rituals be conducted at the Zōjo-ji in Edo (near the modern Tokyō Tower); instructed that a memorial be placed in the Taiju-ji in Mikawa (his birthplace); and decreed that after the first annual memorial service, a shrine (**jinja**) was to be built and his spirit revered as a *kami*. This became the famous **Nikko Tosho-gu**, where he is enshrined as the Tōshō-Dai-Gongen (Great Avatar Light of the East). The shrine belongs to the **Tendai Shinto** tradition. For general reckoning purposes, the Edo period is normally dated as commencing in 1615, just before he died.

TORII. Gate at the entrance to shrine (**jinja**) grounds. *See also* ARCHITECTURE IN SHINTO.

TOYOASHIHARA-NO-MIZUHO-NO-KUNI. Land where the abundant **rice** plants ripen beautifully, the romantic name for Japan in contrast to **Takama-no-hara**, the High Plain of Heaven.

TOYOTOMI HIDEYOSHI (1536–1598). Succeeding **Oda Nobunaga** (1534–1582), and preceding **Tokugawa Ieyasu** (1543–1616), he was the pivotal of the three warlords who enforced the unity of the nation. Oda Nobunaga was concerned primarily with threats to central unity posed by rebellious local leaders and obdurate religious houses.

Hideyoshi was confronted with the potential menace of the invasion of an alien religion as Roman Catholic missionaries began to operate in the country. Jesuits had trod warily, but a wave of Franciscan monks, who had successfully "converted" the Philippines, created concerns. Awareness of Spanish ambitions in Asia, as well as meetings with Dutch traders, convinced him that caution was required. The beginning of Japan's serious suspicion of Western religious motives are attributed to him.

Hideyoshi was buried according to the rites of **Yoshida Shinto** and is enshrined in numerous locations, principally in the Kyōto Hokoku (abundant country) **Jinja** and in other shrines where the same characters read as Toyokuni Jinja. He is even recorded as having been enshrined after the **Meiji Restoration** (1868), when reversion to Japan's patriotic past became part of the modernization process.

The explanation of Japanese religion that Shinto was the root, **Confucianism** the tree, and **Buddhism** the blossom, is attributed to him.

TOYOUKEHIME-NO-KAMI. The enshrined *kami* of the **Gekū** (Outer Shrine) of the **Grand Shrines of Ise** (Ise Jingū). Identified as the *kami* of grain, and the mother of **Amaterasu-ōmikami**, and a form of **Ame-no-minaka-nushi-no-kami**. The exponents of **Watarai Shinto** argued that these were merely the *kami* of Ise that had a composite identity. The separation of identities probably coincided with the popular rise of **Ise Shinto**.

TŌZAN SECT OF SHUGENDŌ. Sect of **mountain** ascetics associated with Kimpusen in Yoshino, which had become a center for **shūgenja** from shrines (**jinja**) and temples around Nara. The group was made up of 36 centers, mostly temples that had strong links with the Kofuku-ji in Nara. The Tozan sect grew out of this assorted group of shrines, temples, and their respective shūgenja. Its name literally means "this mountain," implying equal status with **Honzan**. Headquarters were established at Ozasa on Mount Omine which received cooperation from both the eastern and western halls of the Kofuku-ji.

The Tōzan traced its roots to Shōbō, who founded both the Daigo-ji and the Ono-ha of **Shingon Buddhism**, thus its link with Shingon. A Muromachi era legend claimed that Shobo had received the spiritual seal of **En-no-Gyōja** (Ozunu) and the imperial seal of Emperor Jomei (reigned 629–641). The seal was subsequently entrusted to two shūgenja, Uchiyama, an Oshūku (leading master guide), and Sakuramoto, Ninoshoku (assistant master guide) of the order, another counter-claim to orthodoxy. Shōbō was also said to have led a pilgrimage of the greatest 36 shūgenja into the Omine range of mountains from Yoshino, which was supposed to account for the 36 centers noted. Novices had first to join one of the 36 identified leaders who would present their names to the whole group which assembled at Ozasa.

The image of Shōbō as founder was strengthened in the late Muromachi period (1333–1600), when the group slowly began to separate from the Kofuku-ji and move closer to the Sambo-in (a branch temple) of the Daigo-ji, confirming the link with Shingon Buddhism. Its headquarters remain in the Sambo-in of the Daigo-ji. Other centers of **Shugendō** grew up in different parts of the country, such as the **Dewa Sanzan**, but their attachment to one or another sect or group demonstrates the pre-eminence of the Honzan and Tōzan sects. The structure of Shugendō and the development of the two sects and their various branches as well as their lingering influences is an area of Japanese religion that merits more attention than it has received.

TSUBAKI ŌKAMI YASHIRO. Located in the mountains of Suzuka City, Tsubaki Grand Shrine celebrated the 2000th anniversary of its foundation in 1997. It is the head shrine (hongu) of **Sarutahiko-ōkami**, *kami* of pioneering and guidance, and who is also head of the earthly *kami*. The shrine (**jinja**) precincts contain the **Mifune-no-iwakura**, the point at which **Ninigi-no-mikoto** landed in the land of reed plains in his search for **Ise**. Enshrined also is **Ame-uzume-no-mikoto**, wife of Sarutahiko, who was the heavenly *kami* whose dance enticed **Amaterasu-ōmikami** out of the **Ame-no-iwato**.

Originally known as Chiwaki Jinja, the shrine at the separation of heaven and earth, the many species of wild camellia that grow on the mountain (Nyudogatake) within the shrine prompted **Emperor Nintoku** (reigned 313–399) to recommend a change of name to camellia (tsubaki). The Yamamoto family are hereditary priests and span 97 generations. Tsubaki Grand Shrine also is unique in that it has two branch shrines (**bunsha**) in North America, one in the United States and one in Canada. *See also* KANNAGARA JINJA; SHINTO OUTSIDE JAPAN.

TSUKA. Sacred mounds used for worship or other **ritual** purposes.

TSUKIMACHI. Moon-waiting ceremony held on set dates such as the 15th, 17th, 19th, and 23rd days of the first, fifth, and ninth months of the year.

TSUKINAMI-NO-MATSURI. Ceremonies scheduled for fixed days of the month, when worshippers gather to offer gifts and prayers to the *kami.*

TSUKURI KATAME NAOSU. The restoration of purity to the **soul** in order to elevate spirituality. *See also* ETHICS IN SHINTO.

TSUMI. Impurity, pollution, or uncleanness that requires purification (**harai**). *See also* KEGARE; TATARI.

TSURUGAOKA HACHIMAN-GŪ. Branch shrine of the **Iwashimizu Hachiman-gū** in Kyōto and the **Usa Hachiman-gū** in Kyushū, located in Kamakura. **Hachiman** was favored by **Minamoto Yoritomo** (1141–1199) and enshrined when he set up his military government in Kamakura.

TSUTSUSHIMI. Propriety of attitude toward the *kami*. It was a term favored by **Yamazaki Ansai** (1618–1682), founder of **Suiga Shinto**.

TSŪZOKU SHINTO. Popular Shinto as it was understood among the people during the 18th-century in movements such as **Shingaku**. This was in contrast to the academic tradition that developed in the **Kokugaku** (National Learning) movement.

TWENTY-TWO SHRINES (NIJŪ-NI-SHA). Heian period (794–1185) listing of important shrines (**jinja**) identified for government support. They included the **Grand Shrines of Ise** (Ise Jingū), Iwashimizu, **Upper and Lower Kamo Shrines**, Matsuo, **Hirano, Inari**, the Upper Seven **Kasuga** Shrines, Oharano, Omiwa, Iso no Kami, Oyamato, Hirose, **Tatsuta**, the Middle Seven **Sumiyoshi** shrines, **Hie**, Ume no Miya, Yoshida, Hirota, **Gion**, Kitano, Niu, and the Lower Eight Kifune Shrines. This special ranking of 22 shrines remained in force until the mid-Muromachi period (1333–1600) and functioned as a guideline for both the government and for the common people, whose devotion tended to center around them.

– U –

UBAZOKU-ZENJI. Wandering lay ascetics who were an early form of what later became **yamabushi**, practitioners of formalized **Shugendō** and whose activities flourished particularly during the Kamakura period (1185–1333).

UBUSUNA-NO-KAMI. The tutelary *kami* of the place where a child is born. The child is usually taken for **hatsu-miya-mairi** first shrine (**jinja**) visit, to the shrine in the locality. They child then becomes an ubako, or parishioner of that shrine.

UDA, EMPEROR (867–931). Listed as the 59th emperor, who reigned from 887 to 897 before abdicating in favor of his son Daigo. He was son and successor to Empress Kōkō (830–887; reigned 884–887), who was not closely related to, or allied to, the Fujiwara clan. Although brought to the throne by regent (kampaku) Fujiwara no Mototsune, he successfully challenged Fujiwara at the Ako Incident of 887. He consequently refused to fill the post of kampaku after the death of Mototsune.

Uda tried to broaden the base of the court, and introduced people of other families, notably **Sugawara Michizane** (845–903). Before retiring to enter a monastery, he presented guidelines for his son, entitled *Kampyo Goyukai*. His personal diary, Uda Tenno Gyoki, although incomplete, survives in fragments as a valuable resource for research into court ceremonies and events during his reign.

UDO JINGŪ. Shrine (**jinja**) in Nichinan City, Miyazaki Prefecture, Kyushū, enshrining Ugayafukiaezu-no-mikoto, father of the first **Emperor Jimmu Tenno** (reigned 660–585 B.C.E.), and five other ancient *kami*. The site is thought to be the birthplace of Ugayafukia-ezu-no-mikoto. It was erected during the reign (592–628) of Empress Suiko. Somewhere toward the end of the eighth century, it came under the influence of the Ninno Gokokuji and became known as Udo Gongen (Udo Incarnation). At the separation of **Buddhism** and Shinto, its name was changed to Udo Jingū.

UESHIBA MORIHEI (1883–1969). Founder of **aikido**, born in 1883 of samurai stock during the Meiji period (1868–1912), close to the beginning of Japan's **modernization** period. He grew up in the village of Tanabe in what is now Wakayama Prefecture and in Kumano, one of the most sacred areas of Japan. The sense of spirituality engendered by his environment remained a foundation of his thought.

While he was a soldier, he studied the **martial arts**, but felt dissatisfied with what he found. He began to develop his own techniques that became the foundation of the discipline aikido. After trying unsuccessfully to create a new colony in Hokkaido of people from Tanabe, in 1919, near Kyōto, he met with **Deguchi Onesaburō** (1871–1948), the leading figure of the Shinto sect **Omoto-kyō**. This led to a new direction in life, beginning with a disastrous trip to China: the Great Mongolian Adventure, as it became known. It ended with Deguchi and Ueshiba being arrested, chained, and, after their executions had been cancelled, sent back to Japan.

Ueshiba's biographers narrate these and many other interesting aspects of life. After he had created the term aikido in 1942, the essence of the man himself became much clearer. The spirituality he had acquired at Kumano in his youth found mature expression in his vision of aikido as a force intended to enhance defense rather than attack, and to cultivate love at its center. To the end of his life, he maintained links with Ōmoto-kyō which is one manifestation his eclecticism. He is revered in Aiki Jinja in Ibaraki Prefecture, while the hon-dojo, the principal training hall, is in Shinjuku Ward, Tokyō. He died at Iwama on 26 April 1969. His face was so serene, however, that one of his disciples described it as "the face of a *kami*." He is recorded as having said "The world's chaos will worsen. Expect my return."

UJIGAMI. Ancestral *kami* of a clan or family that usually protects the entire community or village under direction of that family. It is a reminder that one root of Shinto was and remains **ancestral reverence**.

UJIKO. Patrons of a shrine (**jinja**) living within the traditional boundaries. Members are part of the Ujiko-kai, the association of supporters in that area.

URABE SHINTO. Older root name for **Yoshida Shinto**, traced to Urabe Kanekata, 13th-century scholar-priest and author of the **Shaku Nihongi**. From it, the family acquired a reputation for preserving the Shinto classics, and for their sound scholarship and profound thought.

Kanekata's work was an attempt to reinstate Shinto and its position in face of the encroachments of **Buddhism** and to teach a type of Shinto that was sophisticated enough to withstand Buddhism and demonstrate that Shinto was the foundation of Japanese culture. Although Kanekata was embroiled in a power struggle with the Shirakawa family, he left sufficient generic ideas behind for **Yoshida Kanetomo** (1435–1511).

After 1378, the name of Yoshida replaced that of Urabe. Urabe gave the school a solid foundation, enabling Kanetomo to put forward a theory of Shinto called **Yuiitsu Genpon Sogen Shinto** ("the one and only original essence Shinto"), also called Yuiitsu Shinto or Yoshida Shinto.

USA HACHIMAN-GŪ. The oldest of the **Hachiman** shrines (**jinja**), located in the city of Usa, in Kyushū, it first demonstrated prominence during the Nara period (710–794) when the imperial court was struggling to deal with a hegemonistic Buddhist hierarchy. It enshrines **Emperor Ōjin** (reigned 270–310), whom it identifies with Hachiman.

UTSUSHIYO. The world in which human beings live, in contrast to the hidden world (kakuriyo), the High Plain of Heaven (**Takama-no-hara**). Although Utsushiyo is not perfect, purification (**harai**) brings it back to the condition in which the *kami* may be worshipped.

UYAMAU. Holding a proper attitude of respect and reverence toward *kami* and other human beings.

– W –

WA. An early name for Japan found in second century Chinese records, still in use and that may be read as Yamato. More commonly used is the character that also means peace or harmony, but it can also be read as wa. It is used in contrast to yo, which refers to things Western, as in washitsu (Japanese-style room), or yōshitsu (Western-style room). *See also* WAKON-YŌSAI.

WAGAKU. The early **Kokugaku** (National Learning) scholar **Keichu** (1640–1701) of the Edo period (1615–1868) used this word to describe Japanese learning.

WAKA. A 31-syllable Japanese poetic form found in the **Man'yōshū**, referred to also as **tanka**.

WAKAMIYA. A shrine containing the branch spirit of a *kami* from a main shrine. They may also be called **bunsha**.

WAKE NO KIYOMARU (733–799). Courtier of the late eighth century and adviser to Emperor Kammu (reigned 781–806), he is best remembered for foiling the scheme of the Buddhist monk **Dōkyō** (died 722), whose entanglement with Empress Kōken (reigned 749–758) had led him to aspire to imperial status. An oracle from the **Usa Hachiman-gū**, delivered by Kiyomaru, brought the incident to an end by declaring Dōkyō's aspirations as false and illusory. But it earned him exile in Osumi, in what is now Kagoshima Prefecture .

Following the death of the empress, Emperor Kōnin (reigned 770–781) succeeded and he recalled Kiyomaru to Nara and honored him. Emperor Konin died in 781 and was succeeded by Emperor Kammu, who had the courtier manage the Province of Settsu (Osaka and Hyogo). He became Minister of the **imperial household** and Minister in Chief of Civil Affairs, in which capacity he achieved numerous important results, most famously, moving the court from Nara to Nagaokakyō in 784, and 794 to Heiankyō (Kyōto) in 794. The goal, not surprisingly, was to prevent further Buddhist interference in court politics.

WAKON-YŌSAI. A **Meiji Restoration** period slogan meaning Western techniques, Eastern (Japanese) spirit. It is thought that it was derived from an older expression, Wakon Kansai (Japanese spirit, Chinese knowledge). The older version has been attributed to **Sugawara Michizane** (845–903), but may have come later. In Meiji period (1868–1912) thought, it was intended to be a guide as to how to adapt and adopt Western ideas into Japanese culture.

WALEY, ARTHUR DAVID (1889–1966, BORN ARTHUR DAVID SCHLOSS). Translator and scholar of Chinese and Japanese literature who made classical and other texts available in English. In relation to Shinto, he translated parts of the **Man'yōshū**, and many **Noh** plays. He also translated the *Genji Monogatari*. In spite of criticism of his work by subsequent academics, he handed on many important insights to later generations, and given the limitations imposed upon him by the period in which he lived, his work was most prodigious.

WATARAI IEYUKI (1255–1351). *See* RUIJI JINGI HONGEN.

WATARAI NOBUYOSHI (1615–1691). He helped to revive the study of **Ise Shinto** with his text **Daijingū Shinto Wakumon**. With the aid of some of the high priests of the **Grand Shrines of Ise**, he set up the Toyomizaki Bunko (Library) for the training of senior priests at the **Gekū** (the Outer Shrine). He also worked tirelessly to rebuild the **sessha** and **massha**, the branch shrines that had been destroyed during the civil war. In his efforts to improve the weakened reputation of the Outer Shrine, he came into conflict with the high priest of the **Naikū** (the Inner Shrine) concerning what kind of inscription should be written on good fortune a mullets distributed by the shrines (**jinja**). He lost the debate, and shortly thereafter, much of his own personal library was destroyed by fire.

The concept of "propriety" about which he was concerned was very much a **Confucian** value. There is much in his thought that is Confucian, and in that regard, he is more typical of the early Edo period (1615–1868) and has some traits in common with the Confucian style Shinto that grew up at the time. Nevertheless, his vigorous affirmation of the claims of Ise Shinto separates him from the other thinkers of the period. The order in which he discussed the Confucian relationships is that preferred by the Edo government, particularly the shogun, **Tokugawa Ieyasu** (1543–1616). He introduced the order to strengthen the moral grip of the government on the social order. He also composed a two-volume work that interprets Shinto in terms of **divination**, and another that argues that the Shinto practiced at Ise was the true origin of Shinto in Japan.

WATARAI SHINTO. A Shinto theory created by **Watarai No-buyoshi** (1615–1691) priest of the **Gekū** (Outer Shrine) of the **Grand Shrines of Ise** (Ise Jingū). He formally rejected any synthesis with **Buddhism** and **Confucianism** and proposed instead a return to the simpler forms of the Shinto of Ise. In pursuing scholarly research Watarai formulated original concepts of his own. He also began serious documentation work, and collected the extant documents of the Grand Shrines, establishing a library and school for priests of the Outer Shrine known as the Toyomiyazaki Bunko.

Watarai researched and revised the classic texts of Shinto and tried vigorously to revive the branch shrines of Ise, many of which had been destroyed and their locations lost or forgotten during the civil wars. The tradition compiled the famous Shinto Gobusho, the Five Canons of Shinto. One interesting aspect of the thought of Watarai Shinto is the search for a primordial creative *kami*, which takes it close to a type of monotheism. The school identified Toyouke with Ame-no-minakushi-no-Mikoto, the *kami* at the Center of High Heaven. By a combination of Chinese cosmological ideas and the argument that the other name of **Toyouke**, namely Miketsukami was derived from mi, meaning water (mizu), the Watarai School claimed that Toyouke was therefore the primal *kami*, even over **Amaterasu-ōmikami**.

The Watarai School was also important in its explicit rejection of the then-contemporary understanding of the **honji-suijaku** theory that Shinto *kami* were simply manifestations of Buddhist deities. It argued, on the contrary, that Buddhist figures were in fact manifestations of Shinto *kami* who were the ultimate reality. This doctrine had the effect of reversing the roles of *kami* and Buddha in **Ryōbu Shinto**. The first major exponent of the doctrines of Watarai Shinto was **Watarai Yukitada** (1236–1305). *See also* DAIJINGŪ SHINTO WAKUMON; ISE SHINTO; RUIJI JINGI HONGEN; SHINTO GO-BUSHO; SHINTO MEIBEN.

WATARAI TSUNEAKIRA (1675–1752). *See* SHINTO MEIBEN.

WATER IN SHINTO. Water (mizu) is universal in its religious usages, but nowhere more central than in Shinto. From ancient times, the Japanese have used water for purification (**harai**). According to ancient Chinese records of the Wei Dynasty, Japanese families bathed themselves in a river after attending a funeral. They long had the custom of taking baths, all of which implies a deep sense of the desire to be ritually pure. This attitude probably lies behind the development of the ascetic practice known as **misogi shūho** where the complete meaning of the use of water is best illustrated in its paradigmatic form, following the first **ritual** act of purification by **Izanagi-no-mikoto**. When he was pursuing his dead wife, Izanami-no-mikoto, he escaped from the land of pollution and death (**Yomi-no-kuni**) and bathed himself in the river Tachibana.

In modern Shinto, harai takes many forms, and may not even use water. In a manner similar to the modification of immersion into sprinkling in Christian baptism, the use of the harai gushi in Shinto, a wand-like device made of masses of paper streams attached to a stick represents water. A waterfall, a river or a pond may also be used. The open sea, because of its salt content, is considered most effective. Immersion in any of these is referred to as misogi.

The great ceremony of **Obarae**, performed initially by imperial command to remove the impurities of the nation entails tearing a strip of holy hemp and the discarding of this into a river to bear away the impurities. At some shrines (**jinja**) that are adjacent to a river, paper figurines bearing the impurities of the believer are thrown into the river for the same reason as part of a purification service.

In January 2000, archaeologists working on the site of Asukamura in Nara Prefecture, discovered a turtle-shaped stone structure, designed apparently for purification rituals involving water. According to the **Nihon Shōki** (720), Empress Saimei (reigned 655–661) ordered the construction of a ritual site referred to as the Ishi no Yamaoka. The Empress is reputed to have been interested in construction and **architecture**, as well as in rituals and ceremonies, as were all ancient incumbents of the imperial office.

The Japanese bath, the washing of entrances to businesses and restaurants before guests arrive, and general concern about cleanliness reflects a disposition toward purity that use of water seems to confirm. *See also* YUDATE.

WAZAWAI. Another word for disaster to be removed by purification (**harai.**)

WEDDINGS IN SHINTO. The division of labor among Japan's religions is clearly seen in preferences for the rites of passage and for important times in life. Children are initiated into society at shines (**jinja**). Funerals are rare in Shinto. The majority are conducted by Buddhist priests because once state support for **Buddhism** had been removed, new sources of income had to be found. Traditionally, weddings were domestic acts of adoption in which a **woman** was brought into a family (or in rare cases the reverse). This was announced at the ancestral grave and recorded in the village register. In modern times, shinzen kekkon, as it is known, began to develop from the Meiji period (1868–1912) on. Large shrines now offer total packages including the wedding ceremony, the reception, gifts for the guests (who normally bring cash in specially prepared envelopes), and even honeymoon travel.

The ceremony itself is very colorful. The bride, wearing the traditional wedding-style kimono, is led along the **sando**, the approach road or path to the building complex, and into the shrine facility in which the wedding will take place. The priest intones an invocation ritual (**norito**) to the *kami*. Small cups of **sake** are drunk and the priest (**kannushi**) prays for the happiness and well-being of the couple whose wedding is reported to the *kami*. There may be a dance by a shrine maiden (**miko**). Photographs are taken, and the family and the newlyweds proceed to the reception party. At the party, it is common to have a cake-cutting ceremony, and for the bride to change into a Western wedding dress, and then into evening wear. Words to be avoided (**imi no kotoba**) are kiru (cut) and deru (go out), which challenges the master of ceremonies to announce the proceedings without using either of these words. The fact that people can be married at a shrine and have a Buddhist funeral is an example of the syncretistic character of Japanese religion and an example of flexibility and tolerance (**kanyō**). *See also* FINANCE OF SHRINES.

WOMEN IN SHINTO. From earliest times, the role of female shamans in Shinto rites is apparent. An incident recorded in the Wei Dynasty records refers to a civil war that was ended when a 13-year-old girl called **Himiko** was made empress. While this may have been an incident in the kingdom of **Yamatai**, women empresses both reigned and ruled, especially **Empress Jingū** (reigned 201–269) until Empress Kōken (reigned 749–758) became involved with the would-be usurper Buddhist monk **Dōkyō** (died 722), after which the office was closed to women.

In spite of Western feminist attacks on the alleged male chauvinism of Japanese society, women in fact have served as priests (**kannushi**), imperial representatives, and in many other offices. Even Japanese Christianity ordained women clergy at least half a century before ordination of women began in a few traditions in Europe and the United States.

Restrictions on women have to do primarily with issues such as menstruation or childbirth, where blood may be found. Blood may be related to new life, but it also may link with death, and therefore creates impurity (**tsumi**) that must be removed by purification (**harai**). This is not a gender issue in the Western sense. The issue is any of the items that create impurity.

While any impurity that women are thought to carry must remain outside the shrines (**jinja**) it should remain even more so outside the **dohyo** in **sumo**. No female body should stand over the purified ring, because women may be impure. An American boxer had to leave his manager outside the ring when the world title fight was fought in the old Kokugikan building, the sumo arena in Tōkyō. Of interest in the 21st century is the issue raised by Ota Fusae, the first elected lady governor of Osaka, who claimed the right to present the Osaka Governor's trophy in person at the Osaka Basho in 2000.

In spite of some feminist arguments coming from within Japan that Shinto is discriminatory in certain respects, taking into consideration of role of early empresses who practiced **shamanism**, and the number of women who in later periods led religious movements, especially among the **New Religions**. Shinto in its history, on the whole, seems to have been relatively open-minded toward women. The position and influence of women seems first to have been challenged and changed with the arrival of the highly male-centered and patriarchal culture of **Buddhism** from the Asian mainland to an extent that has not yet been fully realized or admitted by many scholars of Buddhism. *See also* DEGUCHI NAO; EMPEROR SYSTEM; FEMINISM AND SHINTO; HIMIKO; JINGŪ KŌGŌ, JINGŪ (OR

JINGO), EMPRESS; MIKO; SEX IN SHINTO; SHAMANISM IN SHINTO; TENRI-KYŌ; TENSHŌ KŌTAI JINGŪ-KYŌ.

WORLD WAR II. *See* PACIFIC WAR.

– Y –

YABUSAME. Horse-backed **archery** contest of the **Heian period** (794–1185) used in **divination**. Riders wear Heian period costumes when performing in the contest, which uses three targets. *See also* BOKUSEN.

YAKUBARAI. Purification (**harai**) to calm a troubled *kami*, sometimes mistakenly translated as "exorcism." It involves the performance of the ceremony of oharai in a place where, usually, a sequence of misfortunes has taken place, due to a *kami* who is troubled or distressed.

Classic in Japanese history is the story of **Sugawara Michizane** (845–903), the **Heian period** (794–1185) courtier who was unjustly condemned and who died in exile. Assassinations, earthquakes, and floods struck terror into the people of Kyōto, leading finally to the posthumous restitution of Sugawara, followed by the enshrinement of his **soul** (**tama**) as **Tenjin**, the *kami* of learning.

In modern times, the same rite may be performed on buildings where a number of suicides have taken place, or a site where there have been numerous accidents, as in the housing estate at Takashimadaira in Tokyō during the early 1970s. One famous incident in Japanese baseball took place when the Yomiuri Giants lost a game due to three costly errors made by the third baseman. The Giants management called for a priest (**kannushi**) to perform **yakubarai** on the third base itself.

YAMABUSHI. Literally meaning people who lie down in the **mountains**, it was the term used to refer to mountain ascetics who gathered in various centers around Japan during the **Heian period** (794–1185). *See also* SHUGENDŌ; YAMABUSHI-CHO.

YAMABUSHI-CHŌ. This 13th-century register is one of the main sources of information about the lifestyle and activities of **yama-**

bushi, mountain dwelling ascetics. It lists many practices of the **Kumano** region, for example, **shūgenja** dressed in orange tunics, wearing hakama trousers and special headgear, and carrying wooden boxes on their backs. Three accessories considered necessary for entry to the mountains were a wooden case (carried on the back), a conical-shaped, broad-brimmed hat, and a Shinto harai-gushi. This may have originally been made of paper but, probably because of weather considerations, shūgenja came to carry a suzu, an instrument used for exorcism in India.

It was widely thought by older scholars that yamabushi merely hiked in the mountain ranges from Yoshino to Kumano (or from Kumano to Yoshino), through what is now the Kumano-Yoshino national park, although more recent research suggests that they formed temporary settlements at specific locations. Entry into or exit from the mountains, however, was ritualized. Buddhist and other sacred objects or artifacts were given to the shūgenja.

Rituals and practices slowly became standardized during the Kamakura period (1185–1333), and much of modern **Shugendō** was developed during that time. Formal entry into the mountains commenced with the ritual beating of a novice with a staff to awaken him into awareness of the Tathagata or the Buddha whose power was being sought. This was followed by the confession of sins (which in the case of Kumano was performed by hanging over a cliff by a rope that is briefly released to simulate the drop into hell), and then purification (**harai**) under a waterfall (**misogi**). Consumption of food and water was minimal. Sacred fires using small piles of wood set up in pillars (**hashiramoto goma**) were prepared and lit as a form of purification.

Initiation into esoteric mysteries followed these rituals performed on a regular basis along with instructions on how to draw energy from power places in the mountains. When the designated period was completed, there was a formal departure from the mountains. The concepts underlying disciplines such as **Sen-nichi-kai-hō-gyō** can be traced to these early practices. Two sets of practices are distinguished in the Yamabushi-cho. One was concerned with the life-support activities of the ascetic, while the other pursued the quest for spiritual power.

From the 15th century on, 10 disciplines were made obligatory for anyone wishing to enter the mountains formally for ascetic practice. These included the already mentioned beating to awaken the senses;

the confession of impurities; the weighing of karmic bonds to determine how much guilt was being borne; abstaining from drinking water and from eating cereals; the pouring of water on the body for purification; ritual wrestling; dancing; and hashiramoto goma (sacred fires) with esoteric rites. Each act was considered to correspond to one of the 10 worlds of **Shingon Buddhism** through which people passed on their way to enlightenment and living Buddhahood (soku-shin-jo-butsu). The ten worlds listed by **Kūkai** (773–835) were the worlds of hell, hungry spirits, animals, demons, human beings, heavenly beings, shravakas, pratyeka-Buddhas, bodhisattvas, and finally the world of the Buddhas. A shūgenja who correctly performed the rituals could progress through the ten worlds and attain Buddhahood in the flesh, according to the separate philosophies of Shingon and **Tendai Buddhism**.

In addition, symbolic explanations of both rituals and locations were invented around the same time to intensify the meaning of the rites, displaying yet another interesting feature of Japanese religion. The Omine mountains, for example, were interpreted in terms of **Ryōbu Shinto**, the Kumano end being the Womb Mandala and the Yoshino end being the Diamond Mandala. The pilgrimage route thus carried the shūgenja in a symbolic way, either upwards to enlightenment or downwards to hell, depending upon where he began.

An additional feature of the activities of shūgenja that explains how many grew so rich and powerful was that they acted as guides for the nobility, who made pilgrimages from the **Heian period** (794–1185) on. They led courtiers and samurai, as well as ordinary people performing rituals, offering prayers, and guiding pilgrims through the requirements of the pilgrimage. Shugenja were attached to teachers who owned hostels, which in turn were used to collect revenue. The Kumano guides, for example, travelled all over the country to spread the teachings of the cult, acquiring believers and helping to establish branches of the Kumano tradition. An mound excavation at Nachi records that a shūgenja called Gyoyo toured the country in 1176 and enlisted 69,000 followers. This was probably the peak of that sect, although, as has been noted, Shugendō continued to exist until the Meiji government banned it. The **Kumano Junrei**, like the **Dewa-Sanzan**, was revived after the **Pacific War** (World War II), as was the Tendai discipline of Sen-nichi-kai-hō-gyō. *See also* IKI-BOTOKE; IKIGAMI

YAMAGA SOKO (1622–1685). Famous Confucian scholar, military strategist, and Japanese historian who studied under **Hayashi Razan** (1583–1657). He published a book in 1695 entitled *Seikyō Yoroku* (The Essentials of the Sacred Teachings), from which **Seikyō Shinto** (teaching of the sages, referring to **Confucianism**) was derived. He used this idea to describe Shinto and to insist that imperial reverence was the basis of Shinto.

It was partly the influence of Chinese Confucianism during the Edo period (1600–1868) that led to the development of Shinto thought along ideological lines, with a heavy emphasis placed upon the duties of individuals within the sociopolitical system. Despite the later movements that undertook to establish the content of pure Shinto, the Confucian assumptions remained in the background, although they were never overtly discussed. It was this line of development also that contributed greatly to the deliberate creation of **Kokka Shinto** (State Shinto) as a national ideology to unify the nation following the changes after the **Meiji Restoration** in 1868.

YAMAMOTO SHINSAI (1873–1944). Shinto scholar of the late Meiji period (1868–1912) who declared that Shinto was the idealization of humanity in his work, the *Shinto Koyo*.

YAMAMOTO YUKITAKA (1922–2002). 96th high priest (**gūji**) of the **Tsubaki Ōkami Yashiro** and internationally famous enthusiast for world interfaith dialog. He is the first Shinto priest (**kannushi**) ever to receive an honorary doctorate in theology from an American college, and was also the first Shinto priest to become president of the International Association for Religious Freedom, serving from 1996 to 1999. He authored numerous books on Shinto, and also served as spiritual mentor to Matsushita Konosuke, founder of the Panasonic Corporation, who is enshrined within the precincts of Tsubaki Grand Shrine as the *kami* of management.

YAMATAI. Kingdom believed to have existed in Kyushū, a legendary queendom referred to in the third century Chinese record, the *Wei Zhi* (*Wei Chih*).

YAMATO. Region and kingdom from which the imperial lineage claims descent. It refers also to the Yamato Minzoku, the Yamato race, the original inhabitants of the Japanese archipelago. The kingdom of Yamato is usually divided into two phases. The first, the protohistoric period, was from 300 to 710, during which the first unified state emerged in Japan. The second was from 710 to 794, the Nara period, which saw the creation of various centralized institutions on the Chinese model. The ancient texts, the **Kojiki** (712) and the **Nihon Shōki** (720), contain some references to the historical events of the period. *See also* WA.

YAMATO-DAMASHII. Unique spirit of the Japanese race, a term which first appears in the 11th-century *Genji Monogatari* (The Tale of Genji), where it is the core of Japanese sentiment to which Chinese externals may be added. In the *Konjaku Monogatari* of the same period, it means maturity and good sense. It was not used again until the later **Kokugaku** (National Learning) writers of the Edo period (1600–1868) reconsidered its use. The ideological Shinto thinkers who followed **Hirata Atsutane** (1776–1843) linked it to the slogans of the **Meiji Restoration**, and transformed it into a martial ideal. Pre-war moral education was intended to cultivate the invincible spirit of the Japanese people.

YAMATOHIME-NO-MIKOTO. Princess and daughter of Emperor Suinin (reigned 29 B.C.E.–7 C.E.) and aunt of Prince **Yamatotakeru-no-mikoto**.

YAMATO KOTOBA. Ancient Japanese language as spoken before Chinese influences entered Japan, and still distinguished from spoken forms that bear Chinese influence. For example, the word *kami* is Yamato Kotoba, while the same character for divine being, if read as *shin*, relates to the Chinese word *shen.*

YAMATO-MAI. The **dance** of **Yamato** that originated in the Nara area and that was performed at court events and **festivals**. It is considered part of the **Noh** tradition. Related songs were used in ceremonies at the **Grand Shrines of Ise** (Ise Jingū) and other major shrines (**jinja**). *See also* DRAMATIC ARTS IN SHINTO; MUSIC IN SHINTO.

YAMATOTAKERU-NO-MIKOTO. Legendary prince who helped to unite the people of Japan, and who was one of Japan's tragic hero figures.

YAMAZAKI ANSAI (1618–1682). Founder of the "Shinto of Divine Revelation and Blessing" known as **Suiga Shinto**, perhaps the most aggressive form of anti-Buddhist Shinto outlook. Having studied the ideas of **Yoshikawa Shinto** and **Watarai Shinto**, Yamazaki Ansai claimed that there was but one "way," that of Ohirume-muchi (**Amaterasu-ōmikami**, the *kami* of the sun). There was only one "teaching," namely that of **Sarutahiko-ōkami** who had guided the heavenly grandson from the Plain of Heaven (**Takama-no-hara**) to the land of Japan.

The term Shinto meant the study of the sun-virtue (nittoku) of Amaterasu-ōmikami, whom he claimed was united with the sun in the heavens, amatsuhi. He also added to this the concept of the absolute sovereignty of the emperor as direct descendant of Amaterasu. The greatest power on earth is united with the greatest celestial power of the heavens. Ansai's later disciples such as Ogimachi Kinmichi and Izumoji Keichoku provided additional solid academic support for the imperial loyalists and anti-Bakufu movements of the late Edo period (1615–1868).

YANAGITA KUNIO (1875–1962). The father of Japanese folklore studies (minzokugaku), Yanagita Kunio was the sixth son of Matsuoka Misao, a scholar, educator and Shinto priest. He was a prolific writer who had worked in a number of appointments before dedicating himself, after 1930, to the study of folk traditions to discover what was unique about Japanese culture. Inspired by the **Kokugaku** (National Learning) ideal, he collected and collated masses of information after travel, field work and vast research.

After his death, controversy arose over how he was perceived, and how his work should be continued. Never really an academic purist, he followed an eclectic approach for which some scholars attacked him. Nevertheless, his stature is beyond doubt and his contribution to the better understanding of folk Shinto unquestionable.

YAO YOROZU NO KAMI. The myriad of *kami* as referred to in the words of all Shinto **norito**.

YASAKA JINJA. The shrine (**jinja**) in Kyōto from which the **Gion Matsuri** commences.

YASAKANI-NO-MAGATAMA. The jewel in the **imperial regalia**. *See also* SANSHU-NO-SHINKI.

YASHIKI-GAMI. The *kami* of a household, worshipped usually in a small shrine (**jinja**) within the garden of the house.

YASUKUNI JINJA. Shrine (**jinja**) for the war dead of the **Meiji Restoration** that was used to enshrine all Japanese war dead thereafter. The need for such a shrine was first expressed in 1868 as a place to house the spirits of the 3,588 soldiers who fell during the Meiji Restoration struggles on behalf of the imperial cause.

The original site at Kudanshita in Tokyō, near the old castle of Edo that had become the Imperial Palace, was secured in 1870 and the shrine was erected in 1871. In 1880, it was designated a **Bekkaku-Kampeisha**, having the highest rank of shrine where the *kami* are subjects of the emperor. At the same time, **Emperor Meiji** (reigned 1868–1912) named it Yasukuni (Peaceful Country) Jinja.

The Ministry of the Interior (Naimusho), was responsible for the administration, finances and appointments to the shrine staff, and thus it remained until the disestablishment of **Kokka Shinto** (State Shinto) in 1945. The emperor himself on set occasions would visit the Yasukuni Shrine to show respect and did a great deal to place the shrine and its unconscious symbols deep in the sentiments and the imagination of the masses of rural people from whose ranks most of the infantry was drawn.

By 1911, over 100 **shōkonsha** (shrines for the war dead) were in existence all over the country, and these were special places of devotion for those who had lost sons during the Meiji period (1868–1912). From the perspective of the **Meiji Restoration**, 22 of these are in Yamaguchi, the home of the Choshū clan, and 15 in Kagoshima, the home of the Satsuma clan. Some of these predated the Meiji Restoration, but they were all integrated into the system and helped to bolster local community commitment to the **emperor system** and the state.

After the end of the **Pacific War** (World War II), the Yasukuni Shrine became a private incorporated religious juridical person (**shūkyō hōjin**), but controversy soon arose. The basic issue is whether or not financial responsibility for the shrine should be taken over by the state. Those who favor this approach argue that the state has an obligation to maintain an appropriate memorial of the war dead. This includes the Liberal Democratic Party that draws much support and money from the various associations of bereaved families of the war dead. There are over three million war dead **souls** (**eirei**) enshrined in Yasukuni Jinja.

Opponents charge (quite correctly) that such support would be against the Constitution. Therefore the question of constitutional revision is closely linked with the Yasukuni problem. The governments of Korea and China, whose peoples suffered under the Japanese Imperial Army before the war, as well as opposition parties and religious groups in Japan, are vigilant in commenting on any signs of Yasukuni being specially honored, since to them shrines for the war dead are symbols of militarism and everything they endured. The comments of these groups are similar, that Japan's war dead should not be honored since, in their view, they were predators in Asia who committed crimes against humanity.

That there has been a move toward seeking government support for the shrine is clear. However, public and international reaction seems to have impeded its expected development. Two events however are worthy of note. First was the enshrinement of the 14 leaders of the Pacific War period, in the fall of 1979. These men, including General Tojo Hideki, the perceived war leader, were designated as Class-A defendants at the Tokyō War Crimes Trials. While wanting the men enshrined along with the others who died is understandable in Japanese terms, it shocked some people in Japan and outraged the governments of China and Korea. To add further misunderstanding, the enshrinement took place at night, giving the air of secrecy to the event. However, the movement of an enshrined being from one place to another always takes place at night. Since all were already enshrined in appropriate regional shokonsha, the night transfer was simply in accord with normal procedure.

The other controversial act occurred when Prime Minister Nakasone Yasuhiro visited the Yasukuni Shrine in the company of several cabinet members, an event that takes place annually. Until Nakasone's visit, previous prime ministers signed the book as ordinary citizens, and donated from their own pockets. Nakasone signed "Prime Minister (Sori Daijin) Nakasone Yasuhiro," making the visit official and consequently stirring up considerable controversy. His successor, Prime Minister Takeshita Noboru, avoided the issue by deciding not to make the visit for one year. Prime Minister Koizumi Junichiro restarted the controversy by visiting Yasukuni Jinja six times during his incumbency.

Among the enshrined is former Foreign Minister Matsuoka Yosuke, one of the architects of the Berlin-Rome-Tokyō Axis. The situation becomes ironic when it is remembered that Matsuoka was Christian (a Presbyterian), and that controversy remains about the enshrinement in the Gokoku Jinja in Yamaguchi of a member of the Self-Defense Forces who was Christian.

Problems associated with the Yasukuni Jinja are not easy to grasp because of the emotional delicacy and political complexity associated with the shrine. It cannot be compared to the various international war memorials, such as Arlington in the United States or the Cenotaph in London that were created at later periods. The concept embodied in the Yasukuni Shrine lies deep in Japanese culture and must be viewed in that regard. Reverence for the dead in Japan is observed in ways unique from a Western standpoint.

Some non-Japanese critics and commentators on the Yasukuni problem appear to believe that popular concern over Yasukuni Jinja will lead to the revival of State Shinto (**Kokka Shinto**), or to the rebirth of Japanese militarism. Observers less excited by conspiracy theories see nothing strange in honoring the war dead, even although they died in vain. The late George Furness, one of the defending lawyers in the Tokyō War Crimes Trials and author of the controversial book *Victors' Justice*, challenged orthodox opinion by stating simply that the ultimate crime in war was simply to lose. *See also* CHINKON; SOUL IN SHINTO.

YASURAKEKU. Serenity, a term used by **Kamo no Mabuchi** (1697–1769), the early **Kokugaku** (National Learning) scholar.

YATAGARASU. The black three-legged bird, either a raven or a large crow, that guided **Ninigi-no-mikoto** in his travels to subdue the land of reed plains, the land that became Japan. It acted as a messenger of **Amaterasu-ōmikami**, *kami* of the sun and the ancestor of the imperial family. It was adopted as the symbol of the Japan Football Association (JFA, known in Japanese as the *Nippon Sakka-Kyōkai*) and is worn as a crest on the national team strip. The winner of the annual Emperor's Cup is also permitted to wear the symbol of the Yatagarasu during the following season. *See also* ANIMISIM IN SHINTO; IMPERIAL HOUSEHOLD; KUMANO SHINTO.

YATA-NO-KAGAMI. Mirror in the **imperial regalia**. *See also* SAN-SHU-NO-SHINKI.

YOHAI. Worship from afar toward a *kami* whose location is difficult to access because of location or distance.

YŌMEI, EMPEROR (REIGNED 585–587). The first emperor to recognize both *kami* and Buddha, each of whose ways he is said to have revered equally.

YOMI-NO-KUNI. The polluted land of the dead described in Japanese mythology according to the **Kojiki** (712) and the **Nihon Shōki** (720) to which **Izanagi-no-mikoto** went in order to find his dead wife **Izanami-no-mikoto**. *See also* DEATH IN SHINTO.

YORISHIRO. Medium or symbol of the soul (**tama**) of someone who has died.

YOSHIDA KANEMIGI (1516–1573). The adopted grandson of **Yoshida Kanetomo** (1435–1511) and successor to the **Yoshida Shinto** tradition. Kanemigi undertook substantial documentation of shrines (**jinja**) in various parts of the country and was in possession of specialized knowledge of the **Nijū-ni-sha**, the 22 government-favored shrines of the Heian period (794–1185). Under his influence, the institutional power of the Yoshida family grew such that many Shinto families came to Kyōto to seek affiliation with the Yoshida tradition. This was the result of extensive travels undertaken between 1542 and 1572.

YOSHIDA KANETOMO (1435–1511). Shinto priest (**kannushi**), intellectual creator and transmitter, and pivotal personality of the Yoshida (until 1378, Urabe) tradition. He wrote numerous books expounding his ideas, principal among which were *Yuiitsu Shinto Myōbōshū* (Essentials of the Only One Shinto), *Shinto Yurai-ki* (Records of the Origins of Shinto) and *Shinto Taii* (An Outline of Shinto). His work was intended to build upon the political base established by Kanekata and to oust the Shirakawa family from their position as head of the **Jingikan**.

Kanetomo wrote the *Yuiitsu Shinto Myōbōshū* under the pen name of his ancestor Kanenobu while he claimed that the *Shinto Yu-*

rai-ki was the work of another ancestor, Kanenao. The subterfuge over authorship was designed to strengthen the claim that Yoshida Shinto had developed over a long period of time, and that it was indeed, the original, one, and only true Shinto. The *Shinto Taii* was written in his own name, as the culmination of the tradition he was claiming to expound. The book elaborates his concept of *kami* and its all-pervading presence in heaven and earth and how human beings should respond to it.

He identified three types of Shinto: Honjaku Engi Shinto, Shinto of "true essence and manifestation"; Taishi-Ryū Shinto, also known as **Shotoku Taishi** Shinto, or **Ryōbu** Shugo Shinto; and finally his own Genpon Sogen Shinto. Kanetomo claimed that this form of Shinto drew its authority from the *kami* known as Ame-no-koyane-no-mikoto, and that this was the true source of Japan's unique cultural tradition. **Buddhism** and **Confucianism** were considered to be the flowers and fruits of the true root that was Shinto. *See also* DAIGENGŪ; URABE SHINTO; YOSHIDA SHINTO.

YOSHIDA KENKO (CIRCA 1283–1352). Buddhist priest and author of *Tsurezuregusa*, a famous work (*Essays in Idleness*, circa 1330), of the **Urabe Shinto** family. A distinguished literary figure, poet and thinker, who thought in terms of appreciation of beginnings and endings, not in fulfillment, prefigures later profound Shinto concepts such as **nakaima**, or in the thought of **Motoori Noringa** (1730–1801), leading figure of the **Kokugaku** (National Learning) movement, **mono no aware**.

YOSHIDA SHINTO. The Shinto tradition of the Urabe family, one of the principal families in the **Jingikan**, the Office of Shinto *Kami* during the **Heian period** (794–1185). The family were also priests of the Yoshida Shrine (the **Hirano Jinja**) and the Ume no Miya in Kyōto. Yoshida Kanetomo (1435–1511) developed a version is also known as **Yuiitsu**, the "one and only Shinto." His overall objective was to reverse the doctrine of **honji suijaku**, which implied that *kami* were manifestations of the eternal Buddhas, and stand it on its head. He began to assert the primacy of Shinto, and reversed the relationship with **Buddhism** by claiming that the Buddha and the bodhisattvas were the manifestations of eternal *kami*. This began the long process of rehabilitating the indigenous cult and restoring the prominence it had once enjoyed in ancient times.

In his *Yuiitsu Shinto Myōbōshū* (Essentials of the Only One Shinto), Kanetomo rejects Buddhism but permits purification (**harai**) by fire (goma), invocations (kaji), and a rite of initiation into Shinto borrowed from esoteric Buddhism. While having clear concepts of Shinto to present, he permitted the popular appeal of esoteric Buddhism to remain in the background and within certain rituals and ceremonies of purified Shinto. Politically shrewd, he claimed for himself the title of Supreme Official of the Jingikan and created a system of Writs of Authorization of Shrines that remained in effect until the beginning of the Meiji period (1868–1912).

Kanetomo claimed jurisdiction over four areas, namely transmission of Shinto practices (forms of ceremonies for worship, offerings, and other rituals), priestly status, titles and ranks, priestly dress (**saifiku**, including the kazaore, eboshi, jōe, hashaku, and other items of dress recognizable to the present). The fourth was the kanjo (invitation) and enshrinement of the **go-shintai** (symbols, of the *kami*) in any new shrines to be established in the future.

Kanetomo also created within the Yoshida Shrines what he claimed was the supreme national ritual site. He built a hall of eight *kami* which was to serve as the central place for the proper administration of ceremonials in their honor. The imperial court received lectures on the **Nihon Shōki** (720) which had been discontinued since the **Heian period** (794–1185) and he himself lectured on the **Nakatomi-no-Obarae** to enrich the religious life of the Court. He circulated popular tracts such as the *Sanja Takusen* in order to expand the influence of his ideas. It became the orthodox position, and survived as such until government intrusions of the Meiji period.

YOSHIKAWA KORETARI (1616–1694). Shinto thinker and influential figure in bringing together Shinto and Confucian thought. He was born in Edo (in Nihombashi), and after his father died, he was brought up by a merchant family and was trained for business. He moved to Kamakura in 1651 to study Shinto and in 1653 entered the service of the head of the **Yoshida** family, Hagiwara Kaneyori (1588–1660).

He studied **Yoshida Shinto** and by 1682, having gained the confidence of the Tokugawa family, he was appointed shintokata (director of Shinto affairs of the government), which became a hereditary office until the **Meiji Restoration** brought it to an end. His real influence, although a Yoshida Shinto exponent was on **Yamazaki Ansai** (1618–1682) and how he tried to integrate Shinto and neo-**Confucianism**.

YOSHIKAWA SHINTO. Known as **Rigaku Shinto** (the Study of Rational Principles) it was derived from **Chu Hsi**'s (1132–1200) social thought that became the basis of the Tokugawa social order. *See also* YOSHIKAWA KORETARI.

YOSHIMI YUKIKAZU (1673–1761). A 17th-century imperial loyalist thinker who declared (in his *Izukawa Ki*) that Shinto was the way of the emperor and not easily understood by the subject.

YUDATE. A ceremony in which **water** is boiled in a large cauldron, and sprayed using bamboo leaves on the priests and on the worshippers as an act of purification. *See also* CHINKI-SHIKI; WATER IN SHINTO.

YUIITSU GENPON SHINTO. Another name for **Yoshida** Shinto. *See also* YOSHIDA KANETOMO; YOSHIDA SHINTO.

YUISHŌ. A general term referring to pedigree, but in the case of Shinto, the documented historical lineage of a shrine (**jinja**). Reference was made to cach shrine's yuisho during the **Jinja Gappei** program of the Meiji period (1868–1912) to determine which shrines should be permitted to survive.

YUSOKUGAKU. Motoori Norinaga (1730–1801), the **Kokugaku** (National Learning) scholar, used this term to describe antiquarian study.

– Z –

ZA. A za, or **miya-za** is a committee of laypeople supervising a shrine (**jinja**) where there is normally no resident priest (**kannushi**). The members of the za or miya-za are known as toya or tonin and they rotate in their leadership and responsibilities.

ZEN BUDDHISM AND SHINTO. Zen **Buddhism** in Japan became the spiritual guide of the warrior (samurai) class, particularly because of its cavalier attitude toward death. One of the major contrasts between Zen in China and in Japan is that while in China, Zen followed the idea of paying no respect to the emperor or princes, and was therefore essentially iconoclastic, the Japanese version was espoused to nationalism, as evidenced in an early work by Eisai entitled *Propagation of Zen as Protection of the Nation* (*Kozen Gokoku-Ron*). Out of this root, the links between Zen and militarism at a later date became significant.

Apart from the prominent military aspect, Zen in Japan inspired the development of many arts. Sumi-e (black-and-white ink paintings), karesansui (use of rocks and stones to create cosmic emblems), and the tea ceremony, while not directly derived from Shinto, do display Shinto motifs, particularly in their stress on beauty and elegance. The Japanese garden, a by-product of Zen, is really a horticultural depiction of **kannagara**. The famous karesansui garden of the Ryoan-ji in Kyōto unites the reverence for unique rocks and stones with meditation. Similarly the moss gardens of Kyōto are also designed to use nature to generate feelings of finitude, an aesthetic sensitivity that **Motoori Norinaga** (1730–1801) referred to as **mono no aware**.

While Zen and Shinto have no formal meeting, it has been argued by some scholars (for example Fujisawa Chikao) that the presence of the two in the Japanese cultural psyche symbolizes two poles of influence, and is the framework for the development of Japanese thought. *See also* KYUDO.

ZŌKA-SANSHIN. The three central *kami* of creation, according to the **mythology** as recorded in the **Kojiki** (712) and the **Nihon Shōki** (720).

Bibliography

INTRODUCTION

Shinto has been the subject of more serious attention in the last decade of the 20th century than it has been in the entire period since Japan first began to open its doors to the West in the mid-19th century. Nevertheless, there remains a dearth of materials in English in particular and in Western languages in general. Most of what exists derives from and is colored by the agenda of the Meiji period (1868–1912). Shinto's first encounters with the West were taking place at a time when the Japanese government was seeking to create, in the interests of modernization, a national religion that would serve simultaneously as a national ideology. Hence the image of Shinto that emerged toward the end of the 19th century was that of a religion that consisted of little more than a sterile system of rituals with virtually no spiritual vitality.

Anyone visiting a present-day shrine festival will immediately testify to the inaccuracy of this view. However, images linger, and there is public perception of Shinto as a government-initiated structure focusing on the war dead, the Yasukuni Shrine and the emperor system did much to damage the image as well as the true reality. Shinto itself has undergone a post-World War II revival, largely due to the religious freedom policy put into effect in 1945, because of which much of the ancient spirituality has been regenerated. New movements have emerged and old shrines have come back to life. Consequently, while the bibliography was compiled on strictly academic lines, it became necessary nevertheless to include some popular writings that will bring readers closer to the realities of 21st century Shinto. This is supplemented by some general studies of Japanese culture that in different ways have a bearing upon Shinto.

Among the more recent insightful and enlightening writings that begin to draw attention to aspects of Shinto are the works of Professor Allan G. Grapard, in particular his excellent work *The Protocol of the Gods: A Study of the Kasuga Cult in Japanese History*, 1992. There is also John K. Nelson's book on the life of the Suwa Jinja (*A Year in the Life of a Shinto Shrine*, 1996) and Mark Teeuwen's discussion of Watarai Shinto (*An Intellectual History of the Outer Shrine of Ise*, 2000). Each makes a sizeable contribution to the understanding of an area of Shinto that helps to display the richness and complexity behind its physical presence as well as its various traditions.

The listings close with some websites that might be helpful for those who wish to pursue more empirical lines of inquiry. Perhaps their inclusion should be qualified by a few remarks. Firstly, anyone who has ever used the Internet for research will realize exactly how imperfect, unbalanced, and frequently misleading it can be. Sites may vary in quality, from those designed for official public relations purposes, intended to convey as much accurate information as possible, to those created by well-meaning but either unqualified or incompetent amateurs, analogous to the difference between a well-made documentary and a badly made home video. Shinto websites are no exception. Some are official, some are parts of course materials for academic programs, and some are subjective flights of fantasy. Such is the Internet. For those requiring visual images, there are numerous sites that offer video clips and other relevant materials. I have listed only sites that I believe to be reliable, including some because they provide links to other sites; however, no one can guarantee that the links are all of the same quality. In the case of Shinto, sound reading and actual—rather than virtual—contact will always be the measure against which theory and web images must be judged.

The headings used to categorize the listings were created to assist those who might be looking for materials under a particular theme. Many titles might have been justifiably placed in more than one category, but to do so would have made the bibliography extremely cumbersome. Those used are not the only ones possible, but are probably the most helpful for general study purposes.

GENERAL STUDIES OF JAPANESE RELIGION

Anesaki Masaharu. *History of Japanese Religion.* London: Kegan Paul, 1930.
———. *Art, Life and Nature in Japan.* Boston: Marshall Jones Company, 1932.
———. *Religious Life of the Japanese People.* Tokyo: Japan Cultural Society, 1970.

Armstrong, Robert C. *Just before the Dawn: The Life and Work of Ninomiya Sontoku*. New York: Macmillan, 1912.

Ashida K. "Japan." In *Encyclopaedia of Religion and Ethics*. Edited by James Hastings. Vol VII: 481–489. Edinburgh: T & T Clark, 1914.

Bellah, Robert. *Tokugawa Religion.* Glencoe, IL: Free Press, 1957.

Bernard-Maitre, Henri. "L'Orientaliste Guillaume Postel et al decouverte spirituelle du Japon en 1552." *Monumenta Nipponica* 9 (1954): 83–108.

Borgen, Robert. "Sugawara no Miichizane: Ninth-Century Japanese Court Scholar, Poet and Statesman." Ph.D. dissertation. Ann Arbor: University of Michigan, 1978.

Brumbaugh, T. T. *Religious Values in Japanese Culture*. Tokyo: Kyo Bun Kwan, 1934.

Bunce, William. *Religions in Japan*, Ch. 6–8. Tokyo: Tuttle, 1973.

Chamberlain, Basil Hall. *Classical Poetry of the Japanese.* London: Trubner, 1880.

———. *The Language of Mythology, and Geographical Nomenclature of Japan Viewed in the Light of Aino Studies*. Tokyo: Tokyo Imperial University, 1887.

———. *Things Japanese*. London: K. Pul, Trench, Trubner & C., 1905.

Cousins, Steve. "Culture and Self Perception in Japan and the United States." *Journal of Personality and Social Psychology* 56, no. 1 (1989): 124–131.

Davis, W. "Pilgrimage and World Renewal: A Study of Religion and Social Values in Tokugawa Japan, Part I." *History of Religions* 23, no. 1 (November 1983).

———. "Pilgrimage and World Renewal: A Study of Religion and Social Values in Tokugawa Japan, Part II." *History of Religions* 23, no. 3 (February 1984).

———. *Japanese Religion and Society: Paradigms of Structural Change*. Albany: State University of New York Press, 1992.

Earhart, H. Byron. *Japanese Religion: Unity and Diversity*. Belmont, CA: Wadsworth, 1974.

———. *Religion in the Japanese Experience: Sources and Interpretations.* Belmont, CA: Wadsworth, 1974.

Elison, George, and Bardwell L. Smith, eds. *Warlords, Artists & Commoners: Japan in the Sixteenth Century*. Honolulu: University of Hawaii Press, 1981.

Fisher, Jerry T. "Nakamura Keiu: The Evangelical Ethic in Asia." In *Religious Ferment in Asia*. Edited by Robert J. Miller. Lawrence: University Press of Kansas, 1974.

Fridell, Wilbur M. "Notes on Japanese Tolerance." *Monumenta Nipponica* 27 (1972): 253–271.

———. "Thoughts on Man and Nature in Japan: A Personal Statement." *Japanese Journal of Religious Studies* 5/2–3 (June–September 1978): 186–190.

Griffis, William Elliot. *The Religions of Japan: From the Dawn of History to the Era of Meiji.* New York: Houghton Mifflin, 1901.

Hall, John Whitney, Nagahara Keiji, and Yamamura Kozo, eds. *Japan Before Tokugawa: Political Consolidation and Economic Growth, 1500–1650.* Princeton, NJ: Princeton University Press, 1981.

Hase Akihasa. *Japan's Modern Culture and its Roots.* Tokyo: International Society for Educational Information, 1982.

Havens, T. R. H. "Religion and Agriculture in Nineteenth-Century Japan: Ninomiya Sontoku and the Hotoku Movement." *Japan Christian Quarterly* 38, no. 2 (1972).

————. *Farm and Nation in Modern Japan: Agrarian Nationalism.* Princeton, NJ: Princeton University Press, 1974.

Heaslett, Samuel. *The Mind of Japan and the Religions of the Japanese.* Religions of the East Series, no. 1. London: The Church's Committee for Work among Japanese, 1947.

Hozumi Nobushige. *Ancestor Worship and Japanese Law.* Tokyo: Z. P. Manruya, 913.

Ishida Ichiro. "Mother-Son Deities." *History of Religions* 4, no. 1 (Summer 1964): 30–52.

Kasulis, Thomas P. *Intimacy: A General Orientation in Japanese Religious Values.* Honolulu: University of Hawaii Press, 990.

Ishikawa Hiroyoshi and Noguchi Takenori. *Nihonjin no Sei* (Sex and the Japanese). Tokyo: Burgei Shinju, 1974.

Kato Shuichi, Michael K. Reich, and Robert J. Lifton, eds. *Nihonjin no shisei-kan* (The World of Death of the Japanese), 2 vols. 1977.

Keene, Donald, ed. *Anthology of Japanese Literature: From the Earliest Era to the Mid-Nineteenth Century.* New York: Grove Press, 1955.

————. *Landscapes and Portraits.* New York: Kodansha International, 1971.

Kelsey, W. Michael. "Religion and Nature in Japan: Some Introductory Remarks." *Japanese Journal of Religious Studies* 9, no. 2–3 (Religion and Literature in Japan). Guest Editor W. Michael Kelsey (June–September 1982): 103–114.

Kerr, George H. *Okinawa: The History of an Island People.* Tokyo: Tuttle, 1958.

Kindaichi Haruhiko. *The Japanese Language.* Translated by Hirano Umeyo. Tokyo: Tuttle, 1978.

Kishimoto Hideo, ed. *Japanese Religion in the Meiji Era.* Translated by John F. Howes. Tokyo: Obunsha, 1956.

Kitagawa, Joseph M. "Japan: Religion." *Encyclopaedia Britannica.* Vol. 12, pp. 899–904. London: The Encyclopaedia Britannica Company, 1962.

————. "Religious and Cultural Ethos of Modern Japan." *Asian Studies* 2, no. 33 (December 1964): 334–352.

———. "Japanese Religion." In *A Reader's Guide to the Great Religions*. Edited by Charles J. Adams, New York: Free Press.1965.

———. *Religion in Japanese History.* New York: Columbia University Press, 1966.

———. *On Understanading Japanese Religion*. Princeton. NJ: Princeton University Press, 1987.

Knox, George William. *The Development of Religion in Japan*. New York: T. Y. Crowell & Co., 1907.

Latourette, K. S. *History of Japan*. New York: Macmillan, 1957.

Lewis, David C. *The Unseen Face of Japan.* Tunbridge Wells, England: Monarch Press, 1993.

Longford, Joseph H. "Note on Ninomiya Sontoku." *Transactions of the Asiatic Society of Japan* 22, Part I (1894): 103–108.

Loy, David. *Non-Duality: A Study in Comparative Philosophy*. New Haven, CT: Yale University Press, 1988.

Mass, Jeffrey P. *Warrior Government in Early Medieval Japan.* New Haven, CT: Yale University Press, 1974.

McEwan, J. R. *The Political Writings of Ogyu Sorai*. Cambridge: Cambridge University Press, 1962.

McMullin, N. "Historical and Historiographical Issues in the Study of Pre-Modern Japanese Religions." *Japanese Journal of Religious Studies* 16, no. 1 (1989): 3–40.

Ministry of Education. *Religions in Japan*. Tokyo: Minister of Education, 1963.

Mol, Hans. "The Identity Model of Religion: How It Compares with Nine Other Theories of Religion and How It Might Apply to Japan." *Japanese Journal of Religious Studies*, Proceedings of the 1978 Tokyo Meeting of the Conference Internationale de Sociologie Religieuse 6, no. 1–2 (March–June 1979): 11–38.

Morioka Kiyomi. *Religion in Changing Japanese Society*. Tokyo: University of Tokyo Press, 1975.

———. "The Appearance of 'Ancestor Religion' in Modern Japan: The Years of Transition from the Meiji to the Taisho periods." *Japanese Journal of Religious Studies* 4, no. 2–3 (June–September 1977): 183–212.

Morris, Ivan. *Nationalism and the Right Wing in Japan; A Study of Post-War Trends*. Westport, CT: Greenwood Press, 1974.

———. *The Nobility of Failure*. New York: London: Secker and Warburg, 1976.

Murakami Shigeyoshi. *Japanese Religion in the Modern Century.* Tokyo: University of Tokyo Press, 1980.

Nakamura Hajime. *Ways of Thinking of Eastern Peoples.* Honolulu: East-West Press, 1973.

———. *Development of Japanese Thought.* Tokyo: Japan Society for the Promotion of Science, 1976.

Naumann, N. *Die Einheimliche Religion Japans*, 2 vols. Leiden: E. J. Brill, 1994.

Nebreda, Alfonso M. "The Japanese University Student Confronts Religion." *Monumenta Nipponica* 20 (1965): 15–40, 298–318; *Monumenta Nipponica* 23 (1968): 31–65.

Nielsen, Niels C. *Religion and Philosophy in Contemporary Japan.* Rice Institute Pamphlets, Vol. 43, no. 4. Houston: Rice University Press, 1957.

Nishikawa Kyotaro. *Bugakumen*, 1971. Translated by Monica Bethe as *Bugaku Masks.* 1978.

Nishiyama, Shigeru. "Morioka Kiyomi: From a Structural to a Life-Cycle Theory of Religious Organization." *Japanese Journal of Religious Studies.* Focus on Scholars: Yanagita, Furuno, Aruga, Morioka. Ikado 7, no. 203 (June to September 1980): 167–207.

Nitobe Inazo. *Bushido: The Soul of Japan.* New York: Putnam, 1905.

Norbeck, Edward. *Religion and Society in Modern Japan.* Houston: Rice University Studies, 1970.

Nozaki Kiyoshi. *Kitsune.* Tokyo: Hokuseido Press, 1961.

Ohe Seizo. "Sontoku Renaissance." *Humanities* 11: 211–215. Tokyo: International Christian University, 1978.

Okafor, Fidelis U. "In Defence of Afro-Japanese Ethnophilosophy." *Philosophy East and West* 47 (October 1997).

Okakura Kakuzo. *The Book of Tea.* Edinburgh & New York: Duffield, 1906.

Ooms, H. *Tokugawa Ideology.* Princeton, NJ: Princeton University Press, 1986.

Picken, Stuart D. B. "Jesus, Kierkegaard and Zen." *Japanese Religions* 8, no. 1 (March 1974): 29–46.

———. "The Understanding of Death in Japanese Religion." *Japanese Religions* 9, no. 4 (July 1977): 47–59.

———. "Religiosity and Irreligiosity in Japan: Aspects of *mu-shukyo.*" *Japanese Religions* 11, no. 1 (December 1979): 51–67.

———. *Christianity and Japan: Meeting-Conflict-Hope.* Tokyo: Kodansha International, 1982.

———. "Japanese Religions and the 21st Century: Problems and Prospects." Tokyo: Japan Foundation, Orientation Seminar 24, 1987.

Prasad, S. A. *The Patriotism Thesis and Argument in Tokugawa Japan*, 3 vols. Calcutta, India: Guntur, 1975–1984.

Reader, Ian. *Religion in Contemporary Japan.* Honolulu: University of Hawaii Press, 1991.

———. *Religious Violence in Contemporary Japan: The Case of Aum Shinrikyo.* Honolulu: University of Hawaii Press, 2000.

———. *A Poisonous Cocktail? Aum Shinrikyo's Path to Violence.* Copenhagen: NIAS Books, 1996.

Reischauer, Edwin O. *Japan: Past and Present.* New York: Knopf, 1964.

———. *The Japanese.* Tokyo: Tuttle, 1978.

————. *Japan: Tradition and Transformation* (with Albert M. Craig). Tokyo: Tuttle, 1978.

Reischauer, R. K. *Early Japanese History*, 2 vols. Princeton, NJ: Princeton University Press, 1937.

Robertson, Jennifer. "Sexy Rice: Plant Gender, Far Animals, and Grass-Roots Nativism." *Monumenta Nipponica* 39 (1984): 23–260.

Sakai Atsuharu. "Kaibara Ekken and 'Onna Daigaku.'" *Cultural Nippon* 7, no. 4 (1939): 45–46.

Sanada Takaaki. "After Prophecy Fails: A Reappraisal of the Japanese Case." *Japanese Journal of Religious Studies*. Proceedings of the 1978 Tokyo Meeting of the Conference Internationale de Sociologie Religieuse 6, no. 1–2 (March–June 1979): 217–237.

Sansom, Sir George. *Japan: A Short Cultural History.* New York: The Century Co., 1932.

————. *History of Japan.* 3 vols. Tokyo: Tuttle, 1979.

Shindoda Minoru. *The Founding of the Kamakura Shogunate.* New York: Columbia Unversity Press, 1960.

Smith, Robert J. *Ancestor Worship in Contemporary Japan.* Stanford, CA: Stanford University Press, 1974.

Smith, Robert J., and Richard K. Beardsley, eds. *Japanese Culture: Its Development and Characteristics.* Chicago: Aldine Press, 1962.

Spae, Joseph. *Japanese Religiosity.* Tokyo: Oriens Institute, 1971.

Steensrup, Carl. "The Gokurakuji Letter: Hojo Shigetoki's Competition of Political and Religious Ideas of Thirteenth-Century Japan." *Monumenta Nipponica* 32 (1977): 1–34.

Swyngedouw, Jan. "Reflections on the Secularization Thesis in the Sociology of Religion in Japan." *Japanese Journal of Religious Studies*. Proceedings of the 1978 Tokyo Meeting of the Conference Internationale de Sociologie Religieuse 6, no. 1–2 (March–June 1979): 65–88.

Tsunoda Ryusaku, Wm. Theodore de Bary, and Donald Keene, eds. *Sources of the Japanese Tradition.* New York: Columbia University Press, 1958.

Ueda Makoto. *Literary and Arts Theories in Japan.* Cleveland, OH: Press of Western Reserve University, 1967.

Waley, A. *The Way and its Power.* London: Allen & Unwin, 1934.

Watsuji Tetsuro. *Climate: A Philosophical Study.* Translated by Geoffrey Bownas. Tokyo: University of Tokyo, 1961.

Lafcadio Hearn: Texts and Studies

Dawson, Carl. *Lafcadio Hearn and the Vision of Japan.* Baltimore: Johns Hopkins University Press, 1992.

Goodman, Henry, ed. *The Selected Writings of Lafcadio Hearn.* New York: The Citadel Press, 1949.

Hearn, Lafcadio. *Kokoro: Hints and Echoes of Japanese Inner Life.* Boston & London: Osgood, McIlvaine, 1896.

———. *Exotics and Retrospective.* Boston: Little, Brown & Co., 1898.

———. *In Ghostly Japan.* Boston: Little, Brown & Co., 1899.

———. *Shadowings.* London: Sampson Low, Marston, 1900.

———. *A Japanese Miscellany.* Boston: Little, Brown & Co., 1901.

———. *Japan: An Attempt at Interpretation.* New York: Macmillan, 1904.

———. *Kwaidan.* London: K. Paul, Trench, Trubner, 1904.

Kennard, Nina H. *Lafcadio Hearn.* London: Eveleigh Nash, 1911.

Koizumi Setsuko. *Reminiscences of Lafcadio Hearn.* Boston: Houghton Mifflin, 1918.

Kunst, Arthur E. *Lafcadio Hearn.* New York: Twayne Publishers, 1969.

Stevenson, Elizabeth. *Lafcadio Hearn.* New York: Macmillan, 1961.

PRE-BUDDHIST JAPAN

Beardsley, Richard K. "Japan Before History: A Survey of the Archaeological Record." *The Far Eastern Quarterly* 14, no. 3 (May 1955): 317–346.

Egami Namio. "Light on Japanese Cultural Origins from Historical Archaeology and Legend." In *Japanese Culture: Its Development and Characteristics,* 11–16. Edited by Robert J. Smith and Richard K. Beardsley. Chicago: Aldine Publishing Co., 1962.

Haguenauer, Charles M. *Origines de la civilisation japonaise: Introduction a l'etude de la prehistoire du Japon.* Part I (The Origins of Japanese Civilization: Introduction to Japan's Pre-History). Paris: Imprimiere Nationale—Libraire C. Klincksieck, 1956.

Imehara Suyeji. "Ancient Mirrors and Their Relationship to Early Japanese Culture." *Actsa Asiatica* (Bulletin of the Institute of Eastern Culture, Tokyo) no. 4 (1963): 70–79.

Kidder, J. E. Jr. "A Jomon Pottery Vessel in the Buffalo Museum of Science." *Artibus Asia* 10 (1952).

———. "The Maegaoka Vessels in the City Art Museum, St. Louis." *Artibus Asia* 16 (1953).

———. "Reconstruction of the 'Pre-Pottery' Culture of Japan." *Artibus Asia* 17 (1954): 135–143.

———. *Japan Before Buddhism.* London: Thames and Hudson, 1959.

———. "Haniwa: The Origin and Meaning of Tomb Sculptures." *Transactions of the Asiatic Society of Japan,* Series 3, no. 99 (1966).

Kiley, Cornelius J. "State and Dynasty in Archaic Yamato." *Journal of Asian Studies* 23, no. 1 (1973).

Komatsu Isao. *The Japanese People: Origins of the People and the Language.* Tokyo: The Society for International Culture, 1962.

Matsumoto, Hikoshichiro. "Notes on the Stone Age People of Japan." *American Anthropologist* 23, no. 1 (1921): 50–76.

Matsunaga, Alicia Orloff. "The Land of Natural Affirmation: Pre-Buddhist Japan." *Monumenta Nipponica* 19 (1964): 203–209.

Miki Fumio. *Haniwa: The Clay Sculptures of Protohistoric Japan.* Translated by Roy Andrew Miller. Tokyo: Tuttle, 1960.

———. *Haniwa.* Translated by Gina Lee Barnes. New York: Weatherhill, 1974.

Milne, J. "The Stone Age in Japan." *Journal of the Anthropological Institute of Great Britain and Ireland* 10 (1881): 389–423.

Morse, Edward S. "Shell Mounds of Omori." *Memoirs of the Science Department* (Tokyo Imperial University), vol. I, part 1 (1879).

Yawata Ichiro. "Prehistoric Evidence for Japanese Cultural Origins." In *Japanese Culture: Its Development and Characteristics.* Edited by Robert J. Smith and Richard K. Beardsley, 7–10. Chicago: Aldine Press, 1962.

JAPANESE BUDDHISM

Anesaki Masaharu. *Buddhism and Art in Relation to Buddhist Ideals.* New York: Houghton Mifflin, 1915.

———. "The Foundation of Buddhust Culture in Japan." *Monumenta Nipponica* (1951): 1–13.

———. *Religious Life of the Japanese People.* Revised by Kishimoto Hideo. Tokyo: Kokusai Bunka Shinkokai, 1961.

Armstrong, Robert C. *Buddhism and Buddhists in Japan.* New York: Macmillan, 1927.

Callaway, Tucker N. *Japanese Buddhism and Christianity.* Tokyo: Tuttle, 1957.

Dogen. *Shobo genzo* (1231–1253). Translated by Kosen Nishiyama and John Stevens as *The Eye and Treasury of the True Law.* 2 vols. Sendai: Daihokkaikaku Publishing, 1975 and 1977.

———. *Hokyoki* (1225–1227). Translated by Norman A. Waddell as "Dogen's Hokyoki." *Eastern Buddhist*, 10.2, 11.1 (1978).

Elliot, Sir Charles. *Japanese Buddhism.* London: Routledge & Kegan Paul, 1935.

Hakeda Yoshito S. *Kukai: Major Works.* New York: Columbia University Press, 1972.

Hori Ichiro. "Buddhism in the Life of Japanese People." In *Japan and Buddhism*, 16–17. Tokyo: The Association of the Buddha Jayanti, 1959.

———. "Self-Mummified Buddhas in Japan." *History of Religions* I, no. 2 (Winter 1962): 222–242.

Living Buddhism in Japan. Edited by Yohio Tamura and William P. Woodward. Tokyo: International Institute for the Study of Religions, 1960.

Marcure, Kenneth A. "The Danka System." *Monumenta Nipponica* 24 (1985): 39–67

Marra, Michele. "The Development of Mappo Thought in Japan (II)." *Japanese Journal of Religious Studies* 15, no. 4 (December 1988): 287–305.

Matsunami Yoshihiro. "Conflict within the Development of Buddhism." *Japanese Journal of Religious Studies*, Proceedings of the 1978 Tokyo Meeting of the Conference Internationale de Sociologie Religieuse 6, no. 1–2 (March–June 1979): 329–345.

Nakamura Hajime. "Suuzuki Shosan (1579–1655), and the Spirit of Capitalism in Japanese Buddhism." *Monumenta Nipponica* 22 (1967): 1–14.

Picken, Stuart D. B. *Buddhism: Japan's Cultural Identity.* Tokyo: Kodansha International, 1981.

Reader, Ian. *Making Pilgrimages: Meaning and Practice in Shikoku.* Honolulu: University of Hawaii Press, 2006.

———. *Pilgrimage in Popular Culture.* London: Palgrave Macmilllan, 1992.

Reischauer, August Karl. *Studies in Japanese Buddhism.* New York: Macmillan, 1925.

Sanford, James H. "The Abominable Tachikawa Skull Ritual." *Monumenta Nipponica* 46 (1991): 1–20.

Saunders, E. Dale. *Mudra: A Study of Symbolic Gestures in Japanese Buddhist Sculpture.* New York: Pantheon Books, 1960.

———. *Buddhism in Japan.* Philadelphia: University of Pennsylvania Press, 1964.

Seckel, Dietrich. "Japanese Buddhist Temple Names." *Monumenta Nipponica* 40 (1985): 359–386.

Stevens, John. *Marathon Monks of Mt. Hiei.* Boston: Shambhala Press, 1988.

Takakusu Junichiro. *The Essentials of Buddhist Philosophy.* Honolulu: University of Hawaii Press, 1947.

Ui Hakuju. "A Study of Tendai Buddhism." *Philosophical Studies of Japan*, vol. 1. Edited by Japanese National Commission for UNESCO. Tokyo: Japan Society for the Promotion of Science, 1959. 33–74.

Visser, Marinus Willem de. *Ancient Buddhism in Japan.* 2 vols. Leiden: E. J. Brill, 1935.

SYNCRETISM IN JAPANESE RELIGION

Earhart, Byron. "Mount Fuji and Shugendo." *Japanese Journal of Religious Studies* (theme: Shugendo and Mountain Religion in Japan, Royall Tyler and Paul L. Swanson, eds.) 16, no. 2–3 (December 1988): 205–226.

Fujisawa Chikao. *Zen and Shinto: the Story of Japanese Philosophy.* Westport, CT: Greenwood Press, 1971.

Hori Ichiro. "On the Concept of Hijiri (Holy Man)." *Numen* 5, no. 2 (April 1958): 128–160; and 5, no. 3 (September 1958): 199–232.

Kamstra, J. H. *Encounter or Syncretism: The Initial Growth of Japanese Buddhism.* Leiden: Brill, 1967.

Kitagawa, Joseph M. "The Buddhist Transformation in Japan." *History of Religions* 4, no. 2 (Winter 1965): 319–336.

Matsunaga Alicia. *The Buddhist Philosophy of Assimilation.* Tokyo: Sophia University Press, 1969.

Miyake Hitoshi. "Religious Rituals in Shugendo: A Summary." *Japanese Journal of Religious Studies* (theme: Shugendo and Mountain Religion in Japan, Royall Tyler and Paul L. Swanson, eds.) 16, no. 2–3 (December 1988): 101–116.

Morrell, Robert E. "Muju Ichinen's Shinto-Buddhist Syncretism: Shasekishu, Book 1." In *Monumenta Nipponica,* Tokyo: Sophia University, 1975.

Pearson, Birger A., ed. *Religious Syncretism in Antiquity: Essays in Conversation with Geo Widengren.* Missoula, MT: Scholars Press for the American Academy and the Institute of Religious Studies, University of California, Santa Barbara, 1975.

Plutschow, Herbert E. "Is Poetry Sin? *Honjisuijaku* and Buddhism v. Poetry." In *Oriens Extremus.* Wiesbaden: Kommisionverlag O. Harrasowitz, 1978.

Reader, Ian. *Pilgrimage in Popular Culture.* Edited with Tony Walter. London: Macmillan, 1993.

Sawa Ryuhen. "Shugendo Art." *Japanese Journal of Religious Studies* (theme: Shugendo and Mountain Religion in Japan, Royall Tyler and Paul L. Swanson, eds.) 16, no. 2–3 (December 1988): 195–204.

Tyler, Royall. "Kofuku-ji and Shugendo." *Japanese Journal of Religious Studies* (theme: Shugendo and Mountain Religion in Japan, Royall Tyler and Paul L. Swanson, eds.) 16, no. 2–3 (December 1988): 143–180.

Tyler, Susan. "Honji Suijaku Faith." *Japanese Journal of Religious Studies* (theme: Shugendo and Mountain Religion in Japan, Royall Tyler and Paul L. Swanson, eds.) 16, no. 2–3 (December 1988): 227–250.

Wakamori Taro. "The Hashira-matsu and Shugendo." *Japanese Journal of Religious Studies* (theme: Shugendo and Mountain Religion in Japan, Royall Tyler and Paul L. Swanson, eds.) 16, no. 2–3 (December 1988): 181–194.

GENERAL STUDIES IN SHINTO

Aaland, Mikkel. *The Sword of Heaven.* San Francisco: Travelers' Tales, 2000.

Antoni, Klaus. Shintō und die Konzeption des japanischen Nationalwesens (kokutai): Der religiöse Traditionalismus in Neuzeit und Moderne Japan, *Handbook of Oriental Studies* 5, no. 8. Leiden: Brill, 1998.

Anzu Motohiko. *Shinto as Seen by Foreign Scholars.* Tokyo: Central Federation of Japanese Culture, 1940.

———. *Shinto Gairon* (An Outline of Shinto). Tokyo, 1954.

———. "Geku Shintoron, Shinto Gobusho kara Ieyuki to Chikafusa e" (Shinto Theory of the Outer Shrine, the Five Canonical Books of Shinto from [Watarai] Ieyuki to [Kitabatake] Chikafusa). *Shinto Shukyo* 6, no. 66 (January 1972).

———. "Amaterasu Omikami to Toyouke no Kami ni tsuite no Shiron." (An Essay on Amaterasu-omikami and Toyouke no Kami). *Kokugakuin Daigaku Daigakuin Kuiyo* 10 (1978).

———. *Shinto to Nihonjin* (Shinto and the Japanese). Tokyo: Jinja Shinposha, 1996.

Asoya Masahiko. *Shinto Shiso no Keisei* (The Evolution of Shinto Thought). Tokyo: Perikansha, 1985.

———. *Shinto no Seishikan* (The Shinto View of Death). Tokyo: Perikansha, 1996.

Aston, W. H. *Shinto: The Way of the Gods.* London: Longmans, 1905.

Ballou, Robert O. *Shinto, the Unconquered Enemy.* New York: Viking, 1945.

Beardsley, Richard K. "Shinto Religion and Japanese Cultural Evolution." In *The Science of Culture.* Edited by Gertrude E. Dole and Robert L. Carneiro. New York: Crowell, 1960. 63–78.

Bocking, Brian. *A Popular Dictionary of Shinto.* Richmond, England: Curzon Press, 1995.

Boot, Willem Jan. "Japanese Poetics and the Kokka Hachiron." Asiatica Venetiana 4 (1999): 23–43.

———. "The Death of a Shogun: Deification in Early Modern Japan." In *Shinto in Japanese History.* Edited by John L. Breen and Mark Teeuwen. Honolulu: University of Hawai'i Press, 2000. 144–166.

———. "The Religious Background of the Deification of Tokugawa Ieyasu." In *Rethinking Japan,* vol. II: *Social Sciences, Ideology and Thought.* Edited by Adriana Boscaro, Franco Gatti, and Massimo Raveri. Folkestone, Kent: Sandgate, 1990. 331–337.

Breen, John. "Shintoists in Restoration Japan (1868–1872): Towards a Reassessment." *Modern Asian Studies* 24, no. 3 (1990): 579–602.

——— . "Accomodating the Alien: 'Kuni Takamasa and the Religion of the Lord of Heaven.'" In *Religion and Japan: Arrows to Heaven and Earth.* Edited by P. F. Kornicki and I. J. McMullen. Cambridge: Cambridge University Press, 1996. 179–197.

———. "Nativism Restored." *Monumenta Nipponica* 55, no. 3 (2000): 429–439.

————. *Modern Passings: Death Rites, Politics, and Social Change in Imperial Japan* (review). *Monumenta Nipponica* 63 (2008): 169–172.

Breen, John, and Mark Teeuwen, eds. *Shinto in History: Ways of the Kami*. Richmond, England: Curzon Studies in Asian Religions, 2000.

Breen, John, and Mark Teeuwen. *A New History of Shinto*. New Jersey: John Wiley & Sons Inc, 2009.

Brownlee, John S. Japanese *Historians and the National Myths, 1600–1945: The Age of the Gods and Emperor Jimmu*. Vancouver and Tokyo: University of British Columbia Press and University of Tokyo Press, 1997. 15–67.

————. trans. "The Jeweled Comb-Box: Motoori Norinaga's Tamakushige." *Monumenta Nipponica* 43, no. 1 (1988): 35–61.

Bukkyo Dendo Kyokai. *The World of Shinto*. Tokyo, 1985.

Dumoulin, Heinrich. *Kamo Mabuchi (1697–1769): Ein Beitrag zur japanischen Religions und Geistesgeschichte*. Tokyo: Sophia University Press, 1943.

————. "Zur japanischen Shinto-Forschung." *Monumenta Nipponica* 1 (1945): 576–584.

Earhart, Byron H. "The Ideal of Nature in Japanese Religion and its Possible Significance for Environmental Concerns." *Contemporary Religions in Japan* 11 (1970): 1–2.

Florenz, Karl. "Der Shintoismus." *Die Orientalischen Religionen* (Die Kultur der Gegenwart) Teil I, Ableitung 3, no. 1, Berlin and Leipzig (1906): 194–220.

————. *Die Historischen Quellen der Shinto-Religionen aus dem Altjapanischen und Chinesischen Ubersezt und Erklart*. Gottingen: Vanderhoaek & Ruprecht, 1919.

Fujisawa Chikao. *Concrete Universality of the Japanese Way of Thinking*. Tokyo: Hokuseido Press, 1958.

————. *Zen and Shinto: The Story of Japanese Philosophy*. Westport, CT: Greenwood Press, 1971.

Grapard, Allan. "Shinto." In *Kodansha Encyclopaedia of Japan*. Tokyo: Kodansha International, 1983. 125–132.

Handa Shigeru et al., eds. *An Explanation of Shinto for People of Foreign Lands*. Aichi Prefectural Shinto Youth Association, December 1985.

Harada Tasuku. *The Faith of Japan*. New York: Macmillan, 1914.

Harada Toshiaki. "The Origin of Community Worship." *Religious Studies in Japan* (1959): 213–218.

Haas, Hans. "Shintoismus." *Religion in Geschichte und Gegenwart* 5 (Tubingen): 466–470.

Haydon, A. Eustace. *Biography of the Gods*. New York: Macmillan, 1945.

Hearn, Lafcadio. *Japan's Religions: Shinto and Buddhism*. Tokyo: Tuttle, 1985.

Herbert, Jean. *Shinto: The Fountainhead of Japan*. London: George, Allen & Unwin, 1967.

Hibino Yutaka. *Nippon Shindo Ron or the National Ideals of the Japanese People*. Translated by A. P. McKenzie. Cambridge: Cambridge University Press, 1928.

Hirai Naofusa. *The Concept of Man in Shinto*. MA Thesis. University of Chicago, 1954.

———. "Fundamental Problems of Present Shinto." *Proceedings of the IXth International Congress for the History of Religions* (1960): 303–206.

———. "Studies on Shinto in Pre- and Post-War Japan." *Acta Asiatica* (Toho Gakkai), no. 51 (February 1987): 96–118.

Holtom, D. C. *The National Faith of Japan.* London: Kegan Paul, 1938.

———. *Modern Japan and Shinto Nationalism*. Chicago: University of Chicago Press, 1943.

———. "Shintoism." In *The Great Religions of the Modern World*. Edited by Edward J. Jurji. Princeton, NJ: Princeton University Press, 1946. 141–177.

Ivy, Marilyn. "Ghostlier Demarcations: Textual Phantasm and the Origins of Japanese Nativist Ethnology." In *Culture/Contexture: Explorations in Anthropology and Literary Study*. Edited by E. Valentine and Jeffrey M. Peck. Berkeley: University of California Press, 1996. 296–322.

Jinja Honcho. *An Outline of Shinto Teachings*. The Association of Shinto Shrines Tokyo, produced on behalf of the Japan Committee for the 9th International Congress of the History of Religions, 1958.

Kasulis, Thomas P. *Shinto: The Way Home.* Honolulu: University of Hawaii Press, 2004.

Kato Genchi. *A Study of Shinto.* Tokyo: Meiji Japan Society, 1926.

———. "The Three Stages of the Shinto Religion." *The Japan Christian Quarterly* 3, no. 2 (April 1928): 116–125.

———. "Shinto Worship of Living Human Gods in the Religious History of Japan." 17th International Congress of Orientalists, Oxford, 1928.

———. *What is Shinto?* Tokyo: Maruzen, 1935.

———. "Shinto's Terra Incognita to be Explored Yet." Paper for private circulation, Gotemba, 1958.

———. *A Historical Study of the Religious Development of Shinto*. Translated by Hanayama Shoyu. Japanese National Commission for UNESCO, 1973.

Kato Genchi, with Karl Reitz and Wilhelm Schiffer. *A Bibliography of Shinto in Western Lanugages from the Oldest Times till 1952*. Tokyo: Meiji Jingu Shamusho, 1953.

Kawazoe, Noboru. "The Ise Shrine." *Japan Quarterly* 9, no. 3 (July–September 1962): 285–292.

Kenney, Elizabeth. "Shinto Funerals in the Edo Period." *Japanese Journal of Religious Studies* 27, no. 3–4 (2000): 239–271.

Kitagawa, Joseph M. "Shinto." In *Encyclopaedia Britannica*, Vol. 21. London: The Encyclopaedia Britannica Company, 1962. 517–521.

————. "Some Remarks on Shinto." *History of Religions* 27, no. 3 (February 1988): 227–245.

Kokugakuin University Institute for Japanese Culture and Classics. *Basic Terms of Shinto.* Rev. ed. Tokyo, 1958.

Kono Shozo. "Kannagara no Michi." *Monumenta Nipponica* 3 (1948): 369–391.

Kuroda Toshio. "Shinto in the History of Religion." Translated by J. C. Dobbin and S. Gay. *The Journal of Japanese Studies* 7, no. 1 (Winter) 1981.

Lange, R. "Die Japaner, II. Der Shintoismus." In *Lehrbuch der Religionsgeschichte* I, Tubingen: Mohr, 1905. 41–171.

Littleton, C. Scott. *Shinto: Origins, Rituals, Festivals, Spirits, Sacred Places.* U.S.A.: Oxford University Press, 2002.

Lokowandt, Ernest. "The Revival of State Shinto." *Asiatic Society of Japan.* Lecture, September 1982.

Lowell, Percival. *Occult Japan or the Way of the Gods.* New York: Houghton Mifflin, 1895.

Mason, J. W. T. *The Meaning of Shinto: The Primaeval Foundation of Creative Spirit in Modern Japan.* New York: E. P. Dutton, 1935.

————. *The Spirit of Shinto Mythology.* Tokyo: Fuzambo, 1939.

Minstry of Education, Government of Japan. *Kokuitai no Hongi: Cardinal Principles of the National Entity of Japan.* Translated by John Owen Gauntlett. Cambridge: Cambridge University Press, 1949.

Miyagawa Munenori. "The Status Quo of Shinto Shrines." *The Shinto Bulletin* I (March 1953): 4–6.

Miyake Hitoshi. *Shugendo girei no kenkyu* (Research on the Rituals of Shugendo). 1971.

Morris, J. "A Pilgrimage to Ise." *Transactions of the Japan Society of London* 7 (1905–7): 248–262.

Munakata Taisha Fukko Kisei Kai (publications about the island by Munakata Taisha). *Okinoshima*, MunakataTaisha. 1958–1971.

Muraoka Tsunetsugu. *Studies in Shinto Thought.* Translated by Delmer M. Brown and James T. Araki. Westrport, CT: Greenwood Press, 1964.

Nelson, John K. "Freedom of Expression: The Very Modern Practice of Visiting a Shinto Shrine." *Japanese Journal of Religious Studies* 23, no. 1–2 (1996): 117–153.

Nishitsunoi Masayoshi. "Social and Religious Groups in Shinto." *Religious Studies in Japan* (1959): 219–228.

Nomura, Noriko S. *I am Shinto.* Religions of the World Series. New York: Rosen Publishing Group, 1990.

Okano Haruko. "Women and Sexism in Shinto." *Japan Christian Review* 59 (1992): 27–31.

Ono Sokyo "The Contribution to Japan of Shrine Shinto." *Proceedings of the IXth International Congress for the History of Religions* (1960): 387–392.

————. *Shinto: The Kami Way.* Tokyo: Tuttle, 1962.

Picken, Stuart D. B. "Shinto and the Beginnings of Modernization in Japan." *Transactions of the International Conference of Orientalists in Japan,* no. 22 (1977): 37–43.

————. *Shinto: Japan's Spiritual Roots.* Tokyo: Kodansha International, 1980.

————. *Handbook of Shinto.* Stockton, CA: Tsubaki Grand Shrine of America, 1985.

————. "The Place of Shinto in Japanese Culture." *Institute of Korean Humanistic Sciences International Cultural Symposium.* Seoul: Institute of Korean Humanistic Sciences, 1986.

————. "Shinto." *Oxford Dictionary of Politics.* Oxford: Oxford University Press, 1993.

————. *The Essentials of Shinto.* Westport, CT: Greenwood Press, 1994.

Piggot, Joan R. "Sacral Kingship and Confederacy in Early Izumo." *Monumenta Nipponica* 4, no. 1 (Spring), 1989.

Ponsonby-Fane, R. A. B. *Studies in Shinto and Shinto Shrines.* Kyoto: Ponsonby Memorial Society, 1942.

————. *The Vicissitudes of Shinto.* Kyoto: Ponsonby Memorial Society, 1963.

Price, Willard. *Son of Heaven.* London: William Heinemann, 1945.

Rarick, Charles A. "The Philosophical Impact of Shintoism, Buddhism, and Confucianism on Japanese Management Practices." *International Journal of Value-Based Management* 7 (1994): 219–226.

Reader, Ian. *Religion in Contemporary Japan.* Honolulu: University of Hawaii Press, 1991.

————. *Simple Guide to Shinto.* The Religions of Japan (Simple Guides to World Religions).

Reader, Ian. *Practically Religious: Worldly Benefits and the Common Religion of Japan.* Honolulu: University of Hawaii Press, 1998.

Revon, Michel. *Le Shintoisme.* Paris: E. Heroux, 1907.

Robertson, Jennifer. "Sexy Rice: Plant Gender, Farm Manuals, and Grass-Roots Nativism." *Monumenta Nipponica* 39, no. 3 (1984): 233–260.

Ross, Floyd H. *Shinto: The Way of Japan.* Boston: Beacon Press, 1965.

Sakamaki Shunzo. "Shinto: Japanese Ethnocentrism." *The Japanese Mind.* Edited by Charles Moore. Hawaii: East-West Press, 1967. 24–33.

Sakurai Haruo. "Tradition and Change in Local Community Shrines." *Acta Asiatica* (Toho Gakkai) no. 51 (February 1987): 62–76.

Sato Noriaki. "The Initiation of the Religious Specialists Kamisan: A Few Observations." *Japanese Journal of Religious Studies* 8, no. 3–4 (September–December 1981): 149–186.

Satow, E. M. "The Revival of Pure Shin-tau." *Transactions of the Asiatic Society of Japan* 3 (1875): 1–87.

Schurhammer, Georg. *Shin-To, the Way of the Gods in Japan (According to the Printed and Unprinted Reports of the Jesuit Missionaries in the Sixteenth and Seventeenth Centuries).* Bonn: K. Schoroeder, 1923.

Schwade, Arcadio. *Shinto Bibliography in Western Languages: Bibliography on Shinto and Religious Sects, Intellectual Schools and Movements Influenced by Shintoism.* Leiden: E. J. Brill, 1986.

Smyers, Karen A. "Women and Shinto: the Relation between Purity and Pollution." *Japanese Religions* 12, no. 4: 7–18.

Sonnier, Suzanne. *Shinto, Spirits, and Shrines: Religion in Japan* (Series—Lucent Library of Historical Eras). San Diego, CA: Greenhaven Press, 2007.

Sonoda Minoru. "The Religious Situation in Japan in Relation to Shinto." *Acta Asiatica* (Toho Gakkai), no. 51 (February 1987): 1–21.

Spae, Joseph. *Shinto Man.* Tokyo: Oriens Institute, 1967.

Stiskin, Nahum. *The Looking Glass God: Shinto, Ying-Yang, and a Cosmology for Today.* Tokyo: Weatherhill, 1971.

Supreme Commander for the Allied Powers (SCAP). *Religions in Japan.* Washington, DC: SCAP, 1948.

Swanson, Paul L. "*Shugendo* and the Yoshino-Kumano Pilgrimage." *Monumenta Nipponica* 36, no. 1 (Spring 1981): 58–84.

Tani Shogou. *Shinto Genron* (Basic Shinto Theory). Kogakukan University Publication, 1995.

Teeuwen, Mark. "Attaining Union with the Gods: The Secret Books of Watarai Shinto." *Monumenta Nipponica* 48, no. 2 (1993): 225–246.

———. "Watarai Shinto: An Intellectual History of the Outer Shrine in Ise." Leiden: Research School CNWS, 1996.

———. "Poetry, Sake, and Acrimony: Arakida Hisaoyu and the Kokugaku Movement." *Monumenta Nipponica* 52, no. 3 (1997): 295–325.

Toda Yoshio. "Traditional Tendency of Shintoism and Its New Theoretical Developments." *Religious Studies in Japan* (1959): 229–232.

Tsuda Sokichi. *An Inquiry into the Japanese Mind as Mirrored in Literature.* Translated by Matsuda Fukumatsu. Tokyo: Japan Society for the Promotion of Science, 1970.

Tyler, Susan E. "Is there a Religion called Shinto?" *Rethinking Japan*, 11, no. 30 (1990): 261–270.

Ueda Kenji. "Contemporary Social Change and Shinto Tradition." *Japanese Journal of Religious Studies.* Proceedings of the 1978 Tokyo Meeting of the Conference Internationale de Sociologie Religieuse 6, no. 1–2 (March–June 1979): 70–79.

———. "The Monothetistic Tendency in Shinto Faith." *Acta Asiatica* (Toho Gakkai), no. 51 (February 1987): 77–95.

———. *Shinto Shingaku.* Tokyo: Jinja Shinposha, 1993.

Umehara Suyeji. "Ancient Mirrors and Their Relationship to Early Japanese Culture." *Acta Asiatica* no. 4 (1963): 70–79.

Underwood, A. C. *Shintoism: The Indigenous Religion of Japan.* London: Epworth Press, 1934.

Walthall, Anne. *The Weak Body of a Useless Woman: Matsuo Taseko and the Meiji Restoration.* Chicago: University of Chicago Press, 1998.

———. "Nativism As a Social Movement." In *Shinto in History.* Edited by John L. Breen and Mark Teeuwen. Honolulu: University of Hawai'i Press, 2000. 205–239.

Watanabe Yasutada. *Shinto Art: Ise and Izumo Shrines.* Tokyo: Weatherhill/ Heibonsha, 1974.

Wehmeyer, Ann. Kojiki-den, Book 1. Ithaca: Cornell University East Asia Program, 1997.

The World of Shinto. Tokyo: Bukkyo Dendo Kyokai, 1985.

Yamakage Motohisa. *Shinto: A Mirror Held up to the Cosmos.* Hammatsu: no date.

———. *The Essence of Shinto: Japan's Spiritual Heart.* Tokyo: Kodansha International, 2006.

Yamamoto Yukitaka. *The Kami Way.* Stockton, CA: Tsubaki Grand Shrine of America, 1985, revised 1999.

Yamashita Hideo. *Competitiveness and the Kami Way.* Aldershot: Avebury, 1996.

SHINTO MYTHOLOGY

Ashkenazi Michael. *Handbook of Japanese Mythology.* Oxford: Oxford University Press, 2008.

Anesaki Masaharu. *Japanese Mythology. The Mythology of All Races*, vol. 8. New York: Cooper Square Publishers, 1964.

Elisseeff, Serge. "The Mythology of Japan." In *Asiatic Mythology: A Detailed Description and Explanation of the Mythologies of All the Great Nations of Asia.* 1932.

Florenz, Karl. *Japanische Mythologie, Nihongi, Zeitalter der Gotter.* Tokyo: Druck der Hobunsha, 1901.

Hadland, David F. *Myths and Legends of Japan.* New York: T.Y. Crowell, 2007

Ishida Eiichiro. "Mother-Son Deities." *History of Religions* 4, no. 1 (Summer 1964): 30–52.

Isomae Juin'ichi. "Myth in Metamorphosis: Ancient and Medieval Visions of the Yamatotakeru Legend." *Monumenta Nipponica* 54 (1999): 361–385.

Kitagawa, Joseph M. "Prehistoric Background of Japanese Religion." *History of Religions* 2, no. 2 (Winter) 1963.

Kurosawa Kozo. "Myths and Tale Literature." *Japanese Journal of Religious Studies* 9, no. 2–3 (Religion and Literature in Japan). Guest editor W. Michael Kelsey (June–September 1982): 115–1215.

Neumann, Nelly. Das Umwandeln des Himmelsfpfeilers: Ein japanischer Mythos und seine kulturhistorische Einordnung. *Asian Folklore Studies* (Monograph 5). 1971.

Numazawa, Franz Kiichi. "Die Weltanfange in der japanischen Mythologie." *Internationale Schriftenreihe fur soziale und politishe Wissenschaften, Ethnologische Reihe*, vol. 2, Paris and Lucerne, 1946.

Obayashi Taryo. "Die Amaterasu-Mythe im Alten Japan und die Sonnenfinsternismythe in Sudostasien." *Ethnos* XXV (1960): 20–43.

———. "Origins of Japanese Mythology, Especially of the Myths of the Origin of Death." *Monumenta Nipponica* 25, *Folk Cultures of Japan and East Asia*. 1976.

———. "The Origins of Japanese Mythology. " *Acta Asiatica* (Toho Gakkai), no. 31 (1977).

———. "The Ancient Myths of Korea and Japan." *Acta Asiatica* (Toho Gakkai), no. 61 (February 1991): 68–82.

Roberts, Jeremy. *Japanese Mythology A to Z*. New York: Chelsea House Publications, 2003.

Satow, E. M. "The Mythology and Religious Worship of the Ancient Japanese." *Westminster and Foreign Quarterly Review* (1878): 25–57.

Saunders, E. Dale. "Japanese Mythology." In *Mythologies of the Ancient World*. Edited by Samuel Noah Kramer. Garden City, NY: Doubleday, 1961. 409–442.

Szczesniak, Boleslaw. "The *Sumu-Sanu* Myth." *Monumenta Nipponica* 1 (1945): 107–126.

Uemura Seiji. *Jimmu Tenno.* 1957.

Wheeler, Post. *The Sacred Scriptures of the Japanese.* New York: H. Schuman, 1952.

Yoshida Atsuhiko. "La Mythologie japonaise: essai d'interpretation structurale." *Revue de l'Histoire des Religions.* 160, 161, 163 (1961–1963).

THE JAPANESE CLASSICS AND POETRY

Aso Mizue. *Kakinomoto Hitomaro Ronko* (A Study in Kakinomoto Hitomaro). Tokyo: University of Tokyo, 1962.

Aston, W. G., trans. *Nihongi*. London: Longman and Green, 1905.

Bock, Felicia. *Engishiki.* (tr. Books VI–X), Tokyo: Sophia University, 1972.

Bonneau, Georges. *Le Monument poetique de Heian: le Kokinshu.* 3 vols. Librairie Orientaliste Paul Guenther, 1933–1935.

Brower, R. H., and Earl Miner. *Japanese Court Poetry.* Stanford, CA: Stanford University Press, 1961.

Chamberlain, Basil H. *Kojiki: Records of Ancient Matters.* Tokyo: Tuttle, 1982.

Honda, H. H. *The Man'yoshu.* Tokyo: Hokuseido Press, 1967.

Imbe Hironari, trans. *The Kogoshui: Gleanings from Ancient Stories.* Introduction by Genchi Kato. Tokyo: Meiji Japan Society, 1926.

Kato Genchi and Hikoshiro Hoshino. *The Kogoshui: Gleanings from Ancient Stories.* Tokyo: Meiji Japan Society, 1926.

Konishi Jin'ichi, Robert H. Brower, and Earl Miner. "Association and Progression: Principles of Integration in Anthologies and Sequences of Japanese Court Poetry." *Harvard Journal of Asiatic Studies* 21 (1958).

Levy, Ian Hideo. *The Ten Thousand Leaves: A Translation of the Man'yoshu, Japan's Premier Anthology of Classical Poetry.* Vol. 1. Princeton: Princeton University Press, 1981.

———. *Hitomaru and the Birth of Japanese Lyricism.* Princeton: Princeton University Press, 1984.

Miner, Earl. *An Introduction to Japanese Court Poetry.* Stanford: Stanford University Press, 1968.

———. "Toward a New Approach to Classical Japanese Poetics." Japan P.E.N. Club ed. *Studies in Japanese Culture.* Vol. 1. 1973.

Nakanishi Susumu. *Kakinomoto Hitomaro.* 1970.

Nippon Gakujutsu Shinkokai, trans. *The Man'yoshu: One Thousand Poems* Tokyo: 1940; reprinted, Tokyo: University of Tokyo Press, 1965.

Philippi, Donald L. *Kojiki.* Tokyo: Kokugakuin University Center for the Japanese Classics, 19.

———. *Norito.* (A New Translation of the Ancient Japanese Ritual Prayers). Tokyo: Kokugakuin University Center for the Japanese Classics, 1959.

Picken, Stuart D. B. *Shinto Meditations for Revering the Earth.* Berkeley: Stonebridge Press, 2002.

Pierson, J. L. *The Man'yoshu.* 20 vols. Leiden: E. J. Brill, 1929–1969.

———. *Selected Japanese Poems from the Man'yoshu.* Leiden: E. J. Brill, 1966.

Snellen J. B., trans. *Shoku Nihongi.* "Shoku Nihongi: Chronicles of Japan Continued from 697–779." *Transactions of the Asiatic Society of Japan,* Second Series, 11 (1934): 151–239 and 14 (1937): 209–279.

SHINTO *KAMI* AND CULTS

Anzu Motohiko. "The Concept of Kami." *Proceedings of the IXth International Congress for the History of Religions* (1962): 218–222.

Bender, Ross. "The Hachiman Cult and the Dokyo Incident." *Monumenta Nipponica* 31, no. 2 (Summer 1979): 125–153.

Bock, Felicia G. "The Rites of Renewal at Ise." *Monumenta Nipponica* 19, no. 1 (Spring 1974): 55–68.

Bohner, Hermann. "Massen-Nukemairi." *Monumenta Nipponica* 4 (1949): 486–496.

Buchanan, Daniel C. "Inari, Its Origin, Development and Nature." *Asiatic Society of Japan*, 12 (1935): 1–91.

———. "Some Mikuji of Fusmimi Inari Jinja." *Asiatic Society of Japan* 22 (1946): 518–535.

Deguchi Nobuyoshi. *Ise Daijingu Jin'iki* (A Record of Marvels at the Grand Shrine of Ise). Annotated and translated by Noman Havens. *Kokugakuin Daigaku Nihon Bunka Kenkyujo Kiyo* 74 (September 1994).

Earhart, H. Byron. *A Religious Study of the Mount Haguro Sect of Shugendo*. Tokyo: Sophia University, 1970.

Endo Masajumi. *Ise Shinto: Trajectories of Discourses on Time*. Master's Dissertation, University of California, Santa Barbara, Department of Religious Studies, 1990.

Evans, Ann L. *Shinro Norito: A Book of Prayers*. British Columbia: Matsuri Foundation, 2002.

Grapard, Allan G. "Institution, Ritual, and Ideology. The Twenty-two Shrine-Temple Multiplexes of Heian Period Japan." *History of Religions* 27 (3): 246–269.

———. "The Shinto of Yoshida Kanetomo." *Monumenta Nipponica* 47, no. 1 (Spring 1992): 27–58.

———. trans. *Yuiitsu Shinto Myobo Yoshu, Monumenta Nipponica* 47, no. 2 (Summer 1992): 137–161.

———. *The Protocols of the Gods: A Study of the Kasuga Cult in Japanese History*. Los Angeles: University of California Press, 1992.

Hammitzsch, H. *Yamato-hime no Mikoto Seiki. Bericht uber den Erdenwandel Ihrer Hochheit der Prinzessin Yamato. Eine Quelle zur Fruhgeschichte der Shinto-Religion*. Leipzig, 1937.

Holtom, D. C. "The Meaning of Kami." *Monumenta Nipponica* 3, no 1 (1940): 1–27; also 3, no. 2 (1940): 32–53; and 4, no. 2 (1941): 25–68.

Hori, Ichiro. "On the Concept of Hijiri (Holy Man)." *Numen* (1958).

Iwata, Kenji. "The Evolution of the *Kami* Cult." *Acta Asiatica* (Toho Gakkai), no. 61 (February 1991): 47–67.

Kanda, Christine G. *Shinzo: Hachiman Imagery and Its Development*. Boston: Harvard East Asian Monographs, no.119, 1985

Kawazoe, Noboru. "The Ise Shrine." *Japan Quarterly* 9, no. 3 (July–September, 1962): 285–292.

Kokugakuin University, Institute for Japanese Culture and Classics, Tokyo. Edited by Inoue Nobutaka. "Kami." In *Contemporary Papers in Japanese Religion* 4 (1998).

Kyburz, Josef A. "Le culte d'Ise au debut de l'ere Meiji." *Cipango* 7 (1998): 182–214.

Nagai, Shinichi. *Gods of Kumano.* Tokyo: Kodansha International, 1968.

Nelson, John K. *Enduring Identities: The Guise of Shinto in Contemporary Japan.* Ph.D. thesis, University of California, 1993.

———. *A Year in the Life of a Shinto Shrine.* Seattle: University of Washington Press, 1996.

Nishitakatsuji Nobusada. *Dazaifu Tenmagu.* Shrine Publication, 1982.

Numazawa, Franz Kiichi. "The Fertility Festival; at Toyota Shinto Shrine, Aichi Prefecture, Japan." *Acta Tropica,* supplement 16, no. 3 (1959): 197–217.

Sadler, A. L. *Diary of a Pilgrim to Ise.* Tokyo: Meiji Japan Society, 1940.

Satow, E. M. "The Shinto Shrines of Ise." *Transactions of the Asiatic Society of Japan* 1 (1874): 99–121.

Schwartz, W. L. "The Great Shrine of Idzumo." *Transactions of the Asiatic Society of Japan* 41, Part 4 (October 1913): 493–681.

Smyers, Karen A. "My Own Inari: Personals of the Deity in Inari Worship." *Japanese Journal of Religious Studies* 23, no. 1–2 (1996): 85–116.

———. "Inari Pilgrimages: Following One's Paths on the Mountain." *Japanese Journal of Religious Studies* 24, no. 3–4 (1997): 429–452.

———. *The Fox and the Jewel: Shared and Private Meanings in Contemporary Japanese Inari Worship.* Honolulu: University of Hawaii Press, 1999.

Teeuwen, Mark. *Watarai Shinto: An Intellectual History of the Outer Shrine of Ise.* Leiden: Research School of CNWS, 1996.

Thai, Sarah. *Rearanging the Landscape of the Gods: The Politics of a Pilgrimage Site in Japan, 1573–1912.* Chicago: University of Chicago Press, 2005.

Tyler, Royall. *The Miracles of the Kasuga Deity.* (Records of Civilization, Sources and Studies, no. 98). New York: Columbia University Press, 1990.

Tyler, Susan E. *The Cult of Kasuga Through its Art.* Ann Arbor: University of Michigan, 1992.

Vos, Frits. *A Study of the Ise Monogatari with the Text According to the Den-Teika-hippon and an Annotated Translation.* 2 vols. The Hague: Mouton & Co., 1957.

KOKUGAKU (NATIONAL LEARING) SHINTO AND EDO PERIOD THOUGHT

Burns, Susan Lynn. "Contesting Exegesis: Visions of the Subject and the Social in Tokugawa National Learning." Unpublished Ph.D. dissertation, University of Chicago, 1994.

Brownlee, John. "The Jeweled Comb-Box: Motoori Norinaga's *Tamakushige.*" *Monumenta Nipponica* 43 (1988) 35–61.

Devine, Richard. "Hirata Atsutane and Christian Sources." *Monumenta Nipponica* (Spring) 1981: 37–54.

Dumoulin, Heinrich. *Kamo Mabuchi (1697–1768): Ein Beitrag zur japanischen Religions—und Geistesgeschichte.* Tokyo: Sophia University Press, 1943.

———. "Kamo Mabuchi: Kokuiko—Gedanken über den 'Sinn des landes.'" *Monumenta Nipponica* 2 (1946): 165–192.

———. "Kamo Mabuchis Erklarung des Norito zum Toshigoi-no-matsuri." *Monumenta Nipponica* 12 (1957): 121–156, 269–298.

Dumoulin, Heinrich, Hans Stotle, and William Schiffer. "Die Entwicklung der Kokugaku." *Monumenta Nipponica* 2 (1957): 140–164.

Fessler, Susanna. "The Nature of the Kami: Ueda Akinari and Tandai Shoshin Roku." *Monumenta Nipponica* 51 (1996): 1–16.

Grapard, Alan G. "Lotus in the Mountain, Mountain in the Lotus: *Rokugo Kaizan Nimmon Daibosatsu Hongi*." *Monumenta Nipponica* 41 (1986): 21–50.

Hammitzsch, Horst. "Kangaku und Kokugaku." *Monumenta Nipponica* 2 (1946): 1–23.

———. "Aizawa Seishisai (1782–1863) und sein Werk Shinron." *Monumenta Nipponica* 3 (1948): 61–74.

———. "Shingaku." *Monumenta Nipponica* 4 (1949): 1–32.

Harootunian, Harry D. *Things Seen and Unseen: Discourse and Ideology in Tokugawa Nativism.* Chicago: University of Chicago Press, 1988.

Hirata Atsutane. *Taido Wakumon: Es fragte einer nach dem Grossen Weg.* Translated by Wilhelm Schiffer. *Monumenta Nipponica* 2 (1946): 212–236.

Inoue Minoru. *Kamo no Mabuchi no gakumon* (The Study of Kamo no Mabuchi). Tokyo: 1943.

Ishibashi T., and Heinrich Dumoulin. "Yuiitsu-Shinto Myobu-yoshu: Lehrabriss das Yuitisu-Shinto." *Monumenta Nipponica* 3 (1948): 182–239.

Kamo no Mabuchi Zenshu (The Complete Works of Kamo no Mabuchi, 25 Vols. Zoku Gunsho Ruiji Kansekai, 1977–).

Kato Genchi. "The Shinto Studies of Jiun, the Buddhist Priest, and Moto-ori, the Shinto Savant." *Monumenta Nipponica* 1 (1945): 301–316.

Kobayashi Hideo. *Motoori Norinaga.* Tokyo: Shimehosa, 1977.

Marra, Michele. "Nativist Hermeneutics: The Interpretive Strategies of Motoori Norinaga and Fujitani Mitsue." *Japan Review* 10 (1985): 17–52.

Matsumoto Sannosuke. *Kokugaku seiji shiso no kenkyu* (A Study in the Political Thought of the National Learning Movement). 1957.

Matsumoto Shigeru. *Motoori Norinaga.* Cambridge, MA: Harvard University Press, 1970.

McNally, Mark Thomas. "Phantom History: Hirata Atsutane and Tokugawa Nativism." Unpublished Ph.D. dissertation, University of California, 1998.

Motoori Norinaga. "Naobi no Mitama: Geist der Erneuerung." Translated by Hand Stolte. *Monumenta Nipponica* 2 (1946): 193–211.

Nakanishi Masayuki. "Motoori Norinaga to Ise Jingu: Shiso Keisei to Fudo" (Mootoori Norinaga and the Grand Shrines of Ise: The Development of

Thought and Climate). *Nihon no Tenbo*, 6 *Motoori Norinaga no Sekai*. To-kyo: Akatsuki Shobo, 1978.

Ng, Wai-ming. "The I Ching in the Shinto Thought of Tokugawa Japan." *Philosophy East and West* 48, no. 4 (1998): 568–591.

Nishimura Sey. "First Steps into the Mountains: Motoori Norinaga's Uiyamabumi." *Monumenta Nipponica* 42 (1987): 449–493.

———. "The Way of the Gods: Motoori Norinaga's *Naobi on Mitama*," *Monumenta Nipponica* 46 (1991): 21–41.

Nosco, Peter. "Keichū (1640–1701): Forerunner of National Learning." *Asian Thought and Society* 5, no. 15 (1980): 237–252.

———. "Man'yōshū Studies in Tokugawa Japan." Transactions of the Asiatic Society of Japan, Series 1 (1986): 109–146.

———. "Masuho Zankō (1655–1742): A Shinto Popularizer between Nativism and National Learning." In *Confucianism and Tokugawa Culture*. Edited by Peter Nosco. Honolulu: University of Hawai'i Press, 1984. 106–187.

———. "Nature, Invention, and National Learning: The 'Kokka hachiron' Controversy, 1742–46." *Harvard Journal of Asiatic Studies* 41, no. 1 (1981): 75–91.

———. *Remembering Paradise: Nativism and Nostalgia in Eighteenth-Century Japan*. Cambridge, MA: Council on East Asian Studies, Harvard University, 1990.

———. "Rethinking Tokugawa Thought." In *Rethinking Japan*, Vol. I: *Literature, Visual Arts, and Linguistics*. Edited by Adriana Boscaro, Franco Gatti, and Massimo Raveri et al. New York: St. Martin's Press, 1990. 304–312.

Reitz, Karl. "Die Feuerberuhigungszeremonie das Shinto (Chinka-sai)." *Monumenta Nipponica* 3 (1948): 109–126.

Saegusa Tasutaka. *Kamo no Mabuchi*. Tokyo: Yukawa Kobunsha, 962.

Tajiri Yuichiro. "Medieval and Early Modern Shinto Reconsidered." *Monumenta Nipponica* 53 (1998): 375–382.

Teeuwen, Mark. "Attaining Union with the Gods: The Secret Books of Watarai Shinto." *Monumenta Nipponica* 48 (1993): 225–245.

———. Poetry, Sake, and Acrimony: Arikada Hisaoyu and the Kokugaku Movement." *Monumenta Nipponica* 52 (1997): 295–326.

———. "State Shinto: An 'Independent Religion'?" *Monumenta Nipponica* 54 (1999): 111–121.

Yamamoto Yoshimasa. *Kamo no Mabuchi Ron* (Discussion of Kamo no Mabuchi). 1963.

JAPAN'S EMPEROR SYSTEM AND THE DAIJOSAI

Bock, Felicia G. "The Enthronement Rites: The Text of the *Engishiki*, 927." *Monumenta Nipponica* 45 (1990): 307–337.

————. "The Great Feast of the Enthronement." *Monumenta Nipponica* 45 (1990): 27–38.

Brownlee, John S. *Japanese Historians and the National Myths, 1600–1945: The Age of the Gods and Emperor Jimmu.* Vancouver: University of British Columbia, 1999.

Earl, David. *Emperor and Nation in Japan: Political Thinkers in the Tokugawa Period.* Seattle: University of Washington Press, 1974.

Ellwood, Robert S. *The Feast of Kingship: Accession Ceremonies in Ancient Japan.* Tokyo: Sophia University Press, 1973.

Gluck, Carol N. *Japan's Modern Myth: Ideology in the late Meiji Period.* Princeton, NJ: Princeton University Press, 1985.

Hall, John Whitney. "A Monarch for Modern Japan." In *Political Development of Modern Japan.* Edited by Robert E. Ward. Princeton, NJ: Princeton University Press, 1968.

Holtom, D. C. *The Japanese Enthronement Ceremonies.* Tokyo: Kyo Bun Kwan, 1928.

Inoue Kiyoshi. *Tenno no Senso Sekinin* (The Emperor's War Responsibility). Tokyo: Akaski Shioten, 1975.

Ishida Takeshi. "Popular Attitudes toward the Japanese Emperor." *Asian Survey* 11, no. 2 (April 1956): 29–39.

Jansen, Marius B. "Monarchy and Modernization in Modern Japan." *Journal of Asian Studies* 36, no. 4 (1977).

Japan Christian Quarterly. Daijosai. Summer (56.3) and Fall (56.4), 1990.

Journal of Japanese Religions. Special edition, "The Emperor System and Religion in Japan." 17.2–3 (June–September): 1990.

Kawai Kazuo. "The Divinity of the Japanese Emperor: Political and Psychological Problems." *Political Science* 10, no. 2 (1958).

Kurabayashi Masatsugu. *Tenno no Matsuri: Daijosai Shinron* (The Imperial Festival: A New Discussion of the Daijosai). Tokyo: Daishi Houki Shuppan, 1984.

Kurihara Akira. *"Nihon Minzoku Shukyo to shite No Tennosei."* *Sekei* 526, no. 4 (1989): 92–108. (Japanese Folk Religion and the Emperor System). Translated by Edmund R. Skrzypczakr as "Emperor System as Japanese National Religion: The Emperor System Module in Everyday Consciousness." In *Japanese Journal of Religious Studies* 17, no. 2–3 (June–September 1990): 315–326.

Macé, François. "Les funerailles des souverains japonais." Cahiers d'Extreme-Asie 4 (1988): 157–165.

Mayumi Tsunetada. *Nihon no Matsuri to Daijosai* (Japanese Festivals and the Daijosai). Osaka: Toki Shobo, 1990.

Mosley, Leonard. *Hirohito. Emperor of Japan.* Englewood Cliffs, NJ: Prentice-Hall, 1966.

Nosco, Peter, ed. "The Emperor System and Religion in Japan." *Japanese Journal of Religions* 17, no. 2–3 (June–September 1990). This text is a collection of articles about the imperial accession rites and the emperor system, including some valuable translated papers by Japanese scholars.

Okubo Genji. *Problems of the Emperor System in Post-War Japan.* Tokyo: Japan Institute of Pacific Studies International Publishing Co., 1948.

Origuchi Shinobu. *The True Meaning of the Daijosai, Complete Works.* 3 vols. Tokyo: Chuo Koronsha, 1928.

Osanaga Kanroji. *Hirohito: An Intimate Portrait of the Japanese Emperor.* 1975.

Picken, Stuart D. B. "The Imperial Systems in Traditional China and Japan: A Comparative Analysis of Contrasting Political Philsophies and Their Contemporary Significance." *Journal of Asian Philosophy* 7, no 2 (1997): 109–121.

Ponsonby-Fane, R. A. B. *History of the Imperial House of Japan.* Kyoto: Ponsonby Memorial Society, 1959.

———. *Sovereign and Subject.* Kyoto: Ponsonby Memorial Society, 1960.

Sakurai Katsunoshin. "Tenno to Sokukgirei." *Nihon Shintoron* (Studies in Japanese Shinto, with Nishikawa Masatani and Sonoda Minoru). Tokyo: Gakuseisha, 1990.

Sansom, Sir George B. "The Imperial Edicts in the Shoku Nihongi (700–790 AD)." *Transactions of the Asiatic Society of Japan,* Second Series, I (1924): 5–39.

Takamori Akinori. *Tenno to Tami no Daijosai* (The Emperor and the People's Daijosai). Tokyo: Tentensha, 1990.

Takeda Kiyoko. *Tennosei Shiso to Kyoiku* (The Intellectual History of the Imperial System and Education). 1964.

Titus, David A. *Palace and Politics in Prewar Japan.* New York: Columbia University Press, 1974.

———. "The Making of the 'Symbol Emperor System' in Postwar Japan." *Modern Asian Studies* 14, no. 4 (1980).

Togashi Junji. *Koshitsu Jiten* (A Dictionary of the Imperial Household). 1965.

Varley, H. Paul. *Imperial Restoration in Medieval Japan.* New York: Columbia University Press, 1971.

———. *Chronicles of Gods and Sovereigns: Jinno Shotoki of Kitabatake Chikafusa.* New York: Columbia University Press, 1980.

Yamazaki Tansho. *Tennosei no Kenkyu* (Studies in the Imperial System). 1959.

SHINTO, NATIONALISM, AND POLITICS

Breen, John. *Yasukuni, the War Dead, and Japan's Struggle for the Past.* CA and New York: University Presses of California, Columbia, and Princeton, 2008.

Brownlee, John S. *Political Thought in Japanese Historical Writing from Kojiki 712 to Tokushi Yoron 1712.* Waterloo, Ontario: Wildrid Laurier Press, 1991.

Fridell, Wilbur. *Japanese Shrine Mergers 1906–1912.* Tokyo: Sophia University, 1973.

Hardacre, Helen. *Shinto and the State: 1869–1989.* Princeton, NJ: Princeton University Press, 1989.

Holtom, D. C. *Modern Japan and Shinto Nationalism.* Chicago: University of Chicago Press, 1943.

International Institute for the Study of Religions. *Religion and State in Japan.* Bulletin no. 7, Tokyo, 1959.

International Shinto Foundation, Tokyo. "State Shinto on Scrutiny from Japan, Asia, and Europe." Newsletter no. 5 (July 1999).

Morris, Ivan. *Nationalism and the Right Wing in Japan: A Study of Post-War Trends.* Westport, CT: Greenwood Press, 1974, 1960.

Safier, Joshua. *Yasukuni Shrine and the Constraints on the Discourses of Nationalism in Twentieth Century Japan.* Master's Thesis, University of Kansas, 1997.

Sakamoto Koremaru. "Religion and State in the Early Meiji Period, 1868–1912." *Acta Asiatica* (Toho Gakkai), no. 51 (February 1987): 42–61.

Satomi, K. *Japanese Civilization: Its Significance and Realization, Nichirenism and the Japanese National Principles.* London: Kegan Paul, Trench, Trubner, 1923.

Teeuwen, Mark. "State Shinto: An 'Independent Religion'?" *Monumenta Nipponica* 54 (1999): 111–121.

Yanagihara Tadao. *Religion and Democracy in Modern Japan.* Tokyo: Japan Institute of Pacific Studies, 1948.

SHINTO IN THE POSTWAR PERIOD

Ariga Teysutaro. "Contemporary Apologetics of Shinto." Missionary Research Library, *Occasional Bulletin* 5, no. 4 (April 1954).

Aschoff, Angelus. *Catholicism and Shinto in Japan.* Missionary Academia Studies 4, no. 3. New York, 1946.

Creemers, Wilhelmus. *Shrine Shinto after World War II.* Leiden: E. J. Brill, 1968.

Holtom, D. C. "Shinto in the Postwar World." *Far Eastern Survey* no. 14 (February 14, 1945): 29–33.

International Institute for the Study of Religions. *Religion and Modern Life.* Bulletin no. 5 Part II, Tokyo, 1958.

Kitagawa, Joseph M. "The Contemporary Religious Situation in Japan." *Japanese Religions* 2, no. 2–3 (May 1961): 24–42.

Miyagawa Munenori. "The Status Quo of Shinto Shrines." *The Shinto Bulletin* I (March 1953): 4–6.

Woodward, William P. "The Religious Juridical Persons Law," *Contemporary Japan*, ed. The Foreign Affairs Association of Japan, 1–84. Tokyo: Tuttle, 1960.

SHINTO ART AND ARCHITECTURE

Akiyama Aisaburo. *Shinto and its Architecture*. Kyoto: Kyoto Tourist Association, 1936.

Ienaga Saburo. *Painting in the Yamato Style*. Translated by John M. Shields. New York: Weatherhill, 1973.

Ito Nobuo. "Shinto Architecture." In *Kodansha Encyclopaedia of Japan*. Tokyo: Kodansha International, 1985. 132–134.

Iwai Hiromi. *Koema* (Small Ema). 1966.

———. *Ema*. 1974.

Kageyama Haruki. *The Arts of Shinto*. Tokyo: Weatherhill/Shibundo, 1973.

———. *Shinto Arts: Nature Gods and Man in Japan*. Translated by Christine G. Kanda. New York: Weatherhill, 1976.

Kanda, Christine G. "Shinto Art." *Kodansha Encyclopaedia of Japan*, 134–136. Tokyo: Kodansha International, 1985.

Kawada Sadamu. *Ema (Nihon no Bijutsu)*. Japanese Art, vol. 92, January 1974.

Kidder, J. Edward Jr. *Early Japanese Art: The Great Tombs and their Treasures*. Princeton: Van Nostrand, 1964.

Lokesh, Chandra. *The Esoteric Iconography of Japanese Mandalas*. New Delhi: Sharada Roni, 1971.

Okudaira Hideo. *Narrative Picture Scrolls*. Translated by Elizabeth ten Grotenhuis. New York: Weatherhill, 1973.

Paine, R. T. and A. Soper. *The Art and Architecture of Japan*. Baltimore: Penguin Books, 1974.

Shinshu Nihon Emakimono Zenshu (Complete Collection of Japanese Emakimono). Tokyo: Kadaokawa Shoten, 1975–1979.

Tange Kenzo and Kawazoe Noboru. *Ise: Prototype of Japanese Architecture*. Cambridge, MA: MIT Press, 1965.

SHINTO FESTIVALS, RITUALS, AND NENCHU-GYO-JI

Ashenzaki, Michael. *Matsuri: Festivals of a Japanese Town*. Honolulu: University of Hawai'i Press, 1993.

Blacker, Carmen. "The Religious Traveller in the Edo Period." *Modern Asian Studies* 18, no. 4 (1984).

Boyd, James W. and Ron G. Williams. "Artful Means: An Aesthetic View of Shinto Ritual Practice." *Journal of Ritual Studies* 13, no. 1 (Summer 1999): 37–52.

Erskine, William H. *Japanese Festival and Calendar*. Tokyo, 1933.

Evans, Ann L. *Shinto Norito: A Book of Prayers*. British Columbia: Matsuri Foundation, 2002.

Florenz, Karl. "Ancient Japanese Rituals." *Transactions of the Asiatic Society of Japan* 27, Part 1 (1899): 1–112.

Haga Hideo. *Japanese Folk Festivals Illustrated.* Tokyo: Miura Printing Company, 1970.

Harada Toshiaki. "The Development of Matsuri." In *Philosophical Studies of Japan,* vol. 2. Tokyo: Japanese National Commission for UNESCO, 1961.

Inoue Nobutaka, Komoto Mitsugi, Nakamaki Hirochika, Shioya Masunori, Uno Masato, and Yamazaki Yoshie. "A Festival with Anonymous Kami: The Kobe Matsuri." *Journal of Japanese Religious Studies,* Proceedings of the 1978 Tokyo Meeting of the Conference Internationale de Sociologie Religieuse 6, no. 1–2 (March–June 1979): 163–165.

Institute for Japanese Culture and Classics, Kokugakuin University, Tokyo, ed. Iooe Nobutaka, "Matsuri." In *Contemporary Papers in Japanese Religion* 1 (1991).

Iwamoto Tokuichi. *Shinto saishi no kenkyu* (Research into Japanese Rituals), 1970.

———. "Shinto Rites." *Kodansha Encyclopaedia of Japan,* 136–139. Tokyo: Kodansha International, 1985.

Jinja Honcho. *Jinja Shinto Shrines and Festivals.* Tokyo, 1970.

Kato Genchi. "The Naoe Matsuri." *Transactions of the Asiatic Society of Japan,* Second Series, 8 (December 1931): 113–136.

Kreiner, Josef. *Die Kulturorganisation des Japanischen Dorfes.* Wien: W. Braumuller, 1969.

Kurabayashi Masatsugu. *Matsuri no Kozo* (The Structure of the Festival). 1975.

Matsumoto, Nobuhiro. "Notes on the Deity Festival of Yamatano, Japan." *Southwestern Journal of Anthropology* (Spring 1949): 62–77.

Nishitsunoi Masayoshi. *Nenchu gyoji jiten* (A Dictionary of the Cycle of Yearly Rituals). 1958.

Numazawa, Franz Kiichi. "The Fertility Festival at Toyota Shinto Shrine, Aichi Prefecture, Japan." *Acta Tropica,* Supplement XVI, no. 3 (1959): 197–217.

Okada Shoji. "The Development of State Ritual in Ancient Japan." *Acta Asiatica* (Toho Gakkai), no. 51 (February 1987): 22–41.

O'Neill, P. G. "The Special Ksuga Wakamiya Festival of 1349." *Monumenta Nipponica* (1959): 408–428.

Picken, Stuart D. B. *Shinto Meditations for Revering the Earth.* Berkeley: Stonebridge Press, 2002.

Sakurai Tokutaro. *Japanese Festivals: Annual Rites and Observances.* Tokyo: Tokyo Society for Educational Information Press, 1971.

Satow, E. M. "Ancient Japanese Rituals." *Transactions of the Asiatic Society of Japan,* 7 (1879): 97–132 and 9 (1881): 182–211.

Seced, Susan. *Women of the Sacred Groves: Divine Priestesses of Okinawa.* Oxford: Oxford University Press, 1999.

Yanagita Kunio. *Nihon no Matsuri* (The Festivals of Japan), vol. 10 of *Teihon Yangita Kunioshu*, 1962–71.

BUGAKU, GAGAKU, KAGURA, AND NOH

Averbuch, Irit. *The Gods Come Dancing: A Study of the Ritual Dance of Yamabushi Kagura*. Ithaca, NY: Cornell University East Asian Series, 1995.

Blau, Hagen. *Sarugaku und Shushi, Beitrage zur Ausbildung dramatischer Elemente in weltlichen und religiosen Volkstheater der Heian-Zeit unter besondere Breucksichtigung seiner sozialen Grundlagen* (1966).

Fish, David Lee. "'Edo Sato Kagura': Ritual, Drama, Farce and Music in a Pre-Modern Shinto Theatrical." Unpublished Ph.D. dissertation, University of Michigan, 1994.

Griolet, Pascal. "L'orthographe du japonais et les 'études nationales.'" *Cipango* 3 (1994): 7–36.

Garfias, Robert. *Gagaku: The Music and Dances of the Japanese Imperial Household.* New York: New York Theater Arts Books, 1959.

Gundert, Wilhelm. *Der Shintoismus im Japanischen No-Drama.* Tokyo: Verlag der Deutschen gesellschaft fur nature- und volkerkunde Ostasiens, 1926.

Hincks, M. A. *The Japanese Dance.* London: Heinemann, 1910.

Hoff, Frank. "The 'Evocation' and 'Blessing' of Okina: A performance of Ritual Kagura." *Alcheringa Ethnopoetics* 3, no. 1 (1977).

———. "Shinto and the Performing Arts." *Song, Dance Storytelling: Aspects of the Performing Arts in Japan.* Ithaca, NY: Cornell University East Asian Papers, 15, 1978.

———. *Song, Dance, Storytelling: Aspects of the Performing Arts in Japan.* Ithaca, NY: Cornell University East Asian Papers, 1978.

Honda Yasuji. "Yamabushi Kagura and Bangaku Performance in the Japanese Middle Ages and Folk Performance Today." *Educational Theatre Journal* 26, no. 2 (1974).

Keene, Donald. *No: The Classical Theater of Japan.* Tokyo: Kobunsha International, 1966.

Muller, Gerhild. *Kagura: die Lieder der Kagura am Naishidokoro.* Wiesbaden: Harrasowitz 1971.

Nihon Minzoku Geino Jiten (Dictionary of Japanese Folk Entertaiment Arts). Tokyo: Daiichi Hokui, 1966.

O'Neill, P. G. *Early No Drama, Its Background, Character and Development, 1300–1450.* London, 1959.

Picken, Stuart D. B. "Myth, Ritual and Drama: The Japanese Paradigm. Paper presented at the Center for Hellenic Studies Colloquium, "From Ritual to Drama." Washington DC, August 15–20, 2000.

Turner, Victor. "Frame, Flow and Reflection: Ritual and Drama as Public Liminality." *Japanese Journal of Religious Studies* 6, no. 4 (December 1979): 465–499.

SHINTO AND FOLK RELIGION

Blacker, Carmen. *The Catalpa Bow.* London: Allen & Unwin, 1975.
Buckley, Edmund. *Phallicism in Japan.* Chicago: University of Chicago Press, 1895.
Casal, U. A. "The Goblin, Fox and Badger and Other Witch Animals of Japan." *Folklore Studies* 18 (1959): 1–94.
Dorson, Richard M. *Folk Legends of Japan.* Rutland, VT: Tuttle, 1962.
———. *Studies in Japanese Folklore.* Bloomington: Indiana University Press, 1963.
Eder, Matthias. "Figurliche Darstellungen in der japanischen Volkreligion." *Foklore Studies* 10 (1951): 197–280.
———. "Die 'Reisseele' in Japan und Korea." *Folklore Studies* 14 (1955): 215–244.
———. "Familie, Sippe, Clan und Ahnenverehrung in Japan." *Anthropos* 52 (1957): 813–840.
———. "Shamanismus in Japan." *Paideuma* 7, book 7 (1958): 367–380.
Embree, John F. "Some Social Functions of Religion in Rural Japan." *American Journal of Sociology* 47, no. 2 (1941): 184–189.
Fairchild, William P. "Shamanism in Japan." *Folklore Studies* 21 (1962): 1–122.
Fujitani Toshio. *Okagemairi to Ee-ja-ni-ka* (Okagemari and the Eeejanaika Movement) Iwanami Shinsho, 680. Tokyo: Iwanami Shoten, 1968.
Hirano Toshimasa. "Aruge Kizaaemon: The Household, the Ancestors, and the Tutelary Deities." *Japanese Journal of Religious Studies* 7, no. 2–3 (June–September 1980): 144–166.
Holtom, D. C. "Some Notes on Japanese Tree Worship." *Transactions of the Asiatic Society of Japan*, Second Series, 8 (December 1931): 1–19.
Hori Ichiro. "Mountains and Their Importance for the Idea of the Other World in Japanese Folk Religion." *Japanese Religions* 6, no. 1 (August 1966): 1–23.
———. *Folk Religion in Japan: Continuity and Change.* Chicago: University of Chicago Press, 1968.
———. *Nihon no shamanizumu.* Tokyo: Miraisha, 1971.
Howell, Richard W. "The Classification and Description of Ainu Folklore." *American Journal of Sociology* 64, no. 254 (1951): 361–369.
Ishida Eiichiro. "The Kappa Legend." *Folklore Studies* 9 (1950): 1–152.
Kato Genchi. "Japanese Phallicism." *Transactions of the Asiatic Society of Japan*, I (Supplement), 1924.

Kindaichi Kyosuke. *Ainu Life and Legends*. Tokyo: Tokyo Tourist Board, 1941.

Kokugakuin University, Institute for Japanese Culture and Classics, Tokyo, ed. Inoue Nobutaka, "Folk Beliefs in Modern Japan." In *Contemporary Papers in Japanese Religion* 3, 1996.

Lowe, Michael and Carmen Blacker, eds. *Divination and Oracles*. London: Allen & Unwin, 1981.

McAlpine, Helen with William McAlpine. *Tales from Japan* (Oxford Myths and Legends). Oxford: Oxford University Press, 1958.

Mayer, Fanny Hagin. "Religious Concepts in the Japanese Folk Tale." *Japanese Journal of Religious Studies* 1, no. 1 (March 1974): 73–101.

Miyake Hitoshi. "Folk Religion." In *Japanese Religion*. Edited by Hori Ichiro. 1972.

Mori Koichi. "Yanagita Kunio: An Interpretative Study." *Japanese Journal of Religious Studies* 7, no. 2–3 (June–September 1980): 83–115.

Nakamura Kyoko. "Revelatory Experience in the Female Life Cycle: A Biographical Study of Women Religionists in Modern Japan." *Japanese Journal of Religious Studies* 8, no. 3–4 (September–December 1981): 187–205.

Neumann, Nelly. "Yama no Kami—Die Japanische Berggotheit." *Folklore Studies* 22 (1963): 133–366.

Norbeck, Edward. "Yakudoshi: A Japanese Complex of Supernaturalistic Beliefs." *Southwestern Journal of Anthropology* 8 (Autumn 1952): 269–185.

Opler, Moris E. "Japanese Folk Beliefs Concerning the Snake." *Southwestern Journal of Anthropology* 1 (1945): 249–259.

———. "Japanese Folk Beliefs Concerning the Cat." *Washington Academy of Science Journal* 39 (1945): 269–76.

Revon, Michel. "Ancestor Worship and the Cult of the Dead (Japanese)." In *Encyclopaedia of Religion and Ethics,* vol. 1. Edited by James Hastings, Edinburgh: T & T Clark, 1928. 455–547.

Seki Keigo. *Folk Tales of Japan*. Chicago: University of Chicago Press, 1963.

Tyler, Royall. *Japanese Tales* (Pantheon Fairy Tale and Folklore Library). New York: Random House, 2006.

Visser, M. W. de. "The Tengu." *Transactions of the Asiatic Society of Japan* 36, no. 2 (1908).

Yanagita Kunio. *Minzogaku jiten* (Dictionary of Folklore). 1951.

———. *Japanese Folk Tales*, trans. Fanny Mayer. Tokyo: News Service, 1958.

SHINTO, TAOISM, CONFUCIANISM, AND CHINESE STUDIES

Bock, Felicia G. *Classical Learning and Taoist Practices in Early Japan*. Temple: Arizona State University, 1985.

Boot, W. J. *The Adoption and Adaptation of Neo-Confucianism in Japan: The Role of Fujiwara Seika and Hayashi Razan*. University of Leiden Dissertation, 1982.

Fisher, Galen M. "The Life and Teaching of Nakae Toju, The Sage of Omi." *Transactions of the Asiatic Society of Japan*, vol. 36 (1908).

————. "Kumazawa Banzan, His Life and Ideas." *Transactions of the Asiatic Society of Japan*, Second Series, 16 (1938).

————. Kumazawa Banzan. *Daigaku Wakumon*. tr. as "Daigaku Wakumon: A Discussion of Public Questions in the Light of the Great Learning." *Transactions of the Asiatic Society of Japan*, Second Series, 16 (1938).

Forte, Antonino. "Some Characteristics of Buddhism (Chinese) in East Asia." Seoul, Korea: Institute of Humanistic Sciences and Korean Society of Taoist Research, Symposium, October 1986.

Fukui Fuminasa. "The History of Taoist Studies in Japan and Some Related Issues." *Acta Asiatica* (Toho Gakkai), no. 68 (February 1995): 1–18.

Fung Yu-lan. *Short History of Chinese Philosophy*. New York: Free Press, 1966.

Hayashi Razan. *Hayashi Razan Bunshu* (Kyoto Shisekikai), 1918–19.

————. *Hayashi Razan Shishu* (Kyoto Shisekikai, 1920–21).

Isao Hori, *Hayashi Razan*. (Vol. 18 of a collection of famous thinkers), Yoshikawa Kobun Kan, 1964.

Kitagawa, Joseph M., "One of the Many Faces of China: Maoism as a Quasi-Religion." *Japanese Journal of Religious Studies* 1, no. 2–3 (March 1974): 125–141.

Kobayashi Masayoshi. "The Establishment of the Taoist Religion (*Tao-chiao*) and its Structure." *Acta Asiatica* (Toho Gakkai), no. 68 (February 1995): 19–36.

Maeda Shigeki. "The Evolution of the Way of the Celestial Master: Its Early View of Divinities." *Acta Asiatica* (Toho Gakkai), no. 68 (February 1995): 54–68.

Maruyama Hiroshi. "The Historical Traditions of Contemporary Taoist Ritual." *Acta Asiatica* (Toho Gakkai), no. 68 (February 1995): 84–104.

Nivison, David S., and Arthur Wright, eds. *Confucianism in Action*. Stanford, CA: Stanford University Press, 1959.

Oldstone-Moore, Jennifer. *Confucianism*. New York: Oxford University Press, 2002.

————. *Taoism*. New York: Oxford University Press, 2003.

Ooms, H. "'Primeval Chaos' and 'Mental Void' in Early Tokugawa Ideology: Fujiwara Seika, Suzuki Shosan and Yamazaki Ansai." *Japanese Journal of Religious Studies* 13, no. 4 (1986).

Ozaki Masaharu. "The History of the Evolution of Taoist Scriptures." *Acta Asiatica* (Toho Gakkai), no. 68 (February 1995): 37–53.

Smith, Warren W., Jr. *Confucianism in Contemporary Japan: A Study of Conservatism in Japanese Intellectual History.* Tokyo: Hokuseido Press, 1959.

Yamada Toshiaki. "The Evolution of Taoist Ritual: K'ou Ch'ienchih and Lu Hsiu-ching." *Acta Asiatica* (Toho Gakkai), no. 68 (February 1995): 69–83.

Yang, Lihui. *Handbook of Chinese Mythology.* Oxford: Oxford University Press, 2005.

SECT SHINTO AND THE NEW RELIGIONS

Akaike Noriaki. "The Ontake Cult Association and Local Society: The Case of the Owari—Mikawa Region in Central Japan." *Japanese Journal of Religious Studies* 8, no. 1–2 (March–June 1981): 51–82.

Ariga Teysutaro. "The So-called 'Newly-Arisen Sects' in Japan." Missionary Research Library, *Occasional Bulletin* 5, no. 4 (March 1954).

Bairy, Maurice A. *Japans Neue Religionen in der Nachkriegzeit.* Bonn, 1959.

Doerner, David L. "Comparative Analysis of Life after Death in Folk Shinto and Christianity." *Japanese Journal of Religious Studies* 4, no. 2–3 (June–September 1987): 151–182.

Earhart, Byron (Ben Kingsley, reader). *Shinto & Japanese New Religions* (Audio Series: Religions, Scriptures and Spirituality). Knowledge Products, 2006.

Earhart, H. Byron. *The New Religions of Japan: A Bibliography of Western-Language Materials.* Tokyo: Sophia University, 1975.

———. "Gendatsukai: One Life History and its Significance for Interpreting Japanese New Religions." *Japanese Journal of Religious Studies* 7, no. 2–3 (June–September 1980): 227–257.

———. "New Religions for Old." *Monumenta Nipponica* 36 (1981): 328–334.

Fujieda Masakazu. "The Church of World Messianity." *Contemporary Religions in Japan* 1, no. 4 (December 1960): 24–34.

Hambrick, Charles H. "Tradition and Modernity in the New Religious Movement Structure." *Japanese Journal of Religious Studies* 1, no. 2–3 (1973): 183–197.

Hammer, Raymond. *Japan's Religious Ferment.* New York: Oxford University Press, 1962.

Iwamoto Tokuichi. "Present State of Sectarian Shinto." *Research Papers*, IXth International Congress for the History of Religions, Tokyo, 1958.

Koepping, Klaus-Peter. "Ideologies and New Religious Movements: The Case of Shinreikyō and its Doctrines in Comparative Perspective." *Japanese Journal of Religious Studies* 4, no. 2–3 (June–September 1977): 103–149.

Kokugakuin University, Institute for Japanese Culture and Classics, Tokyo, ed. Inoue Nobutaka. "New Religions." In *Contemporary Papers in Japanese Religions* 2 (1992).

MacFarland, H. Neill. "The New Religions of Japan." *The Perkins School of Theology Journal* 12, no. 1 (Fall 1958): 3–21.
————. *The Rush Hour of the Gods.* New York: Macmillan, 1967.
Morioka Kiyomi. "The Institutionalization of a New Religious Movement." *Japanese Journal of Religious Studies*, Proceedings of the 1978 Tokyo Meeting of the Conference Internationale de Sociologie Religeuse 6, no. 1–2 (March–June 1979): 239–280.
Offner, Clark B., and Henry van Straelen. *Modern Japanese Religions.* New York: Twayne, 1963.
Reader, Ian. *A Poisonous Cocktail? Aum Shinrikyo's Path to Violence.* Copenhagen: Nordic Institute of Asian Studies Books, 1996.
————. *Religious Violence in Contemporary Japan: The Case of Aum Shinrikyo.* Honolulu: University of Hawaii Press, 2000.
Schiffer, Wilhelm. "New Religions in Postwar Japan." *Monumenta Nipponica* 11, no. 1 (April 1955): 1–14.
Schwade, Arcadio. *Shinto Bibliography in Western Languages: Bibliography on Shinto and Religious Sects, Intellectual Schools and Movements Influenced by Shintoism.* Leiden: E. J. Brill, 1986.
Shillony, Ben-Ami. "The Princess of Dragon Palace: A New Shinto Sect Is Born." *Monumenta Nipponica* 39 (1984): 177–1812.
Thomsen, Harry. *The New Religions of Japan.* Tokyo: Tuttle, 1963.
Tsushima Michihito, Nishiyama Shigeru, Shimazono Susumu, and Shiramazu Hiroko. "The Vitalistic Concept of Salvation in Japanese New Religions: An Aspect of Modern Religious Consciousness." *Japanese Journal of Religious Studies*, Proceedings of the 1978 Tokyo Meeting of the Conference Internationale de Sociologie Religeuse 6, no. 1–2 (March–June 1979): 139–161.
Watanabe Baiyu. "Modern Japanese Religions." *Monumenta Nipponica* 13 (1958): 152–162.
Wilson, Bryan R. "The New Religions: Some Preliminary Considerations." *Japanese Journal of Religious Studies*, Proceedings of the 1978 Tokyo Meeting of the Conference Internationale de Sociologie Religeuse 6, no. 1–2 (March–June 1979): 193–216.
Young, Richard Fix. "From Gokyo-dogen to Bankyo-dokon: A Study in the Self-universalization of Omoto." *Japanese Journal of Religious Studies* 15, no. 4 (December 1988): 263–286.
————. "Magic and Morality of Modern Japanese Exorcism: A Study in Mahikari." *Japanese Journal of Religious Studies* 17, no. 1 (March 1990): 29–49.

Kurozumi-kyo

Hardacre, Helen. *Kurozumi-kyo.* Princeton, NJ: Princeton University Press, 1986.

Hepner, Charles William. *The Kurozumi Sect of Shinto.* Tokyo: 1935.
Stoesz, William. *Kurozumi Shinto: An American Dialogue.* Anima, 1989.

Konko-kyo

Konkokyo: A New Religion of Japan. General Headquarters of Konkokyo, 1958.
Fujii Kineo. *Hitowa Mina Kaminoko.* General Headquarters of Konkokyo, 1984.
Matsui Fumio. *Konko Daijin: A Biography.* Konko Churches of America, 1972.
Schneider, Delwin B. *Konkokyo: A Japanese Religion.* Tokyo: ISR Press, 1962.
Yasuda Kozo. *Konkokyo Scriptures.* General Headquarters of Konkokyo, 1983.

Mahikari

Tebecis, A.K. *Mahikari: Thank God for All the Answers.* Tokyo: 1982.

Omoto-kyo

The Omoto Movement, Its Origin, Aims and Objects. Kameoka: 1950.
Deguchi Nao. *Scripture of Omoto.* Kameoka: 1957.
Deguchi Kyotaro. *The Great Onisaburo.* Tokyo: 1973.
Franck, Frederick. *An Encounter with Oomoto.* Cross Currents, 1975.
Murakami Shigeyoshi. *Deguchi Onisaburo.* 1978.
Tucker, Beverley D. "Christian Worship with Omoto-kyo." *Japanese Religions* 9, no. 4 (July 1977): 60–63.

PL Kyodan

PL Kyodan. *Perfect Liberty—How to Lead a Happy Life.* Tondabayashi, 1958.
Yuasa Tatsuki. "PL (Perfect Liberty) *Contemporary Religions in Japan* I, no. 3 (September 1960): 20–29.

Shinrei-kyo

Light from the East. Shinrei-kyo Publications, 1986.
Towards the Dawning World. Shinrei-kyo Publications, 1981.

Tenri-kyo

Masuno Michioki. *Tenrikyo.* Duyusha: Tenrikyo Head Church, 1928.
A Short History of Tenrikyo 1960. Kyoto: Tenrikyo Kyoka Honbu, 1960.

Van Straelen, Henry. *Religion of Divine Wisdom: Japan's Most Powerful Religious Movement.* Kyoto: 1954.

Tensho-Kotai-Jingu-kyo

Guidance to God's Kingdom. Tabuse, 1956.
Tensho-Kotai-Jingu-kyo: The Prophets of Tabuse. Tabuse, 1954.

INTERNET RESOURCES

Major Shrines Listed in the Dictionary

Akama Jingu. 4-1 Amida dera cho, Shimonoseki shi, Yamaguchi 750-0003: www.urban.ne.jp/home/koushi/my_city/infotown/akamajin/akamajig.htm

Akiba Jinja. Akibayama, Ryouke, Haruno machi, Shyuchi gun, Shizuoka 437-0693 sun.ee.kocji-ct.ac.jp/tourism/akiba.html

Atago Jinja. 1 Atago cho, Saga, Ukyoh ku, Kyoto 616-8458: web.kyoto-inet.or.jp/people/kinmei/html-j/atago.html

Atsuta Jingu. 1-1-1 Jingu, Atsuta ku, Nagoya shi, Aichi 456-8585: www.shatchy.ne.jp/cef/english/chubu/comment/Atsuta/html

Awa Jinja. 589 Dai Jingu, Tateyama shi, Chiba 294-0233: www.geocities.co.jp/SilkRoad/4815/awa.html

Chichibu Jinja. 1-1 Banba cho, Chichibu shi, Saitama 368-0041: www.chichibu-jinja.or.jp

Dazaifu Tenmangu. 4-7-1 Zaifu, Dazaifu shi, Fukuoka 818-0195: www.dazaifutenmangu.or.jp/english/index.htm

Dewa Sanzan Jinja. 7 Temukai Haguro cho, Higasi Tagawa gun, Yamagata 997-0292

Fushimi Inari Taisha. 68 Yabuno uchi machi, Fukakusa, Fuchimi ku, Kyoto 612-0882: www.kyoto-np.co.jp/kp/ojikoji/kaido/fushimi/f4.html

Futarasan Jinja. 2307 Yamauchi, Nikko shi, Tochigi, 321-1431: www.mct.gr.jp/world_h/futarasan/honden.html

Hakozakigu. Fukuoka, Kyushu www.jrkyushu.co.jp/travel/zukan/sketch/s9605.htm

Heian Jingu. Tenno-cho, Okazaki Nishi, Sakyoh ku, Kyoto 606-8341: pobox.upenn.edu/~Cheetham.jp.garden/gardens/heian.html

Hie Jinja. Tokyo, Akasaka 2-10-5 Nagata-cho, Chiyoda-ku, Tokyo Japan, Otsu in Shifa: www.mct.gr.jp/nikko/P42_118/P099_hie.html and www.hiejinja.or.jp/eindex.htm

Hikawa Jinja. Omiya, Saitama Prefecture, 1-407 Takahana cho, Omiya shi, Saitama 330-0803

Hirano Jinja. 1 Miyamoto cho, Hirano, Kita ku, Kyoto 603-8322
Hirose Jinja. Ohhito cho, Takata gun, Shizuoka: www.wbs.ne.jp/cmt/ootyu/70oo/index73.htm#12
Hirota Jinja. Nishinomiya shi, Hyogo Prefecture: www.nishi.or.jp/hitori/hirota.html
Ikukunitama Jinja. 13-9 Ikutama cho, Tennouji ku, Osaka 543-0071
Itsukushima Jinja. 1-1 Miyajima cho, Saeki gun, Hiroshima 739-0500: www.hiroshima-cdas.or.jp/miyajima/english/jinja/noshock.htm
Ise Jingu. Ise shi, Mie Prefecture: www.shatchy.ne.jp/cef/english/chubu/comment/Ise.html, courtneymilne.com/jingu.html, and www.isejingu.or.jp/
Isonokami Jinja. 384 Furu cho, Tenri shi, Nara 632-0014: member.nifty.ne.jp/stan/n_isk01.htm
Iwashimizu Hachimangu. 30 Koubou, Hachiman, Hachiman shi, Kyoto 614-8588
Izumo Taisha. 195 Kinetsuki Higashi, Taisha cho, Hakawa gun, Shimane 699-0701: www.joho-shimane.or.jp/pref/nutshell/izumo04-e.html
Kannagara Jinja (Seattle, U.S.). 17720 Crooked Mile Rd., Granite Falls, WA 98252: www.kannagara.org and www.tsubakishrine.org/ceremonies/index.html
Kasuga Taisha. 160 Kasugano cho, Nara shi, Nara 630-8212: hames.keihanna-plaza.co.jp/ICMA596/Travel/tour3/html
Keihi Jinja. 11-68 Akebonocho, Tsuruga-shi, Fukui-ken 914
Kibitsu Jinja. 931 Kibitsu, Okayama shi, Okayama 701-1341: www.harenet.ne.jp/kibitujinja/
Kotohira Jinja. plaza.harmonix.ne.jp/~t nouchi/1.shimo.html.f/shimo.konpira.yago.html and www.konpira.or.jp/exri.htm
Kumano Sanja (See Nachi Taisha). www.asahi-net.or.jp/~DR3Y-TKNK/sansya.htm
Meiji Jingu. Harajuku, Tokyo: meijijingu.or.jp
Miyazaki Jingu. 2-4-1 Jingu, Miyazaki-shi, Miyazaki, Miyazaki Prefecture, Kyushu
Nachi Taisha. 1 Nachiyama, Katsuura cho, Nachi, Higashi Murou gun, Wakayama 649-5301: member.nifty.ne.jp/shouzi/shrine/kinki/nachi/index.html
Nikko Toshogu. 2301 Yamauchi, Nikko shi, Tochigi 321-1431: www.mct.gr.jp/world_h/isan_toushogu.html
Nogi Jinja. 8-11-27 Akasaka, Minato ku, Tokyo, 107-0052: www.tcvb.or.jp/h0/0541.htm
Ogata Jinja. Inuyama City
Tagata Jinja. Komakik, Nagoya City. Aichii Prefecture: yamasa.org/japan/english/destinations/aichi/tagata_jinja.html
Tsubaki Okami Yashiro. 1871 Yamamoto-cho, Suzuka-shi, Mie-ken, 519-0315: www.kannagara.org/Tsubaki.htm

Yasukuni Jinja. Kudanshita, Tokyo: www.yasukuni.or.jp

General Shinto Websites

Cyber Jinja. Sakura Jinja, Setagaya Ward, Tokyo: www.sakura.jingu.net
Online article. "Festival and Sacred Transgression" by Sonoda Minoru of Koku-gakuin University: kokiugakuin.ac.jp/ijcc/wp/cpjr/matsuri/sonoda/html
Kokugakuin University. Institute for Japanese Culture and Classics: www.kokuguin.ac.jp/ijic/ja
Kogakkan University. The Shinto Institute: www.kogakkan-u.ac.jp/eng/ise/index17.html
Shinto and Ecology Biography. Rosemarie Bernard, Harvard University: environment.harvard.edu/re;ligion/Research/Shinto/Biography/html
Shinto Purification Rites. James W. Boyd and Ron. G. Williams: lamar.colstate.edu/cspooner/shinto/ (Professor Boyd and Professor Williams also made an excellent video on Shinto.)

Rituals for Use in Graduate School Programs

Japanese Religions. Personal site by Paul Watt: www.indiana.edu/~japan/Digests/religion.html
Shinto Shrines. An introduction to terms and concepts, with links to shrine sites from Japan-Guide.com: www.japan-guide.com/e/e2059.html
Wikipedia: Shinto. http://en.wikipedia.org/wiki/Shinto
Shinto: Teaching Comparative Religion through Architecture. Resource from the University of California at Berkeley: ias.berkeley.edu/orias/visuals/japan_visuals/shinto.HTM
Koyasan University. www.geocities.co.jp/Berkeley/5873

Shinto Information Sites

General Information on Shinto

www.religioustolerance.org/shinto.htm
www.japan-guide.com/e/e2056.html
Yuzo's Shinto Research Center (personal): www.geocities.co.jp/Berkeley/habo/1317
Dr. George Williams, California State University, Chico, Professor on Shinto: www.csuchico.edu/-georgew/tsa/nl/teaching about.html
www.japan-guide.com/e/e2059.htm
cyberfair.gsn.org/dodson/japan97/shinto.htm
Richard Hooker, personal academic site: www.lib.duk.edu/ias/eac.religion/htm

Note: There are numerous such sites which vary in quality and often express the polemical views of the author.

Encyclopedia Articles about Shinto

www.encyclopaedia.com/articles/11820.html
www.britannica.com/bcom/:eb/article/6/0,5715,108166+105864,00.html
The Columbia Encyclopaedia (6th Edition) "Shinto": search.netscape.com/ google/tmpl.?search-Shinto+Bibliography &start-20
www.jinja.or.jp/english/s-4a.html
Cyber Shrine: www.kiku.com/electric_samurai/cyber-shrine/index.html (site listing numerous illustrated shrines and information)

Festivals

www.gallery.ne.jp/~hatamap/event/ne-e.html
www.gallery.ne.jp/~hatamap/index-e.html
http://www.fujiyoshida.yamanashi.jp/english/firefset.html (Aichi Hadaka Matsuri and other important festivals)
www.happy.gr.jp.atelier/e-taisai.htm (collection of festival images)
www.happy.or.jp/home/uji/pic20e.htm (collection of festival images)
links.asiasociety.org/get_links/default/asia/51

Shrine Buildings in Ichikawa Prefecture

www.pref.ishikawa.jo/bunkazai/e-kenzoubutu.htm

Links to Noh and Shrines

www.links2go.com/more/corpnews.com/dragonball/

Information about the Shinto Priesthood

www.jinja.or.jp/english/s-4b.html

Miscellaneous

Japanese Shinto Ritual Music audio CD, 1997
Esentials of Shinto: http://info.greenwood.com/bookd/0313264/031326417. html

New Religions

Federation of New Religious Organizations of Japan Shisuren Zaidan Hojin,
Shin-Nihon Shukyo Dantai Rengokai, 1-1-2 Yoyogi, Shibuta-ku, Tokyo 151-
0053: jin.jcic.or.jp/jd/org/oo6022117.html

The Japanese New Religions Project Centre for New Religions, Dept. of Theology and Religious Studies, Kings College, University of London, Strand,
London WC2 2LS Tel: 44-171-836454 e-mail: p.b.clarke@uk.ac.kcl.cc.bay
(an academic research project on New Religious Movements activities and
growth outside of Japan)

Shinto and New Religions. www.clas.ufl.edu/users/gthursby/el/shinto.htm

Byakko Shin-Kokai Fuji Sanctuary, Fujinomiya City: www.byakko.org/index.html

Konko-kyo. Konko Headquarters Otani 320, Konko-cho Asakuchi-gun,
Okayama-ken 719-0111, tel: 81-86542-3111, fax: 81-86542-4419: www.
konkokyo.or.jp/eng/ and www.konkokyo.or.jp/eng/bri/hist.html

Konko Churches of America. www.konko.com

Konko Church of Izuo. www.relnet.co.jp/izuo/brief/newtop.htm

Kurozumi-kyo. Munetada Jinja, Okayama city, Okayama Prfecture: www.
kurozumikyo.com

Mahikari Sekai Mahikari Bunmei Kyodan. www.mahikari.org/ship.htm.

Sukyo Mahikari. ctl.virginia.edu/~jkh8x/soc257/nrms/mahikari.html

Omoto-kyo. www.omoto.or.jp webmaster@oomoto.or jp

Church of Perfect Liberty. 2172-1 Shindou, Tondabayashi, Osaka 584-8651,
Japan North America Main Church: 700 S. Adams St., Glendale, CA. 91205,
U.S.A. South America Main Church: Av. PL do Brasil Alt 8000, Arujá, SP
CEP:07400-970 web.perfect-liberty.or.jp

Seicho-No-Ie. www.snitruth.org/ www.snitruth.org/social/links.htm

Sekai Kyusei-kyo. www.terravista.pt/copacabana/1085/topo.htm

Shinrei-kyo. 1-4-19 Aksaka, Minato-ku, Tokyo www.srk.info/index_e.htm

Tenri-kyo. www.tenrikyo.or.jp

Tensho-Kotai-Jingu-Kyo. www.letusreason.org/Cults5.htm

Resource Organizations

Japan Society of the United States. 333 East 44th Street, New York, 10017, tel:
212-832-1155

Shinto: Nature Gods and Man in Japan. (movie by Peter Grilli)

The Association of Shinto Shrines (Jinja Honcho). 1-1-2, Yoyogi, Shibuya-ku,
Tokyo, tel: 03-3379-8016, fax: 03-3379-8299: http://www.jinjahoncho.or.jp

Nihon Minzoku Bunka Eizo Kenkyujo (Japan Audio-Visual Research Insitute
for Folk Culture). This has generated some excellent Japanese language
materials on rituals and ceremoneis.

The International Shinto Foundation. Tanaka Building 3rd Floor, Hirai 5-22-9, Edogawa-ku, Tokyo 132-0035, tel/fax: 03-3610-3975, e-mail: UmedaY@ msn.com www.shinto.org

Shinto-Religion.com. Website for the purchase of Shinto artifacts thaht contains photographs of the principal utensils used in Shinto rituals.

Shinto Online Network Association. This is a non-profit volunteer organization with the objective of publicizing Japanese tradition and a correct understanding of the Shinto religion. Our organisation is run by volunteer Shinto priests affiliated to Jinja Honcho (The Association of Shinto Shrines). There is no direct link, however, between this organization and Jinja Honcho.

Note: Various shrines have movies of their own festivals and buildings (for example, The Grand Shrines of Ise). The *Jinja Honcho* can provide more detailed information, as do the websites listed. Many shrines are still creating sites. Listed above is what was available at the time of publication.

About the Author

Stuart D. B. Picken was educated at Allen Glen's School, Glasgow, and the University of Glasgow, where he majored in philosophy and divinity. He served on the faculty of the International Christian University in Tōkyō for 25 years prior to moving to Nagoya University of Commerce and Business Administration. He served as dean of the faculty of Foreign Languages and Asian Studies since its inception in 1988 and also as dean of the Graduate School of Global Business Communications since its opening in 2002. His prior books include *Shinto: Japan's Spiritual Roots* (1979), *The Essentials of Shinto* (1994), *Historical Dictionary of Shinto* (2001, Scarecrow Press), and *Historical Dictionary of Japanese Business* (2007, Scarecrow Press). He is also the author of over 200 academic paper and articles. From 1985 to 1988, he served as director of the Centre of Japanese Studies at the University of Stirling in Scotland and was instrumental in founding the Japan Society of Scotland. In Japan, he served as a council member of the Japan-British Society from 1981 to 2001. He has been actively involved in interreligious dialogue at many levels and in promoting the better understanding of Shinto and Japanese culture in international Asia and in the West. He served as a special advisor to the president of the International Association for Religious Freedom between 1997 and 2000. He also maintains close connections with the Japan Research Center of the Chinese Academy of Social Science in Beijing. Outside academia, he has functioned as a consultant to various major Japanese corporations, including Mutsui Mining and Smelting Corporation, Kobe Steel, and the Japan Airlines Group. He retired early in 2001 and now lives in Perthshire in Scotland, where he devotes time to research and writing, and is currently Chair of the Council of the Japan Society of Scotland and Chair of the Advisory Board of the International Academic Forum (IAFOR), which is based in Osaka and in Hong Kong. He was awarded the Order of the Sacred Treasure by the emperor of Japan in 2007.

Breinigsville, PA USA
17 December 2010

251609BV00001B/2/P